MW00826376

ORGANIZATIONAL BEHAVIOR TODAY

This exciting new introductory text offers a new perspective on teaching organizational behavior by framing the organization as the vehicle for implementing strategic management processes, while also breaking down how the different components of an organization are designed to work together. Unlike traditional OB texts, *Organizational Behavior Today* emphasizes a "big picture" examination of how organizations function in a Darwinian world, in which the primary goal of an organization is survival.

The book introduces readers to the three stages of the strategic management process: strategy formulation, strategy implementation and strategic control, thereby linking the organization to its mission, vision and strategic goals. Essential OB concepts such as work processes, policy, worker behavior, reward system, change management and leadership development are covered, and the book also highlights the impact of technology on organizations.

To support student comprehension and bring the study of OB to life, the book includes vignettes highlighting real organizations who have implemented OB processes, either successfully or unsuccessfully. End-of-chapter questions ensure that students can apply the information learned effectively. Accompanying online resources for this text include a curated list of relevant video content. The book is suitable for undergraduates and graduate students completing a first course in Organizational Behavior, as well as a practical reference for current managers wishing to optimize organizational performance.

Stanley C. Ross is Associate Professor of Management at Bridgewater State University, USA.

"Author Stanley Ross has done a fantastic job putting together the pieces of the great puzzle of organizational behavior in a way that is accessible to all readers. Students, practitioners, and scholars will benefit from the text's clarity of explanation, real-life case studies, and integration of policy and policy-making. *Organizational Behavior Today* is a must-read."

Dr. Habib Chamoun-Nicolas, *Professor of International Negotiations and Business Development*, University of St Thomas, Houston

"I highly recommend this textbook as it examines the foundational theories and most important concepts of organizational behavior to help students comprehend and apply OB practices in the workplace. The text also provides an overview of the most current OB research along with examples of how real businesses are implementing OB concepts. The text includes illustrations, case studies, and end-of-chapter questions to help enhance student comprehension."

Kennedy Kwabena Amofa, *Assistant Professor of Business Administration*, Columbia College

"*Organizational Behavior Today* is written in a very organized way that's easy to follow. As a business forensics specialist, I deal with organizational behavior regularly. This book will help guide employees and employers to understand how their organization works and how to improve it inside and out."

Johnathon Vermaelen, Review Assistant in E-Discovery and Forensic Accounting, and Author of *Business Forensics 101*

ORGANIZATIONAL BEHAVIOR TODAY

Stanley C. Ross

Routledge
Taylor & Francis Group

NEW YORK AND LONDON

First published 2021
by Routledge
52 Vanderbilt Avenue, New York, NY 10017

and by Routledge
2 Park Square, Milton Park, Abingdon, Oxon, OX14 4RN

Routledge is an imprint of the Taylor & Francis Group, an informa business

© 2021 Taylor & Francis

The right of Stanley C. Ross to be identified as author of this work has been asserted
by him in accordance with sections 77 and 78 of the Copyright, Designs and Patents
Act 1988.

All rights reserved. No part of this book may be reprinted or reproduced or utilised
in any form or by any electronic, mechanical, or other means, now known or hereafter
invented, including photocopying and recording, or in any information storage or
retrieval system, without permission in writing from the publishers.

Trademark notice: Product or corporate names may be trademarks or registered trademarks,
and are used only for identification and explanation without intent to infringe.

Library of Congress Cataloging-in-Publication Data
Names: Ross, Stanley C., author.
Title: Organizational behavior today / Stanley C. Ross.
Description: 1 Edition. | New York: Routledge, 2021. |
Includes bibliographical references and index.
Identifiers: LCCN 2020043087 (print) | LCCN 2020043088 (ebook) |
ISBN 9780367695071 (hardback) | ISBN 9780367695095 (paperback) |
ISBN 9781003142119 (ebook)
Subjects: LCSH: Organizational behavior.
Classification: LCC HD58.7 .R674 2021 (print) |
LCC HD58.7 (ebook) | DDC 302.3/5—dc23
LC record available at https://lccn.loc.gov/2020043087
LC ebook record available at https://lccn.loc.gov/2020043088

ISBN: 978-0-367-69507-1 (hbk)
ISBN: 978-0-367-69509-5 (pbk)
ISBN: 978-1-003-14211-9 (ebk)

Typeset in Palatino
by codeMantra

Access the Support Material: www.routledge.com/9780367695095

CONTENTS

DETAILED TABLE OF CONTENTS

Part III   Management Initiatives   141

Chapter 7   Organizational Culture   143

Part IV   People Dynamics   235

Chapter 11 Team Development and Team Management   237

INTRODUCTION

PREVIEW

There are three ways to write a book about Organizational Behavior (OB). An author(s) can cover the subject from a top-down perspective. This entails describing subjects related to strategic management of the organization, using the strategic management model as a guide. With the emphasis on a top-down presentation, the focus on the individual is not primary. The second approach and the most common method OB author(s) use is a bottom-up viewpoint. Here, the author's focus is mostly about the individual and then strategic issues. Using this approach leaves out much about the critical contextual organizational issues. The third approach is to integrate the two approaches using the strategic management model, with an emphasis on strategy, strategy implementation (organizational issues) and strategic control, but with a bias toward the individual.

In the pursuit of meeting one of the three approaches, something is usually omitted or minimized. But, an OB book and an OB course need to teach students about organizations, the purpose of an organization and the actions associated with the organizing processes linked to achieving the strategic goals of the organization, and be able to survive in a Darwinian World. Left out of most OB texts is what organizations do to implement the organization's strategy. This is an important subject of the strategic management model which encompasses three stages: strategy formulation, strategy implementation and strategic control. Understanding the purpose of strategy and the strategy formulation process is a critical contextual issue that the student of OB needs to understand when studying OB. OB represents the second stage of the strategic management model, strategy implementation. Implementation requires people to do the actual implementing, but to succeed, people in an organization need organizing.

Organizing is an important organizational function that incorporates several critical organizing issues. One issue is how individuals are organized into groups and teams. This is referred to as the structure or design of the organization. Some OB texts devote a chapter on the subject, but many only cover the subject in a section of a chapter. Second, management systems is an important subject to learn about because organizations create many different types of management systems, each system with a designated purpose. Information systems, cost control system and inventory control system are examples of management systems. There are many systems, with large organizations creating more systems and more formal types of systems. It is the unusual OB book that covers the subject of management systems in any detail. Organizations utilize policies to guide decision-making when decision-makers and non-decision-makers confront situations that require a decision. Policies and the policy-making process are important management methods organizations use to guide actions by keeping everyone focused. There is too little discussion about policy and the policy developmental process in traditional OB books. This omission fails to cover an important management subject. Finally, the focus on work processes receives minimal attention in traditional OB books. All tasks performed in an organization are performed as a work process; with sequential stages, each work process has a start point, an end point and stages between these stages. A work process always generates an outcome at the end. Work processes represent the quintessential subject for understanding what goes on in an organization daily. Tasks are preformed through work processes.

CORE MESSAGE

Organizational Behavior in the 21st Century introduces the reader to the study of organizations. Organizations represent the means used by individuals to achieve goals that require the cooperation and coordination among two or more people. Because of the central role of organizations in society, the study of organizations is important to understand how organizations operate the human element in an organization and the methods used by organizations to keep the workforce focused and to coordinate the workforce's work efforts.

A good analogy in understanding how an organization operates is the automobile. Like an automobile, an organization has parts that we refer to as groups (of people), people in a group need to work together and groups of people need to work together to ensure that the organization achieves the strategic goals. People give automobiles purpose (place to go), and people give organizations purpose through identifying the organization's mission (purpose), vision (where to go) and grand strategy (how to reach the destination point). Destination for an organization is the achievement of strategic goals.

Learning about all the parts of an organization, their role and function is critical in understanding how to ensure that the parts work together. Furthermore, by understanding how the parts of an organization are designed, linked and operate together, we learn how to optimize the performance of the organization as well as anticipate the potential problems that can emerge. The reader will learn about the methods organizations typically use to solve organizational problems.

In sum, the reader will understand the most salient point of the book. Every organization fulfills a greater purpose by describing the design and operations of the organization within the context of fulfilling the organization's mission, achieving the strategic goals through implementing the grand strategy to achieve the organization's vision of the future.

VALUE PROPOSITION: Readers will understand the role and functioning of an organization created to fulfill its mission and accomplish the organization's vision.

STATEMENT OF AIMS

Understanding the way an organization is designed and managed is critical to the long-term success of the organization. What is different and unique about the book is that the focus of the book is on an organization's role as the implementation vehicle within the strategic management process. Strategic management encompasses three distinct but interconnected stages: strategy, strategy implementation and strategic control.

- **Strategy** represents the plan an organization selects to achieve the strategic goals of the organization to fulfill the organization's mission and accomplish the vision.

- **Implementation** represents the role the organization as the method for putting the strategy into action.
- **Strategic control** represents the methods an organization develops to monitor the organization's performance to ensure that the organization is on track to succeed in achieving the strategic goals.

Linking the organization to the organization's mission, vision and strategic goals is a different perspective than other OB books because *Organizational Behavior in the 21st Century* emphasizes a "big picture" examination of how organizations function.

The big picture is that an organization operates within a Darwinian World. The overarching goal of all organizations is survival. To survive means to achieve the strategic goals and vision. Success requires that the organization constantly adapts to external environmental conditions to survive and avoid extinction. It is this perspective that makes this book standout among other OB texts.

A. Learning Objectives
    After reading this book, the reader is able to:
    1. Explain the relationship between strategy and strategy implementation.
    2. Describe and explain the role and functions of an organization.
    3. Identify and discuss the reasons organizations regulate worker behavior using formal methods such as *policies.*
    4. Define, analyze and explain how and why organizations develop and use *management systems* to regulate purposeful worker behavior.
    5. Define, analyze and explain how and why organizations develop and use *work processes* to regulate worker behavior.
    6. Define, analyze and explain how and why organizations develop and use policies to regulate *worker behavior.*
    7. Describe and explain how and why organizations facilitate formal, systematic changes within the organization through the use of a variety of change management methodologies.

B. Book Innovations
    The following innovations represent the distinctive features of this book about organizational behavior.
    1. An organization's external world represents a Darwinian World that organizations need to operate within to survive as the goal of all organizations is to survive and prosper. Learning how organizations function in this Darwinian World is essential for students interested in learning about the methods organizations use to achieve success.
    2. An important feature of the book is the way the author helps the reader understand that organizations represent the primary method for implementing an organization's strategy. The reader learns that there are three distinct but interrelated stages to the strategic management process: strategy formulation, strategy implementation and strategic control. Organizations, ranging from large conglomerates to small organizations with fewer than 15 people, seek to keep workers focused in a systematic way. How organizations keep the workforce focused is essential to understanding what constitutes a successful organization and how

successful organizations differ from unsuccessful organizations. The author examines the development and use of management systems, work processes and policies as levers' organizations use to keep the workforce focused.

3. Another important issue is the examination in the use of formal management methods that represent how organizations use officially sanctioned methods to regulate workforce behavior. Within every organization, there is a dynamic social system composed of different types of individuals with different backgrounds, interests and goals. The intent of the formalization process is to create purposeful workforce behavior that benefits the organization and ensures that the workforce remains focused and consistent in performing their job responsibilities.

4. Change management is a topic in all OB books. However, *Organizational Behavior in the 21st Century* emphasizes how organizations change the workforce's behavior through the use and modification of management systems, work processes and organizational policies. The author provides short vignettes to illustrate different types of organizational problems and demonstrates how to solve these problems through the application of change management methods. This is the "show and tell" chapter where the reader learns the role of change agents and how change agents approach solving different types of organizational problems by changing management systems, work processes and policies.

C. Important Themes

The book focuses on the important themes that represent the critical subjects that students of organizations need to understand to become successful managers and organizational change agents.

1. An organization is the strategy implementation agent in the strategic management models described earlier. Strategy is only a plan within the model. Implementation of the strategy is essential to attain success. The book describes the role and functions played by an organization during the strategy implementation process.

2. Organizational activity represents the "effect" of causal factors that influence how an organization operates. Readers need to learn and understand the role of an organization's mission, vision and strategic goals along with the grand strategy to understand what drives an organization's actions.

3. Organizational behavior is frequently referred to as operations, and overseeing the operations is commonly referred to as operations management. The organization uses very specific methods to focus the workforce's efforts and to coordinate the work forces' efforts. Many organizations of different sizes created a chief operations officer position because of the complexity associated with the daily management of an organization.

4. Organizations create and formalize *management systems, work processes* and *policies* to standardize operations to ensure that there is consistent workforce performance.

5. Management systems represent a collection of formal work processes supported by formal policies; each system has a common theme. Readers need

to learn about the value of management systems, the process for creating a management system and how management systems function.

6. Work processes represent the way organizations routinize all forms of work to ensure that the work is performed correctly, consistently, achieves the outcome(s) expected for each work process and that the process operates in a cost-effective way.

7. Policies represent officially sanctioned guidelines the workforce is expected to follow. Readers need to learn about the role of policies, the policy formulation processes and how policies evolve over time.

8. Change management is a critical subject for learners to understand because change in organizations is constant. Learners learn that change occurs through the modification of management systems, work processes and policies. Through the use of different types of vignettes, the reader learns about the application of change management methods for facilitating successful change. Readers learn how organizations utilize training programs as an example of a change management method.

9. The application of change management methods aims to create more purposeful behavior and that change is driven by the need to respond to changes in the organization's external environment that impacts the organization's ability to achieve the mission, vision and strategic goals.

10. Leadership and leadership development are essential subjects in an organizational behavior text because leaders facilitate and direct the activities of the workforce. The text shows how leaders lead within the context of using management systems, work processes and organizational policies.

11. The role of technology in shaping the organization's operations is new to the study of organizational behavior. But the subject is essential to include in an organizational behavior text because of the impact technology has in an organization's efforts at implementing the grand strategy.

12. The study of motivation is essential to any study of organizational behavior, but the focus needs to examine how organizations utilize the reward system and other management systems along with sub-systems to motivate workers. Organizations incorporate various motivation theories within the operations, and readers need to learn the way organizations apply theory.

13. Management models are used throughout the book to guide the reader in understanding the subjects introduced within each chapter. The strategic management process represents one such model. The management systems development model is another example of a model.

CHAPTER SYNOPSES

1. Chapter 1: Organizational Strategy and Organizational Behavior
   - Chapter 1 introduces the reader to the strategic management model and the critical role organizations serve in the implementation of an organization's strategy. The chapter provides the reader with a broad overview of all relevant subjects related to the organization's role in the implementation process.

2. Chapter 2: Strategy Implementation and the Organization's Structure
   - Chapter 2 describes the strategy implementation process in detail and the role and functioning of the organization through organizing the workforce by attempting to follow a logical framework.
3. Chapter 3: Management Systems
   - Organizations represent a systematic approach to achieve the organization's strategic goals. Every organization represents a collection of management systems designed to serve specific purposes in facilitating the workforce's efforts toward achieving the strategic goals and vision. The chapter discusses the purpose of management systems, sub-systems and the process for creating management systems along with managing management systems and methods used to modify existing management systems.
4. Chapter 4: Work Processes
   - Organizations create formal work processes within every management system to ensure that employees perform a job consistently and achieve the expected outcomes. The chapter covers the purpose of a work process; examines the subject of formal and informal work processes and their differences; and management methods used to manage work processes.
5. Chapter 5: Policies
   - Formal policies represent an organization's official view on the accepted way to act in a variety of situations. The reader learns about the purpose of having policies; the function of policies within an organization; the difference between formal and informal policies; and a model describing the policy-making process.
6. Chapter 6: Organizational Design
   - An organization's structure is one type of formal management system that requires special focus because of the unique role an organization's structure serves in coordinating the efforts of the workforce in three ways: workflows, decision-making and communication or information flows. The chapter describes the role and functions of an organization's structure as well as the major types of organizational designs along with a model describing the design creation process.
7. Chapter 7: Organizational Culture
   - Readers need a thorough understanding of the important role an organization's culture serves in the daily life of the workforce as well as the way an organization operates. Culture impacts all actions within an organization because culture reflects the important values of the organization, and values influence the decision-making process and employee behavior as an output of decisions. The chapter examines the role of culture; the effect that an organization's culture can have on employee behavior and describes a model for changing an organization's culture.
8. Chapter 8: Change Management in Organizations
   - Change is ongoing as organizations respond to evolving environmental conditions to successfully implement the organization's strategy. Models of change management methods aid the reader in learning about and understanding how to use the methods available to organizations attempting to facilitate formal changes in their operations. Vignettes of different types of

situations along with the application of different change management methods provide the reader with the knowledge on how to apply the change management methods.

9. Chapter 9: Leadership and Leadership Development
   - Students of organizational behavior need to learn about the concept of leadership and the role of leadership within the organization because leaders make decisions that profoundly impact on an organization's performance. Basic leadership themes are introduced, along with an understanding of the different levels of leadership and the types of leaders; the difference between leaders and managers, formal and informal leaders, a model on how to identify potential leaders and a model describing the leadership development process.
10. Chapter 10: Organizational Development and Training
    - Training represents an organization's most important official change management method used to bring about transformation within the organization. In the 21st century, training has become an essential management function in the support of the ongoing evolution of an organization. A model training program design is introduced to the reader to show readers how trainers approach designing training programs.
11. Chapter 11: Team Development and Team Management
    - Teams represent a common approach organization's use to accomplish a variety of tasks. It is important for the reader to learn about the role and functions of teams and the different types of teams that organizations can use. The reader learns a model that describes a process for creating teams as well as model that describes a process for managing teams. Conflict is endemic within teams because of the differences that can occur among team members with different personal agendas and personalities. The reader learns about the different types of conflict and conflict resolution strategies that ensure a team's success in accomplishing the team's mandated goals.
12. Chapter 12: Group and Individual Decision-Making
    - Decision-making represents an important process within an organization. Organizations seek to routinize decision-making to objectify the process. Organizations also seek to train employees to become more effective decision-makers. Chapter 11 introduces the reader to decision-making models for groups and individuals; compares formal decision-making with informal decision-making; and provides a model for decision-making within the implementation process.
13. Chapter 13: Motivation and Effective Workforce Performance
    - Motivated employees are achievement-oriented, and organizations require a motivated workforce to successfully implement the organization's strategy to achieve the strategic goals. Readers learn a representative sample of motivation theories and how organizations design management systems with the idea of motivating employees through the application of motivation theories.
14. Chapter 14: Communication Management
    - Communication within an organization represents one of the essential systems used by the organization to keep the workforce focused. A variety of communication models enables the reader to learn and understand the way

organizations communicate with employees and communication among employees. The chapter compares the use and purpose of formal communication methods and informal communication methods to influence the flow of information.

15. Chapter 15: Technology and the Organization's Workforce
    - This is the first organizational behavior textbook that examines the role and function of technology in influencing the actions of the workforce and the organization while executing the strategy implementation process.

PART I

STRATEGIC OVERVIEW

Organizational Strategy and Organizational Behavior

OVERVIEW

The creation of an organization is done to fulfill a purpose. We think of an organization as the means to achieving an endpoint. Once the original purpose is achieved, the organization continues to serve as the means for fulfilling new reasons for existing. To understand an organization's overall purpose for existing, we need to examine the context to understand the role an organization plays. The **Strategic Management Model** provides this context, so the reader understands the role an organization plays in supporting the efforts of decision-makers and individuals to achieve the original vision of the decision-makers.

The destiny of any organization is to support the achievement of a vision and to remain in existence if the organization can facilitate the achievement of future visions as determined by an organization's decision-makers. By continuing to achieve, the organization can survive within a Darwinian World that rewards success but provides the ultimate punishment for failure, extinction. This chapter identifies and describes the strategic management model, the strategic management planning process, strategy, the strategy formation stage in the strategic management model and the strategy formulation process. Furthermore, the chapter introduces the reader to the strategy implementation process, to the formal methods organizations utilize to keep employees focused, goal-oriented and motivated to serve the needs of an organization. Strategy implementation encompasses the methods organization's use to influence and focus people; these methods include management systems, work processes, policies and related rules.

CHAPTER 1   LEARNING OBJECTIVES

Readers will achieve the following learning objectives after reading this chapter.

1. Describe and explain the major features of the strategic management model.
2. Describe and explain the strategic management planning process.
3. Identify and explain the meaning of the term "strategy."
4. Identify, describe and explain the differences between the three levels of strategy.
5. Identify and describe the relationship between the strategy formulation process and the strategy implementation process.
6. Identify and describe the meaning of the term's formal, formalization and informal.
7. Discuss the linkage between the size of an organization and the formalization of an organization's actions.
8. Identify and briefly describe the purpose and functions of management systems, work processes and organizational policies.

LEARNING OBJECTIVE #1: MAJOR FEATURES OF THE STRATEGIC MANAGEMENT MODEL

A model serves as a guide. To understand the role and function of an organization, we need to describe the context that leads to the creation and ongoing evolution of an organization. The context provides the reader a "big picture" perspective in learning about an organization's role and function. The **Strategic Management Model** (see Figure 1.1) provides the context for understanding the purpose of an organization. An organization serves as the means used to facilitate the achievement of a goal. After the creation of the organization, the organization serves a dual purpose to identify new goals to accomplish and to support the achievement of the new goals. The achievement of goals serves to accomplish the fundamental goal, the survival of the organization. Organizational members serve to support an organization's efforts to survive. By understanding an organization's people dynamics, the reader understands that people are pivotal to the successful performance of an organization as well as the failure of an organization.

The strategic management model begins with the organization's **Mission** statement. The mission statement represents a formal description of the organization's purpose. Mission statements commonly reference the customer group(s) the organization targets; offers a broad overview of the products, services or products and services provided; and describes unique methods for making products or delivering services. As an organization grows in size, products or services are grouped into broader categories. Each category emphasizes the common feature the products in a category refer to. For example, Figure 1.2 shows a product category Dental

FIGURE 1.1   Strategic Management Model

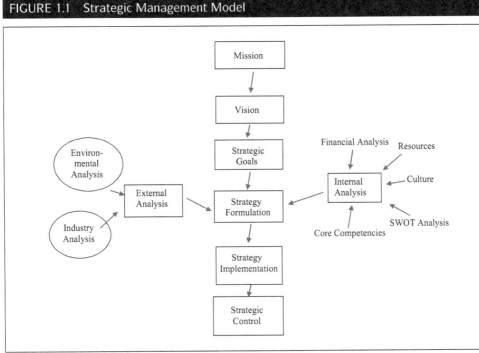

FIGURE 1.2   Example of a Product Category with Sub-Categories of Product Groups

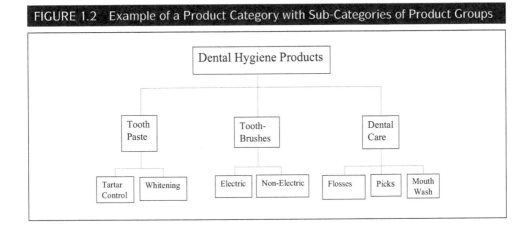

Hygiene product sub-divided into three separate sub-categories. Each sub-category is divided further, ultimately leading to separate product lines, with each product line encompassing several different products.

Following the mission statement is the **Vision** statement. The vision statement articulates the organization's image of the status of the organization within a three to five-year time frame. The vision statement provides focus and acts like a goal without all the properties of goals. The vision has a longer time horizon than do goals. Organizations that operate within a dynamic environment and industry(ies) often have three-year vision statements because of the constant changes that occur. All technology organizations typically have shorter time horizons because of the constant changes with new technology developing circumstances which can impact an organization. Organizations operating in less dynamic situations commonly have longer vision time horizons.

Strategic Goals represent goals aimed at moving the organization forward toward achieving the organization's vision. Strategic goals influence the organization's efforts toward realizing the vision. **SMART Goals** often are the most common types of strategic goals because a SMART goal is **S**pecific, **M**easurable, **A**chievable, **R**ealistic and **T**ime-limited. Measurement enables the organization to track progress and to take corrective action if necessary. Timeliness creates a sense of urgency that keeps the workforce focused.

Strategy represents the plan for achieving the strategic goals. Strategy exemplifies the organization's decision in selecting the optimal course of action to pursue to achieve the strategic goals which will lead to achieving the vision. External and internal analyses provide information that aids in the identification of strategic options to consider and in guiding the strategy selection process for choosing the preferred strategic option.

There are two primary types of external analyses. One is an **Environmental Analysis**. An environmental analysis examines the world within which the organization operates and must adapt to. There are five major dimensions of an environmental analysis. Economic factors, socio-cultural factors, political-legal factors, international factors and technological factors. Economic factors can include the growth rate of the economy, changes in disposable income and interest rates as the primary indicators of economic activity. Socio-cultural factors include changes in demographics, preferred consumer tastes and preferences as well as important values that influence buyer behavior of the target market(s). Political-legal factors refer to laws and government policies that can impact an organization's business. International factors commonly cover potential foreign markets and the potential for outsourcing production or moving production outside of the host country. Technology factors are important because technology can benefit or hurt an organization. There are three forms of technology to possibly consider. Process technology is technology used in manufacturing or in providing a service; there is product features technology or attributes of a product that have a technology focus; and input technology which is new technology that enhances or benefits a product such as gorilla glass for iPhone screens or elastane used in making certain types of clothing.

An **Industry Analysis** is the second major type of external analysis. An industry analysis examines the industry the organization operates in. The industry analysis becomes more complicated as an organization grows, entering other industries. An industry analysis includes examining the power of suppliers over organizations in the industry (or the reciprocal), the power of customers over organizations in the industry (or the reciprocal), substitute products or services provided by organizations outside of the industry; barriers that make entry into the industry challenging for organizations considering entry into the industry; the growth rate of an industry and the analysis of the strategies and related issues of organizations that operate within the industry to assess opportunities and threats.

The **Internal Analysis** encompasses the review of several dimensions associated with the organization. The concept of the **Balanced Scorecard** encompasses three forms of analyses. These include financial analysis of the organization's performance; operational analysis which focuses on monitoring and evaluating operational performance; and market analysis which examines the customer-organization relationship. A **SWOT Analysis** provides insights on the organization's strengths and weaknesses along with a review of the opportunities and threats that an organization must consider. The identification of the organization's **Core Competencies** is an essential issue to consider when developing and assessing strategic options that need to emphasize core competencies. A competency represents something an organization excels in; it is difficult for competitors to emulate an organization's core competencies fully. An example is Wal-Mart's inventory control system or Apple's product development process. **Resource** availability is another internal factor the organization needs to consider when formulating a strategy because resource limitations constrain what an organization is capable of doing. An organization's **Culture** is the last major factor to consider when identifying strategic options and selecting an option because culture represents a set of values, and values shape the decisions and actions of an organization. The collective body of employees promotes and supports an organization's culture. This is one of the important reasons organizational members are important in supporting the longevity of an organization.

Strategy Implementation follows the selection of the corporate strategy. Implementation involves the mobilization of the work force to focus on putting the strategy into effect. The expectation is that successful implementation leads to the achievement of the strategic goals. Implementation represents the organization's operations. Operations encompass all the people activities of the organization. We can identify three operational categories that define operational actions. These operational categories include management systems, formal and informal work processes and formal and informal organizational policies. Each management system includes work processes and organizational policies, all sharing a common theme. For example, an inventory control system focuses on the management of an organization's inventory. Work processes represent established methods or tasks in performing an activity. A policy represents the organization's view on the best way to perform a work process. The workforce's responsibility is instrumental in identifying problems and recommending changes to the management systems, work processes and organizational policies.

The last stage of the strategic management model is **Strategic Control**. Strategic control represents the means an organization uses to determine if the organization is moving toward achieving the strategic goals as well as operational objectives linked to the strategic goals. **Operational Objectives** are SMART type objectives, with a narrow focus and a shorter time horizon than strategic goals. An example of an operational objective is keeping defect rates within acceptable levels. Various types of control systems enable the organization to assess performance-based activities by providing routine performance reports that offer insights about operational performance to decision-makers. The information serves as a catalyst for action depending on the nature of the information.

JDM Flowers on the Go: Part I

John Mulligan, CEO of JDM Flowers on the Go was sitting with Patricia Bennett, the company's CFO. John and Patricia were discussing the future of the company. Since opening in 2005 as a local distributor of flowers in Massachusetts, the company's growth rate was meteoric. Access to large distributors in California and Europe along with well-received customer services contributed to the company's success. Over the years, the company expanded its operations to serve all New England. The business grew largely by leveraging the internet and easy access to the airport in Providence, RI to ship flowers to small, local retailers. However, growth came at a cost. John realized his lack of a business education was limiting his ability to look ahead to the next stage of the business. Patricia began working for the company at the start as a part-time accountant, but she lacked experience as a savvy senior executive. John and Patricia were both ambitious executives looking to ramp up the operations, but they were unsure how to proceed. John and Patricia were discussing an article John read that was written by a former Harvard University business professor. The professor was a strategist. The article described the importance of developing a sound corporate strategy. The article emphasized the important role of strategy in the context of the strategic management model. "What did she mean by the term strategic management model?" asked Patricia.

Questions

1. What does the strategic management model refer to?
2. What are the three major components of the strategic management model?
3. Why should John and Patricia consider following the strategic management model?
4. How is the strategic management model likely to help John and Patricia?
5. Should John and Patricia hire a strategic management consultant? Explain.

LEARNING OBJECTIVE #2: STRATEGIC MANAGEMENT AS A PROCESS

The strategic management model depicted in Figure 1.1 represents a strategic planning process because the organization needs to allocate resources to achieve the strategic goals depicted in the model. To allocate resources necessitates the need to make resource allocation decisions, and making resource allocation decisions requires involving different management levels, each level holding authority over certain types of resource allocation decisions. Moving through the hierarchy or the organization involves multiple decision-making processes. A decision-making process represents a systematic approach to ensure that individuals make optimal decisions regarding the best use of resources, which is necessary since all organizations confront resource constraints.

The strategic planning process is comprehensive because the process requires a systematic approach toward achieving the organization's vision. Decision-makers make decisions to influence future people activities and which represent the best interests of the organization. By creating an overall systematic approach with linked work processes, the organization attempts to generate sufficient information to support making effective decisions. The information collected can vary because the needs of decision-makers can vary. To ensure meeting sufficient current and future information needs, the organization creates different categories of information systems, each system focusing on a type of information. The strategic management model guides decision-makers by identifying the types of information needed required and creates management systems to provide the required information. For example, an environmental analysis involves the collection of certain types of relevant information. Market analyses require certain types of relevant information.

The strategic management model represents an interconnected series of activities linked together to provide a process for ensuring an organization's success in adapting to and succeeding in the Darwinian World all organizations confront. With the mission statement, the organization is confronted with the need to clarify the organization's purpose. Purpose identification involves identify existing markets, products or product categories and work processes that support meeting the needs of the markets and create products and/or services to meet market needs. An organization needs to remain clear about the purpose of the organization to justify the organization's existence. A mission can evolve over time when circumstances warrant an updated mission statement.

The vision is an organization's first showing of the intent to pursue a focus that is future-oriented. There are many options available in the choice of a possible vision, but decision-makers need to make a choice. This choice has important implications for the organization, so careful deliberation is necessary to ensure that a vision is realistic, achievable and focused. The organization creates the necessary information-gathering work processes to import relevant insights from all the major stakeholders of the organization. Consensus on the choice of vision among the stakeholders is essential to avoid the potential for serious differences that can disrupt planning as the organization moves forward in the strategic management planning process.

The organization's vision provides the basis for identifying the organization's strategic goals. Strategic goals are important because achieving the strategic goals moves the organization forward toward achieving the vision. The important role of strategic goals means that the organization needs to be very clear as to the type of goals to select to ensure relevancy in supporting achieving the vision. Examples of strategic goals include market share goals, market development goals, market penetration goals, revenue goals, profitability goals and profit margin goals. Choosing SMART type strategic goals (specific, measurable, achievable, realistic and timely) requires careful consideration to ensure that achieving the goals is feasible within time limits and resource constraints. Careful planning in selecting the goals means that various types of information processes are necessary to provide decision-makers with relevant information in choosing the strategic goals.

The strategy for achieving the goals is the next step in the strategic management planning process. This step includes identifying the strategic options available to the organization and the preferred strategy from the list of strategic options. The goal, during this stage of the planning process, is to identify a limited number of realistic strategic options and then evaluate each of the options; the process culminates in selecting the most advantageous strategic option to consider for achieving the strategic goals. Strategy formulation is a complex stage involving two broad categories of information gathering activities. External and internal types of analyses are the two categories. Each category involves collecting specific types of information that needs assessing for relevancy and usefulness. The two major external information gathering forms of analysis include an environmental analysis and an industry analysis. Strategic planners need to be systematic in identifying relevant information to consider, often choosing to objectify subjective information. The objectifying of information involves creating quantitative rubrics to follow. For example, socio-cultural information, such as the importance of the value health consciousness, is accessible by the statistics that only 14% of the population as of 2011 smokes cigarettes, down from 40% in the 1960s.

Strategy formulation also involves examining information generated by the organization. This is internal analysis. The information needs to be objectified as much as possible because strategic planners and decision-makers need to identify feasible strategic options and then using the gathered information to select one strategic option. Quantitative rubrics serve the organization well in using both objective information (e.g. financial information and operational information) and subjective information (e.g. organizational culture and core competencies) in identifying strategic options, evaluating the strategic options and selecting the optimal strategic option. Careful planning represents the means for systematically conducting the various information gathering processes associated with the strategy formulation stage.

After identifying the strategy for achieving the strategic goals, the next stage is the strategy implementation process. Decision-makers need to formulate action plans to identify operational changes that are necessary to successfully implement the organization's new strategy. Strategy implementation refers to the organization's operations. Operations encompass the organization's management systems, work processes and organizational policies. The operations represent the organization's structure imposed on the workforce to ensure that employees remain focused and to facilitate coordination among the work force. Strategic planners need to show decision-makers, through the use of action plans, the management systems to modify or develop, the work processes to modify or develop and the new and modified policies that guide employees in changing their behavior. Changing the operations provides a new structural configuration to successfully implement the new strategic plan.

Strategic control represents a specific information-generating stage intended to develop control systems that monitor the operational performance of the organization. Achieving operational performance objectives moves the organization forward in achieving the strategic goals. Organizations commonly use operational objectives linked to the strategic goals to assess short-term performance. Control systems monitor progress toward achieving the objectives and serve to identify problems that can prevent achieving the objectives. Early identification of problems can minimize the disruption to the organization's efforts at implementing the strategy and ultimately, achieving the organization's vision. Various types of control systems (e.g. quality control, total quality management and inventory control system), control work processes and control-defining policies represent the organization's systematic efforts to monitor performance by providing relevant performance-based information.

JDM Flowers on the Go: Part II

John and Patricia ended their impromptu meeting with Patricia telling John that she wanted to learn more about the strategic management model. Later, that night, Patricia and her partner, Joanne, were discussing their day when Patricia told Joanne about her conversation with John regarding the strategic management model. Joanne worked for a regional financial services firm located in Boston. Joanne was the operations manager. "I know all about the strategic management model" reported Joanne. "What?" was Patricia's response. "Tell me what you know." said Patricia. Joanne proceed to tell Patricia all about the strategic management model, explaining that strategic management provides organizations with a comprehensive approach intended to further the organization's success. Joanne continued by explaining that the strategic management model outlines a planning process to follow. A process intended to keep an organization focused. Joanne likened the model to a puzzle with pieces that link together, but unlike a puzzle, the pieces follow in a sequence, and the planning process is ongoing, or the expectation is that once started, the process remains ongoing to keep the organization focused and able to continue to be successful under all circumstances. "How is strategic management like a puzzle with a sequence of pieces?" asked Patricia. Joanne went to her desk and pulled out a plan that was a perfect example of the strategic management model and strategic management planning process because her company put the plan together in 2017 when the organization re-vamped their strategy. Joanne continued by showing Patricia the plan and how the plan followed a process, starting with the organization's mission statement. Joanne then highlighted for Patricia the next step was to create a vision of the organization's future in five years. The vision is a "want to be" said Joanne. After identifying the organization's vision, the next step is to select the strategic goals. Strategic goals are SMART type annual goals intended to move the organization forward toward achieving the vision. "Stop" said Patricia. "I am overwhelmed with information. I will bring a copy of the article John discussed with me home tomorrow and we can continue our conversation then."

Questions

1. What makes understanding the strategic management model so difficult to understand?
2. Why is the strategic management model considered a planning method?
3. What stage of the strategic management model should they focus on? Why?
4. Why is the strategic management model considered a change method?
5. How can the model's description be simplified?

LEARNING OBJECTIVE #3: THE MEANING OF THE TERM "STRATEGY"

Strategy identification occurs during the strategy formulation stage of the strategic management planning process. Set into motion during this stage are the strategy identification information systems and strategy identification information gathering processes intended to assist in identifying the strategic options available to the organization. The process of identifying the strategic options and assessing each option involves the use of two primary criteria. First, complete information is required to identify the strategy that impacts the entire organization. The intent is to mobilize employees, directly or indirectly, to be actively involved during the implementation of the strategy. Information is critical in learning the best way to move the organization forward effectively. Second, there is the element of time limitations in which to take advantage of opportunities and to negate threats. Organizations are unable to control what happens outside of the organization and which can impact the organization; the organization must respond either reactively or proactively to opportunities and threats the organization confronts. External circumstances can threaten the organization or represent opportunities to advance competitively. The window of opportunity can close quickly while threats can increase over time without a rapid response. For example, new technology can enable customers to buy a product more readily, but if there is no convenient means available, a competitor could meet this need.

The concept of **Bounded Rationality** is a useful concept because it enables us to understand and appreciate that the organization is always going to suffer from limited information when attempting to identify strategic options and evaluating each option. Assessing impact of a possible strategy and moving fast work at cross-purposes. Bounded rationality teaches us that the demand for information conflicts with the time constraint of needing to make a quick decision. The result is that a compromise must result that only satisfies the criteria without satisfying the requirements of each criterion fully. Organizations need to act sooner and not later.

What does the word strategy really refer to? There are many definitions of strategy, but the most useful and least complex definition (Nickols, 2016) is that strategy is "a general plan of action for achieving... goals and objectives" (p.3). This plan that an organization develops has far-reaching implications, and the most significant is that finding the best strategy leads to survival, but selecting the wrong strategy can lead to the organization's demise.

In sum, to ensure the selection of a successful strategy, organizations create strategy formulation systems and strategy formulation processes to conduct the necessary external and internal analyses; identify the strategic options; evaluate each option; and select one of the strategic options. As organizations grow in size, these systems and processes expand in scope and in complexity because conducting the required analyses becomes more challenging due to the organization's size. With more employees, more products and services, more and more complex management systems, work processes and policies, moving the organization forward becomes more demanding. After all, steering a small boat is a lot easier to direct and operate than steering an ocean liner.

LEARNING OBJECTIVE #4: DIFFERENCES BETWEEN THE THREE LEVELS OF STRATEGY

There are three levels of strategy to develop during the strategy formulation process. So far, the focus has been on the development of the corporate strategy. The corporate strategy refers to the competitive plan that impacts the entire organization. The second level of strategy is a business strategy. At some point, organizations can choose to grow in size by adding more types of businesses that operate under the corporate umbrella. These businesses differ from each other by type of products and services, customer type and perhaps geographic location. The differences require the careful calibration of a competitive plan that guides each of these businesses. Frequently, this type of strategy is referred to as a business strategy to differentiate the strategy from the corporate strategy. Business strategy formulation systems and formulation processes are developed to aid in the search to identify business strategy options and then used to assist in the process for selecting a business strategy. There is an important distinction between identifying the corporate strategy and each business strategy. If it is a cost-focused corporate strategy, the business strategies need to share a cost focus. If uniqueness or differentiation is emphasized in the corporate strategy, uniqueness is necessary in the business strategies. Sharing a common theme is necessary because the implementation management systems, implementation work processes and related policies are typically focused on supporting either a cost-focused or uniqueness-focused corporate strategy. Individual business units are largely responsible for the business-level strategy formulation process. Corporate management assesses the chosen business strategies to ensure each is complementary with the corporate strategy and then approves if supportive or recommends changes if the differences are problematic.

Functional strategies represent the third level of strategy. Each functional strategy represents the organization's plan for that functional area. Functional strategies support the business strategy (if any) and the corporate strategy. Examples of functional areas include marketing, information systems, manufacturing, human resources and accounting. As organizations grow in size and scope, there is a delineation of sub-functions, each of which can have its own strategy. For example, under marketing, there can be a promotion strategy, advertising strategy, sales strategy and market research strategy along with other possible sub-functions. Similar strategy formulation systems and formulation processes emerge to generate the required information needed to enable decision-makers to develop sub-functional strategies.

JDM Flowers on the Go: Part III

John, Patricia and William Yeung, the company's human resource manager, were meeting with Salina Gomez. Salina was a consultant with Hymes Strategic Consultants. Salina came highly recommended by one of John's friends who said that Salina is that rare person who combines education, academic experience and corporate experience. She is a professional specializing in the strategic management model with a focus on strategy and the strategy formulation process.

Salina prepared her PowerPoint presentation with a focus on the strategy formulation process. John, Patricia and William were eager to learn what needs to be done to identify a new growth strategy for the company. What worked in the past, everyone realized, was not going to work anymore. Taking the organization to the next level required more thought and research. The game was for bigger stakes, and their goal was to succeed. Each realized that they knew that they did not know much about the process for identifying a new strategy or what Salina referred to as a "game plan" to follow, but they were anxious to learn. Salina's presentation was the first step in learning how to develop a formal corporate strategy. "Shall we begin?" asked Salina.

Questions

1. How did Salina begin?
2. Why was William Yeung present at this meeting?
3. What is the goal of the meeting? Explain.
4. What does the word formulate mean? Explain.
5. Why do they want a growth strategy? What does a growth strategy refer to?

LEARNING OBJECTIVE #5: THE RELATIONSHIP BETWEEN THE STRATEGY FORMULATION PLANNING PROCESS AND THE STRATEGY IMPLEMENTATION PROCESS

Once an organization identifies a strategy during the strategy formulation planning process, this functions as a catalyst for triggering the strategy implementation systems, implementation processes and implementation policies into action. Initially, decision-makers throughout the organization require clarification of the new strategy to implement and how management systems, work processes and relevant policies must evolve to support the new strategy and any other levels of strategy affected by the change. Information systems and information processes operate to provide information that increases decision-makers understanding of the new strategy along with ideas about how to implement the new strategy.

An alternative view on strategy implementation is operational planning. Because all organizations have some form of hierarchical structure, decision-making associated with operational planning moves from being strategic to a narrower focus of planning down through the lower levels of the organization. Operational planning involves decision-makers determining the type and amount of resources that are necessary, employee specialty skills required, modification of the organizational structure if needed, changes to management systems, modification of work processes, new and/or modified policies as well as reinforcement of organizational cultural values.

The role of an organization's culture in the strategy formation process and strategy implementation process is critical because an organization's culture encompasses the core values that the organization defines in the organization's **Code of Conduct**. Values shape all organizational actions just as values influence the actions of individuals. The type of strategic options any organization considers is influenced by the organization's values. Values influence the design of the strategy formulation management systems, strategy formulation work processes and related organizational policies associated with the strategy formulation process. The system of values shapes the design and application of the strategy implementation management systems, related work processes and organizational policies that support the process for implementing the organization's strategy(ies).

There are strategy formulation management systems, work processes and organizational policies that only operate to facilitate the selection of strategic goals and strategy. Other types of management systems, work processes and policies serve a dual purpose of supporting strategy formulation and strategy implementation. These serve to link strategy formulation with strategy implementation. There are also management systems, work processes and organizational policies that exclusively support the strategy implementation stage. The goal of this network of management systems, work processes and organizational policies is to provide a systematic and comprehensive approach to the strategic management planning process, ensuring maximum effort at successfully accomplishing the organization's vision and ensuring the organization's survival. Survival is the overarching goal of all organizations.

Management systems can be broadly defined as information systems. The purpose of each system is narrowly focused, providing a certain type of information. For example, an organization can create a management system that operates to conduct an environmental analysis as a way of assessing possible strategic options and to assess if a change in a strategy is warranted. Inventory control systems represent another example of systems designed to manage various aspects of an organization's inventory. Information management systems link to decision-making processes because decision-makers need information to make informed decisions. In strategic management information, systems assist in identifying the best strategic options and in selecting an optimal strategy. Information systems provide decision-makers with information on how to best implement a recommended strategy as well. This linkage among management systems helps us understand the dual purpose of management systems, strategy formulation and strategy implementation. Decision-making processes are integrated within every management system, and each management system incorporates multiple work processes and multiple related policies.

Most common failures in achieving an organization's strategic goals and vision occur when there is a bad fit between the organization's strategy and the organization's choice of implementation methods. This includes the communication system used to translate a strategy into operational guidelines throughout the various levels of the organization. The goal of communication is to facilitate the critical role employees play in the strategy implementation process.

LEARNING OBJECTIVE #6: MEANING OF THE TERMS FORMALIZATION AND INFORMAL

Figure 1.3 shows a continuum with two endpoints: formal and informal. The continuum encompasses and explains all possible conditions of an organization's management systems, work processes and organizational policies. Of a continuum, no organization is totally formal or totally informal. All organizations range between these two endpoints. An informal organization refers to a more personal, non-standardized approach in the way an organization organizes the implementation process. Actions differ from prior actions on a non-systematic basis because the systems, work processes and policies are not formally standardized. A formal organization is highly systematized using standardized, sophisticated and detailed management systems; well-defined and structured work processes and detailed policies that cover all contingencies.

FIGURE 1.3   Continuum Showing Range of the Extent an Organization can be Organized

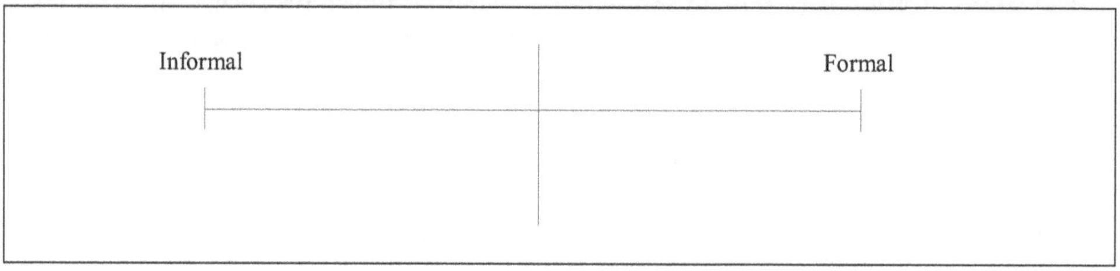

Informal   Formal

JDM Flowers on the Go: Part IV

Samuel Powers is an associate of Salina Gomez. Both work at Hymes Strategic Consultants. Where Salina is an expert in the strategy formulation process, Samuel's expertise is on the strategy implementation process. Prior to joining Hymes, Samuel worked for over 25 years as a COO at several organizations with revenues between 100 and 200 million dollars.

Samuel Prepared a PowerPoint presentation to accompany prepared handouts. The focus of Samuel's presentation was the strategy implementation process. Strategy implementation refers to the process of operationalizing an organization's strategy. The main emphasis in covering implementation is to stress the importance of management systems, work processes and organizational policy as critical concepts that provide order and focus to the strategy implementation process.

Samuel's plan is to discuss the role of strategy implementation within the strategic management model. After an overview on the subject, Samuel intends to cover the concept of organizational structure as an example of a management system aimed at organizing the workforce hierarchically. Next, Samuel plans to cover the subjects of the hiring process and employee performance review process as examples of two types of work processes to illustrate the concept of a work process. The presentation will emphasize formally designed work processes.

Samuel asked if there were any questions prior to starting his presentation on the strategy implementation process.

Questions

1. How is a person with COO experience relevant for the company?
2. What does strategy implementation refer to? Explain.
3. Why is it important to discuss the concept of work processes?
4. What questions do you think they will ask Samuel prior to his presentation? Why?
5. What is meant by the term "formally designed work processes?"

LEARNING OBJECTIVE #7: ORGANIZATIONAL SIZE AND FORMALIZATION

The size of an organization is a trigger or catalyst for initiating the formalization process. Formalization represents a process that systematically creates and organizes the management systems and work processes, along with developing official policies to regulate an increasing complex organization's internal environment. Figure 1.4 shows the relationship between the size of an organization and the formalization process. Size introduces more complexity in overseeing the management of the organization's operations. More products, more different products, more employees, more specialized employees, more and different types of customers and more suppliers all mix together in some combination which leads to an organizational environment that is difficult to manage without utilizing formal methods to keep employees focused. Formalization represents a process for keeping the organization's workforce focused. The management systems, work processes and organizational policies represent the means used to keep employees focused and consistent in the performance of work activities. Formalization of an organization's operations supports efforts to improve organizational performance.

Keeping the workforce focused and consistent in their actions requires routinizing implementation activities. Routinization leads to increased operational predictability. Performance predictability requires identifying specific performance standards and performance goals to achieve to reduce or eliminate performance variability. The creation of performance standards and performance goals aims to influence employee behavior and improve operational performance by achieving specific performance standards and goals. Randomness is incompatible with setting

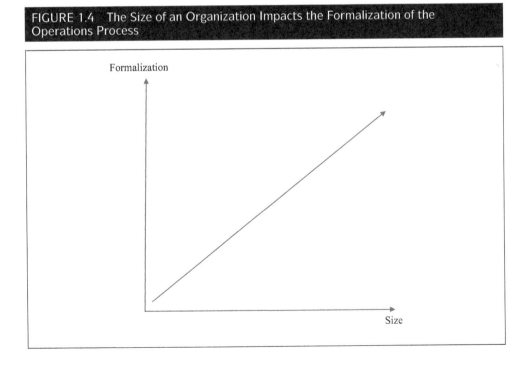

FIGURE 1.4   The Size of an Organization Impacts the Formalization of the Operations Process

performance standards and performance goals. Progress in achieving the standards and goals needs to be measurable and achievable. Measurability provides the focus as objectivity enables decision-makers to assess progress and develop intervention strategies when performance is not optimal.

Systemization through formalization facilitates **Coordination** of employee work efforts. As an organization grows, interdependence increases among the workforce as does increased employee specialization. Work specialization rises because the organization seeks to reduce job complexity to accelerate learning to improve job performance. The need to coordinate work activities hastens the need to systematize coordination to ensure accomplishing work in a time-limited manner. **Cooperation** is another important management issue. Increased organizational size requires greater effort at gaining cooperation among the workforce. **Trust** is an important element in creating a cooperative environment but building trust among the workforce within an organization becomes more challenging as an organization grows because building trust is a personal action. As more individuals are involved in a work project, trust becomes more challenging to achieve, but cooperation becomes more essential. Organizations utilize formalized methods, such as **Teams**, to create cooperation with the expectation that trust will evolve over time. But cooperation to achieve goals is paramount, and this is the primary focus for formalizing work processes.

Oversight is another important management issue that requires increased formalization in an expanding organization. Supervising in a small organization is easier because direct oversight is a more common form of supervision. However, at some point, direct methods of supervision become less practical; formal indirect oversight methods grow in importance to ensure routine oversight of worker activities. Indirect and direct methods of oversight vary according to management's preferences, but systematizing oversight becomes essential in keeping the workforce focused and productive.

Communication methods become more formalized as the organization grows, and the ability to directly communicate becomes more challenging. Also, more challenging is the need for constant messaging to maintain the workforce's focus. Organizations rely more and more on formally written policies; policies that standardize work processes; and policies that guide the development and ongoing management, including oversight, of the management systems. Rule development represents a special sub-set of policies as rules provide greater specificity in guiding employee behavior. Memorandums, emails and policy manuals that cover different subjects along with standardized reports represent traditional methods organizations use to formalize communication with the goal of keeping workers focused and worker behavior consistent.

Systematizing **Decision-making** and the decision-making processes are important because the magnitude of people making decisions increases as the size of an organization increases; therefore, the sheer number of decisions being made grows exponentially. Formalizing decision-making and the decision-making processes help to clarify, keep focus and maintain consistency as the organization expands in size. Creating formal job descriptions that outline decision-making authority along with routinizing the decision-making processes associated with a job contributes to more consistent outcomes and minimizes potential confusion over who has jurisdiction over specific organizational domains.

Finally, the human element is a critical catalyst for systematizing an organization as the organization grows. Even the most motivated employee can lose focus, allow personal goals to dominate and sometimes let personal issues impact their performance. Use of formalization management methods helps employees stay focused and ensures that the organization's goals and objectives remain a top priority. Formal management systems, work processes and policies serve as the primary methods to keep employees focused, consistent and successful in fulfilling their work responsibilities.

LEARNING OBJECTIVE #8: PURPOSE AND FUNCTIONS OF MANAGEMENT SYSTEMS, WORK PROCESSES AND ORGANIZATIONAL POLICIES

Management systems represent a systematic approach for providing order and structure during the strategy implementation process. As stated earlier, as an organization grows, management systems become more prevalent and complex to better support the organization's workforce's efforts at implementing the corporate strategy along with business strategies (if any) and the functional strategies.

Systems serve two primary functions. There are systems created specifically to facilitate the formulation of an organization's strategies. This encompasses all levels of strategies. The second function of management systems is to support the organization's work processes that implement the strategies. Management systems provide value during the strategy formulation and strategy implementation stages of the strategic management model. In designing management systems, the purpose is to reduce the risk of failure by increasing the probability of successfully identifying optimal strategies and successfully implementing the strategies.

A work process provides order to a specific activity by systematizing the process through routinizing the activity. Each process focuses on one type of activity; routinizing the activity in a series of sequential stages, with a start point and an end point. Creating a formalized process is meant to ensure that the process activity gets performed consistently, in accordance with process performance standards codified through the organization's policy(ies). Like a system, the goal in designing a process is to contribute value by achieving performance expectations. Often, there is an objective associated with a work process, and the objective is typically a SMART objective, comparable to SMART goals.

A policy represents an official guideline intended to regulate specific type of behavior. Policies directly and indirectly support the implementation of the organization's strategies. Direct support policies focus on the actual implementation process. Policies shape each work process by standardizing the performance of the work process. Furthermore, policies shape the design and functioning of a management system. Every management system is composed of multiple work processes, all sharing a common theme. Each system incorporates multiple policies because there is at least one policy associated with each work process.

Support policies refer to policies that regulate the lives of the workforce when not directly performing work-related activities. Support policies, such as sexual harassment policy, anti-bullying policy, career ladder opportunities policy and a myriad of other types of support policies are intended to deal with issues that can detract the workforce from performing their work functions. Support policies keep the workforce motivated and focused on work activities directly associated with the strategy implementation process.

Chapter Summary

This chapter describes how the concept of an organization originated as a means for achieving goals that require two or more people to achieve. Once created, an organization continues to strive to achieve greater levels of accomplishments to justify and protect its existence, which is a proxy for serving the personal goals of the workforce too.

The strategic management model serves to provide the reader with a wide-ranging context to better understand that an organization is only one aspect of a giant puzzle. An organization's role is to achieve and maintain. The strategic management model provides focus to direct and guide the efforts of the workforce to benefit the organization and the workforce. Because strategic management represents a process, the reader learns that the strategic management model encompasses a sequence of actions (or stages) such as mission and vision identification stages.

Organizations rely on people to perform the organization's work efforts in support of the achievement of the organization's strategic goals and vision. To keep the workforce focused on the strategic purposes of the organization, the organization incorporates the use of management methods that contribute to creating focused and consistent behavior. These management methods formalize the organization's activities within various management systems. Formalization represents an organization's official actions to standardize and routinize the organization's operations. Organizations create use management systems, work processes and policies as vehicles for influencing individual, group and organizational behavior, with the purpose of supporting the achievement ethic.

Questions

1. Identify and describe the major features of the Strategic Management model.
2. Describe and explain each of the major stages of the Strategic Management Planning process.
3. Identify and explain the meaning of the term "strategy."
4. Identify and briefly explain the three levels of strategy and explain their differences.
5. Identify and describe the relationship between the strategy formulation process and the strategy implementation process.
6. Identify and describe the meaning of the term's formalization and informal.
7. Describe the link between the size of an organization and the formalization process.
8. Identify and briefly describe the purpose and functions of a management system, work process and organization policy.

Bibliography

Brown, P. (2005). The evolving role of strategic management development. *Journal of Management Development*. 24(2). 209–222.

Dunlop, A., Firth, V. & Lurie, R. (2013). *Dynamic Strategy Implementation: Delivering on Your Strategic Ambition*. Deloitte University Press.

Friis, O., Holmgren, J. & Eskildsen, J. K. (2016). A strategy model-better performance through improved work strategy. *Journal of Modelling in Management.* 11(3). 742–762.

Gibbons, P., Scott, P.S. & Fhionnlaoich, C.M. (2015). Strategic management: a perspective on the development of strategic management and the contribution of the Irish Journal of Management. *Irish Journal of Management.* 34(1). 22–41.

Hanasini, Athapaththu H.K.S. (2016). An overview of strategic management: an analysis of the concepts and importance of strategic management. *International Journal of Scientific and Research Publications.* 6(2). 124–127.

Jurevicius, O. (2013). Strategic management & strategic planning process. *Strategic Management Insight.* February 13. 1–12.

Kaplan, R. S. & Norton, D.P. (2001). Transforming the balanced scorecard from performance measurement to strategic management: part II. *Accounting Horizons.* 15(2). 147–160.

Misankova, M. & Kocisova, K. (2013). Strategic implementation as a part of strategic management. *Procedia – Social and Behavioral Sciences.* 110. 861–870.

Nickols, F. (2016). Strategy, strategic management, strategic planning and strategic thinking. *Distance Consulting.* 1–9.

Okumus, F. (2003). A framework to implement strategies in organizations. *Management Decisions.* 41(9). 871–882.

Olson, E.M., Slater, S.F. & Hult, G.T.M. (2005). The importance of structure and process to strategy implementation. *Business Horizons.* 48. 47–54.

Pedrosa, L.F.C. (2010). Processes of strategic management. *Unpublished Manuscript.* 1–23.

Porter, M.E. (1998). *Comparative Strategy: Techniques for Analyzing Industries and Competitors.* New York: Free Press. Chapter 2.

Radomska, J. (2014). The role of manages in effective strategy implementation. *International Journal of Contemporary Management.* 13(3). 77–85.

Zafar, F., Babar, S. & Abbas, H. (2013). The art of strategic management – a key to success in the corporate sector. *European Journal of Research and Reflection in Management Sciences.* 1(1). 15–24.

PART II

OPERATIONAL ISSUES

Strategy Implementation and the Organization

OVERVIEW

Research confirms that the more an organization follows a systematic approach during the strategy implementation process, the more likely the organization will achieve its strategic goals. For those organizations that fail to achieve the strategic goals, the strategy implementation process was singled out as the primary reason. However, even the successful organizations identified the strategy implementation process as the most challenging stage of the strategic management planning process. This chapter examines the strategy implementation process to provide the reader with a better understanding of the purpose and function of the strategy implementation process in detail; the principal constraints associated with the strategy implementation process; and the challenges that make managing the strategy implementation process difficult to successfully follow. The strategy implementation process is essential to understand because strategy implementation is another term for organizational behavior.

What makes the strategy implementation process a successful effort or a failed effort in achieving the expected results? The answer is simple, people! People design the management systems, work processes and policies associated with the implementation process. People are responsible for using the management systems, work processes and heeding the policies. A failed implementation process represents a failure of the people employed by the organization.

What makes people successful or poor implementors? Many factors contribute to either condition. This chapter examines how the implementation process functions knowing fully that this is a people process. Later chapters examine the varied roles of people in contributing to the success or failure of the implementation process in achieving an organization's strategic goals.

CHAPTER 2   LEARNING OBJECTIVES

Readers will achieve the following learning objectives after reading this chapter.

1. List and explain the factors that make up the strategy implementation process.
2. Describe how the strategy formulation process and the strategy implementation process are top-down and bottom-up processes.
3. Identify and explain the reasons why the strategy implementation process leads to challenges.
4. Explain the link between strategy and strategic goals and operational objectives.
5. Discuss the association between the increasing systemization of the strategy implementation process and increasing operational success.
6. Identify and describe how the implementors are organized.
7. Discuss the role of each manager type in the strategy implementation process.
8. Identify and explain the use of performance indicators and the performance review process during the strategy implementation process.
9. Identify and explain the purpose of the reporting process during the strategy implementation process.
10. State and discuss the primary features of a policy (Figure 2.1).

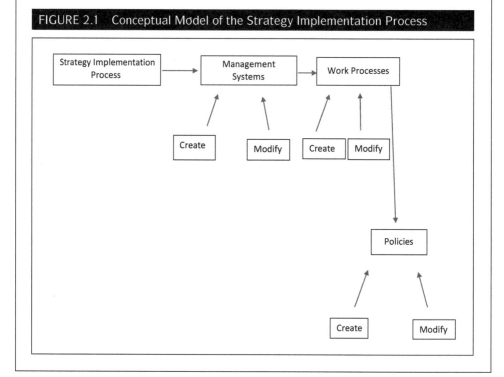

FIGURE 2.1   Conceptual Model of the Strategy Implementation Process

LEARNING OBJECTIVE #1: LIST AND EXPLAIN THE FACTORS THAT MAKE UP THE STRATEGY IMPLEMENTATION PROCESS

Junior et al. (2012) refer to implementation as a "process of translating intentions into actions" (p.21). Intentions represent the organization's strategy for achieving the organization's strategic goals. Implementation is the doing or operational stage that translates the strategy into actionable activities. We can refer to implementation as one large mega-system because the organization attempts to impose rationality on the strategy implementation process. Rationalization represents the efforts of **decision-makers** at routinizing the actions identified as essential to the success of the strategy implementation process. Decision-makers identify various standardized implementation work processes because systematizing the strategy implementation process is the single most important factor contributing to an organization's long-term success.

Systemization is critical in attempting to rationalize the strategy implementation processes. Decision-makers responsible for designing or modifying the existing strategy implementation processes and ensuring the functionality of these implementation processes need to know the critical issues to consider when organizing implementation activities. Table 2.1 identifies the most important implementation issues.

TABLE 2.1   Important Issues Associated with an Effective Strategy Implementation Process

Issues	Reason
• Systems	• A system has a common theme or focus; each system is composed of work processes codified by policies
• Processes	• A process has a common focus; each process represents the organization of activities sequenced in order with a primary outcome expected
• Policies	• A policy represents an official statement on the correct way to structure a system and/or work process
• Organizational Structure	• Structure refers to the way management, functions and people are organized in units and through vertical levels
• Leadership	• Officially designated decision-makers
• Communication	• Sharing information on the performance of management systems, work processes and the achievement of goals and objectives
• Human Resource Skills and Competencies	• The talents of individual members of the workforce
• Organizational Learning	• Represents the attempt by the organization to create systems with the specific purpose of facilitating knowledge acquisition
• Conflict Management	• Creating the capability to successfully manage conflict
• Resource Allocation	• Additional resources are necessary to support the strategy implementation process

Chapter 1 introduced the reader to the concept of management systems. In this chapter, we want to examine how an organization's decision-makers use management systems as the principal management method to systematize the overall strategy implementation process.

Strong leadership throughout the organization is essential to the success in creating and executing the implementation processes because leaders represent the designers who possess the knowledge and expertise to design new management systems and work processes or modify existing management systems and work processes to ensure the successful execution of the strategy implementation process. All levels of leaders, from senior management to supervisory managers, are responsible for systems management that includes designing management systems and work processes. Leaders lead through the use of management systems and bring about change through the use of management systems. At the implementation stage in the strategic management model, management systems function to achieve SMART objectives. SMART objectives operate similarly to SMART goals, but the focus is on improving and measuring operational activities. The use of SMART operational objectives leads to the creation of performance control systems (a type of management system) to keep the work force focused and moving forward toward achieving the SMART operational objectives. Leaders create policies or modify existing policies because it is with policies that leaders influence the behavior of the workforce; management system performance; optimal work process performance is the goal.

Organizational structure is one type of management system organizational structure refers to the formalization of strategy implementation activities by grouping the activities into homogeneous units. Units are organized vertically called levels, beginning with the office of the CEO down to the lowest organizational level. This vertical design represents a hierarchy of authoritative relationships with lower units responsible to units above them either directly or indirectly. Examples of units include Human Resources, Marketing and R&D. Leaders also organize each unit horizontally into specialized sub-units. Examples of sub-units in Marketing include Sales, Promotions and Advertising. Sub-units coordinate with each other. Each sub-unit has operational objectives to achieve; groups of sub-units can have shared operational objectives to achieve; the larger unit encompassing all the sub-units has operational objectives to achieve. Some refer to the hierarchy as a **hierarchy of objectives**. Organizational structure serves as a road map, pinpointing each unit of the organization and the relationship of a unit with other units. Each unit and sub-unit serve a specific purpose. The structure enables decision-makers to locate individuals responsible for an activity(ies), hastening their ability to solve operational problems and facilitate **coordination** among units and sub-units. Figure 2.2 presents an example of an organizational structure with levels, units and sub-units.

The **communication system** represents another factor associated with the strategy implementation process. A formalized information system standardizes various forms of communication processes used to disseminate and collect information that serve four purposes. First, information helps to **clarify** the decision-makers' intentions during the process of implementing the corporate and functional strategies. Second, communication processes help to **convey** how best individuals can organize management systems and work processes to facilitate the strategy implementation process. Third, communication processes provide **reports** on ongoing implementation successes and to identify implementation problems to resolve.

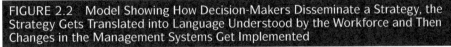

FIGURE 2.2   Model Showing How Decision-Makers Disseminate a Strategy, the Strategy Gets Translated into Language Understood by the Workforce and Then Changes in the Management Systems Get Implemented

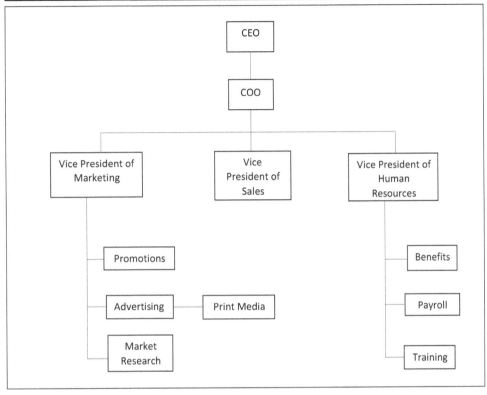

Finally, communication processes serve to **engage** all parties involved in the strategy implementation process to support coordination efforts.

Communication can take one of two forms: written and oral. Written communication serves as a reference or historical record to reference. Written communication is clear and concise, helping to clarify the message sent by the sender to the receiver. Oral communication is for immediate purposes when time is of the essence, and there is the need to clarify verbally the written communication or hasten an action that requires an immediate response.

Another important factor in the implementation process is an **organization's culture**. Culture represents an organization's collective set of values reflected in the management systems, work processes and policies. Values influence all actions of individuals; values influence all programmatic actions of an organization. For example, if cost containment is deemed a critical value, the organization will devote considerable effort in developing cost control systems and the important work processes associated with these cost control systems. Policies codify the changes to existing work processes, represent the creation of new work processes and regulate employee relations.

Another factor is the **human resources skills and competencies** that provide the expertise needed by the organization to optimize the strategy implementation process. The skills and competencies can be vested in leaders and non-leaders, but what is essential is that the organization possesses the human resource skills and competencies needed to successfully oversee the implementation process.

Organizations confront new circumstances that can impede the strategy implementation process. This can include unforeseen problems. The faster the organization can respond to the new circumstances, the greater the likelihood for success during the implementation process. Developing an organization's capabilities to learn is important because building capabilities accelerates the process of learning how to resolve problems. **Organizational learning** is developed through the creation of learning systems that serve the purpose of facilitating learning. **Training** represents the organization's efforts at routinizing the process of enhancing the organization's capabilities to learn.

Conflict management is a necessity because differences of opinion frequently occur during the strategy implementation process. Conflict often revolves around the issue of the "best way" to execute an activity. Individuals in conflict underlying personal motives are often present, appearing in the differences on the best way to do something. Getting past personal agenda is an important goal of conflict management. Building the capability to act quickly and responsibly helps to engage the parties in a conflict resolution process. Preventing conflict is the first line of defense but an unrealistic expectation in all situations. Resolving conflict successfully and speedily moves the organization forward. Human Resources often plays a central role in conflict management either through direct intervention or training organizational members in learning how to use conflict resolution strategies.

Resource allocation decisions are an important factor in supporting a successful strategy implementation process because the allocation of resources provides the means to support implementation with human and monetary resources. Implementation activities often involve doing something different. As a consequence, creating the capabilities to succeed in the strategy implementation process is critical. Just as the military needs to devote extra resources to support an offensive action or buttress a defensive position, organizations need to create resource allocation processes that ensures sufficient people and monetary resources support that can contribute to a successful strategy implementation process.

LEARNING OBJECTIVE #2: DESCRIBE HOW THE STRATEGY FORMULATION PROCESS AND THE STRATEGY IMPLEMENTATION PROCESS ARE TOP-DOWN AND BOTTOM-UP PROCESSES

Top-down refers to actions initiated by senior management including the CEO. Bottom-up refers to actions initiated at the lowest levels of the organization with non-managers reaching out to the lowest supervisory management level. Non-managers and supervisory managers' report issues up through the other management levels if the importance of the issue warrants the attention of more senior managers. Middle management represents the dividing point between senior management and lower management levels as well as non-managers.

Work processes link to other processes in an unbroken chain of processes. The strategy formulation process and strategy implementation process link together. Because each process is a stage in the strategic management model, it is natural that the two processes form a link. Linkage breakdowns represent serious problems if unresolved because there is an inter-dependency between the two processes.

We begin by examining new top-down influences on the strategy formulation and strategy implementation processes. Senior management, as part of their work responsibilities, initiates changes that can impact the entire organization. Developing the **vision** statement is a common responsibility of senior management because senior management's role is to create a path to follow and an end to achieve. The end is the vision. Senior management can seek buy-in from subordinates throughout the organization, but the starting point occurs among senior management.

Because senior management's traditional role is to have a strategic big-picture perspective, it is senior management's responsibility to identify the long-term **strategic goals** of the organization. After selecting the strategic goals, senior management initiates the strategy formulation process. The strategy formulation process becomes the catalyst for involving various information gathering processes within the **information management system**. Information gathering occurs at the upper levels of the organization, with the strategic planners responsible for gathering information, analyzing the information and interpreting the information with senior management. Subordinate managers conduct relevant operational analyses and forward this information up to the strategic planners via information processes.

After selecting the strategy for achieving the strategic goals, senior management communicates the strategy to middle managers. Middle managers translate the strategy into areas of responsibility that are then parceled out to subordinates in the organization who become responsible for implementing their assigned responsibilities. Senior management identifies management systems that need to change to support the new strategy. Modified management systems require modifying work processes and related policies impacted by the new strategy need to change. Senior management identifies the management systems, work processes and policies that need to change, but middle management and their subordinates are responsible for identifying how the management systems, work processes and relevant policies need to change.

Bottom-up involves non-managers and supervisory managers who are directly responsible for overseeing the operations of the organization. Operations have a short-term focus because operations typically focus on achieving short-term objectives. Short-term is emphasized in operations because the organization wants to ensure that movement toward achieving the strategic goals is progressing as planned. This represents an **incremental** approach. Achieving the objectives means the strategy is working, but if not, there is time to modify the operations that achieve the operational objectives.

Lower-level supervisory management and non-managers determine how best to operationalize the strategy to ensure a successful strategy implementation process. It is at this level that specific changes to the management systems, work processes and related policies mostly occur. Recommended changes at this level are communicated up to middle management, usually in the form of performance reports. Middle management's responsibility is to translate the recommended changes into terms senior management understands. This process can continue through several iterations until there is acceptance among the relevant parties that operations are working as expected.

The lower levels of the organization commonly submit routine operational reports that can include recommendations for making improvements to the operations directly associated with implementing the strategies. These reports move up to middle management. Middle management interprets the report contents and explains the intent of the changes requested along with recommending actions to consider to senior management. Generally, the recommended changes to the operations focus on meeting the performance expectations. Senior management relies on the insights provided by subordinates because lower-level managers are mostly familiar with the performance of their respective units. Frequently, initiatives for changing the operations involve modifying management systems, work processes and related policies directly associated with implementation activities. Policy is particularly important because policy guides the management of a management system and related work processes. Ineffective policies have a detrimental effect on achieving the operational objectives which will impact the organization's ability to achieve the strategic goals (Figure 2.3).

FIGURE 2.3   Goal–Strategy–Resource Allocation Relationship

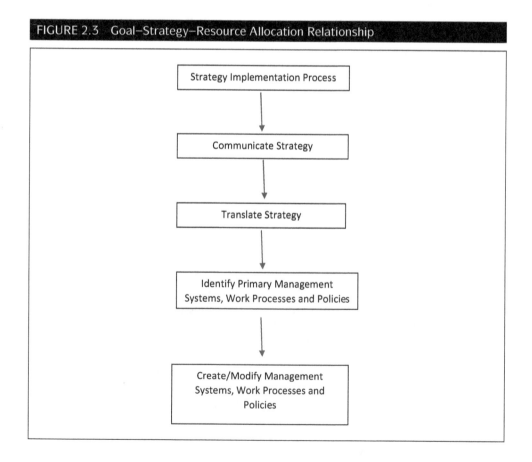

Newcastle Call Center – Part 1

Bob Watson owned Newcastle Call Center for a year, purchasing the firm from Amanda Bates in 2017. Amanda started the business 25 years earlier. The organization grew over the years because Amanda was good at knowing how to successfully build the business. Bob spent the year learning the business from Amanda. But Amanda officially stepped aside the prior month. Bob saw several opportunities to grow the business but decided on a cautious growth strategy to avoid unnecessary risks. However, he was confronted with a dilemma. Bob was uncertain of the next step. He knew things needed to change to implement the new strategy, but he was uncertain how to begin. Amanda told him to always feel free to contact her. Up to this point he did not want to bother her, but now, his uncertainty created a lot of personal angst. Bob called Amanda. They talked for over an hour. Now Bob knew what he needed to do to implement the new strategy. First, he reviewed Amanda's suggestions.

Questions

1. What were Amanda's suggestions?
2. What were Bob's concerns?
3. Who else should Bob consult with? Why?
4. Why does Bob need to understand the strategy better?
5. What makes deciding difficult for Bob?

LEARNING OBJECTIVE #3: IDENTIFY AND EXPLAIN THE REASONS WHY THE STRATEGY IMPLEMENTATION PROCESS LEADS TO CHALLENGES

Several factors make the strategy implementation process challenging to manage. Converting the corporate strategy and related functional strategies into action steps or operational activities requires a thorough understanding of the strategies and the ability to translate these strategies into specific operational guidelines to understand and be able to respond to by designing the impacted management systems, work processes and relevant policies. (These represent the important action steps.) This leads to two additional challenges. The organization needs leaders who can guide the strategy implementation process by demonstrating an understanding of the type of action steps necessary to implement the organization's strategies. Leadership requires the ability to translate strategy into action steps, but equally important, leaders need effective communication skills to present and describe the roadmap of actions required of implementors. The inability to communicate effectively and in a consistent way likely will lead to inaction, hasty actions or actions that fail to contribute to a successful strategy implementation process.

By definition, a new strategy emphasizes the need for the organization to act differently to achieve strategic goals that are not yet achievable. Change is disruptive, no matter if the changes are minor or major. Overcoming **resistance** to change is a challenge. Implementors may be unwilling to act differently for fear of the unknown, fear failure or fear of loss of advantages by upsetting the status quo. Overcoming the resistance is one of the important challenges leaders and implementors need to confront.

Another challenge is an organization's size and the difficulty in managing the change process successfully. The larger the organization, the more complex is the organization's operations. Here, complexity refers to numerous and sophisticated management systems, numerous and complex work processes along with a myriad of formal and detailed organizational policies associated with the many management systems and work processes. Because of this complicated network of management systems and work processes, the organization's strategies tend to be less ambitious because of the challenge associated with managing the changes to the operations during the strategy implementation process.

Providing sufficient resources to support the strategy implementation process is another important challenge that requires attention. Often, leadership can underestimate the adequacy of resources in supporting the strategy implementation process. Skilled staff and financial resources need to be adequate to the task. What is adequate is difficult to estimate; managers need to communicate the adequacy to make the case for additional resources. Also, leadership and implementors need to ensure the best use of resources.

Strategy incompatibility with organizational capabilities is a common challenge for leaders to address because leaders too often underestimate the required resources needed during the strategy implementation process. This situation is not totally unexpected because underestimating is a frequent occurrence during the planning process because the future cannot be predicted with 100% certainty. But, hastening the ability to upgrade an organization's capabilities to successfully implement the strategies is essential to achieve the strategic goals.

Implementing new strategies is disruptive to the established order. Resistance will occur for the reasons stated earlier. One of the primary strategies for overcoming resistance is to offer **incentives** to encourage resisters to embrace the change process associated with strategy implementation. Knowing what incentives work best is an important challenge to resolve to engage the leaders and implementors in the change process. Resistance to change can occur from ignorance of the issues associated with the change process. **Education** is one of the most effective strategies an organization can use to overcome resistance associated with ignorance. Training programs are important for educating everyone associated with the change process.

Organizations continually evolve, often moving from having relatively undeveloped management systems, work processes and policies to more developed types of management systems, work processes and organizational policies. An aggressive growth strategy frequently reveals an organization's operational shortcomings associated with a developed strategy implementation process. The challenge is to push forward to create a more sophisticated strategy implementation process; this entails making the implementation process better organized and systematic.

Leadership oversight of the strategy implementation process is always a challenge because of the inability of the organization to provide direct and continuous oversight in monitoring the strategy implementation process. Leaders and implementors need to design performance monitoring management systems along with the relevant work processes and policies that reflect selected monitoring methods used to assess the performance of the management systems and work processes associated with the strategy implementation process. As strategies become more ambitious, the strategy implementation process becomes more complex to mirror the strategies to implement. The use of technology to provide enhanced monitoring capabilities is a must for any but the simplest strategy implementation process. Technology, used thoughtfully, can facilitate performance monitoring and reduce the need for direct oversight. This explains why management systems are referred to as sociotechnical entitles that combine people with technology.

An organization's **culture** offers the type of values that support the existing strategy implementation process. However, a new strategy, for example, an aggressive growth strategy, will necessitate additional values and strengthening of supportive existing values. For example, being cost conscious through keeping costs steady and cost savings by lowering costs is an example of how an organization can strengthen a value. Values shape all behavior. Identifying actions associated with specific values and designing the operations to reflect the associated value(s) is another challenge.

Newcastle Call Center – Part 2

Bob's efforts at implementing the new strategy led to several unexpected challenges that he had not considered, and Amanda's suggestions failed to address. Bob decided not to bother Amanda again as he needed to learn how to manage the business and deal with the consequences of his decisions. Bob decided that the first step was to write down a list of the challenges associated with implementing the new strategy. Once he created the list, the next step was to rank the challenges from most important to deal with immediately to least important. Once Bob decided on this plan, he determined that the best approach was to prepare the list at home, free from work distractions. Bob was eager to get started because he knew that failing to respond with a plan to deal with the immediate challenges would lead to a failed strategy.

Questions

1. What were the major challenges Bob identified?
2. Why did Bob decide to prepare the list of challenges at home?
3. Bob needs guidance in preparing the plan. What do you advise?
4. What type of goals should Bob use? Explain.
5. What type of objectives should Bob use? Explain.

LEARNING OBJECTIVE #4: EXPLAIN THE LINK BETWEEN STRATEGY AND STRATEGIC GOALS AND OPERATIONAL OBJECTIVES

An organization exits to serve a purpose. That purpose is to achieve something. Often, the terms **"vision or goal"** are used to define that something, and the goal frequently is framed as a metric. For example, successfully introduce a new product to society and eliminate a medical problem such as polio or build a state-wide system of roads represent examples of vision statements. After identifying a vision, the next step is to galvanize effort to garner the resources needed to achieve the vision. The resources collected may or may not be sufficient to achieve the original vision but as long as the resources are adequate to achieve a limited version of the vision and the resources can keep the organization in existence, this is sufficient (Figure 2.4 shows the ongoing process of goal identification and resource allocation). However, there is a stage needed because a vision or goal alone is insufficient. The strategic management model shows the stage needed for achieving both the vision and one or more strategic goals. This is the strategy formulation stage where the organization conducts a series of analyses that leads to the identification of strategic options and then analyzing the options to select the preferred option for achieving the strategic goals (linked to the vision). The choice of a strategy is the selection of a plan that shows the greatest promise for achieving the strategic goals. The resource allocation process begins at this point; the strategy formulation process includes identifying the resources needed and subsequently how the resources need to be used in support of the strategy implementation process.

Certain types of strategic goals are preferable for assessing if the strategy is working and that the resources are adequate and utilized effectively. SMART strategic goals are the best type of goals. SMART goals are defined in Chapter 1. SMART goals represent the ideal goal type because this type of goal functions as a performance standard, with metrics, to assess the organization's strategy implementation efforts toward achieving the strategic goals.

Within the context of the strategic management model, operational objectives serve to focus the strategy implementation process. Objectives are SMART type but differ from SMART strategic goals in that the objectives are short-term (e.g. under one year) and are strictly operational. This means that objectives are an important aspect in the design of management systems and work processes, serving as

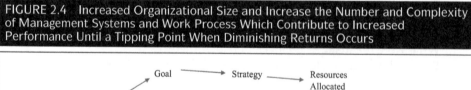

FIGURE 2.4 Increased Organizational Size and Increase the Number and Complexity of Management Systems and Work Process Which Contribute to Increased Performance Until a Tipping Point When Diminishing Returns Occurs

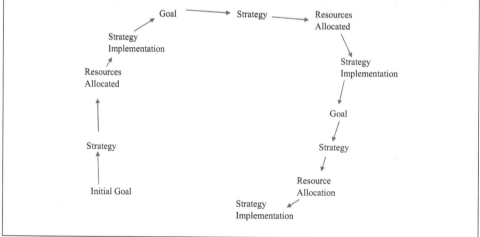

performance standards to assess the effectiveness of the management systems and work processes. As performance standards, the organization can assess the performance of a management system and work process. Success in achieving the operational objectives represents movement toward achieving the strategic goals and achieving the strategic goals represents movement toward achieving the vision. Success in achieving the operational objectives and strategic goals affirms that the selected strategy is working as expected.

Newcastle Call Center – Part 3

During the next several days, Bob considered his situation, debating how best to change the operations to successfully implement the new strategy. As Bob pondered the situation, it became clearer to him that providing more focus to certain aspects of the business' operations was essential. He identified the strategic goals: a 5% increase in revenue in 2019; a modest 3% decline in total costs in 2019; and a 2% increase in revenue per customer. Bob recalled that Amanda often referred to something called "operational objectives" and that objectives are important to link to the strategic goals. He was not certain about the association between goals and objectives nor was he clear about the purpose of operational objectives. As he sat in his office thinking on the subject, his cell rang. Amanda was calling. What a coincidence, he thought. During his conversation with Amanda, she explained the link between goals and operational objectives; the importance of having measurable objectives; and the role the measurable operational objectives play in monitoring different aspects of the business' operations.

Questions

1. How are goals and objectives related?
2. What is an operational objective?
3. Why did Amanda stress the importance of measurable objectives?
4. What is the role played by measurable objectives in the monitoring process?
5. What do you recommend for how Bob should begin?

LEARNING OBJECTIVE #5: DISCUSS THE ASSOCIATION BETWEEN THE INCREASING SYSTEMIZATION OF THE STRATEGY IMPLEMENTATION PROCESS AND INCREASING OPERATIONAL SUCCESS

Research supports the view that organizations associated with being systematic in their business practices are more effective in achieving their goals. Furthermore, as systems become more systemized, performance continues to improve. There are several factors associated with the systematizing process that represent essential issues that contribute to an organization's ability to continue meeting performance expectations. One factor is an **organization's culture** which embodies a collection of values that influence the organization's internal environment and relations with external stakeholders; culture manifests itself by acting as a hidden hand, influencing the orientation of all operational activities. One such value is self-improvement; the process of continual emphasis on making the operations function better.

Associated with self-improvement is a **performance value** orientation. Self-improvement is measured using **performance metrics**. Numbers count and performance metrics enable users to set **SMART objectives** to measure performance and calibrate operational activities to achieve the operational objectives. Measurement enables users to assess performance, and the timeliness of the objective imposes a sense of urgency over the strategy implementation process by minimizing wasted time and resources in achieving the operational objectives.

Organization is the quintessential value associated with being systematic. Being organized is like having a desk with no clutter, everything has a special place on the desk. Whereas disorganization is the complete opposite. Most often, the look of the desk reflects a stage in the process of becoming more organized. The desk metaphor helps to understand that operations represent an organizing process, but unlike the desk metaphor, operations continue to evolve by being more organized as a consequence of changing strategies, the need for greater efficiencies and in response to changing external circumstances. Environmental, industry and market forces are frequent catalysts for forcing the organization to change. The larger the organization, the greater the likelihood of needing to change, and the scope of the change is greater. In short, the change in the operations of large organizations is more complex than in smaller organizations.

Successfully responding to the need to change means that instead of rigid thinking, one way only to operate philosophy, the organization acts **pragmatically** and **flexibly**, the two important values for any organization to include as part of the organization's culture. Pragmatism refers to the avoidance of a dogmatic approach to managing an organization's operations. Theory or one best way to manage is secondary to being open to a wider range of possible change options. Flexibility is important because an openness to change is merely a first step in a two-step process. The organization needs to initiate change and to embrace change as a necessity for the long-term success of the organization. There is no one "right way" or "we need to hold steady, circumstances will change" mentality.

Rigid thinking often is pervasive with an organization's reward system; the reward system represents the primary ways organizations use to motivate the workforce. Unfortunately, an organization's reward system loses much of its effectiveness as a motivator of the workforce because the rewards are considered automatic; merely by holding a position in the organization and gaining seniority status in each position held deserve a reward. Organizations that promote the use of **incentive systems** understand the dilemma associated with the reward system's limitations by developing single purpose incentive programs to motivate the workforce to achieve SMART objectives. Achieve and earn and as long as the objective is achievable and realistic, the workforce will strive toward being successful. A corollary value is the value of **self-motivation**. A workforce composed of mostly self-motivated individuals represents a workforce committed to the value **achieving** because the end product of self-motivation is achieving an objective. People with a strong sense of **self-worth** commonly are self-motivated and achievement-oriented because they demonstrate the self-confidence to achieve operational objectives.

Associated with a motivated and self-confident workforce is a leadership team with the same characteristics but who also possess the dual values of **objectivity** and **decisiveness**. Being objective is demonstrated by using a rational approach to decision-making. Being rational involves creating an information system designed to draw information from varied sources; offering decision-makers a diverse range of perspectives to aid them in making decisions. Objectivity emphasizes the use of performance metrics and data because performance is a proxy for defining degrees of success. Hard data is the measure of a result-oriented leadership team. Performance assessment functions as a catalyst for more action, even if the trend is positive. Success in achieving operational objectives allows leaders to raise the performance bar continually. Decisiveness is associated with effective leadership because leaders need to act on their decisions. Arriving at a decision and acting on the decision is a two-step process. Indecisiveness avoids making a decision and acting on that decision. There is a saying that captures the importance of being decisive and acting decisively. "He who hesitates is lost."

Finally, a successful strategy implementation process is often associated with the **integration of management systems**. Too often, management systems operate like islands; treated like islands when all the organization's management systems must link directly and indirectly in a spiderweb like network system. The more the management systems are linked together, the greater the probability of the organization achieving the strategic goals. Faulty linkage will always show up through visible symptoms of management system dysfunction that a **well-designed information and performance management system** will diagnose, signaling the need for remedial action.

Figure 2.5 shows the association between the increasing size of an organization and the shift toward formalizing the organization's management systems and work processes which contribute toward improved organizational success.

FIGURE 2.5   Example of a Simple Organizational Design

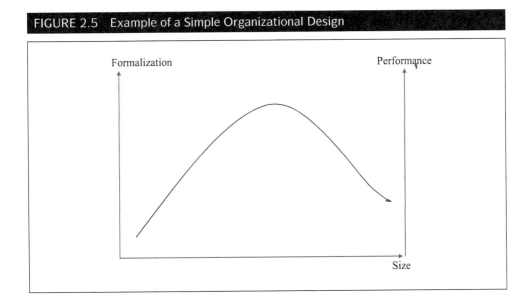

However, there is a tipping point where formalization becomes increasingly counter-productive. When formalization becomes an end in itself instead of the means to an end, the tipping point is reached. It is when the organization reaches the tipping point, then the organization's performance begins to suffer. At the tipping point and beyond, diminishing returns is the end result until the organization shifts focus again to emphasize the use of pragmatic strategy implementation process to achieve the strategic goals and operational objectives. Performance assessment is the critical management system to assess when the organization reaches the tipping point.

LEARNING OBJECTIVE #6: IDENTIFY AND DESCRIBE HOW THE IMPLEMENTORS ARE ORGANIZED

There are seven types of **organizational designs** used to organize strategy implementors. The seven designs serve to facilitate decision-making and communication (A.K.A. reporting relationships) throughout the organization as well as designating a location for each employee. Location identification helps decision-makers easily locate an individual who is responsible for specific work responsibilities. Each design organizes implementors into a **vertical hierarchy,** with levels; each level guided by decision-makers; each decision-maker is responsible for making decisions for a particular unit within the hierarchy. We can think of this arrangement as a vertical **chain of authority**; each lower-level subordinate reports to the level immediately preceding this level. Within each level, implementors are organized into **horizonal units**. Each horizontal unit is labeled to denote its specific function. For example, a unit could be labeled as marketing. Another unit might be Human Resources. All implementors within the marketing unit share the common frame of reference, marketing.

Within each horizontal unit, there usually are sub-units. For example, within the marketing unit, there can be a market research unit, sales unit, promotions unit and advertising unit. Implementors within each sub-unit share that function in common. The purpose in creating horizontal units and sub-units is to organize specialties into homogeneous groups to facilitate coordination of relevant goal and objective-oriented activities. Furthermore, the design can facilitate coordination among horizontal units and sub-units if routine cross-unit coordination is necessary.

The hierarchy maintains a degree of control over subordinate units. Control reflects the authority conferred at that level for making decisions and overseeing the workforce within that unit. Organizations can either be **centralized** with most decision-making authority vested among senior managers or **de-centralized**, where authority to make many types of decisions dispersed among lower levels of managers. We can think of the concepts, centralization and de-centralization as two ends of an authority continuum. Senior decision-makers determine if more immediate decisions are necessary to respond to external issues (then, decision-making is more de-centralized) or if decision-makers do not need to make quick decisions in responding to external issues (then decision-making is more centralized).

Coordination is emphasized among horizontal units and sub-units because coordination of operational activities is essential between vertical levels. Each level has responsibilities associated with the strategy implementation process, but because each level has a specific role to play in the strategy implementation process, coordination between levels is necessary. Coordination requires some degree of **co-operation** among sub-units within a unit, between units and between levels of units. Co-operation represents the need to work together toward achieving a shared purpose. Organizations use goals, objectives, job descriptions, performance reviews and incentives, among the various management methods available, to promote co-operation among implementors.

Within each organizational design are planned, formal **communication processes**. There are both formal and informal communication processes. The intention of communication processes is to provide information and guidance to decision-makers to enhance each unit's and each level's ability to perform their assigned duties. A **formal communication process** is a process officially sanctioned as an official means for sharing information within the organization. Information can move downward between levels, upward through levels to upper management and horizontally between units and between sub-units within a larger unit. Common forms of formal communication methods include reports, PowerPoint presentations and emails. Emails for official use are formal because these are retrievable and constitute part of the organization's official records. Informal communication methods do not receive official sanction by the organization. Frequently, informal communication processes provide meaningless information or misleading information. Often problematic, informal communication processes wield considerable influence on the workforce until the organization responds with a clarifying statement.

Figures 2.6–2.12 show examples of each type of organizational design. The designs include the following.

- **Simple Design**: Typical of organizations with few than 15 employees; usually two primary levels, a CEO and all others. The lowest level is most commonly organized in semi-formal structural arrangement.
- **Functional Design**: A common form of organizational design. The workforce is grouped into functional units such as marketing, information systems and accounting; within a unit, the workforce is grouped by function within a function (i.e. market research within marketing).
- **Product Design**: Organizations with a large number of diverse products sometimes can group segments of the workforce by product category; the unique characteristics of each product category require the workers to specialize in that product category.
- **Market Design**: Organizations with very different types of customers sometimes group segments of the workforce by customer type because the workers need to specialize in knowing how to work with a customer-type possessing unique characteristics and needs.
- **Geographic Design**: Organizations that operate in different geographic areas, each area presenting unique characteristics, will organize segments of the workforce by geographic regions and sub-geographic regions to enable the workforce to respond quicker to regional situations.

- **Divisional Design**: Some large organizations, especially conglomerates, grew by acquiring other companies; often, these acquisitions differed from each other. Overseeing these acquisitions is strengthened by treating each acquisition as a separate division to make corporate oversight and performance management easier.
- **Matrix Design**: Typically, part of a functional design; a matrix is included in those organizations where projects and project management are common strategies used in developing new products; enhance coordination and co-operation among functions as well as make better use of resources (i.e. people primarily).

FIGURE 2.6   Example of a Functional Organizational Design

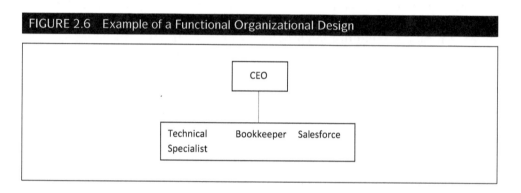

FIGURE 2.7   Example of a Product-Functional Organizational Design

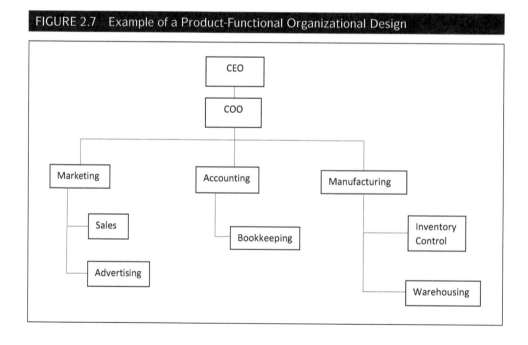

FIGURE 2.8   Example of a Market-Functional Organizational Design

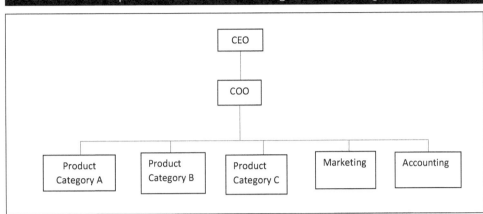

FIGURE 2.9   **Example of a Market-Functional Organizational Design**

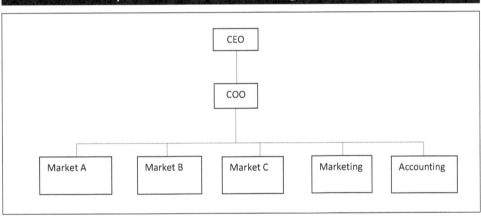

FIGURE 2.10   **Example of a Geographic-Functional Organizational Design**

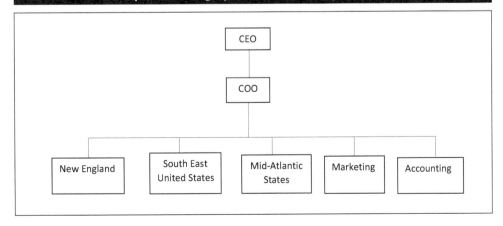

FIGURE 2.11   **Example of a Divisional Organizational Design**

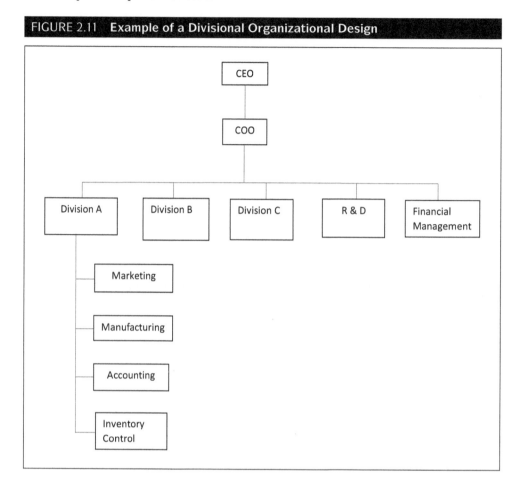

LEARNING OBJECTIVE #7: DISCUSS THE ROLE OF EACH MANAGER TYPE IN THE STRATEGY IMPLEMENTATION PROCESS

Organizations create management positions to oversee and supervise the strategy implementation process. There are three primary levels of managers. **Senior managers** are responsible for overseeing the strategic direction of the strategy implementation process because senior managers bear the responsibility of recommending the organization's corporate strategy along with other strategies (e.g. functional strategies). **Middle managers** serve a pivotal role in the implementation process in four important ways. First, middle managers **translate** strategy to ensure that members of the organization at lower levels learn their responsibilities during the strategy implementation process. Second, middle managers routinely **oversee** the strategy implementation process to ensure that the operations function as planned. Third, middle managers determine if operations **deviate from expectations** and working with responsible individuals to undertake corrective actions to ensure that the strategy implementation process remains on track. Finally, middle managers serve as a **conduit of information** sharing between senior management and lower levels

FIGURE 2.12   Example of a Matrix-Functional Organizational Design

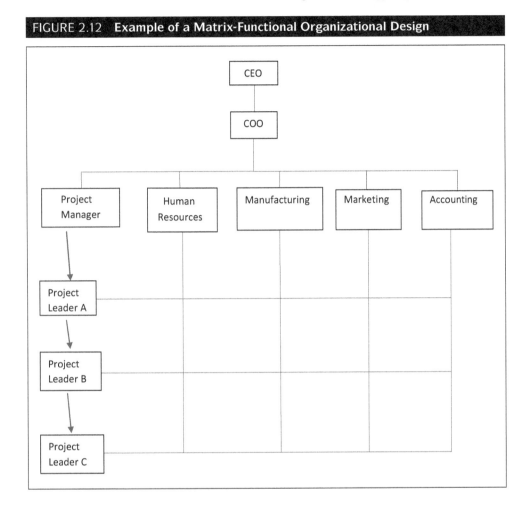

of supervisor managers and non-managers. **Supervisory managers** represent the lowest management level. Supervisory managers determine how best to implement the strategic plan by following the guidelines provided by middle managers. Supervisory managers represent the frontline management ranks, working directly with non-managers to certify a high-performance operation and to report to middle managers where problems or opportunities exist for making operational improvements.

LEARNING OBJECTIVE #8: IDENTIFY AND EXPLAIN THE USE OF PERFORMANCE INDICATORS AND PERFORMANCE REVIEW PROCESS DURING THE STRATEGY IMPLEMENTATION PROCESS (SMART OBJECTIVES)

There is a category of management systems referred to as **performance control systems**. The purpose of performance control systems is to assess if the operational changes to the management systems associated with the strategy implementation process are working. **Performance indicators** represent a critical dimension of a performance control system because the performance indicators represent metrics used both to assess change and for facilitating change. First, indicators use SMART objectives which are similar to SMART goals except that the objectives are operational objectives. Examples include defect rates, turnover rates of new hires, units produced per hour, average time spent on the phone answering calls, number of calls made per hour and so forth. The list of possible objectives is almost endless.

Metrics are used to facilitate change using operational objectives which represent targets to achieve. Achieving the targets warrants changing the relevant operations. The choice of targets is made by decision-makers in consultation with non-decision-makers directly involved with the work process to determine the work processes and management systems linked directly to an organization's strategy. As a reminder to the reader, organizations can have multiple strategies so that impacted management systems must change during the strategy implementation process. The management systems along with work processes focused are those showing the greatest potential for impacting the organization's performance when executing a strategy. An organization's performance, measured by assessments of the operations, showing movement in the right direction, indicates the likelihood of achieving the strategic goals.

Performance control systems are a means for comparing actual results with expected results. Therefore, the use of performance metrics is essential because objectivity aids the measurement process better than subjective, non-measurable information prone to bias. Every work process generates a measurable outcome easily converted into an objective. Think of driving home at night from work. The drive represents the process (as a non-business issue we refer to this as a routine) that encompasses stages that culminates in arriving home by a certain time. The time taken commonly is consistent within a range of several times recorded after making the drive. This average time becomes the driver's baseline. However, the driver can seek to shorten the time by reviewing the stages to learn how to save time. Of course, a simple way to save time is to incorporate technology through the use of GPS to program the GPS for the route that leads to the best time. Being more creative, the driver might consider leaving work earlier or later to avoid peak travel conditions. Eventually, the law of diminishing returns prevails. The driver cannot save more time unless there is a fundamental shift in circumstances.

Important organizational metrics can encompass gathering customer information such as table turnover rates at a restaurant; costs, for example, advertising costs per email; average profit margin per bottle; rate of production such as the number of units produced per hour or number of calls answered per hour. Organizations create numerous work processes, but decision-makers need to determine the work processes that capture the output of other intermediate types of work processes that link to more significant work processes. As the reader can surmise, work processes link with decision-making systems and information systems to provide decision-makers with routine information about a work process to monitor performance of other work processes. For example, time spent integrating a new employee can encompass the recruitment process, hiring process and the onboarding process. The work process is the important focus point within a system composed of one or more work processes. What makes this important to understand is that work processes link with other work processes within a management system, and management systems link to other management systems through their respective work processes. The entire network completes the strategy implementation process.

Newcastle Call Center – Part 4

One of the projects Amanda intended to introduce was an upgrade to all the technology used in each of the three rooms with operators. Amanda's goal was to introduce state-of-the-art technology to monitor various work processes in each of the three rooms. Each room operated 16 hours a day, 7 days a week. Amanda wanted to track a variety of work processes with the goal of improving the operations of the call center rooms. She knew that without the new technology, she was limited in setting performance targets and developing new work processes and training programs with the intent at improving the performance of the operators. Once Amanda decided to retire, this plan was put in abeyance, but the plan was not forgotten. In a recent conversation with Bob, Amanda discussed the plan with Bob. Bob asked several questions. What work processes did she want to focus on? How were the operational objectives relevant? What did she mean when she mentioned performance standards and performance objectives? Amanda and Bob arranged to meet for lunch to respond to Bob's questions.

Questions

1. In a call center, what is one-work process to evaluate? Explain.
2. What did she say about why operational objectives are important?
3. What did she say about performance standards?
4. What did she say about the need for performance objectives?
5. Why is it essential in using technology?

LEARNING OBJECTIVE #9: IDENTIFY AND EXPLAIN THE PURPOSE OF THE REPORTING PROCESS DURING THE STRATEGY IMPLEMENTATION PROCESS

A new strategy sets in motion changes within the organization as the organization attempts to implement the new strategy (along with multiple support functional strategies). A strategy introduces anticipated and unanticipated changes that will generate a multiplier effect on the operations. Decision-makers expect and plan for pre-determined changes to occur because the changes are part of the change process associated with implementing the new strategy. But setting in motion operational changes, once begun, often can trigger unanticipated changes because of the network of interconnected management systems and work processes. Decision-makers need to monitor the results of the strategy implementation process to determine the effectiveness of the process for implementing the new strategy(ies). Decision-makers also need to monitor the unanticipated impact during the strategy implementation process. The most common method decision-makers use to learn about impact is using formal, **standardized reports**.

Formal, standardized reports represent a common communication method organizations use to disseminate information to designated recipients. A formal type of report represents the organization's officially approved method for reporting performance metrics associated with the strategy implementation process. Formal, standardized, routinized reporting typically meets certain guidelines defined in a policy(ies). First, there is a report's frequency, such as daily, weekly, monthly or some other pre-determined time frame. Second, the organization determines the individual position(s) responsible for submitting the report. One job might be responsible for submitting a report, or several jobs need to submit a group or team report. Third, often, the organization defines the report's content. There might be places for open-ended types of responses, but more commonly, reports require very specific types of metric-based information. For example, defect rates of black dry erase markers averaging six defects per 1000 tested for the week of November 30, 20XX.

Decision-makers typically use reports to learn about the performance of subordinates responsible for developing and implementing changes in their unit's operations. The driving force for change is implementing the subordinate's operational responsibilities associated with the strategy implementation process. The network of reporting methods represents the organization's preferred means for monitoring the work processes and the amount of success in successfully changing these work processes in achieving the operational objectives. Reporting can occur through face-to-face meetings as well as routine presentations. Most often there is a written component. Either a follow-up "minutes of the meeting" or PowerPoint slides can accompany a presentation. Documentation becomes essential as an organization grows, and the need to track activities becomes more challenging because of the increased complexity of the operations.

The reader begins to understand how reports and the reporting process represent the linkage among different types of information processes and the performance management systems. This linkage of work processes, part of a network of different types of management systems, continues to evolve in scope and complexity as the organization expands and pursues more ambitious strategies for achieving more ambitious strategic goals.

LEARNING OBJECTIVE #10: STATE AND DISCUSS THE FEATURES OF A POLICY

Policy represents the quintessential management method used to guide employee behavior. An organization's official policy is a statement that presents the organization's official position covering an organizational issue with expectations that the impacted workforce conforms to the guidelines outlined in the policy. An official, formal policy becomes official once the governing agents of the organization sanctify the policy. Organizations can have unofficial policies that evolve when there is no official policy or an existing policy is insufficient. Organizational decision-makers typically lag in their efforts at formalizing an unofficial policy or revising an existing policy to gain time to determine if a change is actually warranted and to decide on the actual type of changes to make. The reason organizations need to create policies is to hasten the decision-making process when repetitive circumstances occur and a decision on how to act becomes necessary. With a policy in place, decision-makers can act quickly by following the guidelines embedded in the policy. Speedy decisions move the organization forward, avoiding unnecessary delays in making decisions because a policy deals with situations which are like past policy-creating circumstances.

A policy encompasses several features. First, every policy focuses on **one theme** as its point of focus. For example, anti-sexual harassment policy, anti-bully policy, inventory monitoring policy, customer returns policy and dressing room management policy. Second, a policy can deal with **one or more related issues**, each issue links to the primary theme of the policy. For example, an anti-sexual harassment policy could include the definition of sexual harassment, reporting sexual harassment process, the process for adjudicating if sexual harassment occurred, penalties for sexual harassment and reporting process after presenting the findings of the adjudication process. Third, a policy is written to influence behavior in **pre-determined ways**. Fourth, a policy is meant to support or promote an **organization's values**. Fifth, a policy provides **an outline of the needed work processes** to implement the policy. Finally, a policy needs to be sufficiently **clear** to avoid ambiguities in policy enforcement but flexible enough to enable decision-makers to deal with unique circumstances.

The policy-making process begins with either a problem, new situation or the realization that an existing policy is inadequate in dealing with a new situation. A change in organizational values, change in laws, change in customer interests, change in economic conditions and change within the competitive environment represent examples of reasons for developing a new policy or modifying an existing policy. Decision-makers determine the need for action and assign responsibility to subordinates who have the expertise to develop a model policy. Subordinates conduct research and develop a draft policy for review. After careful consideration, a final version of the policy is developed and approval sought from decision-makers.

Decision-makers need to assess if a policy is a "good" policy. A good policy demonstrates certain characteristics that convince decision-makers to conclude that the policy is sufficient. First, a good policy achieves one or more **objectives** associated with the policy. Therefore, SMART objectives are essential because SMART objectives provide performance indicators to measure success in implementing the policy. For example, a policy outlining a new hiring process leads to a decline in the turnover rate among new hires. Second, a good policy always identifies the **scope** of the policy; what is covered and what subjects are not included in the policy statement. Third, a good policy results in **consistent results** and either complements other policies or does not negatively impact other policies. Fourth, a good policy is **logical** and based on **commonsense** grounded in solid business theory. Fifth, a good policy reflects existing organizational **values** or promotes new values. Finally, a good policy is written to provide decision-makers with **documentation** to refer to when the need to enforce a policy arises.

Chapter Summary

This chapter introduced the reader to the strategy implementation process by identifying and describing the management methods organizations use to successfully implement an organization's strategies. Organizations create formal links between the strategy formulation process and the strategy implementation process to ensure a smooth adjustment from creating a strategy to the implementation of the overall corporate strategy. Creating a new strategy represents the organization's effort to compete differently. The need to complete in response to external demands imposes challenges to the organization to overcome. Challenges refer to the necessity to modify existing management practices to ensure that the challenges do not impede the strategy implementation process. Systematizing an organization's operations is the primary focus of the strategy implementation process because research shows that an organization's efforts at systematizing its operations are associated with successful organizational performance.

Successful performance means achieving the strategic goals. The chapter covers the important role of strategic goals and operational objectives as performance standards used to keep the workforce focused. Furthermore, the chapter examines the role of managers in the strategy implementation process; the use of management systems as an organizing method; work processes as a means of routinizing activities to promote uniform and consistent management practices; and the role of policy in the design and functioning of the various management systems and work processes.

Questions

1. Describe the strategy implementation process.
2. Explain how the strategy formulation process and the strategy implementation process are both top-town and bottom-up processes.
3. Explain why the strategy implementation process presents challenges to decision-makers.
4. Identify and briefly explain the reasons why strategy, strategic goals and operational objectives are linked.
5. Why does systematizing the strategy implementation process lead to organizational success.

6. Explain why the strategy implementors need to be organized.
7. Describe the role of each level of managers in the strategy implementation process.
8. Performance indicators and the performance review process are integral to the strategy implementation process. Explain why.
9. Describe the importance of communication during the strategy implementation process.
10. Identify and describe the primary features of a policy.

Bibliography

Aaltonen, P. & Ikavalko, H. (2002). Implementing strategies successfully. *Integrated Manufacturing Systems.* 13(1). 415–418.

Heracleous, L. (2000). The role of strategy implementation in organization development. *Organization Development Journal.* 18(3). 75–86.

HTTPS://eLibrary.net/management/policy. 2018.

Junior, V.M., Pascucci, L. & Murphy, J.P. (2012). Implementing strategies in complex systems: lessons from Brazilian hospitals. *Brazilian Administration Review.* 9(2). 19–37.

Ogunmokun, G., Hopper, T. & Mcclyymont, H. (2005). Strategy implementation and organizational performance: a study of private hospitals. *Proceedings of ARBSA Conference.* August 5–7. 20–28.

Radomska, J. (2015). The concept of sustainable strategy implementation. *Sustainability.* 7. 15847–15856.

Ramadan, M. A. (2015). The impact of strategy implementation drivers on projects effectiveness in non-governmental organizations. *International Journal of Academic Research in Management.* 4(2). 35–47.

Management Systems

OVERVIEW

A management system represents an organized arrangement of standardized work processes guided by the management system's policies. There are broad categories of management systems with sub-systems and specialized groups of management systems that can include more specialized sub-systems. For example, a performance control system encompasses all specialized management systems associated with maintaining and controlling the performance of various types of relevant organizational functions. Information management system encompasses specialized sub-systems that provide access to specific types of information that enable decision-makers and non-decision-makers to perform their jobs more effectively. In short, "a management system represents a formal method for systematically organizing various related work processes." Decision-makers create management systems, oversee the evolution of a management system and regulate the functioning of a management system along with assessing a management system's performance by assessing the most important work processes associated with a management system. The use of the management system methodology provides a framework that endows an organization with consistent action, often lacking in a disorganized organization. Consistency is driven by the need to be efficient and effective in achieving the operational objectives of a management system.

The organization is frequently considered as a mega-management system, encompassing a network of management systems and related sub-systems; a sub-system can and does incorporate separate, but related, more specialized sub-systems. Each system and sub-system focus on implementing one common business function. Within every management system, there is a network of interconnected work processes. Work processes link to each other directly or indirectly. Work processes in a management system can link with work processes in other management systems to create a system of linked management systems. This mega-management system is commonly referred to as an **organizational structure and network of management systems**.

Decision-makers use policies to provide the procedural guidelines to create a management system and sub-systems; decision-makers use policies to design the initial work processes that make management systems operational;

decision-makers use policies to link management system with other management systems. A policy serves as a guide for decision-makers to create an assessment process or specialized performance system and possible sub-systems for the organization's decision-makers to use in assessing the overall performance of the organization along with the performance of individual management systems and sub-systems.

In addition, all management systems incorporate policies that are an integral part of a management system. Decision-makers include more policies in each management system on a per need basis. The creation of a policy results in a new work process(es) and/or modification of an existing work process(es).

CHAPTER 3   LEARNING OBJECTIVES

Readers will achieve the following learning objectives after reading this chapter.

1. Explain the purpose and function of a management system.
2. Identify and describe the elements of a management system.
3. Identify and explain the use of categories of management systems.
4. Identify, describe and explain the primary purpose of decision-making and information management systems.
5. Identify, describe and explain the process for creating a management system.
6. Describe the networking of an organization's management systems.
7. Explain the difference between primary management systems and support management systems.
8. Identify and describe the functioning of a process for assessing the performance of a management system.
9. Explain the role of policy in the creation and ongoing management of a management system.
10. Explain the role of work processes within a management system.

LEARNING OBJECTIVE #1: EXPLAIN THE PURPOSE AND FUNCTION OF A MANAGEMENT SYSTEM

The goal in designing a management system is to satisfy those who benefit from the outcomes generated from the management system. There are management systems designed specifically to support identifying the organization's corporate strategy along with designing functional strategies that support the corporate strategy. These management systems are part of the strategy formulation stage in the Strategic Management model. There are management systems designed specifically to encompass the strategy implementation stage in the Strategic Management model. These management systems represent the organization's core operations. There are management systems designed solely to facilitate the linkage between the strategy formulation stage and the strategy implementation stage in an attempt at creating a seamless connection between the two stages (of the Strategic Management model).

In designing management systems, the designers' goal is to create the means to generate an expected outcome(s) and reduce operational risks by organizing work activities through the creation of work processes. Work processes symbolize the designer's intent to design a management system that operates in a rational, predictable and systematic way. A systems approach aims to generate outcomes that increase the predictability of what decision-makers can expect from a management system.

The management system's framework offers additional benefits to the organization. A management system serves the needs of its customers. There are external customers such as businesses that supply inputs to the organization or end users who purchase products or services from the organization. There are internal types of customers. Internal customers are members of the workforce who benefit from the outcomes generated by a management system.

Management systems operate through the involvement the workforce, which utilizes some form of technology to fulfill their work responsibilities. The designers of a management system expect to enable the participants to perform their work responsibilities efficiently and effectively as well as leveraging the use of technology to enhance work performance. This person-technology relationship leads to referencing a management system as a **sociotechnical system**.

Another benefit of a planned management system is the minimization of conflict among participants because the management system's designers attempt to create an organized management system, with all work processes working together per policy guidelines. Though in reality this is not the case, the potential for conflict is lessened because the designers of a management system attempted to minimize conflict among management system participants.

Finally, the designers of a planned management system attempt to identify and organize all the initial work processes that make up a new management system into a network of interconnected work processes, linked together so that the output of one work process represents the input of another work process. Policy serves as the guide over the work process design and operation.

LEARNING OBJECTIVE #2: IDENTIFY AND DESCRIBE THE ELEMENTS OF A MANAGEMENT SYSTEM

We can think of a management system as a composition of a network of **elements**; the elements link together to serve a common purpose. The common purpose of a management system is the **subject** or focus of a management system. For example, a training management system, cost control management system and inventory control management system show that the subject or focus of the management system or management sub-systems is part of a larger system. Second, every management system has the same types of basic elements though the form each element takes differs because the subject of a management system differs.

Policies are one of the primary elements of a management system, representing an important building block of a management system. A set of policies associated with a management system can vary in scope, with a broad or narrow focus.

A policy represents the organization's official codification leading to either the creation of a management system or the evolution of an existing management system's work processes. Policy guides management system designers throughout the management system design process by adhering to decision-maker policy edicts. Policy provides a structured framework for management systems designers to follow. As an organization's circumstances change, policy changes in response, so must a management system's work processes evolve to reflect new conditions associated with the new policy.

As stated earlier, management systems function through **work processes**. Each work process has a specific subject to focus on. The intention of a work process is to achieve a particular outcome through a series of action stages ordered in a prescribed way because a work process represents a formalized, systematic approach, incorporating a sequence of stages. There is a beginning stage, a final stage and any number of stages between the first and last stages. Each work process generates an outcome which is another work process input. Work processes link to one or more different work processes within a management system and can link to one or more work processes in other management systems. For example, with individuals, a process is commonly referred to as a routine. Getting ready for work follows a personal management process with several linked routines (equivalent to work processes). There are sub-systems such as shaving (for a male), preparing breakfast, eating breakfast, cleaning up and so on. Each of these stages represents a sub-system within the overall routine of getting ready for work. The individual's personal policy guides the creation and management of the individual's personal management system of getting ready for work.

Using a **common language** is a third element of a management system. Language shared among all management system designers and strategy implementers is essential to ensure that the designers and strategy implementers understand their mutual needs and responsibilities. Designing a management system is a challenge, but the need to add the responsibility of translating concepts and other forms of language in terms that participants understand makes the task more challenging. Having a universal language hastens the management systems design and strategy implementation processes and eliminates any confusion over terminology.

Support work processes represent a type of work process. There are **primary or core work processes** responsible for ensuring the success of a management system. Support work processes represent processes designed with the intention to ensure that the core work processes function according to plan. Training is an example of a support process intended to build knowledge, skill enhancement or develop the personal abilities of the individuals responsible for performing a work process. For example, a support routine for preparing to get ready for work is food shopping at another time to ensure there is sufficient food in the house for breakfast.

Each management system and each work process require SMART type of operational objectives because management systems associated with strategy implementation are operational and core management systems. Every management system and each work process generate an outcome. Achieving the correct outcomes provides focus to work process managers. We can create benchmark measures from the outcomes for any management system and work process. These benchmarks function as a basis for identifying **SMART type operational objectives**. SMART operational objectives need to be measurable and time-limited. This is not an issue because each work process creates a measurable outcome(s). For example, defect rates per 1000 tested, units produced per hour and average time spent per call per call center operator.

Outcomes enable the designers of a management system to create **performance measurement processes** within the **performance measurement sub-system** that is integral within every management system in some form. The benchmark outcomes and the SMART operational objectives serve as performance metrics used to assess the performance of a management system and each related work process. A performance measurement sub-system is a support system used to assess if a management system and the system's work processes meet performance expectations (based on achieving SMART operational objectives).

Another element of a management system is the **linkage among the work processes within a management system and the linkage between management systems**. As stated earlier, the output of a work process represents the input of another work process. Management systems do not operate independently. Management systems are meant to be interdependent. Supporting and promoting linkage among management systems is one of the most important functions decision-makers and designers of management systems can perform.

Another **element is individuals** responsible for the operation of a management system through the various work processes. Individuals are essential because people make an organization successful. A management system functioning with unqualified people will result in an underperforming management system. Individuals need to demonstrate and apply the important values of the organization; possess sufficient knowledge required; demonstrate the necessary skills needed; show the personal abilities necessary to meet expectations (e.g. problem-solving skills, self-motivation and keeping focused); and be motivated to perform their work responsibilities to achieve the SMART operational objectives.

LEARNING OBJECTIVE #3: IDENTIFY AND EXPLAIN THE USE OF CATEGORIES OF MANAGEMENT SYSTEMS

A management system is a management method used to organize various work processes. Only work processes that share a common focus are incorporated within a management system. Each management system has a common theme or subject of focus. As organizations expand, the number of management systems and management sub-systems increases, and the management systems become more complex. The ongoing process of systematically organizing management systems evolves along with an expanding organization leading to the creation of broad categories of different types of management systems. These broad categories enable the decision-makers to label and place new management systems into a logical framework, a network of management systems. The model used to organize management systems is derived from the method organizations use to group products and/or services. For example, an organization can begin with a single product and add related products that are grouped into a product line. Adding new, different types of products leads to the creation of a second product line. Creating unrelated products leads to additional product lines, but the organization can create a broader product category to encompass related product lines. For example, a company can have a product line of "winter shovels" and a product line of "gardening shovels" grouped into a broader category of "shovels." The process of organizing products into broader categories continues as an organization attempts to maintain control and oversight over their expanding family of products and/or services.

There are six generic categories of management systems. **Information management systems** encompass two sub-categories of information systems: **executive information management systems** and **administrative management information systems**. Information systems interface with all management systems work processes in support of work process management. Providing timely, relevant information in the form required abets the successful management of a work process. We distinguish between two types of information systems because there are information systems devoted exclusively to supporting executive decision-making, providing information that focuses on strategic issues. There are administrative management information systems that provide operational information primarily for middle and lower management to support decision-making associated with operations management.

Decision support management systems represents another generic category of management system. Closely linked to the information systems, decision support management systems organize work processes designed to facilitate decision-making among all managerial ranks. Decision support management systems need to be closely linked to the information systems because decision-makers make decisions primarily on information gathered from external and internal sources. Because there are two sub-categories of information management systems, decision support systems mirror this grouping with senior managers involved in making strategic types of decisions, while lower-level managers (i.e. middle managers and below) are responsible for operational decisions.

Another generic category of management system is **transaction processing systems**. This category encompasses all the operational activities of the organization. For example, making products, delivering services and any other activities are the primary focus of the organization. A sub-category is transactional support work systems. Transactional support systems represent systems and associate work processes directed toward ensuring that transaction processing systems and transaction processing systems personnel remain focused on their primary work responsibilities and achieve their objectives. As an example, human resources are a typical support **function** that represents a transaction support system.

Performance management systems is another generic management system. Often referred to as a performance control system, performance control systems are divided into at least two sub-categories: **performance administration management systems** and **quality management systems**. Each sub-category focuses on the operations of the organization. We distinguish between the two categories in the following way. The purpose of performance administration management systems is to increase the organization's operational effectiveness by indirectly facilitating the organizing of work processes by assessing the achievement of each work process outcome objectives. Quality management systems focus on an organization's customers by ensuring that the organization continues to add value to their (output) to satisfy customer requirements.

Knowledge management systems represent another generic management system intended to enhance an organization's learning capabilities. Organizations that are fast learners are better able to pursue new opportunities quickly and deal effectively with potential threats if the organization is capable of leveraging its depository of knowledge to identify new competitive strategies and operational improvements more quickly than competitors.

LEARNING OBJECTIVE #4: IDENTIFY AND DESCRIBE THE PRIMARY PURPOSE AND FUNCTIONING OF DECISION-MAKING AND INFORMATION MANAGEMENT SYSTEMS

The primary purpose in creating and managing **decision-making management systems** is to rationalize decision-making throughout the organization. Rationalization occurs through the process of systematizing decision-making by creating routine decision-making work processes. The goal in structuring decision-making work processes throughout the organization is to strengthen the decision-making capabilities of decision-makers who rely primarily on management systems and work processes designed specifically to support making decisions.

The decision-making management system and the **information and knowledge management systems** are linked because information is the most important input in the decision-making process. Knowledge management systems lead to the development of a learning organization that can use new knowledge as well as the organization's library of existing knowledge to better support decision-makers in making decisions. Policies are an integral part of every management system, and decision-making management systems are no exception. Policy guides the process in creating decision-making work processes; policy exists to guide the decision-making process for dealing with re-occurring situations (referred to as programmed decisions); policy also aids decision-makers in dealing with non-re-occurring or new situations (referred to as non-programmed decisions) because a policy serves as a start-point for decision-makers, there is no need to totally re-invent the wheel.

Senior-level decision-makers are responsible for keeping the organization focused; other levels of decision-makers are responsible for keeping the workforce focused by organizing everyone into functional operational units. One important decision-making work process is a process(es) for creating an organization's vision. Senior decision-makers follow a work process(es) for identifying strategic goals as well as a process(es) for evaluating performance of the organization and a process(es) for deciding how to respond to the findings derived from a performance assessment. At lower management levels, decision-making work processes help to identify functional unit goals, unit operational objectives; work process(es) objectives; and design performance assessment work processes to assess unit performance. Furthermore, decision-makers throughout the organization need to create strategies and plans for achieving the goals and objectives, encompassing the entire organization down to the smallest unit. Strategy identification processes fall under the aegis of decision-making management systems because strategy represents a game plan for influencing the future actions of the organization. Finally, all decision-makers need to develop additional policies when confronted with new situations, and these new situations are determined to likely re-occur in the future. The alternative is to modify existing policies when new variants of prior situations require a change in policy. There are policies governing the entire organization and policies unique to each individual operating unit. Senior-level decision-makers need to participate at some point when creating operating unit policies to ensure consistency with the organization's cultural norms and organization-wide policies.

The **information management system** is a generic system composed of a collection of sub-systems that denotes a systematic way to collect data, transform data into information and disseminate information to support decision-making and the knowledge creation. The goal in designing an information management system is to select methods for collecting data on a routine basis from sources outside and inside the organization. The type of external sources is pre-planned so that decision-makers can conduct an environmental, industry and market analyses. Internal sources of data and information are all operational units because operational units generate non-monetary operational outcomes and financial data.

A basic information management system's work processes and associate policies focus on the routine collection of data, analyzing the data by converting the data into information and transforming the information into knowledge through individual's cognitive-processing abilities and then disseminating the knowledge to decision-making management support systems. The knowledge then becomes information for the decision-making management support system. For example, data can include declining GDP rate and declining customer sales that parallel the declining GDP rate. The data is organized into information that declining sales is due primarily to a declining economy. Knowledge is interpreting the information that customers are price sensitive because their consumption rates fall faster than expected because of a decline in GDP. Price sensitive customers' sales trends become information to decision-makers who then need to decide how the organization will respond to the trend. Leaders can select a short-term response if the trend is viewed as temporary or with a decision(s) that has long-term consequences if the trend is determined to last a long time.

Technology is a critical tool used in the information management support systems. The use of technology helps in data collection activities; link computer systems together; converting data to information (application of artificial intelligence operations); and disseminating the knowledge after analyzing the information. The knowledge becomes an input to the decision-making management support system in the form of information to use to create additional knowledge to utilize in support of making decisions within the decision-making support systems and decision-making management systems.

Jordan Marsh Department Store: Part 1

Paul Birkwood, Chief Executive Officer, was meeting with Kim Baker, Senior Executive Vice president of Marketing and Sam Decker, Senior Executive Vice President of Information Systems. They were discussing product sales, product categories, tracking product performance and inventory control. Paul had lunched a few days prior with the CEO of a regional grocery chain. The CEO described their product tracking system and how the system let to greater efficiencies and substantial increases in revenue. Paul wanted to develop a similar system. He wanted to learn from Kim and Sam how to begin and what to do.

Questions

1. Why does Paul want to track the performance of individual products and product groups?
2. How is the inventory control system relevant?
3. What would be the benefits to creating such a system? Explain.
4. What is the first step? Explain.
5. What are the issues to focus on during the first planning meeting?

LEARNING OBJECTIVE #5: IDENTIFY, DESCRIBE AND EXPLAIN THE PROCESS FOR CREATING A MANAGEMENT SYSTEM

The development of a management system begins with a need, and the need is always derived from a problem with an existing system or recognition that there is a gap in performance that warrants creating a new management system. Either an existing management system is not achieving its operating objectives or decision-makers recognize that implementing a new strategy requires another type of management system(s) or the failure of an existing management system occurs because the management system is expected to perform functions different from the original intention. **Empirical** evidence is always the most important determinant in deciding if an existing management system requires modification or create a new management system (see Figure 3.1).

The focus in this section is to describe how to develop a new management system. Steps to change in an existing management system are like the process associated with designing a new management system. First, decision-makers need to identify the **operational objectives** that the management system needs to accomplish. After identifying the operational objectives, the next step is to identify the policies that dictate the type of **work processes** needed as well as drafting an outline of the stages for each work process (see Figure 3.2). Decision-makers review the **policies** and drafts describing each work process. After reviewing the policies and

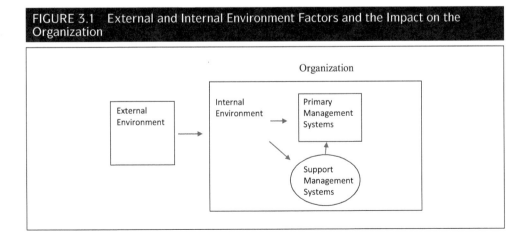

FIGURE 3.1   External and Internal Environment Factors and the Impact on the Organization

FIGURE 3.2   Stages in the Design of a Management System

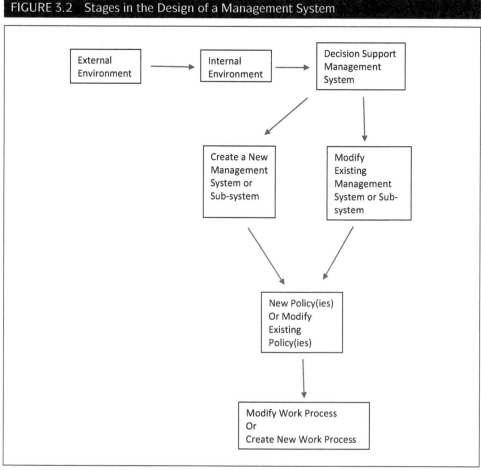

work processes, decision-makers work on a resource allocation process to determine the type and amount of resources needed to ensure the success of the management system. The people with the requisite knowledge, skills and experience needed are identified, and after the decision-makers approve, leaders begin the process of allocating and/or acquiring the resources needed.

Performance measures need to be identified to assess that the management system and associate work processes perform to expectations. Operational objectives serve as the expectations, and every work process has performance benchmarks identified. The **performance monitoring process**, representing a management system support work process, is identified to ensure routine performance monitoring that includes **performance reporting** which is a component to every management system.

Every **management system is linked** to other management systems. A new management system requires one or more work processes to link the management system to other management systems, creating a seamless connection. Also, within a management system, each work process links directly or indirectly to other work processes to create a network of interconnected work processes.

FIGURE 3.3 Overview of the Process of Changing a Management System and the Impact

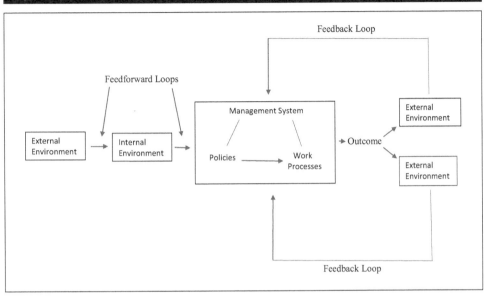

A component of the performance monitoring process is a **self-development work process** whereby issues with the work processes of the management system and associate policies are identified so that the leadership of the management system pursue **self-corrective** actions to improve the work process(es) affected along with the guiding policies (if necessary).

With any new management system or a modification of an existing management system, the changes often do not work completely as planned. This is not necessarily the fault of the planners. It is an inherent issue associated with planning when predicting the future comes face-to-face with the application of the plan; issues then can become apparent. A pro-active self-corrective work process goal is to modify the plan to ensure a properly functioning management system (see Figure 3.3).

LEARNING OBJECTIVE #6: DESCRIBE THE NETWORKING OF AN ORGANIZATION'S MANAGEMENT SYSTEMS

Organizing each management system into self-contained units, each system with a unique focus lays the foundation for a serious operational problem. Management systems can function like silos, designed to operate independently. The application of the silo model hurts the organization because management systems need to link in a network of management systems to facilitate coordination among all decision-makers. To overcome the "silo effect" or island mentality, decision-makers apply systems theory to justify the importance of networking all the management systems together. An offshoot of systems theory is the theory of organizing (covered in detail in Chapter 4), which involves the need to create processes that link management systems together by linking select work processes within a management system together with select work processes in other management systems. We describe the entity created to encompass this network of interconnected management systems as an organization.

The less management systems link together, the more self-directed are the management systems. This is not beneficial to the organization where coordination among operational units is essential to achieve the strategic goals and operational objectives. Weak organizational performance results from non-linkage or work processes poorly linked. A reduction in a management system's performance affects the performance of other management systems culminating in the organization's reduced ability to provide value to the organization's external and internal customers.

The organization's external world acts as a catalyst for promoting greater coordination and cooperation among the linked management systems. Customers, suppliers, competitors and government make up the external world. Customers and suppliers generate the greatest pressure on the organization to ensure that the organization's management systems link with these external stakeholders and work together harmoniously with the management systems of the external customers if customers are organizations. Mutual benefits represent the incentives for linking joint management systems together. Monopolistic or oligopolistic industry conditions lessen the impact of external stakeholders on the organization's need to change to ensure providing value to customers.

The organization's internal world composed of stakeholders associated with management systems functions as a catalyst for countering the silo effect by encouraging coordination and cooperation among the organization's management systems. The pressure to coordinate and cooperate is great because the success of a management system in achieving its operational objectives is dependent in part on integrating with other management systems. Systematically, linking the management systems together is a management approach intended to provide a consistent, predictable relationship among management systems.

A management method used to link management systems is the use of support management systems. The role of **support management systems** is to ensure that primary management systems function according to performance expectations. Support management systems facilitate the linkage among management systems and monitor the linkage to ensure the linkage functions to the benefit of the organization.

An important management method a leader uses to link management systems is an **organization's structural arrangement**. Covered earlier, the premise behind designing an organizational structure into one of several possible types is to identify functional management units (e.g. marketing, accounting and finance) and sub-management units and link these in an arrangement that subordinates all the functions and sub-functions in a **vertical arrangement** with authority figures leading each management function and sub-function. Supplemental management methods that fall under the category of **coordinating management methods or integrating management methods** are used to complement the use of an organizational design because of well-known design limitations. The use of teams, job descriptions, coordination units and shared objectives represents some of the management methods used to facilitate coordination and cooperation among management functions.

Criteria to consider when determining which management systems and functions needing to link together directly and the extent to which the management systems and functions need to work together include the following.

- **Interdependent actions**: A management system and management functions primary work together.
- **Cognitive efficiency improvements**: Simplification of the work by routinizing the link among management systems and functions.
- **Costs**: Costs fall when management systems and management functions coordination increases.
- **Decision-makers:** Gain greater operational control when management systems and management functions link together.
- **Routinizing**: The link among management systems and management functions reduces the potential for conflict because standardization formalizes relationships.
- **Greater cooperation**: Cooperation increases the likelihood that the management systems and management functions will achieve their objectives.
- **Value**: The organization benefits when management systems and management functions link together.

LEARNING OBJECTIVE #7: EXPLAIN THE DIFFERENCE BETWEEN PRIMARY MANAGEMENT SYSTEMS AND SUPPORT MANAGEMENT SYSTEMS

Management systems can be grouped into two main categories: primary management systems and support management systems. Primary management systems focus on providing direct value to external and internal customers. Primary management systems serve to make an organization's products or deliver an organization's services to a customer.

Support management systems beneficiaries are internal customers working in the primary management systems. The vision statements each support management system emphasize ensuring that the primary management systems meet the expectations of the organization and the end user.

This section of the chapter helps the reader learn about the role and function of support management systems, less well-known but essential to an organization's success.

Work processes of support management systems are designed to enable the organizations' primary management systems to achieve the organization's overall vision by achieving the organization's strategic goals. The mandate for support management systems is to assist in creating the orderly functioning within a primary management system and among the network of primary management systems; ensure consistent management system performance; keep the primary management systems focused on achieving its vision; and as a consequence of their interventions, increase the probability of primary management systems meeting the organization's performance expectations.

To implement their mandate of assisting the primary management systems, the designers of support management systems seek to achieve several goals. First, designers want to ensure that support systems have the **capability** of monitoring the performance of primary management systems to detect when there is a problem or potential problem. After analyzing the information, the support management system will recommend a course of action to pursue to improve a primary management system's operational performance. Though designed to coordinate remedial actions with a primary management system, support management systems can confront resistance to their efforts because their authority to intervene directly is often constrained by the organization's policies. Second, a **formal or informal action plan** to improve the performance of a primary management system is formulated. If resistance to the plan occurs, the support management system might reach out to decision-makers to intervene in helping to overcome the resistance. Benchmark performance trends for all primary management systems and their main work processes help the support management systems monitor performance routinely using support-based information management systems designed to provide benchmark performance information. The design for information gathering functions like a patient hooked up to a heart monitoring device.

Third, support management systems focus on **work process improvements** in a primary management system because work processes represent the major activity of every management system. The support management systems have the expertise in process management that primary management systems personnel typically lack.

Fourth, support management systems can focus on increasing **workforce motivation**. Motivating the workforce is a fundamental management action for improving an organization's performance. Support management systems personnel have the expertise to recommend to decision-makers the management methods designed specifically to motivate the workforce. **Conflict management** is another area of focus for support management systems. Conflict is a common fact of life among human interactions. It is essential that primary management systems decision-makers leverage the support management systems conflict resolution expertise to successfully intervene in resolving the conflict.

Finally, support management systems serve as the means to provide **the knowledge** necessary to improve the operating performance of the work systems within a primary management system. Support management systems can assist in developing the knowledge and skills of a primary management system's workforce or improve the personal abilities of the workforce (e.g. problem-solving, communication and brainstorming) through training or assisting in the recruitment of individuals with the required knowledge, skills and personal abilities (e.g. human resources hiring assistance).

Jordan Marsh Department Stores: Part 2

Paula Daniels, Senior Executive Vice President of Human Resources, was meeting with Edward Burke, Vice President of Training and Karen Butters, Senior Executive Vice President of Marketing and Mallory Kindle, Vice President of Sales. The meeting was arranged because Edward and Mallory were concerned about the performance of the sales force. For the past six months, sales volume per salesperson was trending down. An impromptu survey of the sales force turned up no specific reasons for the results. Edward and Mallory concluded that the sales force needed a re-fresher course in Sales 101.

Questions

1. What does Karen and Mallory need to learn from Paula and Edward?
2. What does Paula and Edward need to learn from Karen and Mallory?
3. How will Edward begin? What is the process Edward will follow? Explain.
4. How will everyone learn if training was successful? Explain.

LEARNING OBJECTIVE #8: IDENTIFY AND DESCRIBE THE FUNCTIONING OF A PROCESS FOR ASSESSING THE PERFORMANCE OF A MANAGEMENT SYSTEM

Every management system includes some form of self-assessment process, whether formal or informal. Organizations also create management systems dedicated to monitoring and assessing the performance of other management systems. Why create separate performance management systems? In a single word, bias. Having an unbiased, objective-based self-assessment process is not easy to create. As much as we try to design management systems rationally, logically and objectively, people design the systems on; and people can interpret the data and make interpretations that do not represent reality because of bias.

The organization creates independent performance assessment management systems to impose a degree of objectivity in evaluating the performance of all systems, but the major focus is on primary management systems because primary management systems are directly responsible for executing the organization's strategies. Unfortunately, even the performance management systems are not immune from bias because decision-makers' vested interests can lead to actions contrary to what might be expected in a totally objective-based management system.

The concept of a **balanced scorecard** is a useful management method for designing performance management systems. The three aspects of the balanced scorecard most relevant are **financial analyses**, which utilize **feedback loops** to assess performance of a management system and its operations. **Operational analyses** represent another type of analysis. Here, the organization uses **concurrent feedback loops** to assess the ongoing execution of the organization's strategies by assessing operational performance. For example, the organization can assess defect rates periodically; time spent on the phone by call center operators; and units produced per hour. Benchmarks are easy to create and apply to compare with ongoing performance trends. Third, organizations can create **feedforward feedback loops** that focus on the customer and customer interests, customer needs and a customer's impressions of the product and/or services the customer uses. Feedforward efforts attempt to anticipate changes to avoid negative consequences that eventually show in operational trends and financial performance. **Customer information** provides relevant information on how the primary management systems might need to change in response to the information from the customer.

Designers of performance management systems follow the same model used in designing other types of management systems; the elements of a management system do not change only the details for each element change. For example, objectives will differ because the management system's focus differs. An essential element for a primary management system and a performance management system is the need to have benchmark data to assess performance. Benchmarking is the numeric equivalent of the expected performance of a management system operating under normal conditions. All management systems' work processes create measurable outcomes, and performance standards can be determined from the outcomes to create benchmarks to assess actual performance compared to the benchmarks in each work process. Benchmark measures represent targets of accepted levels of performance derived over a pre-determined time frame. Use of benchmarking helps to identify performance gaps which then initiate signals that indicate the need for a response to address the problem(s). Benchmarks also serve the purpose of identifying operational objectives to focus on to improve performance. The increase in a benchmark standard with the concomitant response to achieve the benchmark standard results in improved performance management system and work processes.

LEARNING OBJECTIVE #9: EXPLAIN THE ROLE OF POLICY IN THE CREATION AND ONGOING MANAGEMENT OF A MANAGEMENT SYSTEM

To fully grasp the purpose and functioning of a management system requires full understanding of the subject of policy. Policy leads to the creation of a management system and the ongoing changes to a management system by changing to a management system's work processes. Any modification of a policy impacts a work process(es).

As a review, recall that policy acts as a guideline or set of guidelines that pertain to a subject of interest to the organization. A policy is meant to influence behavior, acting similarly to a rule, but broader in scope. Official policy represents the organization's position on what is acceptable behavior within the context of the circumstances defined by the policy. For example, a sexual harassment policy can define sexual harassment. A definition provides the guidance to differentiate between acceptable and unacceptable behavior.

A sexual harassment policy is an element of a safe practices management system or some other comparable employee-oriented support management system. A policy can range in complexity, having a single focus or containing several parts with various foci but one overall theme. What a policy is intended to do is to make the case for the need for a work process or multiple work processes (or variations to existing work processes). Using a sexual harassment policy as an example, the sexual harassment policy can encompass the reporting of sexual harassment process, an adjudication of a complaint process, reporting the results of an adjudication process and a process in meting out a penalty. Each part results in the creation of separate, but related work process. A policy states general issues a work process needs to cover. The actual design of a work process is the responsibility of decision-makers and non-decision-makers who design the work process(s) to meet the expectations associated with the intent of the policy and decision-makers interests.

The design or modification of a work process represents the product of the policy development process. A work process represents the planned approach for implementing a policy or a component of a policy. The goals in developing a policy aim to ensure consistent behavior; lead to greater efficiencies in performing an action and improving operational performance. Using sexual harassment policy as an example, a report process is designed to ensure that employees know how to report incidents; the ability to resolve the situation is increased by making the reporting process simple to follow and uniform in the stages a victim needs to follow. The policy is intended to encourage reporting of incidents over the short-run but reduce the number of incidents reported over the long-run by having a detailed sexual harassment policy. Over time employees learn the policy, and they are less distracted by these incidents of sexual harassment, resulting in improved employee work performance.

Jordan Marsh Department Stores: Part 3

Karen Butters, Senior Executive Vice President of Marketing, was meeting with her management team. The agenda was the current policy about dressing room management at all retail locations. Customer theft was on the rise, and there were numerous complaints about the dressing rooms. Complaints ranged from clothes left in the rooms, no salesclerk was available to ask for help and scheduled use of the dressing rooms was chaotic. The perception was that customers used the dressing rooms to steal clothes.

Questions

1. Is the current policy the problem? Explain.
2. If the policy is acceptable, what is the problem? Explain.
3. What work processes does the policy cover? Explain.
4. What do you recommend Karen and her staff do next? Explain.

LEARNING OBJECTIVE #10: EXPLAIN THE ROLE OF WORK PROCESSES WITHIN A MANAGEMENT SYSTEM

As described earlier, work processes represent how organizations execute policy to achieve the objectives of the organization. Policy represents general guidelines about how to act in a specific situation and what is necessary. A work process(es) represents the organization's determination on how best to implement a management system's policy(ies). A work process(es) represents the use of a systematic approach to execute a policy. As an example, if you were driving home from work to home directly, the objectives in driving home from work are to arrive safely and to arrive at a set time (or within a range of times). The individual's personal policy can include such issues as the time to leave work, roads to follow and dealing with possible emergency situations. Then the individual creates a routine with a start point, and the end point is arriving home with stages between the starting stage and the end stage. Organizing a routine is a universal method individuals follow to increase cognitive efficiency by reducing the complexity of a situation through the creation of a standardized routine. Organizations follow this model except that organizations refer to work processes instead of routines; each work process becomes standardized through accepted and official organization policy.

In sum, a work process represents a method for solving a problem or a response to a new situation by having one or more people performing a work process, often with the aid of technology.

Identifying the components of a work process provides a rubric to model in creating work processes or re-designing an existing work process. First, every work process links to another work process with one work process' output the input of another work process. For example, the job description design process links with the recruitment process. Second, a work process is purposeful. Third, a work process always creates measurable outputs; the organization uses outputs to identify a work process performance objective. Also, a work process is composed of stages: each stage represents a definable activity associated with one part of the work process; the stages are sequenced with a starting and ending stage and one or more additional stages between the first and last stages. Every work process stage can represent a sub-work process that is ancillary to the overall work process. For example, the routine of getting ready for work in the morning can include a "showering stage," and the act of showering itself follows a process with stages.

A work process can involve the use of one or more of the generic management systems. These include the information system, communication system, decision-making system, the control system, the quality management system and the performance assessment system. Every management system involved with a work process formally supports the individuals involved in performing a work process to ensure satisfactory execution of each stage of the work process.

In addition to promoting cognitive efficiency, there are other benefits to standardizing a work process. Reduced conflict among work process participants is a benefit because each stage of a work process and the sequence of stages are planned to leave little to disagree about. Differences of opinion can emerge when the stages and their sequence incorporate some degree of flexibility in performing a work process. Another benefit of a routinized, planned work process is that standardization provides greater stability in performing the work process because the work process is a known entity, and a stable work process leads to a predictable work process with a predictable outcome(s). The greater the predictability of the outcome(s) of a work process, the easier it is to maintain performance expectations.

Jordan Marsh Department Stores: Part 4

John Simpson, the hiring manager was sitting at his desk Friday afternoon. He was re-reading the retention management report. For the last year, the number of new hires who quit or were let go during the first three months of employment exceeded the average benchmark considerably. John knew that the problem was not the recruitment process. Most new hires were let go because of poor qualifications and/or poor attitude. During the exit interviews, the new hires complained about the workload and the job requirements. John figured that the problem was with the hiring process. Now he needed to identify the problem(s) with the process and solutions to the problems.

Questions

1. Identify two possible problems. Explain.
2. What new steps are necessary? Explain.
3. What existing steps need improving? Explain.
4. How can John learn if the changes to the hiring process were effective? Explain.

Chapter Summary

The focus of this chapter is to provide a comprehensive overview about the concept of management systems. The chapter examines the purpose of a management system, how a management system functions; generic types of management systems; the elements within a management system along with an explanation that describes an organization as a network of interconnected specialized management systems. The chapter's learning objectives cover each of the important issues associated with management systems, enabling the reader to understand the important role management systems play in contributing to the functioning and ongoing success of an organization.

In addition, management systems represent an essential management concept and management method associated with senior leadership's efforts to organize the strategy implementation process. The strategy implementation process has an operational focus with successful execution of the process goal. Management systems represent one of the critical management methods used to create and manage and support the strategy implementation process. The creation of a network of management systems with associate policies and work processes provides the foundation for all future leaderships' efforts at successfully implementing the organization's strategy.

Questions

1. What is the purpose and function of a management system?
2. Identify and briefly describe the elements of a management system.
3. Why categorize management systems?
4. What is the primary purpose of each of the following: decision-making management system, information management system, performance management system and quality management system?
5. What are the steps in the process for creating a management system?
6. What is the purpose in linking all the management systems of an organization?
7. How do primary management systems differ from support management systems?
8. Describe the process for assessing the performance of a management system.
9. How is policy used to create a management system and manage a management system?
10. What is the role of a work process within a management system?

Bibliography

Abrahamsson, S., Tosterby, J. & Isaksson, R. (2017). Integrated management systems: testing model for integration. Conference Proceedings. 14th Toulon-Verona Conference on Excellence in Services.

Alavi, M. & Leidner, D.E. (2001). Review: knowledge management and knowledge management systems: conceptual foundations and research issues. *MIS Quarterly.* 25(1). 107–136.

Alter, S. (2011). The work system method: systems thinking for business professionals. *Business Analytics and Information Systems*. Paper 32.

Alter, S. (2002). The work system method for understanding information systems and information system research. *Communications of the Association for Information Systems*. 9. 90–104.

Andriachuk, B. (2013). Building effective management systems. (June 5). Enbridge Liquid Pipelines.

Bonnema, G. M. & Broenink, J. F. (2016). Thinking tracks for multidisciplinary systems design. *Systems*. 4(36). 1–17.

El-Bakry, H.M., Riadd, A.E.M., Asem, A.S., El Hoseny, M. & Mastorakis, N. (2010). Design and implementation of total quality assurance management system for universities. *Proceedings of the 4th WSEAS International Conference of Business Administration (ICBA'10)*. University of Cambridge (February 20–22). 89–103.

Feldman, M.S. & Pentland, B.T. (2003). Reconceptualizing organizational routines as a source of flexibility and change. *Administrative Science Quarterly*. 48. 94–118.

Jones, G. (2005). Is the management plan achieving its objectives? In G. Worboys, M. Lockwood & T. DeLacy (Eds.). *Protected Area Management: Principles and Practice*. 2nd Edition. Oxford University Press. 555–557.

Jorgensen, T.H., Remmen, A. & Mellado, M.D. (2006). Integrated management systems – three different levels of integration. *Journal of Cleaner Production*. 14(8). 713–722.

Ladinsky, J. (2015). Developing an effective performance management system: lessons for the implementation of WIOA. *Mathematica-MPR.COM*. (August). 1–7.

Latham, J.R. (2012). Management system design for sustainable excellence: framework, practices, and considerations. *The Quality Management Journal*. 19(2). 7–21.

Pardy, W. & Andrews, T. (2009). Integrated management systems: leading strategies and solutions. *Government Institutes*. The Scarecrow Press, Inc. Chapters 1–2.

Potocki, K.A. & Brocato, R. C. (1995). A system of management for organizational improvement. *John Hopkins APL. Technical Digest*. 16(4). 402–412.

Redman, N. (2018). Module 2: why have an integrated management system? *International Atomic Energy Agency*. 1–21.

Smorol, E. & Aurrichio, P. (2010). Designing, developing, and implementing a management system: an overview. *IBM Management System Podcast*. (April). 1–9.

Truex, D. P., Lakw, N., Alter, S. & Sarkar, S. (2011). Extending a systems analysis method for business professionals. *Communications in Computer and Information Science. European Design Science Symposium*. (October). 15–26.

Truex, D., Alter, S. & Long, C. 2010). Systems analysis for everyone else: empowering business professionals through a systems analysis method that fits their needs. *Proceeding of 18th European Conference on Information Systems*. Pretoria, South Africa.

Work Processes

OVERVIEW

Work processes represent an essential management method that organizations use to perform all organizational operations. However, for the reader to understand the concept of work processes, the reader needs an introduction to a theory about organizing proposed by Weick and Sutcliffe (2005). The theory of organizing is fundamental in framing the discussion about work processes; explaining why organizations use work processes to achieve the organization's mission, vision and strategic goals. This chapter describes the functioning of a work process and the manner in which a typical work process operates. The chapter identifies and describes the basic criteria used to identify a work process and an example of an assessment model for evaluating a work process effectiveness. In addition, the chapter describes primary or core work processes and secondary work process; explaining the importance of each type of work process and how these two types of work processes differ.

Work process proceeds through a work process life cycle, with an originating start point, and evolves over time, with a strong probability of eventually becoming obsolete and then eliminated. This work process maturation process discussion is meant to enable the reader to understand that work processes are not static but dynamic, evolving over time. The evolution of a work process occurs in part because of problems associated with performing a work process. Identified and described are examples of common forms of work process problems along with common management methods used to solve work process problems.

Every action in an organization reflects the organization's cultural influence. An organization's culture encompasses the important values that an organization codifies in the organization's official code of ethics and formal management practices. To understand why an organization designs work processes a particular way and emphasizes developing certain types of work processes requires understanding an organization's culture. Finally, this chapter offers insights about the role of technology associated with many work processes. Technology complements the human element in performing a work process.

CHAPTER 4   LEARNING OBJECTIVES

Readers will achieve the following learning objectives after reading this chapter.

1. Identify and explain Weick's theory of organizing and work processes.
2. Describe and explain how a work process functions.
3. Identify and describe the criteria for identifying a work process.
4. Identify and describe the methods used to evaluate a work process performance.
5. Identify and explain the process for creating a work process.
6. Describe and explain the difference between primary and secondary work processes.
7. Describe and explain the maturation process of a work process (different iterations).
8. Identify and describe common work process problems.
9. Identify and describe the management methods for resolving work process problems.
10. Explain the relationship between organizational values and work processes.
11. Describe the relationship between technology and work process functioning.

LEARNING OBJECTIVE #1: IDENTIFY AND EXPLAIN WEICK'S THEORY OF ORGANIZING AND WORK PROCESSES

To know and understand the concept of work processes requires learning the theoretical model that is the foundation that explains the need for work processes and offers the rationale for using work processes as an organizing management method. A work process or procedure (both represent the same principle, but a process indicates the concept of stages that make up a process) represents a method for creating **order**. Order is necessary for the best use of resources and to achieve goals. Weick and Sutcliff (2005) advance a useful theory of organizing that offers insights on the origin of work processes and provide explanations for why organizations create work processes and why individuals create the equivalent routines.

The theory of organizing encompasses a three-step process. The steps are sensemaking, interpretation or provide meaning and then acting. **Sensemaking** is when individuals in an organization confront some phenomena. The phenomena, if new, overwhelm the individual. This overwhelming effect is explained by the concept of **cognitive complexity**. Each individual confronts cognitive limitations, and to avoid being overwhelmed, individuals follow a process of simplification to make sense of the observed phenomena. This method of sensemaking includes a process of ordering the phenomena into categories to help in comprehending the phenomena to know how best to respond. For example, categories can include important, somewhat important and not important. Categories such as snow shovels, garden shovels and construction shovels can be organized into a broader category called shovels. Labels are used for categories because using labels is a common method for creating meaning, a practiced method for sorting and rating phenomena. Our perceptions, shaped by past experiences, and how we interpret phenomena observed, determine how to respond. For example, if we use the categories, urgent and not urgent, then we know an immediate action is necessary if we interpret the observed phenomena as urgent. The type of response can be categorized as well, short-term response type and long-term response type.

Individuals need to understand the phenomena observed to learn how best to respond. Responding to phenomena can proceed along several different paths if the individual does not know what the phenomena represent. By providing meaning to the phenomena, individuals also reduce **cognitive complexity** which often leads to being cognitively overwhelmed. Individuals seek to achieve four goals to create order. The first goal is to avoid **cognitive dysfunction**. Cognitive dysfunction occurs when phenomena taxes the individual's cognitive capabilities. The second goal is to achieve **cognitive efficiency**. Individuals want to be economical in the use of their time in performing an action.

Making sense of phenomena enables the individual to create a process to respond to the phenomena; this process conforms to the individual's belief in knowing how best to respond. The third goal is an **achievement goal**. Individuals seek results that meet personal expectations. Individuals create a response to meaningful phenomena that is expected to achieve the intended results. Finally, individuals prefer to perform actions on a **consistent basis**. Consistency means responding with a familiar, practiced action to perform in response to each time the individual confronts the same or similar phenomena. In short, individuals create a quiver full of standard responses. For example, the alarm rings to start the day in preparing to leave for work. The alarm is a phenomenon that is known to the individual because this is part of the individual's routine for getting ready for work. Responding to the alarm triggers a series of steps or stages that culminates in leaving the house. The sequence of stages is referred to as a routine. This routine links to the next routine of getting to work. Individuals create routines to provide a semi-automatic process for achieving the goals of getting ready for work by a certain time, minimize wasted time and avoid feeling overwhelmed. When the unexpected occurs that disrupts the routine, the individual begins to feel stressed and attempts to create order to stop feeling stress.

Individuals apply the principles associated with the process for developing and applying routines to organizations, but refer to routines as work processes instead. Work processes differ from routines in that the organization creates formal, established policies for the creation of a work process, the operation of a work process, assessing a work process performance and for modifying a work process. Organizations create formal policies to guide more than one person in performing a work process(es), whereas in a non-organizational setting, individuals use informal policies to focus on developing and implementing personal routines.

LEARNING OBJECTIVE #2: DESCRIBE AND EXPLAIN HOW A WORK PROCESS FUNCTIONS

Each work process has a singular purpose and functions in a systematic way to achieve that purpose. Creating a systematic work process is important to an organization because the goal of a work process is to achieve a pre-defined outcome efficiently, operate on a consistent basis and to meet the organization's performance expectations.

An ordered work process underscores the importance of operating efficiently. The designers of a work process intend to achieve the goal of creating order to a work activity. An orderly work process keeps individuals focused on performing the work process to ensuring that the performance of a work process meets the organization's expectations. The work process participants work experience provides the knowledge about the basic functioning of a work process. This knowledge contributes to the organization's ongoing efforts at ensuring consistent work process performance underscored by the basic value of **continuous and ongoing improvement**, a value associated with all management systems. Organizations attempt to apply the value of continuous and ongoing improvement. Some organizations are more effective than others at applying the value of continuous and ongoing improvement because of the level of commitment to the value varies.

A work process operates with stages. Stages are sequenced with a starting point and an ending point. Work processes connect with other work processes (see Figure 4.1).

FIGURE 4.1   Model of the Application of Weick's Theory of Organizing

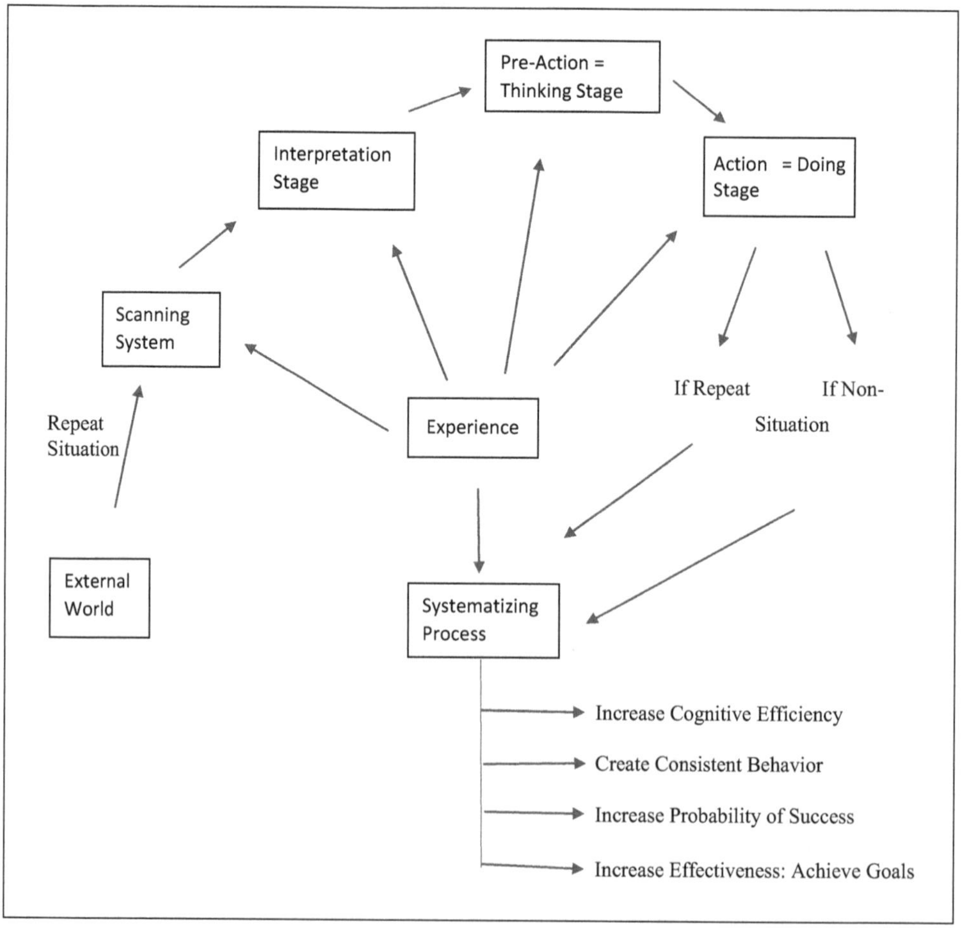

FIGURE 4.2   Model of a Typical Work Process Design

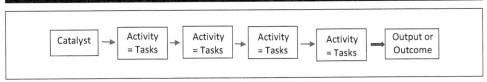

A work process typically generates at least one and perhaps more measurable outcomes. One work process outcome(s) is another work process input(s). For example, resume screening leads to a specific number of acceptable candidates to move forward to the next stage of the hiring process.

The number of stages between the starting point and the end point is determined by the decision-makers ability to narrowly define a stage; each stage should be a single, homogeneous activity. Within a stage are tasks associated with performing the activities of the stage; the outcome or output of a stage is the input to the next stage. Each stage converts an input into an output (or outcome). We can think of a stage as a process within a process and that each work process is part of a network of interconnected work processes (Figure 4.2).

The hiring process is a useful example to illustrate the functioning of a typical work process. The hiring process connects with the recruitment process. The output of the recruitment process is a collection or resumes and applications to review. The input for the hiring process is the collection of resumes and applications for review. The first stage of the hiring process is a review of the resumes and applications. The output of this stage is a select number of applicants to forward to stage two, telephone interviews. The tasks associated with stage one involves the review of resumes and applications to finalize on the selection of candidates to pass on to stage two. The tasks within stage one follows a logical sequence of stages because the fundamental premise underlying the development of a management systems and work processes is to design each work process systematically, this includes each stage of a work process as well.

The hiring process continues through as many stages as necessary to finish up with the hiring of a candidate(s). The outcome or output of the hiring process becomes the input to the next work process. As stated earlier, all work processes link together to form a network of work processes within a management system; each management system is part of a large network of management systems organized as a mega-organizational structure (Figure 4.3).

Roselli's Italian Cuisine: Part 1

Claire Bonsano, the restaurant manager, was meeting with Ken Shields and Amy Klatch, assistant managers. Claire called the meeting to discuss the hostesses. Customer complaints about the hostess behavior along with complaints from the waitstaff led to the need for the meeting. Prior to meeting, Amy met with the hostesses to get their insights about the complaints. What Claire, Ken and Amy realized was that the hostesses never had a formal routine to follow in performing their job. Each hostess chose to perform the hostess duties their own way. Claire, Ken and Amy decided that creating a routine for the hostesses to follow would standardize their actions; hopefully, everyone would be happy, the customers.

Questions

1. What were some of the problems that led to unhappy customers and waitstaff?
2. What are the goals for creating a standard routine for the hostesses to follow?
3. Identify the important activities a hostess needs to perform.
4. Should the managers present their proposal to the hostesses and waitstaff? Explain.
5. How will the managers know if the new routine is a success? Explain.

FIGURE 4.3   Example of a Typical Hiring Process (Work Process Example)

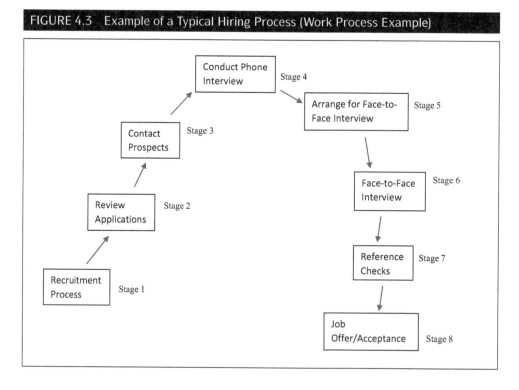

LEARNING OBJECTIVE #3: IDENTIFY AND DESCRIBE THE CRITERIA FOR IDENTIFYING A WORK PROCESS

One of the easiest criteria to use in the process of identifying a work process is to look for a **task**, any type of task. This process is referred to as task analysis, and task analysis involves identifying a task or tasks because each work process has a task to perform. Identifying a task leads to the identification of a work process. Finding a particular work process involves including other criteria. Searching for a work process means looking for a work process that generates a particular **outcome**. By identifying an outcome, the search moves forward by determining the **functional area** associated with the outcome. Labeling, discussed in the prior section, helps to sort through the functions (e.g. marketing) and sub-functions (e.g. advertising) to learn the work process functional location.

Knowing that a work process represents the organization's attempt to standardize a process that creates an output from an input helps in the search for a specific work process. Standardizing a work process occurs once the organization creates an **official policy**. Having an official policy ensures that a work process operates consistently, following a set schedule.

Frequency of task activities is another search criterion to use in guiding the search process because repetition is one of the markers of a work process. In sum, frequency of the activities of a stage and repetition of the same activities of a stage represent indicators of a work process. **Repetition of activities** includes the repetition of tasks associated with each stage.

After identifying an activity, we know that this activity represents a stage of a work process. Logic dictates there are prior stages and succeeding stages. The need to systematize that the search process is important to establish a methodology to follow in future searches. Because each stage generates an output and receives an input, the direction of the search process is not relevant. Starting with identifying an activity, locating the source of the activity's input means that the search leads to a prior stage. Moving in the other direction, the activity generates an output for the next stage of the work process; the stage that is the beneficiary of that output is identified as the succeeding stage.

The search process continues incrementally forward from the initial activity uncovered to each subsequent activity stage. Each stage generates an output (or outcome) as the search moves forward to identify the output of the work process. The output of the work process is known because of the use of a performance benchmark for each work process. Finding the output associated with the performance benchmark means that the final stage of the work process is identified as well as the identification of the first stage of the connecting work process unless the output is for the non-organizational customer. Moving backward from the identified stage (or activity), the input represents the output of the prior stage. The work process puzzle is getting filled in. We know that the first stage of a work process is connected to the final stage of a linked work process. Knowledge of the benchmark measure of the connected work process, the search for the end stage is simplified. After identifying the final stage of a prior work process, then, we know the first stage of the connecting work process that we want to identify because we know the first activity stage associated with the work process. Once identified, a label is used to refer to the stage (e.g. hiring process, job design process and site location process).

Using the hiring process as an example, if we arbitrarily begin the search process at the first interview stage, logic and theory about hiring tell us that there is at least a prior activity stage and at least one following activity stage. Logic and theory dictate that there is a work process linked to the hiring process that provides an input to the hiring process and that there is a connecting work process that uses the output of the hiring process as its input.

After identifying the work process, the search ends. But what makes identifying the stages of a work process, the sequence of the stages and the tasks performed within a stage and the connecting work processes important to learn about? The search process reflects a model for locating a work process. After pinpointing the work process, decision-makers can begin to focus on improving the work process. For example, if the turnover rate of new hires exceeds the industry average, the search for a solution can focus on at least the hiring process without necessarily excluding such other related work processes such as recruitment, job description creation and benefits package development as possible factors contributing to the unacceptable level of turnover among newly hired employees.

LEARNING OBJECTIVE #4: IDENTIFY AND DESCRIBE THE METHODS USED TO EVALUATE A WORK PROCESS PERFORMANCE

An organization's leadership has access to a variety of management methods to use in evaluating the effectiveness of a work process. One common method is to use **SMART performance objectives**. Because each work process generates some type of an outcome, decision-makers can identify performance objectives to represent performance benchmarks to achieve. The preference to use SMART objectives is because this type of objective is measurable and time limited. Measurement is a quantitative feature that is tractable. Timeliness, an attribute of a SMART objective, creates a sense of urgency in galvanizing the workforce's efforts to ensure that the performance meets expectations.

Related to the use of SMART performance, objectives is the use of a system of **performance indicators**. The goal in designing a system of performance indicators is to standardize the operations around a method for gathering information to assess the performance of a work process; this includes assessing a collection of related work processes as well. Using standardized approaches can include the use of performance benchmarks, formal reporting process that includes defining milestones to accomplish, that indicate progress in achieving the objective and a time element for the frequency in submitting a routine report.

Customer surveys and **customer interviews** represent two management methods used to assess work processes directly connected to the end user. These management methods represent direct approaches for learning how well the work processes outcome(s) satisfy end user expectations. **Customer trend analysis** is an indirect management method used to assess customer satisfaction by measuring customer purchasing behavior as a proxy for customer satisfaction and customer loyalty. Examples for assessing customer satisfaction through the use of customer trend analysis include the number of complaints logged compared to a benchmark for complaints; brand loyalty as measure by the number of months a customer actively buys from the organization compared to a brand loyalty benchmark; the frequency of orders submitted and the size of an order or the number of items purchased compared to a benchmark.

Senior-level decision-makers direct **middle managers** in overseeing the workforce's efforts in performing work processes. Middle managers can use direct oversight methods such as face-to-face meetings or use indirect oversight methods, such as reports, in monitoring the execution of a work process and ensuring that the work process meets expectations. Expectations are set through the use of performance benchmarks and performance indicators (using SMART objectives).

Decision-makers use **formal policies**, another type of management method, to regulate the design of a work process, the functioning of a work process and the way to assess a work process performance.

Process management represents another management method used to oversee the functioning of a work process. Process management is a more inclusive approach in evaluating a work process because in addition to the evaluative component, process management includes explanations for operating a work process and designing actions associated with creating a work process or making changes to an existing work process.

Process simulation is a management method used to model a work process prior to implementing the work process. The intent of process simulation is to identify possible flaws in the design of a work process or re-design of a work process. Problems are disruptive to work process operations. The preference is to avoid as many problems associated with the design of a work process prior to making the work process operational.

Roselli's Italian Cuisine: Part 2

Claire Bonsano, the restaurant manager, was meeting with Ken Shields and Amy Klatch, the assistant managers. Waitstaff and customers were complaining about delays in getting their food on time. In addition to providing food late, the food came reported as lukewarm. Amy was assigned the responsibility of observing the food preparation process to better understand the function of the process and to identify problems that led to the delays.

Questions

1. How should Amy proceed? Explain.
2. What type of performance indicators should Amy consider? Explain.
3. Should Amy interview any of the food preparation management team? If yes, why and if not why?
4. Should Amy review the policies related to the food preparation process? Explain.

LEARNING OBJECTIVE #5: IDENTIFY AND EXPLAIN THE PROCESS FOR CREATING A WORK PROCESS

The first step in the process for designing a new work process or re-designing an existing work process is the need to notify decision-makers about the circumstances requiring this action. This step occurs prior to creating or re-designing the work process because subordinates must bring to decision-makers attention that there is a **policy issue** which is inconsistent with providing accurate performance information. The recognition that there is a policy issue comes from feedback either directly or indirectly from either external customers, internal customers or government agencies.

Policy shapes the form of a work process to generate the preferred outcome. As the reader recalls, policy represents the method an organization uses to guide action. Action here refers to creating/re-designing a work process. Decision-makers must decide if a new policy is necessary or an existing policy needs modification. Decision-makers need to be cognizant of the need to carefully craft a policy, so the work process generates the sought-after outcome.

Modifying the policy provides the focus to begin the next step, designing a news work process or re-designing an existing work process. The initial step is to identify a **preferred work process outcome**. Every work process generates an outcome (or output). Decision-makers need to determine the type of outcome the work process needs to generate and a quantitative performance indicator that reflects this outcome. Decision-makers at this point develop ideas on a performance benchmark or performance target for the work process to achieve consistently. The benchmark estimate is tentative at this point, evolving as the design of the work process moves toward a final form, ready to become operational.

Once decision-makers establish a policy position and performance outcomes, the next step is to begin creating or modifying the work process to reflect the decision-makers intentions. Work process designers begin by identifying the important **activities** a work process needs to perform to generate the performance outcome(s). Using the hiring process as an example, an important activity is the review of resumes and applications. Within each activity (or stage of a work process) are tasks to perform to achieve the expected outcome associated with the activity (stage). The outcome of a review of resumes and applications is a select number of candidates to move on to the next activity (stage). Tasks associated with the screening of the applicant's resume review stage, after creating a screening rubric, follow a candidate screening process. After identifying the tasks associated with each activity (stage), the next step in designing the work process is to sequence the activities (stages) into a sequence of **stages**. To make this sequencing process easier, designers **label** each stage (e.g. resume/application review stage). After identifying the labels to use, the next step is to put the stages, each represented by an activity, in a sequence that represents the organization's rational thinking on how to perform the hiring process. Being rationale provides the supporting logic to create an orderly hiring process to follow. **Technology** is always a factor to consider in aiding and abetting the functioning of a work process. Work process designers need to consider the type of technology to incorporate into the work process and how best to use the technology. For example, technology is available to assist in the process of screening candidate resumes and applications.

A process to follow within an activity is referred to as a sub-process. An activity can and often does include multiple sub-processes to achieve the intended outcome of an activity (stage). For example, a sub-process during a telephone or zoom interview stage (or activity) is preparing standard questions to ask.

After designing the work process, **personnel** responsible for performing the work process is identified as well as selecting the **decision-maker(s)** to be responsible for overseeing the work process. **Job descriptions** might require modification to incorporate an individual's role in implementing the work process and to identify work process areas of responsibility.

A **reporting process** associated with a work process is necessary to keep decision-makers updated on the performance results of the work process. Reporting is a component of the performance management system, the system responsible for tracking all the core work processes in an organization. The reporting process, like any process, is a work process that follows the basic work process model. The outcome is information provided to decision-makers on the performance of the work process. Decision-makers use the reports to assess whether work process meets performance benchmark requirements or an underperforming work process.

Because **all work processes link together** with other work processes, a new work process requires identifying partner work processes to link to. Finding a partner involves identifying a work process whose output is the new work process input. At the other end, the work process output represents the linked work process input. These work process linkages require a seamless connection. For example, the prior work process to the hiring process is the recruitment process. The process after the hiring work process could be the paperwork completion work process to officially integrate the new hire(s) to the organization.

A **work process simulation** is a management method used to review the planned operation of the work process. A visual model, presented in the form of a flowchart, helps to visualize the movement of the work process activities. Once satisfied with the work process design, the next step is to **execute** the work process by making the new work process operational.

LEARNING OBJECTIVE #6: DESCRIBE AND EXPLAIN THE DIFFERENCE BETWEEN PRIMARY AND SECONDARY WORK PROCESSES

Organizations create two types of work processes: primary and secondary. There are important characteristics that distinguish between each type of work process. A **primary work process** is distinguishable in that the outcome(s) benefit external customers or benefit internal customers that interact with external customers. For example, sales work processes that link to customers of the organization represent a primary group of work processes. Work process outcomes that contribute to the success of a work process involving external customers are a primary work process. A customer support work process that provides direct assistance to external customers or to those others who aid external customers is a primary work process.

A primary work process level of importance to the organization is measurable using four criteria. First, **direct contact** with the organization's external customers. Second, **frequency of activity** involved in working with external customers is a signal of the importance of the activity involving external customers. Third, the **allocation of resources** signals the importance the organization places on a work process among the different primary work processes. Finally, **governance** or the conferring of decision-making authority to higher-ranked decision-makers over interactions with the external customers and all work processes linked to the external customers indicates the organization's way of valuing the importance of the work process.

A sub-set of primary work processes that contribute to an organization's success, but indirectly linked with an organization's external customers are the **strategy formulation** group of work processes and the **strategic control** group of work processes. Each type of work process grouping represents a stage in the **strategic management model**. Identifying a new strategy along with a vision and strategic goals are essential big-picture actions that provide the strategic focus for an organization to follow. Because of the importance of providing strategic focus, the work processes fall into the category of primary work processes. Strategic control represents another important group of work process because strategic control focuses on monitoring an organization's performance toward achieving the strategic goals with the final determinant the achievement of the organization's vision. Monitoring performance is an important activity that ensures that the organization remains focused on the important priorities that are crucial to an organization's success.

Secondary work processes represent work processes that support the efforts of individuals responsible for performing the primary work processes. Human Resources and all the related specialties such as training program work processes, benefits work processes and reward system work processes represent examples of support work processes. Legal work processes of various types as well as certain marketing work processes (e.g. advertising and promotions) along with logistics work processes represent other examples of support work processes.

Distinguishing between primary and secondary work processes is important because an organization needs to ensure that the primary work processes function at their best because of the important role primary work processes play in contributing to an organization's efforts in working with external customers.

At this point, a detailed example of a work process that encompasses primary and secondary support work processes helps to illustrate the connections and differences between the two types of work processes. Using a medium-priced restaurant as an example, the table management work process is an example of a primary work process where the waitstaff work directly with customers. The secondary work processes that link to the table management work process include the hostess management work process, the drinks and bread management process, the table clean-up management process, the set-up table management process, the cooking management process and the pots and pans and dishes clean-up management process. Each of the secondary work processes link directly or indirectly with the primary management process, the table management process.

Roselli's Italian Cuisine: Part 3

During a meeting among the managers and staff, Claire, the restaurant manager, was discussing the issue of routines in performing various activities. Claire was explaining the differences between primary routines (A.K.A. primary work processes) and secondary routines (A.K.A. secondary work processes). Pam, one of the waitstaff raised her hand to ask Claire a question. Pam wanted to know "How are primary and secondary routines related and could Claire provide examples of each type of routine?"

Questions

1. How did Claire respond in answering Pam's question?
2. What might Claire have said is a primary routine? Explain.

3. What might Claire have said is a secondary routine? Explain.
4. Why is understanding the link between primary and secondary routines important to understand?
5. What can management do with the information about primary and secondary routines? Explain.

LEARNING OBJECTIVE #7: DESCRIBE AND EXPLAIN THE MATURATION PROCESS OF A WORK PROCESS (DIFFERENT ITERATIONS)

Because an organization represents a network of management systems that contain numerous work processes, any changes in an organization's goals and strategies for achieving the goals act as a catalyst, triggering changes among work processes that cascade throughout the organization. The change in an organization's strategic goals means that the strategies for achieving these goals must change. The magnitude of possible changes follows a **change continuum** with no changes at one end of the continuum to major changes at the other end of the continuum. The range of possible changes occurs between each of the continuum's end points.

The changes in an organization's goals and the strategies for achieving the goals initiate the need for a new policy(ies) and for the modification of existing policies to support the new initiatives. Policies initiate organizational actions because policies reflect the organization's expectations about a subject(s). Since the organization's work processes represent the organization's capabilities to perform to meet the requirements of a policy, new work processes or changes to existing work processes become a necessity. The goal is to improve an organization's capabilities by increasing a work process effectiveness which means increasing a work process output.

The evolution of a work process evolution follows a simple design model: there is a need, design the work process, implement the work process, assess the functioning of the work process and modify the work process to achieve performance benchmark targets, assuming that a change is necessary. A work process evolves over time as the needs associated with the work process change. The evolution of a work process is described as a **maturation process** because the initial work process typically represents a simplistic design. Once a work process becomes established, decision-makers and non-decision-makers associated with implementing the work process might recognize limitations to the initial work process design.

Need triggers a review of the work process performance. The outcome of the review process is the decision to re-design the work process. Changes to the work process can be minor or major. A work process matures through various iterations as the performance expectations change. The organization can seek a more efficient work process, or a work process needs to generate greater output or a work process needs to be more efficient and productive.

Work process maturation moves through phases, with each phase of a work process differing from its predecessor. At some point, decision-makers can and do determine that an existing work process is obsolete, either as a consequence of technology that can replace a work process or a combination of new technology and the superior performance of another work process makes the existing work process redundant.

Because change is disruptive, resistance to changing a work process is likely. To counter resistance, the organization often offers incentives to encourage resisters to support the changes. Incentives range from positive performance reviews, bonuses, promotions, greater job responsibilities with increased authority, and other forms of incentives intended to encourage support in making changes to a work process.

LEARNING OBJECTIVE #8: IDENTIFY AND DESCRIBE COMMON WORK PROCESS PROBLEMS

There are two major types of work process problems. There are work process problems that are a direct result of designer omissions, inconsistencies or as a consequence of not following the model for designing a work process. The other type of problems encompasses operational problems associated with the implementation of a work process that does not perform to the intended expectations. Some work process issues encompass both types of problems.

There are a number of identifiable design problems associated with designing a work process.

- The designer(s) might not identify all the necessary activities that a complete work process requires. Since each stage of a work process is an activity, the result is that some stages are missing.
- Design flaws such as bottlenecks between stages in a work process and between linked work processes can occur. These bottlenecks lengthen the overall time to complete a work process and the time to complete the connecting work process.
- The failure to consider the role of performance benchmarks in designing a work process is problematic in assessing a work process performance along with evaluating the performance of a network of linked work processes (each network sharing a common theme).
- The failure to create a reporting process means work process performance information such as report content and frequency of reports is left open-ended.
- Insufficient resources make operating a work process difficult, resulting in underperformance.
- The design of a work process is overly complex which increases cognitive complexity, the anti-thesis in designing a work process.
- The linkage between work processes does not lead to a seamless connection.
- Governance roles and rules are not clearly defined for managing the performance of a work process.
- The work process is not standardized sufficiently; the performance of each stage of the work process and the sequential order of the stages is too variable and open to chance that the stages will operate together as intended.

Work process operational types of problems can include the following.

- Re-designing a work process and/or changing the way work processes link can lead to resistance from implementors of the work process(s) who prefer the status quo.
- Reporting the performance of a work process is essential to ensure consistency of the work process. Irregular reporting leads to the potential for not identifying work process problems soon enough.

- Primary work processes may not benefit from support work processes that are intended to assist in the optimal performance of the primary work process(es).
- Coordination among linked work processes may be irregular or disrupted in some way.
- Technology might be insufficient to ensure optimal work process efficiency.
- Work process governance roles and rules might not be uniformly applied.
- Work process output might be at variance with customer expectations.
- Activities performed within a work process are performed inconsistently in comparison with the intentions of the designers.

LEARNING OBJECTIVE #9: IDENTIFY AND DESCRIBE THE MANAGEMENT METHODS FOR RESOLVING WORK PROCESS PROBLEMS

There are a variety of management methods available to decision-makers to resolve work process problems.

- Visual simulation represents a flowchart visual representation of the identified work process stages sequenced according to the plan. Visualization offers decision-makers a visual image to determine if the model work process is fully representative of what decision-makers required for the work process to meet performance expectations.
- Incentives offered to work process designers and work process implementors can help to overcome any hesitation in designing or implementing a new or re-designed work process.
- By ensuring that the implementation of a work process is part of an implementors performance review, decision-makers put implementors on notice that the work process is an important priority to the organization.
- Including implementors of a new work process during the design or re-design phase of the work process commits these individuals to ensuring that the work process meets the performance expectations of decision-makers.
- Job descriptions of implementors of a work process need to include the need to adhere to the work process performance reporting requirement and perform the role of coordinating between linked work processes.
- Use governance rules to guide the functioning of the work process and the roles of work process implementors to limit the potential for problems associated with work process ambiguities.
- Training implementors of a work process helps to clarify implementor roles and responsibilities in overseeing the functioning of a work process; clarity can often overcome resistance to performing the work process.
- With a work process performance metrics clearly defined and monitored, work process implementors know that problems associated with the performance of a work process are detectable.
- A resource review prior to implementing a new or re-designed work process represents a final check to ensure the adequate allocation of resources to ensure the successful performance of the work process.

LEARNING OBJECTIVE #10: EXPLAIN THE RELATIONSHIP BETWEEN ORGANIZATIONAL VALUES AND WORK PROCESSES

Understanding the values associated with the development and use of work processes is important because values are fundamental to all organizations. This is because the main role of values is to shape every action taken by an organization.

Values represent standards to follow, something that individuals and organizations consider important. Identifying an organization's values is important because values symbolize what is far-reaching to the organization, the prioritizing of all organizational actions. All actions of an organization reflect the values that are important to an organization. The more an organization conducts certain actions, the more we can learn which are the organization's core values. Organizational change, manifested through the actions of the organization, reflects the values underlying the changes along with promoting new values and/or strengthening the existing values. For example, an organization might put a high priority on cost efficiency, but during a recession, cost efficiency becomes a greater priority. The organization can develop programs associated with reducing costs to increase profit margins. Cost decline is an example of raising the standard associated with the value, cost efficiency.

Common values associated with management systems and work processes include the following.

- **Awareness** or alternatively **mindfulness** to the need for a new work process or modification to an existing work process.
- Work processes require a strong commitment to pursuing a **systematic** approach in designing work processes because a successful work process requires careful organizing.
- Being **role-oriented** is an important value for an organization that stresses the importance of a work process with a specific purpose because a carefully crafted policy provides the guidance in designing each work process.
- One of the important reasons associated with designing a work process is to solve a problem(s). Being **problem-oriented** is an important value because organizations always experience problems.
- Being **goal-oriented** keeps decision-makers and non-decision-makers focused and influences the approaches used in designing work processes with measurable outcomes.
- Work process designers have a strong **achievement** orientation; a value that puts a work process in a context of work to accomplish to achieve a specific outcome.
- Belief in the importance of **change** and **change-management** is an important value because designing a work process and re-designing a work process represent changes to the status quo.
- Work process management is more than maintaining the status quo. Work process management is about improving the efficiency and/or the effectiveness of a work process. This theme is supported by **quality management** with the focus on continuous and ongoing improvement.
- A **customer-focus** is a critical value because success in meeting customer needs supports the longevity of an organization and its management systems and work processes.

- A commitment to the important role of **technology** and work process performance is a fundamental value associated with all work processes because technology, ranging from simple to complex, is associated with creating an effective work process.
- Being **process-oriented** ranks work process design and work process management as two critical management issues because each is associated with using a process to oversee processes.
- Work process designers use **simplicity** as a guiding influence in designing a work process to minimize problems associated with managing a complex work process.
- The use of **models** in work process design and work process management enables the designers and decision-makers to create a representation of a work process that identifies process flows prior to implementing the work process.

Roselli's Italian Cuisine: Part 4

Paul Roselli, the owner of Roselli's Italian Cuisine, was meeting with his management team. Paul told everyone that he planned to retire within 1–2 years depending on when he sells the business. His plan was to find a buyer who will keep the tradition of a family-oriented restaurant and remain for a year to give the new owner guidance in overseeing the management of the restaurant. In his discussion, Paul discussed the important values that contributed to the restaurant's success. Surviving for 33 years was a statement about the values that guided the restaurant's operations. Many customers were loyal customers; often, other family members visited routinely; many of the staff worked at Roselli's for years. Pamela, the cashier, started with Paul.

Questions

1. What are the values that made Roselli's a success? Explain.
2. Select a value from your response in Q1 and identify a work process impacted by the value. Describe how the value influenced the work routine.
3. Select another value from your response to Q1 and respond the same way as in Q2.
4. When meeting with a new owner, what does Paul Roselli need to say? Explain.
5. Why is it important to be careful in selecting a new owner? Explain.

LEARNING OBJECTIVE #11: DESCRIBE THE RELATIONSHIP BETWEEN TECHNOLOGY AND WORK PROCESS FUNCTIONING

Process technology is the type of technology often associated with aiding the functioning of a work process. Process technology represents technology that enhances the performance of a work process. The application of technology along with people in performing a work process is meant to strengthen the performance of the people. For example, during the hiring process, technology is useful in providing the initial screening of resumes that are either sent digitally or scanned. The initial screening enables evaluators to screen large numbers of resumes quickly and objectively because the technology is programmed to screen for certain features of an applicant's background.

Process technology is beneficial in three ways. First, an individual performing a work process or work process stage is more efficient working with technology that enhances the individual's ability to perform their job. Second, if a team performs a work process, the team's performance is improved through the use of process technology. Finally, process technology used throughout the organization's numerous work processes strengthens an organization's overall performance.

There are two principal categories of process technology. There is process technology associated with work process that directly meets the needs of customers. For example, self-help checkout stations at a supermarket. Second, there is process technology associated with support management system's work processes that abet the performance of a management system's work processes that directly impact customers. For example, flashing signs that indicate special sales in a supermarket. Support types of management systems can include performance management systems, reporting management systems and information manipulation management systems, as examples of management systems where process technology is useful.

An inventory control management system is another example involving the use of process technology. Process technology can link with other process technology where there is a sender-receiver interaction. One application of technology is the sending of information on inventory levels for different products, and the receiving technology is programmable to respond by re-ordering more of each item in the quantity required to maintain pre-determined inventory levels.

Process technology can automate the data collection process, such as when a cashier at a store enters items bought. Process technology can help in collecting data, analyzing the data and automatically respond with an action such as ordering more of an item or reducing the re-ordering quantity of an item. The automation of these types of work processes does not exclude the human element. The human element is removed from mundane, repetitive types of tasks that process technology is better able to perform. One of the principle benefits of process technology is to reduce problems associated with an individual's need to perform tedious, repetitive tasks that are de-motivating for individuals. The result is a more motivated employee committed to better work performance.

Other examples in the use of process technology to complement a work process include:

- Improving communication within the organization and between the organization and suppliers and between the organization and customers.
- Process technology can aid in the design of a work process by providing the ability to create a visual simulation of a work process and each of the stages of the work process.

- The use of process technology among the various performance management systems automates the monitoring of work process operations routinely to ensure that the work process meets performance expectations and enables the organization to respond more quickly to dysfunctional work processes.

Chapter Summary

The study of work processes is important because work processes represent the procedures used to implement organizational policies. Work process management along with work process assessment represents the core operational activities associated with the implementation of organizational strategies. By understanding that work processes represent the critical focus in implementing an organization's strategies, the reader is in a position to understand how organizations function.

The chapter describes a theory about organizing that is fundamental in framing any discussion about the concept of organizing and the use of work processes to conduct different functions associated with the strategy implementation process (a stage of the strategic management model). Because of the central role of work processes during the strategy implementation process, the chapter examines the subject in great detail. Two topics covered include learning how to identify and describe the criteria used to recognize a work process. The second topic introduces management methods used to evaluate a work process effectiveness.

The chapter examines primary and secondary types of work processes. Primary work processes are essential in serving the needs of customers. Secondary work processes serve the needs of individuals associated with performing the primary work processes. Another important topic describes how work processes evolve. The evolution of a work process is referred to as the maturation process. Decision-makers monitor the functioning of a work process with the goal of continuing to improve the performance of the work process. The continued improvements of a work process represent the stages in the maturation of a work process over an extended period of time.

Work processes experience certain types of problems associated with the functioning of a work process. Work process problems identified in the chapter can hinder the success of an organization if left unattended. Discussed in the chapter are management methods associated with solving common work process problems.

The chapter examines how organizational values prioritize important work processes from less important work processes, impact the design of work processes and influence the management of work processes. Examining values associated with work processes enables the reader to learn about the values that drive all aspects of work process management from the choice of work process goals, the design of a work process, the performance of a work process and the assessment of a work process performance.

Finally, the chapter examines the association between process technology and work processes. All work processes involve the use of some form of technology. The role of process technology is to assist in the operation of a work process, leading to greater work process efficiencies and strengthening a work process effectiveness in the strategy implementation process.

Questions

1. Describe the theory of organizing.
2. Describe how a work process functions.
3. Identify the important criteria used in identifying a work process.

4. What are the methods used to evaluate the performance of a work process?

5. Identify the steps in the work process design process.

6. How are primary and secondary work processes different?

7. What does the maturation of a work process mean?

8. Identify and briefly describe typical work process problems.

9. What are the management methods used to solve common work process problems?

10. Why do we associate organizational values with work processes?

11. Describe the relationship between process technology and work processes.

Bibliography

Armistead, C., Pritchard, J.-P. & Martinelli, D. P. (2013). Business process management: a systematic approach? *Business Process Management Journal.* 19(4). 698–714.

Bititci, V.S. & Muir, D. (1997). Business process definition: a bottom-up approach. *International Journal of Operations and Production Management.* 17(4). 365–374.

Brocke, J.V. & Rosemann, M. (2014). Business process management. *Wiley Encyclopedia of Management.* 7. *Management Information Systems.* 1–15.

Brocke, J.V., Schmiedel, T., Reckler, J.C., Trkman, P., Mertens, W. & Viaene, S. (2014). Ten principles of good business process management. *Business Process Management Journal.* 20(4). 530–548.

Damij, N. & Damij, T. (2014). Business process in process management in Nadja Damij and Talib Damij (Eds.). *Progress in IS.* Chapter Two. Springer-Verlag Berlin Heidelberg. 7–24.

Feldman, M.S. & Pentland, B.T. (2003). Reconceptualizing organizational routines as a source of flexibility and change. *Administrative Science Quarterly.* 48. 94–118.

Oliveira, W. (2015). The nine principles of process design. *Business Process Management.* https://www.heflo.com/blog/bpm/business-process-design-principles/. (December 11).

Rosemann, M. & Brocke, J.V. (2010). The six core elements of business process management in J. von Brocke and M. Rosemann (Eds.). *Handbook on Business Process Management 1, International Handbook on Information Systems.* 107–122.

Ross, J. (2018). 6 techniques for creating engaging business processes. *Nintex Promap* p. 1–10. https://www.promapp.com/resources/-6-techniques-for-creating-engaging-business-processes/.

Segatto, M., de Padua, S.I.D. & Martinelli, D.P. (2013). Business process management: a systematic approach? *Business Process Management Journal.* 19(4). 698–714.

Smart, P.A., Maddern, H. & Maull, R.S. (2009). Understanding business process management: implications for theory and practice discussion in *Management Paper Number 07/08.* 1–35.

Trkman, P. (2010). The critical success factors of business process management. *International Journal of Information Management.* 30. 125–134.

Weick, K.E. & Sutcliffe, K.M. (2005). Organizing and the process of sensemaking. *Organizational Science.* 16(4). 409–421.

Organizations, Policy and the Policy-Making Process

OVERVIEW

The great irony in studying different subjects in organizational behavior textbooks is the failure to cover one of the most common and important management subjects, policy. Organizations of all sizes have hundreds of policies; small organizations typically have informal policies, but as an organization expands, there are more policies to match the expansion, and the policies become formal policies. Policies cover every organizational issue imaginable. But when it comes to studying the subject, scant coverage exists to educate students of business about the subject of policy.

This chapter covers all aspects of the subject, policy, because an organization's policies guide all features of an organization's operations, including governance activities. Because the role of policy is fundamental to the operations of an organization, the chapter describes the purpose and function of the subject in detail. The study of policy includes the identification and description of each of the elements that constitutes an organization's policy.

The development of a policy follows to a formal process referred to as the policy design process. The overview of the policy design process includes an explanation of the importance an organization places on creating policies. After a policy receives official sanctioning, the organization proceeds to implement the policy. The chapter introduces the reader to the different methods organizations use to implement a policy.

Despite an organization's best intentions, there are limits associated with developing and implementing a policy. The limitations associated with policy are identified and discussed. Understanding policy limitations requires learning about what makes a policy effective. The chapter identifies criteria often used to recognize effective organizational policies, and the chapter describes the differences between effective and ineffective policies.

An organization's culture is one of the primary determining factors in creating certain types of policies and the level of specificity of a policy. The chapter offers the reader an introduction to the subject of organizational culture, as reflected by the organization's values and policies. Critical policies, as indicated by the values associated with a policy, frequently result in the organization designing and implementing training programs. Training is meant to ensure that employees understand the policy and become committed to implementing the policy.

The importance of having a policy and procedure manual is essential in providing an institutional memory to reference by decision-makers seeking to apply a policy correctly. The chapter discusses the role of a policy and procedures manual along with identifying and describing common types of categories of organizational policies.

CHAPTER 5 LEARNING OBJECTIVES

Readers will achieve the following learning objectives after reading this chapter.

1. Explain the purpose and function of a policy.
2. Identify and describe the elements of a policy.
3. Identify and describe the criteria to identify a good policy.
4. Identify and describe the policy design process.
5. Identify, describe and explain the policy implementation process.
6. Identify and describe methods for identifying effective organizational policies.
7. Identify and explain the limitations of organizational policy.
8. Explain the relationship between an organization's policies and organizational culture.
9. Describe the design and implementation of training programs covering organizational policies.
10. Describe the purpose and importance of a policy and procedures manual.
11. Identify and describe common types of categories of organizational policies.

LEARNING OBJECTIVE #1: EXPLAIN THE PURPOSE AND FUNCTION OF A POLICY

Policies provide the workforce with work processes to follow in the ongoing governance and management of an organization. Policies **define** and **guide** the organization's efforts at creating and managing official work processes that reflect the organization's formal sanctioning of the policy and policy-guided work processes. The creation and management of work processes promotes the goal of increased organizational efficiencies along with supporting the organization's efforts at achieving the strategic goals; achieving the strategic goals requires a smooth-functioning strategy implementation process. In sum, the use of policies is intended to influence employee thinking and employee behavior in ways that serve the best interests of the organization.

Policy functions as a way to **mobilize** the workforce as part of the organization's overall strategy implementation process. Policy implementation requires individuals to focus on performing their work responsibilities. Because workers interact with other workers to fulfill their job requirements, the organization seeks to regulate **interactions** using policies to optimize individual effectiveness. Also, workers often need to work together in teams. Some policies deal with the **integration** of workers within the context of a team; the intent is to promote efficient and effective team performance.

Another important function of an organization's policies is to create, maintain and enhance an **organization's culture**. Policies reflect several different, though related, actions an organization can pursue to support the culture of an organization. First, policy reflects the important organizational values because policies convey a message about the specific values that are important. Policies are used to promote the values the organization considers important and influence employee behaviors to reflect the application of the values. Policies can reinforce an organization's values by modifying a policy in ways that stress the importance of a specific value. Modifying existing policies represents an opportunity for an organization to focus on introducing new values as well as developing or modifying policies with the intention of strengthening the organization's commitment to a specific value(s). For example, if the organization lacks an anti-sexual harassment policy, the creation of this type of policy reflects a greater commitment to the safety and well-being of the workforce. Modifying an existing anti-sexual harassment policy to promote clearer guidelines and increased sensitivity to the issues associated with sexual harassment demonstrate a commitment to reinforcing the organization's commitment to the safety and well-being of the workforce by re-framing existing policies to support the organization's regard for employee safety. Of course, having a policy is only the first step. Applying the policy is the critical next step to demonstrate the organization's actual commitment to the value(s).

Some policies represent the organization's response to external influences that require an organization to conform to **laws and regulations**. National, state and local governments create laws and regulations to influence individual and organizational behavior. Organizations respond by developing policies that demonstrate the adherence to the laws and regulations. These policies set the minimum that an organization must adhere to, but an organization can have stricter policies that extend beyond the minimum legal requirements. For example, safety requirements can exceed the legal requirements on regulating the use of safety equipment. Often, when an organization creates a policy that exceeds the legal requirements, the organization does this to protect the organization from legal complaints and offers a higher threshold of controls that increases the safety of workers.

Policies serve to **facilitate** decision-making when managers confront reoccurring situations. Managers make frequent decisions, major and minor types of decisions, that demand a manager's time to assess the circumstances. Many decisions deal with situations that occur on a regular basis. Having an established policy in place provides managers with the organization's officially sanctioned guidelines to assist the decision-maker in making a decision. Policy simplifies decision-making; policy promotes consistency in actions and fairness in planning; and policy validates the fairness of the decision-making process described in the policy.

A policy provides the workforce with guidance in performing a work process when there is any doubt on how to act in different situations. Policy guidelines can include the type of assistance an employee can expect from the organization; the process to follow in seeking organizational assistance; the way an organization can be expected to respond as well as the responsibilities of the organization and employees to each other. Policy guidelines frequently place limits to the obligations of individual's and the organization with each other so each party knows what to expect from the other.

Fahey Enterprises: Part 1

James, Jack, and their uncle Paul were eating breakfast on Sunday at their favorite North End eatery. James, the owner of Fahey Enterprises, and his brother Jack asked Paul to join them for breakfast. Quickly, Paul sensed some tension between James and Jack. Paul asked "Okay folks, what's up? Please do not avoid my question. I can feel the vibes and they don't feel good." Jack opened by explaining that the business was struggling. Paul asked "Financially?" Jack said no, not yet but this is coming. James mentioned that employees were leaving; employees were shirking their duties; employees were complaining about pay, the work load and that James tells them one thing one day, something different another day and that both James and Jack tell them different things to do on the same job. Jack complained that there is no financial discipline and that their administrative assistant quit and filed a lawsuit complaining about constant swearing, sexism and being asked to do different jobs from what she was hired to do without any change in pay. Paul's response was to explain that the business is no longer a mom and pop operation. "The business needs organizing and one of the important management methods used to facilitate a well-managed organization is the use of policies." At the same time, James and Jack asked "What are policies? Tell us more!"

Questions

1. What did Paul say?
2. Why did Paul suggest the need for policies? Explain.
3. Policies are an important management method for managing a business. Assume Paul told James and Jack this. What were his reasons?
4. How did Paul know that formal policies were necessary? What were the clues?
5. What questions did James and Jack ask Paul? Why these questions?

LEARNING OBJECTIVE #2: IDENTIFY AND DESCRIBE THE ELEMENTS OF A POLICY

A complete organizational policy encompasses several elements that policy writers need to consider when drafting a policy. Whether a policy's focus is on a major issue or a minor issue, a policy needs to cover certain elements to ensure that the policy is complete and to certify that the policy is comprehensive.

The first element of a policy to include in a policy statement is to state the **purpose** of the policy. The purpose statement can be general or refer to the **goal** of the policy or the statement can be more inclusive, combining a purpose statement along with a specific goal. After identifying the purpose of the policy and/or the policy goal, the policy needs to state the **objectives** of the policy. For example, the goal of an anti-bully policy is to improve workforce safety from harassment through the regulation of employee relations. Objectives can include the elimination of all forms of bullying behavior, ensuring that every employee knows what comprises (the definition) bullying behavior, and employees rate treatment by other employees in a survey as good or better.

A third element of a policy involves identifying the **scope** of the policy. Scope can include the entire organization, a specific unit or department of an organization or specific types of individuals (e.g. maintenance workers, administrative assistants and professors). Using the anti-bully policy as an example, the scope in applying this type of policy is the entire organization.

The fourth element of a policy is the actual **statement** that articulates the policy. The statement can be brief, or the statement can include multiple sections. The range of detail in a policy statement depends on the significance of the policy to the organization. Because an anti-bullying policy has far-reaching significance for the entire organization, the policy likely will include multiple sections. Examples of sections can include a definition of bullying behavior, the reporting of bullying process to follow, the adjudication process for handling a complaint and the process for identifying penalty options and the application of penalties. The policy statement also needs to cover the **procedures** to follow and the responsibilities of designated decision-makers. Using the anti-bully policy as an example, the reporting of bullying represents a procedure to follow for the reporter as well as designating the individual(s) to report bullying (e.g. direct superior) to along with this individual's obligations and responsibilities once a complaint of bullying is received. An anti-bully policy includes several different types of procedures associated with this type of policy; included with the procedures are the roles and responsibilities of individuals associated with each procedure.

A policy requires **definitions of terms** because the use of technical jargon sometimes is inescapable, and clarity of terminology is helped by defining terms. For example, the terms "bullying" and "anti-bullying" can have different interpretations to different people. By providing definitions, the organization offers a standardized interpretation of the terms to reduce possible confusion over the meaning of the terms. Process or procedures are other terms often included in a policy statement. Again, interpretations can vary among different people. Clarity of a term's meaning is important to prevent or eliminate misunderstandings.

The **contact information** of important decision-makers associated with a policy is important to include with the policy statement. Contact information offers everyone clarity as to who are the responsible parties to address issues to. A **reference(s)** is often provided to support the policy. An existing organizational policy is useful in providing the foundation supporting the need for a complementary or a supplemental policy. External sources, such as government laws and regulations, are common examples of references that support the need for certain types of policies or specific subjects of a policy. For example, anti-discrimination laws help support the creation and application of an anti-bully policy.

Providing an **effective policy implementation date** puts the workforce on notice that the policy becomes applicable to all employees that the policy applies to. Another element of a policy is to include in the policy a **review date** to create a sense of urgency among decision-makers that a policy needs reviewing periodically. Finally, the policy needs to include a statement that identifies the **policy approving authority along with the date of approval**. Organization-wide policies often get approved by the Board of Directors. Unit-level policies or policies applicable to individuals typically are approved by the CEO and perhaps one or more other senior executives such as the CFO.

Fahey Enterprises: Part 2

James, Jack and Paul decided to meet the next day to continue the conversation. Sunday evening, Paul reviewed several articles that describe different viewpoints about policies. Paul met James and Jack at their office at 7:00 am. Paul reviewed what everyone decided was the subject of the meeting. The company needed to be organized, and hiring policies seemed like a good place to start. Jack mentioned that policies were necessary to provide the type of consistency and focus that was lacking. "We need to discipline ourselves," said Jack. Paul agreed. James asked, "How do we begin?" Paul said:

> Let us first begin by identifying subjects to cover. What is important to change to ensure work gets done right? If employees act the way you want; you guys act the way you need to act; employees will feel happier.

Jack asked about the next step once the subjects are identified. "What do we do then?" said Jack. Paul said, "We need to start by creating policies." James asked, "How do we go about creating a policy?"

Questions

1. How does the application of policies impose discipline? Explain.
2. Why did Paul suggest the need for hiring policies? Explain.
3. What were the top three subjects where policies are necessary? Why these subjects?
4. What is the first step in creating a policy? Explain.
5. What are the elements of a policy, according to Paul?

LEARNING OBJECTIVE #3: IDENTIFY AND DESCRIBE THE CRITERIA TO IDENTIFY A GOOD POLICY

Distinguishing between a **good policy** and a bad or ineffective policy is an important ability for policy designers because this can be the difference between designing an effective or an ineffective policy. There are several criteria that identify a good policy. A good policy pertains to the design features of a policy and not the specific subject of a policy. As a reminder, a policy is applicable at one of three levels: a policy can apply to the entire organization; a policy can apply to a unit within the organization; and the policy can apply to a select group of individuals.

One criterion in identifying a good policy is that the policy is **specific**. For example, a dress code policy defines what constitutes appropriate dress and inappropriate dress, giving specific examples of each form of dress. The **consequences** for individuals identified as inappropriately dressed are presented along with **future actions** if repeat incidents occur. The policy would apply to the entire organization and state different forms of dress for different categories of employees if warranted. Specificity is essential to avoid misunderstandings and to ensure fairness in the application of the policy.

A **clear** policy is important to ensure that individuals understand the intent of the policy, including the various sections of a policy. This requires a policy written free of jargon, or if jargon is necessary, the jargon is defined and explained. For example, a dress code policy might make a distinction between summer business attire and winter business attire. Each type of business attire requires a brief explanation to ensure each type is clear to decision-makers and non-decision-makers.

A good policy sets a standard of behavior that can be **uniformly** applied at any level of the organization that is the focus of the policy. For example, if business attire for workers is stated as applying throughout the organization, variation in the application of the dress code policy is not acceptable unless the policy standard on correct business attire is ambiguous about the required standard.

The policy needs to be **relevant** or **appropriate** to the circumstances to make the policy a good policy. Creating a policy just to have a policy is not a useful practice as this form of policy often can result in non-conformance. The need for a dress code policy must be in response to circumstances that occur routinely and leads to problems for the organization. For example, a service company where service providers visit a home, wearing the official company uniform with identity badge is important to demonstrate that the individual is the official representative of the organization; official business is being conducted and that the individual projects a professional image as defined in the policy.

A good policy is a policy that is **simple and easy to understand** because the policy avoids using a convoluted writing style with unexplained or poorly defined jargon. Dress code policies too often leave individuals unclear as to what constitutes proper, accepted dress. Because dress has become more varied for men and women, between older and younger men and women and between affluent and less affluent men and women as well as cultural differences, defining proper dress is more challenging but not impossible. A confusing dress code policy is a byproduct of a hasty policy-development process unless policy designers take careful consideration of the circumstance; policy designers need to draft a policy that policy-followers can understand and are willing and able to adhere to the guidelines of the policy to fulfill the spirit of the policy.

Inclusiveness of a policy is one of the hallmarks of a good policy statement because the policy targets who the policy applies to; the application of the policy needs to cover everyone identified in the policy. Going back to the levels of a policy's focus, if the policy is meant to apply throughout the organization, the application must include the entire workforce. If the dress code policy, for example, applies to a unit (such as the maintenance department), the policy applies to everyone in that unit. If the policy applies to a select group of individuals, such as financial advisors, the policy of proper business dress applies to all financial advisors.

A policy that is consistent represents a **stable** policy because the policy does not lead to indecisiveness on the part of policy implementors. A policy where confusion exists over how to apply the policy and/or when to apply a policy indicates a flawed policy that contributes to an uneven application of the policy. Think about a dress code policy that is vague. Policy implementors apply the policy according to their personal interpretation of the policy. The result is confusion and feelings of resentment by those who bear the brunt of the uneven application of the dress code policy.

LEARNING OBJECTIVE #4: IDENTIFY AND DESCRIBE THE POLICY DESIGN PROCESS

The policy design process has two distinct stages. The **pre-stage** provides the foundation for the actual policy design process stage. Almost all policy initiatives originate from management though the ideas for a policy or changes to a policy can originate from non-managers. Senior managers or middle managers confront a situation in which a decision is made. Management recognizes after-the-fact that a policy is necessary because management recognizes that the situation is going to continue to repeat itself. Consequently, a policy is necessary to standardize a response to re-occurring situation, provide a consistent response and to minimize unnecessary time delays. Sometimes, the catalyst for a policy originates from external sources, often governmental agencies. Governments create laws and regulations, some of which impact an organization, who then need to respond with a policy or need to modify an existing policy(ies). For example, creation of anti-discrimination laws requires organizations above a certain size to have a relevant anti-discrimination policy in-place that meets the minimum legal requirements.

The first step in the **policy design process** is the creation of a **policy formulation team**. The team composition includes managers with familiarity with the circumstances warranting a particular policy. For example, if there is recognition that the budget review process needs a formal policy to guide the process, the criteria for selecting team members should include individuals associated with the entire budgeting process. The first major activity of the team is the **collection of data**. Using the budget review process as an example, the team would interview and survey individuals directly and indirectly associated with the budget review process. Qualitative and quantitative data are collected and then converted into information to analyze. The goal in analyzing the information is to determine the **dimensions** of the problem a policy needs to respond to. Dimensions refer to the **scope** of the problem to address, **security issues** to cover along with the sought-after **impact** of the new policy. For example, scope of the budget review process could include the types of participants with a role in the process, the time-frame to identify along with the range of issues to consider during the budget review process. Security refers to the limit on the access to the information to a select group of individuals. Impact in creating a formal budget review process can include creating guidelines for keeping within budget projections, re-allocation decisions, pace of the budget review process and sequential stages of the budget review process. These are examples of subjects to consider when drafting a formal policy covering the budget review process.

Policy team members use brainstorming; a management method used to generate ideas to consider. The goal of brainstorming is to identify all the subjects to contemplate when designing a policy. Policies often include multiple, related parts to ensure that the policy, once written, covers all the important **policy-related issues**.

Brainstorming is typically a two-step process. Generate ideas first and then evaluate the ideas. Evaluating the ideas after generating ideas comes second to avoid limiting the generation of ideas as a result of criticism, which stifles idea-generating.

After identifying the subjects to include in a policy, the team needs to identify **performance objectives** to guide the policy design process as well as **performance objectives** a policy needs to achieve after implementing the policy. Using the budget review process as an example, performance objectives can include identifying personnel to include during the process, expected duration to complete the process, the form of approval of the final budget. Performance objectives a policy needs to achieve during implementation can include meeting review deadlines, limiting the number of revised budgets within the allocated timeframe and completing the entire budget review process within a specified time frame. These are examples of policy performance objectives that proper policy implementation can accomplish.

After identifying performance objectives, the team begins the next stage of the policy design process, designing the **policy content** using the subjects identified during the brainstorming session as the basis for creating the specifics. Often, policy designers include an opening **statement** that sets the tone of a policy, reflecting the intent of the decision-makers. After writing the initial statement of purpose the team writes the specifics for each section of the policy. After writing each section of the policy, the team works on the **policy implementation process**. Decision-makers need guidance in knowing how to implement the policy and to ensure that during the policy implementation process, implementors follow the policy directives correctly, adhering to the policy guidelines. After finalizing the draft of the policy, in consultation with relevant decision-makers, the policy is **reviewed, revised, approved** and an **effective date** for implementing the policy identified.

LEARNING OBJECTIVE #5: IDENTIFY, DESCRIBE AND EXPLAIN THE POLICY IMPLEMENTATION PROCESS

The **policy implementation process** varies according to the level of an organization that a policy applies to. As a reminder, there are three levels of policy. A policy can apply to everyone in an organization; a policy can apply to everyone within a unit of an organization; and a policy can apply to a select group of individuals within an organization.

There is no one standardized policy implementation process. The policy implementation process can and often does vary from organization to organization and within an organization. However, there are several common features associated with all policy implementation processes. The importance of a policy to organization decision-makers often dictates whether additional, supplemental steps to the policy implementation process are necessary.

For an **organization-wide critical policy** the CEO delivers a live speech or provides a video presentation discussing the strategic importance of the new policy. The oral presentation is commonly followed by an email with an attachment letter along with a separate attachment that presents the policy. The letter covers the reasons for the policy, the goals the policy is expected to achieve; how the organization will benefit from the policy and if externally driven, the legal reasons that led to the development of the policy. Training often coincides with a critical policy to ensure employees know the policy and indicate this by signing an attendance form that is placed in each employees personnel file. A **non-critical policy** is often presented through a video presentation by the CEO or a representative, followed by an email with a letter outlining the reasons for the policy; the goals the policy is expected to accomplish; and how the policy benefits the organization. The policy is included with the email as an attachment.

A **department-wide critical policy** is often presented by a live speech by the department head or through a video presentation. An email is sent with two attachments. One attachment is a letter co-signed by the CEO and department head. The letter covers the reasons for the policy, the goals associated with the policy and how the policy benefits the department and the organization. Training is typically part of the policy implementation process for a critical department-wide policy. For a **department-wide, non-critical policy** implementation process, a letter from the department head stating the reasons for the policy, the goals of the policy and how the department benefits from the policy is attached to an email. The actual policy is another attachment sent with the same email.

A **policy targeting individuals** is a **targeted policy** that applies to individuals sharing something in common. For example, an organization with accountants and accounting assistants might have a critical policy for these individuals. A common practice in implementing this type of policy is to provide a video presentation from a senior manager, such as the CFO in this example, discussing the new policy, the reasons for the policy, the goals of the policy and any other relevant information. A follow-up email accompanied by an attached letter summarizing the substance of the video along with another attachment presenting the actual policy is sent to coincide with the video presentation. Training is common because most often, this type of policy deals with a technical issue that requires assurance that the targeted individuals understand the policy and know how to implement the policy correctly. For a non-critical policy, a letter and the policy statement that are attached to an email sent to individuals are often sufficient.

Fahey Enterprises: Part 3

Three weeks later, James, Jack and Paul met for breakfast to discuss what Paul agreed to do since their last meeting. Paul had three loose-leaf binders with him. Each binder was sub-divided by labels, with each label identified a policy category. James and Jack spent 20 minutes quickly reviewing what Paul prepared. James and Jack peppered Paul with questions. Most of the questions were about wording and how to get everyone to follow the policies. Paul stated that the next step is an important step. "Guys, the next step involves implementing the policies." James and Jack looked perplexed and then Jack said, "What does that involve Paul?" "Okay," said Paul. "Let me describe what I think is an effective way to apply the policies." After describing the policy implementation process and what James and Jack need to do, Paul said that "we need to talk about creating short and to the point training programs that cover each of the policies in the binder."

Questions

1. Explain why Paul chose to create categories of policies.
2. Paul mentioned an effective way to apply policies. What did he say to James and Jack?
3. Paul suggested that the next step was to create brief training programs. Why? Why brief?
4. Should a training program cover one policy or several policies? Explain.
5. What type of policies needs to be prioritized for initial training (identify five)? Why these?

LEARNING OBJECTIVE #6: IDENTIFY AND DESCRIBE METHODS FOR IDENTIFYING EFFECTIVE ORGANIZATIONAL POLICIES

Policy is meant to have an impact through the creation of work processes that lead to the type of changes in performance that achieve the goals of the policy. The target of a policy's impact is either the entire organization, a unit(s) of an organization (e.g. human resources) or a select group of individuals in an organization (e.g. computer programmers, business analysts, hiring specialists and security guards). The intent of policy impact is to change performance in measurable ways.

The **impact** of a policy follows a three-step process. Policy is meant to change **attitudes** toward a subject. Changing employee attitudes is the *significant* first step because a change in attitude results in a change in employee **behavior**. The intent of a policy is to change the status quo in a particular way. Doing something different from the present "norm" aims to create a new "norm," and a new norm represents different actions in the form of changes in employee behavior. Changing employee behavior should lead to **measurable performance results**. The use of SMART goals provides the organization with performance indicators to use to assess if the change in attitude has sufficiently impacted behavior that results in achieving the policy's goal(s) or at least movement toward achieving the policy's goal(s).

There are a wide range of performance indicators that can reflect the results that indicate an effective policy. Examples of performance indicators include the following.

- Profit margins are increasing at the rate expected.
- Revenues are increasing at the rate expected.
- Costs are decreasing at an increasing rate that achieved the goal.
- Production within the time allocated, such as in producing a product upgrade or to complete a work process within the time allocated (e.g. call center operation is monitoring a client's caller time per call).
- The number of lawsuits initiated by external parties (e.g. customers, suppliers and government agencies) declined from previous levels, achieving the goal.
- The number of lawsuits initiated by employees declined, achieving the goal.
- Public perceptions of the organization improved from prior perceptions according to survey results.

- The number of incident (e.g. injuries and reported incidents of inaccurate billing) declined from the prior year, achieving the goal.
- Attitudes changed for the better according to survey results.
- Perceptions changed for the better according to survey results.

What is important when designing a policy is to frame the policy to enable decision-makers to measure impact. This enables the organization to assess the effectiveness of a policy.

LEARNING OBJECTIVE #7: IDENTIFY AND EXPLAIN THE LIMITATIONS OF ORGANIZATIONAL POLICY

There are common problems associated with any organization's policies. These problems fall within three broad categories.

- The failure to create a policy management program.
- Issues with the policy design process.
- Policy implementation issues.

The failure to create a policy that establishes a **policy management program** is a serious omission that results in the following consequences.

- Policies often become outdated, failing to remain current with prevailing circumstances.
- There is no formal policy review process or there is a haphazard policy review process that does not include a time frame to review a policy, the required participants in the review process or criteria to use in evaluating a policy.
- There are no pre-established criteria for aiding decision-makers in identifying design flaws in a policy.
- Policies lack a central location, such as a policy and procedures manual in an organization's website. There is no one location for offering employees the opportunity to review all organizational policies.

Sometimes, decision-makers act in **haste in designing a policy**. The consequences of a hasty process follow.

- Policy standards are very rigid, reducing the ability of decision-makers to respond to situations that require a flexible response.
- There are times when policies limit the extent to which a decision-maker can act to promote greater organizational efficiencies.
- There are times when policy designers succumb to organizational politics. The result is a policy that is not in the best long-term interest of the organization.
- In their haste to respond to new business situations, policy designers design a policy that is a "reactive policy" and not a policy that improves the organization's ability to respond to competitive conditions.
- The tendency of policy designers to design a reactive policy reflects a hasty decision that often fails to consider and include a strategic or big-picture perspective to the policy.

Finally, there are **policy implementation issues** that can undercut the value of an organization's policies.

- An organization can have a policy that is not implemented seriously. For example, there is the glass ceiling effect. A company can have a non-discrimination policy related to the promotion of minorities and women into management positions, but there are no minorities or female managers in management positions or are underrepresented.
- Policies imposed by senior management or from external sources (e.g. government agencies) often lead to resistance by those most impacted if the policy is considered unfair and not relevant.
- An unprepared workforce is likely to resist a policy that pushes employees outside of their comfort zone too soon as a consequence of a hasty policy implementation process.
- Sometimes the design of a policy does not reflect actual business conditions; implementors hesitate to implement the policy either fully or even partially.
- Implementation of an official organizational policy can clash with an "unofficial policy," resulting in conflict because the policies were never reconciled during the policy design process.

LEARNING OBJECTIVE #8: EXPLAIN THE RELATIONSHIP BETWEEN AN ORGANIZATION'S POLICIES AND ORGANIZATIONAL CULTURE

Every action an organization undertakes symbolizes one or more **values** that the organization seeks to promote. The collection of values and the types of values represent an organization's **culture**. If a start-up, the founder(s) of the organization provide the initial impetus in creating the organization's culture. The founder(s) impose their personal values on the organization through their actions. Over time, the founder(s) values become embedded through the process of formalizing organizational actions. Policies represent one of the principle formalization methods organizations use to develop and solidify the organization's culture.

Policies can and often do reflect the promotion of new values and reinforce existing values. For example, controlling costs is a business value. Creating a cost control management system that incorporates relevant policies that proscribe work processes reflect the importance of this value. Introducing more cost control policies, such as creating the use of cost-related performance indicators and making existing cost control policies more detailed, are examples of endorsing a value and providing additions support to an existing value.

Values are critical to the functioning of any organization. Policies represent one of the principle management methods use to promote values. Policies are important because policies are meant to influence attitudes and behavior. Policies shape behavior by establishing performance guidelines that convey the organization's efforts at distinguishing between acceptable and non-acceptable behavior. For example, an anti-sexual harassment policy brings to everyone's attention to not act in certain ways with co-workers or customers. A definition that defines sexual harassment creates standards that define what is not an acceptable behavior toward others.

Policies typically do not state specific values. Values are implicit within a policy. If safety of workers is important, the organization promulgates policies that emphasize employee safety. If customer service is a critical value, the organization creates policies for individuals that work directly with customers that emphasize preferred types of customer service.

A value's importance gets emphasized by the level of detail in the policy. When new leaders assume control, often, the new leaders, if current employees, promote important, established values. If leaders are recruited from outside of the organization, the Board of Directors is intent on crafting and implementing new values in the organization's culture. New leaders frequently will initiate changes to existing policies as well as new policies to reflect the values that new leaders deem important in achieving their agenda.

Because the goal of policies is to alter behavior, policies serve as behavioral guidelines that provide the impacted workers behavior standards to adhere to. Because these types of policies are intended to promote certain types of behaviors, the policies need to be clear about the organization's expectations about acceptable employee behavior.

Some organization policies reflect important societal values reflected in government laws and regulations. Organizations need to embrace these values and meet the legal requirements imposed by the government. However, if a value is imposed on an organization from external sources is important to the organization, the organization will develop a policy(ies) that extends well past the minimum requirements of a law or regulation(s).

LEARNING OBJECTIVE #9: DESCRIBE THE DESIGN AND IMPLEMENTATION OF TRAINING PROGRAMS COVERING ORGANIZATIONAL POLICIES

Organizations offer formal training programs that cover an organizational policy when the policy is considered a major policy, warranting direct training in lieu of communicating the policy through email or video. A major policy is a policy viewed as integral to the successful policy implementation process. Training programs are expensive to design and conduct. To maximize the benefits of training, the design of a training program needs to be thorough, encompassing all the important training program issues (e.g. learning objectives, subjects to cover, instructional methods and assessment methods).

To start, we need to understand trainees because an organization's trainees are adults, and the training program designers need to understand that adult learners learn differently from non-adult learners. The theory of andragogy provides insights about working with the adult learner and their preferences for how to learn. Briefly, adult learners prefer using personal experiences and to learn from the personal experiences of others. Dealing with specific types of problems or situations that are relevant to the adult learners' current job represents motivating factors that encourage and promote adult learning. Also, the organization needs to demonstrate to the adult learner that the training program will benefit their career aspirations.

While training about policy has a policy focus, the policy focus is either providing trainees with additional **knowledge** (e.g. new anti-discrimination policy) or **skill-based** training (e.g. policy on writing formal memorandums). Knowledge-based or skill-based training can focus on how well a trainee knows a subject or how to perform something or how to perform something proficiently. Each represents a performance standard. Using the word "correctly" implies the use of performance standards during training because the policy incorporates a performance standard. For example, trainees could follow a policy on the correct procedures to follow in using a mechanical wood chopper for a landscaping business.

A formal training program design encompasses four major themes along with two complementary issues. Every training program includes **learning objectives** that provide focus to the training. Trainees need to achieve the learning objectives to ensure a successful training program. Any policy-oriented training program needs to cover the following issues in the learning objectives.

- Trainees need to learn and understand the purpose of a policy.
- Trainees need to learn and understand the goals of the policy.
- Trainees need to know and understand the circumstances that warranted the need for a new policy or change to an existing policy.
- Trainees need to know and understand the expected behavior after implementing the policy.
- Trainees need to know and understand the expected performance standard, if any, associated with the policy.
- If a policy is externally driven, trainees need to know the laws or regulations linked to the policy along with the reason(s) for the laws or regulations.

Instructional methods represent one of the major themes associated with designing training programs. Instructional methods serve two purposes. First, instructional methods facilitate trainee learning. The adult learner prefers the use of certain types of instructional methods during the training process. Second, motivating types of instructional methods are preferable to ensure the motivation of the adult trainees. Andragogy is a useful guide in the selection of instructional methods to incorporate in a training program because andragogy focuses on how best to educate the adult learner. Examples of instructional methods for the adult learner follow.

- The use of relevant case studies provides actual scenarios to learn from.
- The use of brief vignettes enables trainees to cover more and different types of situations to facilitate learning.
- The use of groups or teams is optimal as adult learners prefer learning from and with other adults.
- Exercises involving hands-on types of learning exercises. Hands-on learning paired with another trainee keeps trainees motivated to learn.
- Instructional methods that draw on a trainee's personal experiences along with learning from the experiences of other trainees serve to motivate the trainee to learn.

Formal and/or informal **assessment methods** enable the trainer to learn if trainees achieved the learning objectives. Trainees need to demonstrate achieving the learning objectives because decision-makers and trainers need to know if the training program achieved the training goals associated with the learning objectives. There are a variety of assessment methods to consider. Examples include the following.

- Multiple choice tests.
- Hands-on or performance types of tests.

- Applied exercises with performance targets to achieve.
- Team or group presentations.
- Answering open-ended questions.

Designing training programs always involves the need to consider trade-offs. The most significant trade-off involves the range of **subjects** to cover and the **time** allocated for training. Frequently, training program designers never have enough time allocated by decision-makers. The time limitations force the training program designer to identify the most important subjects to cover and the amount of time to cover a subject. Using handouts helps as a supplement, filling the gap in covering non-essential but necessary subjects for the trainees to learn.

Lesser issues that a training program designer needs to consider is the **time** to allocate for each subject area; the **sequencing of subjects** if subjects serve as building blocks to learn other subjects; and **topics** to cover within each subject area.

Fahey Enterprises: Part 4

The following week, James, Jack and Paul met again. Jack was eager to begin putting the policies into effect. James was somewhat non-committal as James was still trying to understand what is going to happen and the impact on him. Paul explained to James and Jack that putting policies into effect puts more discipline into the organization. "Everyone is going to be affected once you begin to apply the policies. Everyone needs to follow the policies, especially the two of you" said Paul. James asked about problems with applying policies. Paul told James that problems are inevitable because the policies are ideas and not operational yet. Paul explained that one way to reduce the likelihood of problems is to train everyone on existing policies.

> You guys need to decide which policies to implement first and then create training programs on these policies. Training reduces the risk of problems occurring. We need to create a training schedule to train the employees and both of you.

James and Jack asked, "Who creates the training programs?" Everyone laughed at the question. "Why, I will create the training programs and conduct the actual training" said Paul. James and Jack were relieved, but then, they asked about training. James wanted to know how Paul planned to create the training programs.

Questions

1. Why do James and Jack need to follow policies? Explain.
2. What types of problems are likely to occur during the policy implementation process?
3. Why will training reduce the risk of problems? Explain.
4. Is it a good idea for Paul to conduct the training? Explain.
5. How was Paul planning to design the training programs? Is there a model? Explain.

LEARNING OBJECTIVE #10: DESCRIBE THE PURPOSE AND IMPORTANCE OF A POLICY AND PROCEDURES MANUAL

The purpose for keeping policies centrally located in a **policy and procedure manual** is to provide easy access to decision-makers and non-decision-makers. Accessibility is enhanced in today's organizations by digitalizing the manual. With quick access to the manual, decision-makers can quickly reference the manual to facilitate rapid decision-making. Easy access encourages decision-makers to avoid making random, hasty decisions that might vary from the organization's official policies. The manual includes essential policy-guided work processes to assist decision-makers in following the official work process when implementing a policy. Adhering to official work processes protects the organization and employees from detrimental decisions that can have serious ramifications.

A policy and procedures manual is a useful instructional tool to use during training if organized and presented in a way that makes training easier for the trainers and learning easier for the trainees. The manual should cover official, major work processes that are part of the policy(ies) associated with these work processes. A well-written policy enables trainees to understand the logic associated with the policy, along with the work processes that reflect a logical and systematic method to follow when implementing the policy.

Though there are several models to follow in creating a policy and procedures manual, there are universal criteria to consider following during the creation of a manual that can enhance the effectiveness of the policy and procedures manual.

- The manual should include the goals the organization expects to achieve in having an official and formal policy and procedures manual.
- Including the organization's official code of conduct in the beginning section of the manual provides the reader with the opportunity to reflect on the values that serve as the foundation for all the policies and work processes (A.K.A. work procedures) described in the manual.
- An effective manual is organized by categories that reflect the type of policies reported. This approach provides the reader with a systematic and logical method for accessing a category of policies and then a specific policy(ies) within a category. Examples of categories include:
  - Customer Service Policies
  - Employment Policies
  - Budgeting Policies
  - Credit Policies
  - Workplace Safety Policies
- An effective manual is most effective if written in clear, concise terms; there is a minimum of technical jargon, but when jargon becomes necessary, definitions are provided.
- The format of the manual is standardized throughout, offering the reader a clear, consistent and easy-to-follow presentation of the policies and work processes.
- The manual needs to be organized and written with consideration of the reader, treating the reader as a "customer" to serve correctly.

- Contact information enables the reader to reach out to relevant individuals with questions to ask.
- A policy within the policy and procedures manual needs to cover the policy and procedures policy review process. This helps the reader learn that the organization is pro-active in ensuring that the policy and work processes remain relevant.

LEARNING OBJECTIVE #11: IDENTIFY AND DESCRIBE COMMON TYPES OF CATEGORIES OF ORGANIZATIONAL POLICIES

As organizations expand through the addition of more products and/or services, there is a concomitant increase in the number of employees along with the diversity of the workforce. The growth in the number and type of employees results in an increasing complex work environment to manage. Because of this complexity, the number of policies increases along with the evolution of existing policies; changing from less to more complex policies as the need for more and more detailed work processes increases to support the management of a growing organization.

Because organizing increases in complexity in parallel with the growth, organizations often respond by systematizing operations to facilitate greater operational efficiencies. One operational area requiring a more systematic approach is decision-making. Decision-makers throughout the organization confront a myriad of situations associated with growth that require decisions. Many of these situations frequently repeat. Consequently, organizations regulate decision-making when re-occurring situations occur to make decision-making easier to conduct, quicken response time and provide a standardized uniform response. Under the circumstances with repeating situations, organizations regulate decision-making by developing policies and applying these policies.

Policies proliferate quickly in support of a strategy implementation process associated with an expanding organization. To ensure rapid and sustained growth through responsive decision-making, adding policies and organizing policies represent one approach in support of decision-making. The most common approach used to organize policies is to use the **category model**. Categories provide a framework that allows for easy inclusion of new policies and the modification of existing policies. Categorization makes for easier access to policies for decision-makers because a simple system is necessary to make decision-making responsive to the circumstances; such circumstances often require a quick response.

Examples of categories of policies include the following.

- Customer Service Policies
- Employment Policies
- Safety Policies
- Communication and Security Policies
- Financial Management Policies

Below is a detailed categorization model to illustrate a complex, systematic approach that enables the policy management process to function at a high level. The model shows the level of detail associated with the application of the categorization model.

1. Employment Policies
   1.1 Hiring Policies
       1.1.1 Recruitment Policies
       1.1.1 A Policy on Using Outside Vendors
       1.1.1 A.1 Contract Policy
   1.2 Benefits Policies
       1.2.1 Compensation Policies
       1.2.1 A Overtime Guidelines Policies
       1.2.1 A.1 Maximum Overtime Hours Policy

As the reader notes, the categorization model provides a formal, structured framework to incorporate more and more detailed policies. Organizing policies through the use of a systematic process make decision-makers more accountable for their decisions.

Chapter Summary

Policy represents one of the most important management methods used to guide employee behavior in ways that represent an organization's official position on how to act correctly. This chapter examines and explains why organizations develop policies and the role policy plays in an organization. Policy represents a management method for creating work processes that represent the means organizations used to implement and standardize all operational activities targeted by a policy. Policies play an important role in the strategy implementation process. The strategy implementation process represents the operational focus to an organization's efforts at achieving the strategic goals that the strategy was designed to accomplish.

Because policy is an important management method, the chapter examines all aspects of an organization's policies. This includes the identification of the elements that form a policy, the criteria that define a good policy and the process for creating a policy. By standardizing the policy design process and including the elements that an effective policy needs to consist of, organizations are better able to create policies that achieve a policy(ies) objective(s).

Designing a policy represents only one important step. Implementing a policy involves a process that can enable the organization to make a good policy effective. Though there is not a one right way to implement a policy, the policy implementation process needs to follow a consistent approach to ensure a successful adaptation of the policy by the organization.

Knowing how to recognize an effective policy is essential because a failed policy can hinder an organization's progress in achieving the policy's objective(s). Methods for identifying an effective policy help in limiting the ongoing use of an ineffective policy and lead to corrective measures that hasten an organization's responsiveness. Success is not always about pursuing the right course of action immediately; success is being able to recognize policy-related problems and taking policy-relevant corrective actions immediately.

Even a good policy has limits if there are more strategic types of organizational problems. Knowing how to recognize the limitations of a policy enable the organization to apply additional management methods to complement the policy's shortcomings.

This chapter examines the role of an organization's culture and the important positive role of policy plays in an organization's culture. Each organization has their own unique culture. Values symbolize the critical element that collectively represents an organization's culture. Values underly all actions of an organization. Values provide the justification for the initiatives of an organization. Culture is essential in the choice of policies to enact; the form of a policy and the objective(s) of a policy symbolize. Each policy represents one or more organizational values.

This chapter describes the design of training programs intended to teach a policy to members of the workforce. Organizations create training programs to educate the workforce on major new policy initiatives or a re-designed policy, so the policy implementors have a clear understanding of the policy and the expectations of decision-makers on the policy's intended impact.

Finally, the chapter examines policy management and how policy management becomes more challenging to orchestrate as an organization grows because along with this growth is the proliferation of organizational policies. The expansion in the number of policies includes the greater diversity of policies. To maintain the organization's commitment to continue a systematic approach to managing the operations, policy management needs to reflect this focus through systems management. Developing a policy manual with detailed categories of policies reflects the organization's systematic approach to support growth by centralizing policies using a policy and procedures manual. A policy and procedures manual provides decision-makers and non-decision-makers with an easily accessible central location for all organizational policies.

Questions

1. What is the purpose and function of a policy?
2. What are the criteria used to identify a good policy?
3. Describe the policy design process.
4. Identify and briefly describe the steps in the policy implementation process.
5. Identify and briefly describe the methods used to identify an effective organizational policy.
6. What are the limitations of organizational policy?
7. How are organizational policies and organizational culture linked?
8. Identify and briefly describe the important features of a training program used in training employees on an organizational policy.
9. What are the reasons for having a policy and procedures manual?
10. Briefly explain the importance of categorizing an organization's policies.

Bibliography

Anderson, T.J. & Hallin, C.A. (2017). The adaptive organization and fast-slow systems. *Oxford Research Encyclopedia of Business and Management.* Oxford University Press. 1–24.

Bianca, A. (2018). The importance of organizational policies. https://yourbusiness. azcentral.com/importance-organizational-policieis-9849.html? (April 13).

Bizmanualz.om. What business policies does every company need? https://www.bizmanualz.com/imporove-commpany-governance/what-business-policies-does-every-company=need/.

DiffereneBetween.net. (2018). Differences between policy and strategy. http://www. differencebetween.net/business/-differences-between-policy-and-strategy/ (June 8).

Gasior, M. (2017). How to write policies and procedures. https://www.powerdms. com/blog/how-to-wrie-policies-and-procedures.

Gray, E.R. (2019). Policies and policy making. https://www.referenceforbusiness.com/ encyclopedia/per-pro/policies-and-policy-making/.

Hoskisson, R.E., Hitt, M.A., Wan, W.P. & Yiu, D. (1999). Theory and research in strategic management: swings of a pendulum. *Journal of Management.* 25(3). 417–456.

Kerschberg, B. How to develop and implement a new company policy. *Society for Human Resource Management.* https://www.shrm.org/resourcesandtools/-tools-and-samples/how-to-guides/pages/howtodevelopandimplementanewcompanypolicy/.

Kokemuller, N. (2018). What is the purpose of a workplace policy? https://smallbusiness.chron.com/purpose-workplace-policy-416001.html/ (October 22).

Kothari, A. Policy management: what is it and why is it important? https://tallyfy.com/policy-management/what/is/it/and/why/is/it/important/.

Leonard, K. (2018). Importance of business policy. Smallbusiness.chron.com. https://smallbusiness.chron.com/-importance-business-policy-10199.html/ (August 20).

Lotich, P. (2016). 7 reasons to write business policies and procedures. https://thethrivingsmallbusiness.com/7-advantages-to-writing-business-policies-and-procedures/ (January 20).

National & Community Service. (2018). *Workbook: Establishing Effective Policies, Procedures, and Management Controls.* AmeriCorps. 1–27.

Neideck, S. (2016). 5 key reasons why it's important to have policies and procedures. https://Community.hrdaily.com.au/profiles/blogs/5-key-reasons-why-it-s-important-to-have-policies-and-procedures/ (July 19).

Ontario Human Rights Commission. Developing organizational policies, programs and procedures. https://www.ohrc.on.ca/en/book/export/html/11144/.

Organizational Policy Examples.PDF. https://www.examples.com/business/policy/-organizational-policy-examples.html/.

Pacific Crest Group. Are your policies and procedures a barrier to growing your company? https://www.pcg-services.com/are-your-policies-and-procedures-a-barrier-to-growing-your-company/.

Policies and Procedures Team. (1994). Guide to writing policy and procedure documents. Office of Planning and Budget. (Internal Working Draft). 1–14. (December 2).

Ross, S. (2019). *Training and Development in Organizations: An Essential Guide for Trainers.* Routledge.

Turnpenny, J.R., Jordan, A.J., Benson, D. & Rayner, T. (2015). The tools of policy formulation: an introduction. https://www.econstor.eu/bitstream/10419/182379/1/-978-1-78347-704-3.pdf/. 3–29.

Universalclass.com. Tips for creating effective policies and procedures. https://www.universalclass.com/articles/business/-tips-to-creating-effective-policy-and-procedures/.

Universalclass.com. Why your organization needs a well-written policy and procedure manual – and how to create one. https://www.universalclass.com/articles/business/writing-effective-policy-and-procedure-manual/.

CHAPTER **6**

Organizational Design

OVERVIEW

This chapter examines the important role of organizational structure in the strategy implementation process. As such, strategy implementation encompasses every issue associated with organizational behavior. An organization's structure is an important management method used to organize the organization's functional activities. Frequently, an alternative view of the structure of an organization is that it is a management method used to organize the workforce. Both views are accurate but self-limiting in explaining the purpose of an organization's structure. This chapter examines the issue of organizational structure by examining the context; organizational structure (or design) represents a strategic approach, representing the foundation in providing support in the ongoing evolution of the organization. The evolution of the organization's structure responds to changes to an organization's strategy.

An organization's structure is often referred to as a "hierarchy of authority". This is because the organization's structure represents an approach to organize all functional activities and people who perform the various functional activities with management positions that oversee the performance of the functional activities (or tasks). Oversight involves having some amount of decision-making authority. Circumstances determine if most authority within the hierarchy is centralized among the upper management levels of the organization; circumstances can dictate if authority to make decisions needs to be de-centralized by dispersing decision-making authority among lower management levels of the organization; or authority to make decisions can represent a process with decision-making authority between management levels dictated by external business circumstances. The chapter examines the issue of authority by covering the subjects, centralization and de-centralization to explain the importance of the locus of authority in designing an organization's structure.

The size of an organization is an important issue to consider in determining how to design an organization's structure. The chapter examines how decision-makers respond to the subject of size and how size can influence the design of an organization's structure. Included in the discussion about the effort of an organization's size (or the number of employees) and the organization's structure is the impact of an organization's range of products and services along with the diversity of markets and how these issues influence decision-makers thinking when configuring the organization to better implement the organization's strategies. The range of products and services along with the diversity of markets introduces the reader to the subject of complexity and how the subject of complexity influences how decision-makers follow a process to use when designing an organization's structure.

The chapter identifies and describes additional issues that influence organizational design considerations. One issue is external business conditions that decision-makers need to consider in designing the organization's structure. Internal organizational factors represent additional issues decision-makers need to consider when designing the organization's structure. The organization's management systems represent the internal elements that also influence design considerations.

This chapter identifies and describes seven major types of traditional organizational structures. Each type is a basic model from which variations of the structure can evolve. Because changes to an organization's structure are disruptive, a solid foundation is necessary to avoid major changes, with incremental, selective types of changes most common.

An organization's structure represents one type of management system. However, no management system is sufficient. Decision-makers need to make trade-offs during the design of an organization's structure; as such, decision-makers need to include other management systems that interface with and become a component to the organization's structure. This chapter provides the reader with insights on the limitations of an organization's structure to illustrate the approaches decision-makers must consider in confronting the limitations. The chapter identifies and describes the most common management methods decision-makers consider to successfully manage an organization's structural limitations.

Because an organization's structure is intended to drive the performance of the organization to achieve the organization's strategic goals, one of the important design considerations is the organization's performance management system. The chapter examines the role of the performance management system as one of the specific types of management systems that decision-makers need to consider during the design of the organization's structure.

The lifeblood of every organization is the organization's ability to re-invent itself through the development of new products, new services and identify new markets to serve. The chapter examines innovation management, a sub-system of the knowledge management system, because the role of innovation management is to enable the organization to survive in this Darwinian world that every organization confronts. Organizational decision-makers attempt to incorporate innovation management within the design of an organization's structure, sometimes successfully but sometimes with the wrong results.

CHAPTER 6   LEARNING OBJECTIVES

Readers will achieve the following learning objectives after reading this chapter.

1. Explain the purpose and function of organizational design.
2. Identify and describe the factors that influence whether to centralize or de-centralize decision-making authority.
3. Describe how the size of an organization influences the design of an organization's structure.
4. Describe how the range of products and the diversity of markets influence the design of an organization's structure.
5. Describe how external factors influence the design of an organization's structure.
6. Explain how management systems influence the design of an organization's structure.
7. Identify and describe the major types of organizational structures.
8. Identify, describe and explain the consequences of an organization's structural limitations.
9. Identify and describe the management methods used to supplement an organization's structural limitations.
10. Explain the relationship between an organization's structure and performance management.
11. Describe and explain the role of organizational structure in innovation management.

LEARNING OBJECTIVE #1: EXPLAIN THE PURPOSE AND FUNCTION OF ORGANIZATIONAL DESIGN

The purpose of an **organizational design** is to influence the strategy implementation process. Design in this context is a strategic, process-focused approach with the goal of creating a process-oriented organizational structure with the intention of making the best use of organizational resources to achieve the organization's strategic priorities, pursuing growth opportunities that result from following an organizational design process. The organizational design process focuses on achieving two specific goals. Designing an organizational structure enables the organization to be **effective** in achieving the organization's strategic goals. Second, decision-makers focus on the best use of organizational resources by designing an organization's structure that contributes to an **efficient** operation.

Organizational decision-makers (or designers) **formalize** the organization's design process to ensure that the design process focuses on the goals of enabling an organization to be more effective (i.e. by achieving the strategic goals) and efficient (i.e. best use of resources). Formalization entails standardizing the design process to ensure that the process functions systematically. The organization's structure is the product of the design process. The organizational structure represents a formalized approach at differentiating the organization into homogeneous units and at the same time integrating the homogeneous units into one uniform organizational structure.

Formalization represents a management viewpoint, with the intent of promoting the use of standardization to influence individual and group behavior in supporting the organization's efforts at achieving the organization's strategic goals through the best use of resources. Organizations advance standardization using policies that focus on specific narrow themes, which result in the creation of relevant work processes that help to routinize the process for implementing a policy. For example, an organization can create a policy on the hiring process to follow in hiring senior executives. Such a hiring policy can include creating a recruitment process, hiring process and orientation or onboarding process. Within each process, there are sub-processes to further systematize the policy (e.g. create an interview protocol within the hiring process).

In creating homogeneous units, the underlying principle that guides this process is differentiation or the **division of labor**. Division of labor involves sub-dividing a large task into definable parts. The more complex the task, the more definable parts are necessary. Specific jobs have one or more tasks associated with the job. The more complex the job the more tasks and the more tasks the greater the need to sub-divide tasks. The goal in applying the concept of division of labor is to create an efficient operation by avoiding overly complex jobs. At the same time, the decision-makers divide a job into tasks and tasks into sub-tasks, the greater the need to integrate the sub-tasks and integrate the tasks. **Integration** is meant to ensure the optimal performance of a job that involves more than one person. Division of labor extends beyond individual jobs to groups of jobs that share a common theme. This leads to the creation of functional units. For example, cost accountants can be grouped into a unit called cost accounting; advertising specialists can be grouped within the category advertising; and inventory control specialists can be grouped within the inventory control unit.

As an organization increases in **size**, the organization becomes a more complex operation because the workforce becomes more diverse because of the proliferation of products/services and new markets. There are different types of workers because the organization requires individuals with specialized knowledge and/or skills linked to the new products/services and markets. Work specialization typically leads to fragmenting the workforce, resulting in potential efficiency problems, increasing the challenge of the organization's efforts to achieve the strategic goals. Decision-makers focus on organizing the workforce into homogeneous groups to provide group members with a common focus, but the decision-makers also need to consider integration methods to ensure that the fragmented, specialized units work together and work with large groups.

The information management system, performance management system and decision-making management system represent three primary means decision-makers use to integrate specialists within units, between units and among the hierarchy of units. The **information management system** represents a standardized approach to sharing required information following some pre-determined routines. Decision-makers define the type of information to share, the form information sharing needs to take and the schedule in sharing the information (i.e. reporting process). Work processes serve to link sub-tasks within a task, link tasks within a larger work process and link work processes within a network of work processes. For example, preparing questions to ask is a sub-task within the task of interviewing which is a stage in the hiring process (an example of a work process) within a network of work processes. In sum, all work processes connect with other work processes in a large network of work processes.

Decision-making represents another integrating management system that functions among sub-units within a unit and between levels of units. Decision-makers recognize the need to ensure that control over all resources is maintained to ensure the best use of resources in the pursuit of achieving the strategic goals. Decision-makers confer decision-making responsibilities and authority to positions when creating job descriptions. Jobs are grouped into units with one position's job description including decision-making authority over a group of jobs within a sub-unit. Moving up through the hierarchy, there is always one individual assigned decision-making authority over the unit within the individual's job responsibilities. The design process allocating decision-making authority continues up through the hierarchy to include the highest level of the organization. Decision-makers, through their efforts, make certain there is always a position with decision-making authority over all organizational resources. The **performance management system** focuses on ensuring that individuals and units remain accountable for their actions. A well-designed performance management system creates the work processes that ensure that units and individuals are working toward achieving the operational objectives. Achieving operational objectives contributes to achieving the strategic goals.

McCarthy Engineers: Part 1

John and Karen McCarthy were discussing certain organizational problems with Stan Black, a management consultant with Bridgewater Associates. John and Karen described how they assumed control of the business from their father five years earlier. John always worked for his dad even during engineering school. Karen worked as an engineer at another company until her dad asked her to join John. John and Karen saw lots of growth potential and began expanding the business, adding more services after hiring additional specialists with certain types of expertise. Adding new clients was easy because of the firm's reputation. Within the past year, customer complaints as well as complaints from many employees indicated they had a problem of an undetermined nature. The complaints, as best as they could determine involved customers complaining about delays in starting work, delays in completing projects on time, slow responses to calls and emails. Employee complaints involved no clear project responsibility, overlapping responsibilities and slow responses in answering customer queries. After further discussion and in response to Stan's questions, Stan provided John and Karen with a brief overview of his impressions about the situation. Stan discussed the issues of designing an organizational structure to increase operational effectiveness; the importance of locating decision-making authority with the right people and the importance of coordinating the efforts of different specialists.

Questions

1. Why did Stan think the organization's structure is important?
2. How is an organization's structure linked with operational effectiveness?
3. How is decision-making authority relevant?
4. What did Stan mean by "the right people?"
5. Why is coordinating a relevant issue for John and Karen?

LEARNING OBJECTIVE #2: IDENTIFY AND DESCRIBE THE FACTORS THAT INFLUENCE WHETHER TO CENTRALIZE OR DECENTRALIZE DECISION-MAKING AUTHORITY

An organization's structure reflects the different **levels of decision-making authority** created to enable the organization to respond to external environmental factors and to manage internal environmental factors (i.e. occurring within the organization) that can impede an organization's efforts at achieving the strategic goals. Authority refers to the process of delegating the authority to make certain types of decisions within a position. This includes all management positions as well as select specialist's jobs. The organization's structure represents a hierarchy or levels of decision-makers with decision-making authority. At each level of the hierarchy, the organization confers more decision-making authority on a management position(s) along with more responsibilities.

    Centralization refers to the consolidation of the largest part of decision-making authority among the senior management levels of the organization. **Decentralization** refers to the extent to which the organization disburses certain types of decision-making authority among non-senior management positions. The natural inclination of senior leaders is to retain complete decision-making authority among senior managers because with decision-making authority comes the ability to influence the behavior and actions of the workforce. Figure 6.1 shows a U-shaped curve reflecting the relationship between the organization's size and the extent to which decision-making authority is dispersed.

    The smaller the organization, the fewer the employees and the easier for ownership/senior management to centralize decision-making authority among themselves. Greater reliance on formal policies and work processes aids in controlling the workforce's behavior under these circumstances. But what forces an organization's leadership to begin to disburse decision-making authority among non-senior managers is largely due to the growth in the size of the organization and the interactions with the organization's external environment. When senior leaders confront an increasingly dynamic external world, senior management is less able to respond quickly enough to the organization's benefit. Learning about the circumstances and responding takes senior leaders too long to make decisions in responding. The external world creates uncertainty which is associated with risk, and senior leaders counter the **uncertainty-risk paradox** by attempting to impose certainty by centralizing decision-making authority and increasing the

FIGURE 6.1   U-Shape Curve and the Relationship Between an Organization's Size and the Effect of Size on the Dispersion of Decision-Making Authority

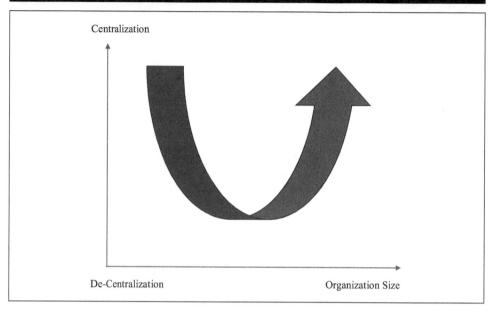

formalization of work processes (through adding policies and making policies more concise). However, as the organization formulates ambitious strategic goals, success at achieving goals causes the organization's size to increase because the workforce increases to manage the additional products, services and markets along with more support staff to help line staff deal with such issues as retirement planning, selecting and managing healthcare benefits and improving safety practices. The growth of the workforce aids the organization's efforts to manage the growth and to continue to succeed in achieving the strategic goals. However, success in achieving the strategic goals confronts the organization with a conundrum. The desire to hold onto decision-making authority among senior management confronts the pressure to disperse decision-making authority among lower levels of non-senior managers and specialists as the organization expands, adding more managers, specialists and non-manager types of employees. The expansion forces the decision-makers to organize the workforce into more and more groupings referred to as units (e.g. accounting and human resources (HR)) and sub-units (e.g. accounts payable, accounts receivables and job analysts).

Adding more specialized positions and non-specialized positions and organizing these positions into more units and levels of units within a unit results in an internal dynamic that leads to a more uncertain, less practical environment because there are more people to manage. This dynamic internal environment is matched by an increasingly complex external environment that becomes more dynamic with changing economic conditions, socio-cultural complexity (with more markets to deal with) and the evolution of process and product technologies becoming more varied, matching the increased diversity of the organization. The demands on organizational leaders increase because of the increased uncertainty in knowing how to respond to competitive conditions. For example, fluctuating economic conditions impacts organizations reliant on more diverse products and services. Socio-cultural factors can refer to changing demographics, changes in societal values and changes in tastes that can impact the organization in different ways. Finally, changes in process and product technologies can represent opportunities if pursued but threats if competitors take advantage of the technological opportunities. The result is that decision-makers confront greater uncertainty over how to guide the organization forward. This uncertainty exceeds senior management's ability to respond quickly because the process of gathering all the facts slows the decision-making process.

As a starting point, small organizations respond to uncertainty by isolating decision-making authority among senior management. As stated earlier, as an organization grows, uncertainty can increase because of the greater complexity of the operations due to the growth. The organization's initial response is to begin disbursing decision-making authority and responsibilities among lower management levels. At a certain undefinable point, the organization responds to the management challenge by shifting more decision-making authority away from lower management levels to senior managers of the organization, but to retain the ability to act quickly, the organization often pursues several actions. First, the ranks of middle managers are reduced, so more senior managers are in closer contact with the lower management levels and non-managers. Second, senior management uses more objective-based performance indicators to assess performance of lower organizational levels. Performance indicators represent operational objectives to achieve. This keeps the workforce focused because the performance management system and information management system are modified to ensure routine monitoring and reporting of performance even at the lowest unit level. Third, senior management re-aligns the reward system with the performance management system to strengthen the commitment to achieving the operational objectives associated with the performance objectives. Finally, senior management begins to change the job descriptions of the workforce to focus greater efforts at recruiting personnel motivated primarily through intrinsic forms of motivation. These individuals are self-driven and require less direct supervision.

LEARNING OBJECTIVE #3: DESCRIBE HOW THE SIZE OF AN ORGANIZATION INFLUENCES THE DESIGN OF AN ORGANIZATION'S STRUCTURE

The study of bees serves as a microcosm in understanding the adaptive behavior of people in achieving a goal. Bees are hardwired to behave in predictable ways but are also adaptable if environmental circumstances change, such as an opening to the nest gets blocked, bees find or create a new opening. Bees hardwiring imposes structure on themselves, and this structure creates **order**, enabling the bees to achieve the goal of sustaining the life of the bee's nest. We can think of a bee's nest as equivalent to an organization with an imposed structure that creates order.

The creation of an organization is done to achieve a goal(s) just like the bees. As a small organization with a small workforce, the organization relies more on informal management methods to create order. Order symbolizes a process for creating a stable, predictable operation, enabling people to work together to achieve the organization's goals. Creating order represents a process for increasing the effectiveness of the organization.

As the organization achieves the goals, senior leadership selects more ambitious goals. Ambitious goals lead to an organization increasing in size by adding more people to assist in achieving new goals. Organizations increase the workforce for two reasons. The workload to perform the tasks associated with the need to achieve the new goals exceeds the capabilities of the existing workforce, despite efforts to improve worker productivity. For example, one bookkeeper no longer has the capacity to manage all the transactions because of the organization adding more customers. The organization hires additional bookkeepers. The organization also hires individuals with specialized skills and/or knowledge because the existing workers do not possess enough expertise demanded by the need to achieve the new goals and the operational objectives associated with the goals.

With the expansion of the workforce, decision-makers need to impose greater structure on the workforce to continue to provide stability and predictability to the operations (equivalent to order). Direct management methods of control over the workforce begin to lessen in importance, replaced by indirect management control methods. Creating an organizational structure enables managers to influence the decision-making process and information sharing process in predictable ways. Structure represents the attempt at creating a process for influencing workforce behavior in **predictable ways**.

Organizational decision-makers leverage two additional management methods to influence workforce behavior. Creating **vertical levels** represents a method for guiding the decision-making process by creating levels of decision-makers who oversee organizational units. Each unit includes workers that share one function in common. For example, the accounting functional unit can have sub-units labeled accounts payable and accounts receivables. These sub-units represent two examples with common themes. The creation of units and sub-units is based on the concept of **job specialization**. Managers are assigned to oversee each unit and each sub-unit within a large unit. How many units a manager oversees and how many people a manager supervises depend on the complexity of the work involved within the unit. The greater the complexity of the work, the narrower the **span of control** used and the greater the need for more levels. Job specialization also leads to **horizontal differentiation**. Growing organizations add more workers to the workforce, and many of the new additions provide specialized knowledge and skills to enable the organization to be more successful. These workers work at the same level but differ from colleagues in related areas. For example, accounting creates sub-units accounts payable and accounts receivables, but designers create another sub-unit, cost control, because cost containment becomes an important operational objective. Levels of sub-units can continue when decision-makers as designers determine the need for a specialized control function such as cost control. Cost control can be subdivided by types of costs. For example, direct labor costs, indirect labor costs and input costs.

Figures 6.2–6.6 show the linkage between the increase in an organization's size and the way size influences the design of an organization's structure as decision-makers seek to maintain an orderly and predictable operation. The use of formal management methods represents the use of practices used to help standardize work performance. The goal is to create an orderly operation. The purpose in creating order is to enable the organization to achieve the strategic goals along with increasing greater operational efficiency in the use of organizational resources.

LEARNING OBJECTIVE #4: DESCRIBE HOW THE RANGE OF PRODUCTS AND THE DIVERSITY OF MARKETS INFLUENCES THE DESIGN OF AN ORGANIZATION'S STRUCTURE

Designing an organization's structure reflects the organization's efforts at managing complexity by maintaining control over the organization's varied activities. Structure represents the organization's efforts at organizing tasks performed by an organization's work processes. The end point in creating a systematic framework (i.e. organizational structure) is to strengthen the organization's ability to achieve the strategic goals through the efficient use of an organization's resources. Ambitious

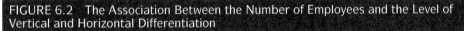

FIGURE 6.2   The Association Between the Number of Employees and the Level of Vertical and Horizontal Differentiation

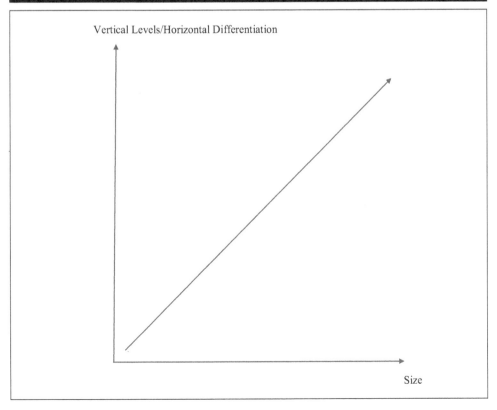

Vertical Levels/Horizontal Differentiation

Size

FIGURE 6.3   The Association Between the Number of Employees and the Complexity of the Decision-Making Process

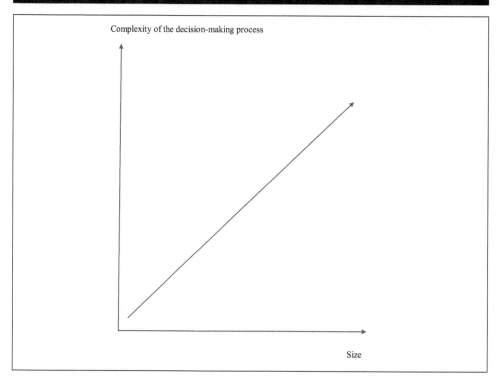

FIGURE 6.4   The Association Between the Number of Employees and the Complexity of the Communication Process

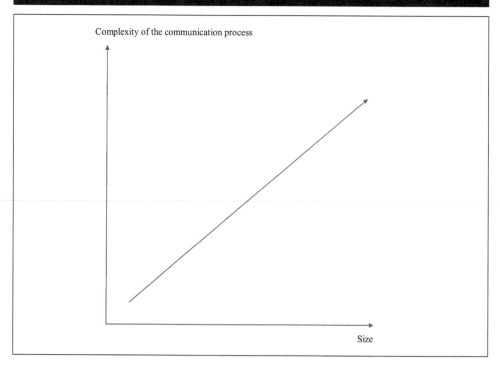

FIGURE 6.5   The Association Between the Number of Employees and the Complexity of the Control Process

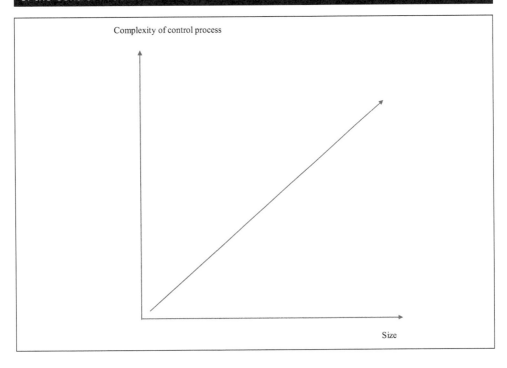

FIGURE 6.6   The Association Between the Number of Employees and the Complexity of the Management Integration Methods Used

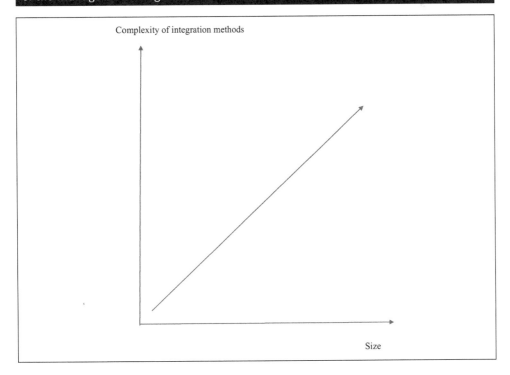

organizations demonstrate their ambitions through the selection of goals that force the organization to develop a new strategy to achieve the strategic goals. A new strategy imposes change on an organization because a new strategy obligates the organization to modify the strategy implementation process, which includes an organization's structure, if the organization expects to successfully implement the strategy. Ambitious strategic goals typically lead to a strategy associated with adding new products, new services and/or expanding within existing markets or entering new markets. An example helps to demonstrate the evolution in the ongoing process of designing an organization's structure as part of the strategy implementation process.

Let's say that Patricia starts a business from her home. The business is making customized golf shirts for men. Patricia designs, makes the shirts and sells six shirts a week to a nearby pro shop located at a private golf course. Recently, a pro shop at another private golf course asked her for five shirts per week for the next three summer months. Patricia manages the business herself. In July Patricia receives a call from two other pro shops at private golf courses requesting orders for the same type of golf shirt. Patricia expanded her hours of operation to accommodate the demand. A pro shop at a private golf course in the next county ordered shirts for the months of August and September. The shop inquired about ordering another type of shirt for female golfers. She immediately designed the shirt and produced a small sample. She shipped the order because of the distance involved. Patricia received a call from the shop manager requesting five shirts of each type, male and female. In early spring of the following year, Patricia reached out to the pro shop managers about new orders. All the shops increased their order size along with ordering the female shirt as well. Patricia realized that the orders exceeded her **capacity** to fill the orders within the time frames required. Patricia decided to hire a part-time bookkeeper and another person to work full time making the shirts with her. Gradually, more orders came from pro shops at other private golf courses throughout the state. Expansion came from word-of-mouth advertising. Many of the store managers asked about other types of clothing along with other types of shirts and if she did custom work too. Over the next four years, Patricia's business expanded rapidly. She leased a building to re-locate her office and production facilities. She hired a designer who specialized in designing golf pants. She hired another full-time bookkeeper and a part-time accountant. Patricia added ten new production workers along with a production manager. She hired two people as customer service representatives. Patricia hired two people to produce customized items only along with a supervisor to oversee their work. Patricia sub-contracted work to a Chinese firm to manufacture a line of golf socks. She employed the people to oversee shipping, with one person as the supervisor. She decided to hire someone as general manager to oversee day-to-day activities while she concentrated on new business development and working with customers who want other types of golf products. Recently, Patricia received orders from several sportswear retail regional chains that sold exclusive sportswear clothing within the region.

Patricia knew that the rapid growth of the business meant that she needed to organize her staff differently to strengthen the organizations' ability to meet existing business requirements and respond to future business requirements. It was only a matter of time before the business would expand into states outside the region along with increases in order sizes from regional sportswear chains. Patricia was very ambitious, setting growth-oriented goals that were always achieved. Patricia realized that she needed to allocate her resources more systematically, and to ensure that, everyone was accountable for a task and that there was a manager responsible to oversee each specific area of the operations. In addition, coordination of activities among the workforce was becoming more and more important because of the growth in the number of products, increased customizing services and meeting the needs of different types of customers.

Patricia created what she learned later was a **functional organizational structure** that included specialized functional areas such as shipping and receiving, production and accounting with managers overseeing each functional area. The general manager was responsible for supervising all line personnel while Patricia added to her responsibilities by supervising staff. She knew that creating a Human Resource department was necessary.

What this example demonstrates is that expanding products, creating product lines, adding services and working with different types of customers forced Patricia to add more people to the workforce who had specialized knowledge and skills to meet the customer's needs. Expansion exerts pressure on the organization to be better organized to successfully achieve the strategic goals and operational objectives. Goals and the strategy linked to achieving the goals impose the need for an ongoing, systematic approach to organize an organization's resources; an organization's structure represents one of the essential management methods used to perform the task of effectively using an organization's resources to achieve the strategic goals.

McCarthy Engineers: Part 2

At the next meeting with John and Karen, Stan mentioned that he had the opportunity to meet with a random group of employees. He wanted a broad range of perspectives to understand the issues better. Stan learned that adding the additional services came in response to opportunities that came about when working on various projects. Business was lost to competitors because the firm did not offer the services the clients wanted. Stan understood why John and Karen jumped at the chance to capture more business, especially because business was available when working on certain types of projects. Stan stated that expanding services and hiring more employees sounded like a great idea but that the additional employees and services had a huge impact on the way people now had to deliver the services. Stan went into a full discussion on the organizational issue associated with expansion.

Questions

1. What issue did Stan start discussing? Explain.
2. What was the second issue that Stan discussed? Explain.
3. What was the third issue that Stan discussed? Explain.
4. Why does expansion lead to problems? Explain.
5. Should John and Karen stop expanding? Explain.

LEARNING OBJECTIVE #5: DESCRIBE HOW EXTERNAL FACTORS INFLUENCE THE DESIGN OF AN ORGANIZATION'S STRUCTURE

Organizations operate in a world without the ability to control circumstances beyond an organization's borders. This world is often referred to as the organization's **external environment**. The organization is expected to develop the capabilities to take advantage of opportunities presented by the external environment and to successfully counter threatening situations. Opportunities pursued can benefit an organization's ability to survive and grow. Dealing successfully with threats enables the organization to survive and maintain its competitive position.

There are four primary dimensions in the external environment to guide the organization's efforts at identifying opportunities and threats. **Dimensions** serve as guides that enable the organization to consider how best to take advantage of opportunities and to defend against threats. The **economy** represents a critical dimension as all organizations thrive in either a growing economy or an economy in decline, with some organizations benefitting from both growth and decline (e.g. pawn shops can pay low prices for high quality items in a recession and sell items at high prices in an expanding economy). GDP, unemployment rate, inflation rate and interest rates are important indicators of economic activity that organizations monitor and plan around.

Socio-cultural factors represent another external environmental dimension. Demographic trends (e.g. aging of the population and the increase in medical problems) and changes in values (e.g. concern for the environment and eating healthy) can have a profound impact on an organization's ability to prosper. For example, increased interest in eating healthy foods requires supermarkets to offer health foods to customers or Pepsi selling health beverages.

Political-legal factors represent a third external environmental dimension. Laws and regulations can directly impact an organization's operations (e.g. hiring practices, policies on employee rights and food ingredients used).

Technology factors represent another important external environmental dimension. There are three major categories of technology an organization can consider. There is technology that an organization can incorporate as a **product feature** (e.g. Apple's use of a new type of camera in the iPhone). There is **process technology** that an organization can incorporate within the process of making a product or delivering a service, increasing efficiency (e.g. use of robots and use of voice software). Another type of technology is **input technology**. Inputs used in making a product (e.g. gorilla glass used to make cell phone screens and modal used in clothing).

The external environment has the potential to de-stabilize an organization even if confronted with an opportunity because the organization needs to respond to the opportunity because a non-response turns an opportunity into a threat potentially pursued by a competitor. A non-response represents a bad decision because the possible result increases the uncertainty of future success in the organization's competitive world.

An organization creates an organizational structure to increase certainty by regulating the actions of the workforce in predictable ways, with the goal of increasing organizational effectiveness (by achieving strategic goals) and organizational efficiencies (by achieving operational objectives). The potential for disruptions originating from the external environment threatens the organization's efforts to increase certainty and reducing risk. Organizational decision-makers heed the potential of the external environment as well as the chance for problems by incorporating into the organizational structure adaptive features that serve to protect the organization and hasten the pursuit of opportunities and counter threats. Structure reflects the intent of the organization to acquire and manage knowledge, and the external environment represents an important source of knowledge to access. **Knowledge management** represents the creation of a systematic process at coordinating decision-making and important management activities to enable the organization to respond in a timely manner to opportunities and threats from the external environment. The pursuit of opportunities and confronting threats is incorporated in an organization's overall structure.

Knowledge acquisition incorporates the use of varied management methods as part of an organization's structure. Designing job descriptions include scanning the external environment and creating sub-units responsible for scanning the external environment; information systems designed to provide routine information for the organization to collect, interpret and make use of are examples of structural techniques organizational decision-makers use in designing an organization's structure in support of knowledge management.

LEARNING OBJECTIVE #6: EXPLAIN HOW MANAGEMENT SYSTEMS INFLUENCE THE DESIGN OF AN ORGANIZATION

The goal in designing an organization's structure is to improve the performance of the organization's management systems (an organization's structure represents one of the management systems). The different management systems constitute management methods used to organize organizational policies and work processes by categories of function (e.g. quality management system and cost control system); each work process serves a specific function (e.g. hiring process, recruitment process and job analysis process). Structure creates order within a management system and between management systems and among management systems to achieve the goal of improving an organization's performance. The emphasis on improving performance focus' attention on making work processes operate optimally, and each management system operates according to the organization's performance expectations.

The focus on management systems is because management systems represent one of the most important management methods used in the **formalization process**. Decision-makers use formalization to assert greater influence over the workforce to ensure that workforce's performance meets the organization's expectations, measured by achieving the strategic goals and operational objectives. The organization's structure serves as the organization's **supra-system** among all the other management systems, functioning like an overseer. Structure exemplifies the means for directing and coordinating the actions of the workforce involved in implementing the management systems through performing specific work processes outlined by an organization's policies. Every work process linked to a policy is subordinate to the management system it operates within.

Decision-making represents one of the management systems. Organizational structure represents the decision-makers approach to organizing decision-making throughout an organization by allocating authority hierarchically. Decision-making represents one of the principal ways the organization controls the behavior of the workforce. Decision-makers are assigned the responsibility of keeping subordinates focused and goal-directed.

Resource management represents another type of management system. The organization represents a collection of resources. Because resources are finite, the organization needs to ensure the best use of resources to aid in achieving the organization's strategic goals.

Performance management is another management system designed to keep the workforce focused. Focus means working to achieve the operational objectives linked to the strategic goals. For example, meeting deadlines is a type of operational objective. Meeting a deadline can mean fulfilling a customer's requirements to realize a sale. There is no limit to identifying operational objectives other than common-sense dictates the prioritizing those operational objectives that contribute the most toward achieving the organization's strategic goals.

The **motivation system** represents the organization's efforts at formalizing the process of using extrinsic and intrinsic rewards to reward individual and unit performance. The goal is to keep individuals and units focused.

The **information management system** represents a formalized approach used by organizations to create a network of reporting types of work processes. Information provides the organization with feedback on the performance of work processes; each work process generates objective types of performance information (e.g. the recruitment process generates applicants). Information enables the organization to learn how well a work process functions, problem work processes and the results from taking remedial actions to improve a work process. Information management covers such issues as the frequency of a report, the content requirements of a report, the recipient(s) of a report and any response requirements. These examples of actions of a work process are dictated by a policy. Information management can include verbal reports as well as written reports. Information management governs the design and operation of work processes using policies.

The **control management system** functions to ensure that work processes perform according to organizational expectations. A **cost control system** is an example of a control system designed to monitor costs and to keep costs within pre-determined limits (i.e. operational objectives). There are sub-systems within a control system. An inventory control system oversees the organization's inventory. An **inventory control system** monitors if there is excess inventory, inventory shortages and if inventory levels are maintained at expected levels (i.e. operational objective). **Workforce management** represents another type of control system. For example, employee turnover rates, absenteeism rates and dismissal rates represent types of performance indicators an organization would track to identify possible problems or to anticipate potential problems.

Knowledge management is a management system that focuses on developing the organization's ability to access knowledge and to prioritize superordinate knowledge intended to improve the organization's effectiveness as well as assist the organization in the efficient use of resources. Knowledge management is an important management system for decision-makers when designing the organization's structure because of the need to access knowledge from sources within the organization and from sources external to the organization. Knowledge is critical to the long-term survival of the organization because knowledge management facilitates organizational learning.

In sum, an organization's structure is designed to facilitate the coordination among the above-mentioned management systems. Structure is the primary method used to integrate the management systems and to ensure that the individuals and organizational units coordinate their efforts for the common good.

LEARNING OBJECTIVE #7: IDENTIFY AND DESCRIBE THE MAJOR TYPES OF ORGANIZATIONAL STRUCTURES

Most common types of organizational structures are represented by one of seven basic designs with three of the types of designs overlapping with the functional design described below. Essentially, all organizations started with the **simple design**. The configuration of a simple design requires that there is more than one person employed by the organization. Simple designs have a leader at the top of the hierarchy who directly oversees all other employees. There may be some degree of job specialization for each employee, but typically, all employees are responsible for several different and often unrelated tasks. For example, an employee might be responsible for financial management that includes budget development and budget oversight, bookkeeping, accounts payable, accounts receivable and hiring. The organization's resources do not warrant more individual job specialization. The speed of growth of the organization dictates the rate at which job specialization among the workforce evolves.

If an organization pursues rapid growth, the simple design rapidly morphs into a **functionally designed** organizational structure. A functional organizational structure reflects the organization's efforts at organizing the workforce by functional areas. The move to a functional design mirrors the move toward job specialization. The progression of a business's growth influences the extent to which jobs become more specialized. Job specialization means that the scope of each job becomes narrower; the emphasis on job specialization reflects the organization's efforts at promoting rapid learning that leads to increases in job performance. For example, a large organization will have at least one individual responsible for the budget development process, the budget oversight process, bookkeeping, accounts payable and accounts receivable. As the organization expands, these tasks become further specialized because the workload associated with each task exceeds the capacity of any one individual to perform the assigned task competently. For example, accounts receivables can be organized by size of a customer, by geographic area, by size of a customer and geographic area or another type of permutation that reflect the need to create additional specialized positions to perform the relevant tasks associated with the work process. Along with increased job specialization comes the need for managers to oversee each of these specialized jobs.

A functionally designed organization can evolve into a **divisional** organizational structure through the acquisition of other companies; acquiring a division from another organization or expanding the range of related products into a product group. The purpose in creating a divisional organizational structure is to assess performance of each division where a non-divisional design does not offer the organization an effective performance evaluation model. Frequently, a division design represents a group of related products that are unrelated to the products of other divisions in the organization. For example, General Electric has an engine manufacturing division and a financial services division and formerly had an appliance division among its family of divisions. A variation of the division design is **strategic business units** (SBUs). SBUs represent a large division that has product groups that are related but different enough to create smaller divisions. For example, General Electric's appliance division could easily have been an SBU with small divisions organized around such product groups as refrigerators, stoves, washing machines and dryers and microwave ovens. Divisions often include most of the various functions to truly make a division semi-autonomous. The parent company has some basic functional capabilities to support the corporate office. Sometimes, the parent center centralizes R&D under the corporate umbrella to efficiently use resources for new product development activities.

A **hybrid design** commonly encompasses one of three variations. A hybrid design will typically include separate functional units, but then part of the organization can be grouped by **products**, or by **customers** or by **geographic areas**. The selection of a hybrid variant is determined by the extent to which the organization needs to specialize by products, customers or geographic areas. The uniqueness of a hybrid variant design can challenge the organization's efforts at retaining the functional design. The decision-makers determine that there is a need to organize part of the workforce by a category such as a product group. For example, the former appliance division of GE could easily be grouped by product category, such as washing machines, clothes dryers, stoves and refrigerators if these product groups do not warrant being an SBU. Again, we can refer to the examples of a hybrid as a product functional.

The **matrix design** is another type of organizational design. A matrix design is mostly found where the organization is challenged to fully utilize functional resources, and there is a project focus to the business. Projects can include developing new products, developing new drugs and designing buildings, and the project requires the temporary allocation of functional resources to successfully complete the project. Functional resources represented by functional specialists are grouped under project coordinators who report to a project manager. Once a project terminates, functional specialists return to their functional areas until ready for assignment to another project.

In every organizational structure, there are common areas with a defined focus. At the top of the hierarchy is the **strategic group**. The strategic group's membership includes all senior leaders including the CEO, COO and the strategic planning group. The legal unit is part of the strategic group. **Middle management** represents another section of the organization. Middle managers interpret the decisions of senior leaders as well as organizational policies for the benefit of the **operational core**. Middle managers oversee the operational core by guiding the core in implementing the decisions of senior leaders and report back to senior leaders their findings on the degree of success in implementing the senior leader's decisions and policies.

The operational core is composed of lower-level managers and non-managers, organized by functions unless part of a hybrid organization. The operational core is responsible for the work to produce a product and/or service. **Support staff** exemplified by the **Human Resources** function work on behalf of **line personnel** who make up the operational core. Support staff seek to make the life of line personnel easier so that they can concentrate on performing their job tasks. Finally, there are the **technical specialists**. Technical specialists meet the analytical needs of the organization. Technical specialists contribute technical knowledge and skills to the organization. Technical specialists are often dispersed throughout the organization, grouped into small, specialized units. For example, cost analysts, computer programmers and statisticians.

McCarthy Engineers: Part 3

In the next meeting, senior managers were invited to participate in the discussion with John, Karen and Stan. Stan planned to discuss an alternative type of method to organize the workforce and oversight of projects. In preparation for the meeting, Stan sent a handout that described a functional-matrix design along with a visual representation of the design. Stan's handout included reasons for this design; advantages the design offered the firm; potential pitfalls to deal with and if the proposed design was accepted, a plan for implementing the design. The handout included an outline of training programs.

Questions

1. Why is Stan recommending a functional-matrix design?
2. What are the top two benefits of the proposed design? Explain.
3. What are the top two pitfalls associated with the proposed design? Explain.
4. What is the first step in implementing the design? Explain.
5. Why is training necessary? Explain.

LEARNING OBJECTIVE #8: IDENTIFY, DESCRIBE AND EXPLAIN THE CONSEQUENCES OF AN ORGANIZATION'S STRUCTURAL LIMITATIONS

As an organization increases in size, the most common response by decision-makers is to emphasize a greater use of formalization methods to create order over an increasingly more complex organization. Without order, there is a greater likelihood for chaos to occur. A chaotic organization increases the level of business uncertainty which results in greater risk of making bad business decisions which will negatively impact the organization's performance. Research shows that an organization's performance benefits from a progression of formalization to regulate and control the behavior of the workforce.

A non-response at formalizing a growing organization or a slow response cab results in negative consequences for the organization. Organizations operate within an external environment with little to no ability to control external events. The organization can only control how it responds to external circumstances. The external world offers both opportunities to consider and threats to deal with. Opportunities usually have a time limit, and competitors' faster response can turn an opportunity into a threat. A slow response to threats usually results in greater negative consequences for the organization.

Organizational structure represents the organization's formal approach in organizing work processes. Organizational structure provides work focus through task specialization, increasing the use of job specialization (i.e. job descriptions) of each employee and then using management methods to coordinate the specialized tasks among a network of specialized jobs. The result is a network of interconnected work processes organized as a structured organization. Management uses policy as the principle management method for creating work processes and for modifying existing work processes. A slow response or non-response in changing to confront external circumstances reduces an organization's effectiveness because the organization follows outdated policies and work processes.

An organization's structural limitations, which contribute to inadequate response to external situations, handicap the knowledge management system in many ways.

- The innovation process of incorporating new forms of technology into work processes and product improvements is handicapped because structure often serves to support the status quo of maintaining routines, discouraging innovativeness through new initiatives.
- Decision-making is handicapped because of the need to centralize or decentralize the authority to make both important and routine types of decisions. Consequently, inaction, an inadequate response or a tardy response hurt the organization's effort at pursuing opportunities and dealing with threats.
- Another consequence of being tardy or non-responsiveness is the negative impact on the communication system where the associated work processes transform information into knowledge, enabling decision-makers to act based on the information provided.
- Performance management and the reward system are not synchronized to support initiatives that focus on knowledge acquisition which is associated with being innovative. Frequently, the result is that the workforce is rewarded for non-essential work, no longer relevant in the organization's efforts to pursue new opportunities and avoid threats.
- Resource management can become dysfunctional through the continued allocation of resources in supporting non-essential actions instead of prioritizing the allocation of limited resources to support actions linked to achieving the organization's strategic goals.

LEARNING OBJECTIVE #9: IDENTIFY AND DESCRIBE THE MANAGEMENT METHODS USED TO SUPPLEMENT AN ORGANIZATION'S STRUCTURAL LIMITATIONS

Limitations associated with an organization's structure require the use of additional management methods to offset these limitations. The goal in using supplemental management methods is to better integrate the units within the organization because the process of creating an organizational structure results in creating separate, homogeneous units. The organization needs these units, organized by special functions, to work cooperatively with other units.

Cross-functional teams is a common integration method. Cross-functional team membership includes technical specialists with the needed knowledge and experience that enable the team to successfully achieve the goals the team needs to achieve. There are additional types of teams. Some are teams with a **single purpose** and with a short time frame. Upon achieving the team's goal, the team dissolves. There are permanent teams with no specific duration because this type of team's agenda is open-ended, with the goals dictated by the organization's ongoing needs. Team membership can vary according to circumstances, but the team itself continues indefinitely until circumstances dictate otherwise.

Organizations often create **coordinator** positions. A coordinator's job description includes the responsibility to pull together the efforts of different units or sub-units of the organization with a specific goal in mind. There are times when a coordinating position is permanent because the need to oversee the coordination efforts among units is ongoing. For example, if the organization wants to create a reporting process that involves several units to be involved in the continuing reporting process, a coordinator helps to negotiate with the leadership of each unit, with the goal of creating a shared reporting process. Some organizations create coordinating units. Each unit is composed of individuals responsible for coordinating among other units and then pulling all the coordinating work processes among the multifarious work units together. For example, a unit can be responsible for overseeing supply-chain management by coordinating the needs of individual units with a variety of suppliers, ensuring that there is an adequate supply secure achieving operational objectives.

Span of control is another type of integration method. Span of control involves the exercise of decision-making authority. An organization can decide to widen spans of control of managers. **Widening the span of control** entails increasing the number of individuals who report directly to a manager. The organization typically would either take people from units to create a larger unit or place more units under a manager and enlarging the manager's position, conferring more authority over a larger number of workers. A **narrow span of control** reduces the number of workers that a manager has authority over. A narrow span of control is common where there is a great deal of technical sophistication among workers, and a manager is not expected to have the technical expertise needed to oversee large numbers of people with technical expertise.

The organization can create new **policies** or modify existing policies to require units to work together routinely. Policies lead to the creation of new work processes or modification of existing work processes. Through the policy development process, the organization can require units to work together. For example, an organization can formalize the budget development process, requiring units within a larger unit to work more closely to synchronize the development of the unit's budget. A policy can require different sub-units to follow a process that requires a formal approach to work on a large unit's budget (working with levels of sub-units).

Changing **job descriptions** is a common management integration method. Enlarging an individual's job to include the need to work with others in different units is a common corporate practice. **Job enlargement** involves adding more tasks and responsibilities to a job; this includes involving individuals within a unit to work together. Job enlargement can include requiring individuals that work in sub-units within a larger unit to work together. For example, in accounting, if there are no sub-units but there are specialists such as accounts payable clerks, accounts receivable clerks, sales expenses clerks and cost accounting clerks, the organization might want these positions to coordinate their efforts to speed up the process of aggregating the information generated by each individual into a larger financial report. In a large organization, these specialties might be organized into sub-units (e.g. accounts payable department and accounts receivables department). The goal of speeding up the reporting process and developing a comprehensive report requires that the sub-units work together by formalizing the work process that results in a pooled report.

Changing a **report creation process** is an example of another type of management integration method. Creating a report is part of the organization's information management system. Linking parts of the organization together occurs by changing the policy regarding the type of information required in a report. The intent is to involve other units that generate related information in the reporting process. A variation to this approach is to require sub-units that work together in a work process to jointly report the results of this combined effort routinely. All work processes generate outcomes and almost all outcomes are measurable in some form. The report can include the outcomes of the various work processes on a regular basis.

The use of **SMART type goals** and **SMART type operational objectives** represent additional management integration methods. By requiring specialists, sub-units and units to achieve goals or objectives that require a pooled effort, the organization enforces the need to work together to achieve the goals and/or operational objectives. This counters a natural inclination to work autonomously.

The use of **incentive programs** combined with **performance assessments** represents additional management integration methods the organization can use to facilitate coordination among individuals, sub-units or units. Incentive programs require the use of a SMART type of goal or SMART type of operational objective that includes a time limit for achieving the goal or objective. The goal/objective needs to be realistic, achievable and the reward worth the effort to generate the motivation to achieve the goal/objective. This is a more complicated integration method because all participants need to agree with the goal/objective and that the reward is worth the effort to achieve the goal/objective.

LEARNING OBJECTIVE #10: EXPLAIN THE RELATIONSHIP BETWEEN AN ORGANIZATION'S STRUCTURE AND PERFORMANCE MANAGEMENT

An organization's structural configuration needs to link with the organization's performance management system. The structural linkage among individuals, sub-units and larger units is meant to ensure that all parts of the organization work together, synchronously, with the goal of increasing the organization's effectiveness, as measured by the performance management system.

The **performance management system** includes two important components, the use of **performance indicators (associated with strategic goals and operational objectives)** and the **reward system or motivation system**. Each component is meant to work together, with performance indicators keeping the workforce focused and the reward system reinforcing success at meeting the organization's expectations (achieving the strategic goals and operational objectives). The organization uses **SMART strategic goals** and **SMART operational objectives to** represent an organization's expectations. Strategic goals apply to the entire organization whereas operational objectives apply to units, sub-units and individuals. Operational objectives need to link directly or indirectly with the strategic goals. The intention of an organization's structure is to make achieving the goals and objectives easier to accomplish.

Decision-makers design an organization's structure partly due to recognizing the importance of the **knowledge management system's** role in contributing to the organization's chances of achieving the strategic goals. Knowledge management, discussed above, is associated with the process of acquiring information, converting the information into knowledge and applying the knowledge to increase an organization's effectiveness. Knowledge management focuses on creating a learning organization. Speed in the process of acquiring information, methods used to convert the information into knowledge and diffusing the knowledge throughout the organization quickly; all depend on the way decision-makers designed the organization's structure (including the other management systems).

Performance indicators provide decision-makers with signals for what is working when operational objectives are achieved and what is not working. Symptoms, whereby the performance indicators show a failure to achieve the objectives, indicate problems for decision-makers to identify and fix. By using metric-type performance indicators, decision-makers can quickly identify the problems (causal factors) and pursue remedial actions. Successful performance triggers the reward system to reinforce success and support future performance in meeting the organization's expectations. Success often leads to the organization raising the expectations by identifying more challenging operational objectives.

Performance management for individuals becomes the responsibility of Human Resources (HR) to manage once an organization reaches a certain size. The right size is arbitrary, but when an organization creates a separate HR function, one of the specialty functions is to develop an individual-focused performance management system. HR works with units to develop performance management practices because of HR's expertise in the field. Policies and the associate work processes related to the design and implementation of performance management throughout the organization becomes the responsibility of HR.

Performance management for sub-units within a functional area (e.g. Advertising within the Marketing function) often is the responsibility of the functional parent (e.g. Accounting). Performance management of a functional specialty (e.g. accounting, R&D and marketing) is often a shared responsibility between the function manager(s) and senior leadership. There is no "one right way" for locating the responsibility for the performance management system other than by tradition and the prerogative of senior leaders.

McCarthy Engineers: Part 4

The meeting with John, Karen, Stan and the senior managers lasted several hours. There were lots of questions asked, but by the end of the meeting, everyone unanimously supported Stan's recommendation to create a functional-matrix organizational design. The agenda for the next meeting between John, Karen and Stan was to discuss the process for implementing the new design and how to involve senior managers in the process. At the meeting's start, John and Karen mentioned to Stan that an issue arose after the previous meeting. No one knew how to organize and oversee the project teams that were a component of the new organizational design. Stan discussed a possible process to follow to create project teams and the common methods used manage, supervise and assess the effectiveness of project teams.

Questions

1. Identify and describe the process to follow in creating project teams.
2. What is a common method for managing project teams? Explain.
3. What is a common management method to use in supervising project teams? Explain.
4. What is a typical management method for judging a project team's effectiveness? Explain.
5. What subjects should the initial training program cover? Explain.

LEARNING OBJECTIVE #11: DESCRIBE AND EXPLAIN THE ROLE OF ORGANIZATIONAL STRUCTURE IN INNOVATION MANAGEMENT

One of the primary decision-makers design an organization's structure is to facilitate the coordination among and between various management functions. But to what purpose? Because coordination is a means to an end and not the end. The design of an organization's structure is meant to influence and guide the organization's knowledge management system's work processes to facilitate the organization's **innovation management system**.

The innovation management system serves two purposes. First, innovation focuses on developing new products and/or services or improves existing products and services. The purpose of this form of innovation is to improve an organization's effectiveness by achieving the organization's strategic goals. Second, innovation management focuses on improving the work processes to enable the organization to be more efficient. Innovation comes in two forms: developing and applying **technology** and developing new **organizational policies** to influence an organization's work processes. Structure aims to improve the knowledge management system so that innovation management, an important attribute of the knowledge management system, performs better. Improved performance means the expanded use of technology throughout the organization to improve an organization's efficiency along with changing management policies that increases an organization's control over operational costs.

The external environment has a major impact on the knowledge management system through the design and functioning of the organization's structure. Competition and the changing external world of the organization force an organization to respond or suffer the consequences associated with a non-response or too little too late response. Increased competition and greater uncertainty require rapid responses to keep the organization competitive. This scenario makes the case for a **de-centralized** organizational structure so that the various functions of the organization can respond more quickly to increased competition and environmental uncertainty (e.g. economic fluctuations and changes in customer values). A less turbulent external environment leads to great levels of certainty, resulting in an organizational structure that centralizes decision-making to increase senior leadership's control over the operations. Greater control provides leaders with more predictable types of actions by the organization. Increased control reduces the risk factor associated with decision-making.

To facilitate the management of the innovation management system, knowledge management's focus is to increase learning throughout the organization. Typically, a de-centralized organization is more likely to be associated with work processes designed to maximize organizational learning. This is because decision-making authority among lower management levels allows for a quicker organizational response to deal with immediate issues that arise. **Organizational learning** benefits from a strong linkage between the organizations' performance management system and the reward system. This is because decision-makers link achieving SMART operational objectives and earning rewards. **Incentive programs** are optimal forms of reward programs because the reward is linked to a measurable, targeted result (e.g. SMART operational objectives and SMART goals).

Organizational structure also represents the organization's effort at systematizing knowledge management because a more formal organizational structure is associated with greater organizational success, as measured by achieving the strategic goals and improved operational efficiencies. Knowledge management benefits from an **organizational culture** that reflects the **values** strongly associated with creating a knowledge management system that facilitates organizational learning. Examples of values include knowledge acquisition, setting learning goals, rewarding successful learning, training to increase learning and rewarding "outside the box" thinking.

Chapter Summary

This chapter provides an in-depth overview describing the purpose and function of organizational design. Organizational design has a strategic purpose. Organizational design is meant to describe the approach taken in designing an organization's structure. An organization's structure represents a management system whose purpose is to organize the various units and sub-units of an organization in a systematic arrangement. The intent in aligning the organization's units and sub-units is to facilitate cooperation and coordination among the various units. Furthermore, organizational designers and decision-makers must consider how best to mold the important management systems within an organization's structure. The overarching goal in designing an organization's structure is to leverage all the management systems to focus on supporting the organization's efforts at achieving the strategic goals and operational objectives.

There are a variety of issues designers, and decision-makers must consider in planning to design an organization's structure. One issue is the role of external environmental issues, and how the organization needs to consider the external world of the organization because how the organization responds can make the difference between success and failure. Organizations must organize the organization's capabilities to respond to external environmental issue by doing so as an organization and not individually. An internal organizational issue impacting what designers and decision-makers approach designing an organizational structure is the effect of an organization's size and design considerations. Size is an important issue as the organization must determine whether to create a centralized organizational structure, a de-centralized organizational structure or utilize other management methods to deal with increased organizational complexity associated with size and how best to manage this complex operation successfully.

Chapter Questions

1. What is the purpose of organizational design?
2. Identify and briefly describe two factors that determine the need to centralize or de-centralize decision-making authority.
3. What are two reasons why the size of an organization influences the design of an organization's structure?
4. How does the range of products and diversity of markets influence designers?
5. Identify and describe the external dimensions that influence organizational designers thinking.
6. Identify and briefly explain three ways management systems that influence the design of an organization's structure.
7. Identify and briefly describe any three types of organizational structures.
8. What are the three consequences of an organization's structural limitations?
9. Identify and describe any three management methods use to supplement an organization's structure.
10. Briefly identify and describe three factors linking performance management and an organization's structure.
11. Identify and describe the ways the organizations influence innovation management when designing and organization.

Bibliography

Aghion, P., Bloom, N., Lucking, B., Sadun, R. & Van Reenan, J. (2017). Turbulence, firm decentralization and growth in bad times. *National Bureau of Economic Research*. Working Paper 23354. 1–61.

Ahmady, G.A., Mehrpovr, M. & Nikoora-vesh, A. (2016). Organizational structure. *Procedia-Social and Behavioral Sciences*. 230. 455–462.

Allen, R.K. (2012). What is organizational design? http://www.centerod.com/2012/02/what-is-organizational-design/.

Alonso, R., Dessein, W. & Matouschek, N. (2008). When does coordination require centralization? *American Economic Review*. 98(1). 145–179.

Aronowitz, S., Smet, A.D. & McGinty, D. (2015). Getting organizational design right. *McKinsey & Company Organization*. June 1. 1–11.

Bloom, N., Sadun, R. & Van Reenen, J. (2012). The organization of firms across countries. *The Quarterly Journal of Economics*. September 7. 1663–1705.

Bloom, N., Sadun, R. & Van Reenen, J. (2017). Management as a technology? *Working Paper* 16–133. Harvard Business School. 1–59.

Bloom, N. & Van Reenen, J. (2010). Why do management practices differ across firms and countries? *Journal of Economic Perspectives*. 24(1). 203–224.

Capponi, J. (2017). The importance of god organizational structure to grow and profitability.https://www.linkedin.com/pulse/importance-good-organizational-structure-growth-Timothy/. September 20.

Chand, S. 8 types of organizational structures: their advantages and disadvantages. https://www.yourarticlelibrary.com/organization/8-types-organizational-structurre-their-advantages-and-disadvantages/.

Clawson, J. G. (2008). Leading organizational design. *Darden Business Publishing/University of Virginia*. UV-OB-0657. 1–19.

Colombo, M.G., Delmastro, M. & Rabbiosi, L. (2012). Organizational design and firm performance. *Oxford Handbook of Managerial Economics*. Oxford University Publishing. Chapter 17.

DeCanio, S. J., Dibble, C. & Amir-Atefi, K. (2000). The importance of organizational structure. *Management Science*. 46(10). 1285–1299.

Engert, O., Kaetzler, B., Kordestani, K. & MacLean, A. *What Is Culture?* McKinsey & Company Organization. 1–7.

Hart, O. & Moore, J. (1999). On the design of hierarchies: coordination versus specialization. *National Bureau of Economic Research*. Working Paper 7388. 1–52.

Hernaus, T., Aleksic, A. & Klindzic, M. (2013). Organizing for competitiveness-structural and process characteristics of organizational design. *Contemporary Economics*. 7(4). 41–56.

Hill, B. (2019). The importance of a good organizational structure. https://smallbusiness.chron.com/importance-good-organizational-structure-3792.html/. March 07.

Ingram, D. (2017). How does organizational structure affect performance measurement? https://yourbusiness.azcentral.com/organizational-structure-affect-performance-measurement/.

Khan, R. Technical report on organizational design decisions: short research paper. Unpublished. 1–7.

Luebke, T. (2011). The importance of organizational design & structure. Faith Technologies Blog. https://www.blog.faithtechnologies.com/Blog_entries/-the-importance-of-organizational-design-and-structure/.

McGrath, R.G. (2012). How the growth outliers do it. *Harvard Business Review*. January–February. 1–13.

Mutti, C.D.N. & Hughes, W. (2001). Contemporary organizational theory in the management of construction projects. In: A. Akintoye (Ed.). 17th Annual ARCOM Conference. 5–7. September 2001, University of Salford. *Association of Researchers in Construction Management*. 1. 455–465.

Rennie, M., Meaney, M., Hazlewood, J., Jumra, G. & Dias, A.K. (2016). *Agility and Organizational Design*. McKinsey & Company Organization.

Serifi, V. & Dasic, P. (2012). Characteristics of traditional and contemporary models of organizational structures. *7th International Conference ICQME*. 333–339.

Shooshtarian, L.M. (2014). The effects of organizational structure on organizational trust and effectiveness. *Polish Journal of Management Studies*. 10(2). 73–84.

Tran, Q. & Tian, Y. (2013) Organizational structure: influencing factors and impact on the firm. *American Journal of Industrial and Business Management*. 3. 229–236.

Zheng, W., Yang, B. & McLean, G.N. (2009). Linking organizational culture, structure, strategy, and organizational effectiveness: mediating role of knowledge management. *Journal of Business Research*. 30. 1–9.

PART III

MANAGEMENT INITIATIVES

Organizational Culture

OVERVIEW

This chapter focuses on providing important insights on the subject, organizational culture. The concept of organizational culture often elicits two common reactions. First, everyone thinks they understand the meaning of the term and consider an organization's culture to be an important factor that contributes to the success of an organization as well as a contributing factor when organizations struggle to achieve the organization's strategic goals. Second, when asked to define organizational culture and explain how organizations create and maintain an organization's culture, the ability to provide answers is often elusive and varied.

This chapter provides the reader with a better understanding of the subject organizational culture by offering a definition of the term and a detailed overview describing the role an organization's culture plays in the success or failure of an organization. An organization's values represent the primary feature associated with organizational culture. The purpose of values is described because of the importance of values to an organization.

The concept, organizational culture, is simple to understand but challenging to describe in detail. This conundrum occurs because organizational culture is a multi-dimensional concept. The chapter identifies and describes the important dimensions and the impact organizational culture has on an organization's performance. Added to the description of the dimensions is a detailed overview of the different levels to an organization's culture. These levels contribute not only to the meaningfulness of an organization's culture but also to the complexity of an organization's culture; this analysis helps the reader understand the challenge an organization confronts in promoting organizational change because there are several layers to an organization's culture that require attention.

Because an organization's culture is a valuable contributor to the success of an organization, researchers and managers attempt to understand the process to follow in creating an organization's culture of success along with learning how to provide the type of support to maintain an organization's culture linked to a successful organization. The chapter introduces the different approaches often considered important in establishing a culture linked to a successful organization. Included in the analysis is a discussion on how an organization's culture affects an organization's performance. This is an important related issue because performance results are the primary indicator of a successful organization.

Because organization's need to adapt to external environmental factors, part of this adaptation process involves changing an organization's culture to better support the needs of the organization. Levers for changing an organization's culture are identified and described. One lever is the important role of leadership in the development and ongoing sustenance of an organization's culture. This is an important topic to understand because leadership is fundamental to an organization's success or failure.

The Lewin Model is an example of a method often used to bring about changes to an organization's culture. The model, described in detail, provides the reader with the understanding of the need for a process to apply to bring about change, using SMART goals as performance measures to learn when change is successful. Once changes to an organization's culture occur, the need to maintain the changes is a requisite requirement to avoid recidivism. The chapter identifies and describes different management methods to use in maintaining an organization's culture.

CHAPTER 7 LEARNING OBJECTIVES

Readers will achieve the following learning objectives after reading this chapter.

1. Define organizational culture and discuss the importance of organizational culture.
2. Identify and describe the role and source of values to an organization's culture.
3. Identify and describe the dimensions of an organization's culture and the impact of culture on an organization's performance.
4. Identify and describe the different levels of an organization's culture.
5. Identify and examine the different approaches to create and maintain an organization's culture.
6. Discuss how an organization's culture impacts an organization's performance.
7. Identify, describe and explain the levers used to change an organization's culture.
8. Discuss the relationship between leadership and organizational culture.
9. Discuss the application of the Lewin Model in changing an organization's culture.
10. Identify and describe the management methods used for maintaining an organization's culture.

LEARNING OBJECTIVE #1: DEFINE ORGANIZATIONAL CULTURE AND DISCUSS THE IMPORTANCE OF ORGANIZATIONAL CULTURE

With over 60 definitions of organizational culture, the ability to offer one universal definition remains challenging. Researchers often discuss the concept in general, but simple terms. Many researchers refer to organizational culture as the "glue" that binds the parts of the organization together and strengthens the commitment of individuals to the organization.

But what does the term organizational culture mean? The most common interpretation of organizational culture is that an organization's culture represents a **collection of values** developed in conjunction with the process of learning what business practices work and what business practices did not work in the organization's ongoing efforts to achieve the organization's strategic goals. Values evident during successful periods reinforce the organization's commitment to the values identified during these periods. The organization attempts to discard values linked with times that the organization was not successful, though often not soon enough.

Once values become embedded within the organization's operations, the values become ubiquitous. The workforce shares the core values that become codified in an organization's **Code of Conduct** and further strengthened by organizational policies (linked to values) that define specific work processes.

Researchers and organizational decision-makers may disagree on how to define the term, organizational culture, but all agree that an organization's culture and the values that make an organization's culture is an important contributing factor in an organization's efforts to successfully convert competitive opportunities into actual benefits to the organization.

LEARNING OBJECTIVE #2: IDENTIFY AND DESCRIBE THE ROLE AND SOURCE OF VALUES TO AN ORGANIZATION'S CULTURE

If an organization's culture is primarily a value-based concept, and an organization's culture instrumental in creating a successful organization, then values are the basis for a successful organization.

Once learned, the workforce remains committed to the organization's values. Like the Pavlovian model, an action leads to a response; if the response leads to success, success is rewarding either extrinsically, intrinsically or in both ways. The values associated with being successful are strengthened because of the association. Values influence the **perceptions** of the workforce. Perceptions involve judging some object or situation in through value-based lenses. In short, values filter an individual's perceptions who then interprets the perceptions in a value-influenced way. Once interpreted, the individual acts. Therefore, values influence behavior and that explains why most organizations create a **code of conduct** and ancillary value propositions. A value is a strongly held conviction; a value or group of values provide standards to follow.

A code of conduct is insufficient to influence workforce behavior. Organization's attempt to strengthen the commitment of the workforce to **core values** designing and implementing management systems that embody the core values. Core values are the complements to the Code. Management systems incorporate values to support the use of management systems used to influence behavior. Values serve to prioritize what is important to focus on, ensuring that the workforce remains committed to meeting the expectations associated with each type of management system. Every management system represents a collection of policies with a common theme. Policies identify specific types of work processes as part of the effort to regulate behavior in prescribed ways. Policies reflect the priorities of the organization. Policies and work processes reflect specific values that represent the organization's core values.

Shared values increase the commitment of the workforce, with the strongest appeal to employee intrinsic motivation because intrinsic motivation taps what is fundamentally important to individuals. A highly motivated workforce is reflected by the workforce's commitment to making the organization a success. Leadership's role is to harness this commitment by guiding the workforce as the workforce commits to the organization's mission statement, vision, strategic goals, strategies and strategy implementation methods (i.e. organizational structure). **Organizational structure** reflects the organizing model perceived as the optimal way to coordinate the efforts of the workforce. The former provides the focus that represents systematic methods to keep the workforce focused and committed to making the organization a success. Underlying each of these methods are the core values.

The **information management system** (i.e. reporting system) reflected by the organization's values if the values encourage closer cooperation, then there are increased attempts at coordinating the work efforts of units and sub-units within the organization. Sharing information in a timely manner helps facilitate **organizational learning** which is the primary role of the **knowledge management system**. The linkage between the information management system and knowledge management system is essential because together, the systems enable the organization's **innovation management system** to pursue new opportunities. Innovation management focuses on the pursuit of new opportunities by developing of new products and services. Again, core values promote the use of different integration methods to support increased coordination among all units in the organization.

Organizational values bind the workforce together by identifying and emphasizing acceptable forms of behavior. One of the most important forms of behavior is working together cooperatively. Cooperative work efforts reflect values of being goal-oriented and win-win oriented. Linking goals among the workforce ensures a bonded and committed workforce.

Common shared goals, reflecting core values, provide the following benefits.

1. **Goal-oriented**: Goals provide focus by setting targets to achieve through the efficient use of organizational resources.
2. **Concern for the workforce**: The workforce performs the work required to achieve the goals. Caring for the well-being of the workforce ensures reciprocity with the workforce committed to the success of the organization.
3. **Team-oriented:** job specialization means that no one individual provides a service or creates a product. Individuals need to work together if the organization is to succeed in achieving the strategic goals.
4. **Result-driven:** performance is essential to an organization's success and this means achieving the strategic goals and operational objectives.

5. **Reduce uncertainty:** a stable internal organizational environment relatively free of crises and workforce turmoil enables the workforce to focus on its primary mission, creating and supporting a successful organization.
6. **Innovative:** managed risk-taking practices reduces uncertainty but still encourages initiative within the workforce. Removing fear associated with what can happen with failure encourages the workforce to initiate ideas about new products and services as well as recommend different methods for creating operational efficiencies.

There are three primary sources that contribute to an organization's values. **Founders** of an organization possess values that serve as the basis for creating, building and maintaining an organization. As founders move on, new leadership assumes the leadership mantle. Senior leaders promoted from within the organization often are chosen to provide the continuity by keeping the values. Senior leaders selected from outside the organization frequently are recruited to promote an alternative set of values. Second, the **hiring processes** used to hire managers and non-managers follow **criteria** for selecting employees that will make a good fit within the existing culture or help influence a transition from the existing culture. The new criteria represent the values that the organization seeks to promote. Finally, through the **crucible of competing**, the organization learns the values associated with being successful. These values become part of the Code that moves the organization forward through the process of competing within a turbulent external environment.

Gillette: Part 1

A slow but steady decline in the stock price indicated that not was well at Gillette. Analysts retained positive ratings, noting the great dividend yield, the company's stock buyback program and rising sales as all positives. Several members of the Board of Directors were apprehensive about the company's future performance though. Dividends and the buyback program had their limits. Analysts were beginning to probe further into the company's finances and business practices. Huge bonuses for senior executives meant that there must be positive results unless the bonus program rewards business practices that benefitted the executives in the short run but hurt the company over the long-term. Discrete inquires turned up several serious concerns. First, costs were increasing at a higher rate than sales. Second, profit margins continued to decline. This trend was evident over the past several years. Third, stories about major retail customers complaining about being forced to order larger quantities of popular products and less popular products, less than wanted or end-user demand dictated. Apparently, the retailers were threatened with severe order restrictions if they did not accept the orders. The result led to excess inventory and the need to reduce prices to reduce inventory. Sales hurt profits because the retailers received no discounts on the larger orders. The board members arranged to meet privately at a nearby restaurant. Their agenda was simple. They wanted to understand the business practices at Gillette better.

Questions

1. Why were the Board members concerned about the business practices? Explain.
2. What are the values associated with the business practices?
3. Explain the problem with the bonus system.
4. Is trust an issue? Explain.
5. Why were the analysts fooled?

LEARNING OBJECTIVE #3: IDENTIFY AND DESCRIBE THE DIMENSIONS OF AN ORGANIZATION'S CULTURE AND THE IMPACT OF CULTURE ON AN ORGANIZATION'S PERFORMANCE

Another way to understand the concept, organizational culture, is to view an organization's culture from a **dimension's** perspective. Organizational culture is a complex concept to understand. The dimension's perspective is a useful methodology for understanding and explaining the important themes of an organization's culture. Using a dimension's model adds a cause-effect view in understanding how the issue of dimensions is useful in learning about an organization's culture. A dimension viewpoint describes a type of organizational action. Every dimension can be viewed as part of a continuum. As an organization moves toward one end of the continuum, the organization's response is greater or lesser depending on the direction the organization moves toward.

Involvement represents one type of dimension. Involvement represents the extent to which the organization's workforce is engaged and committed to an organization's success. Movement toward greater commitment means the workforce demonstrates a higher level of motivation in support of the organization's efforts to be successful. More than an intellectual commitment, the workforce's actions demonstrate great involvement. Greater involvement leads to the creation of work processes that increase the workforce's level of participation in organizational activities. The greater the participation of the workforce, the greater the organization's chances of success.

Adaptability is a dimension that reflects the ability of an organization to respond to external environmental issues by making strategic and/or operational changes. A non-response or slow response to external circumstances can undercut an organization's competitive efforts because of the unwillingness to change or a slow, tardy approach to change. The only constant is change, and the organization's external environment's dynamic nature guarantees the need to adjust, even if the changes are minor operational changes. The failure to adapt or a slow response puts the organization in a vulnerable position against competitors.

Organizations seek to function on a **consistent** basis. The management systems represent management methods developed to promote a consistent, stable, internal business environment. Consistency refers to work processes that operate in a predictable way, providing a predictable work environment that reduces risk associated with erratic business practices. Consistency helps a workforce spend less time on operational dysfunctions and more time working to achieve the strategic goals and operational objectives.

A **mission-driven** workforce represents another dimension of an organization's culture. Mission refers to an organization's sense of purpose, a reason for the organization's existence. An organization's mission commonly focuses on customers, products and unique ways to make products or deliver services. A vague or non-existent mission leaves the workforce with the only option available; each member of the workforce focuses on fulfilling personal reasons for being members of the organization.

An **innovative** organization is an organization on the move in two ways. An innovative organization is ambitious and demonstrates ambition through the development of new products and services. Innovation does not stop at this point. Innovative organizations also seek to leverage process technology along with management methods to create organizational efficiencies that achieve more challenging operational objectives.

An **assertive** organization represents an organization that is proactive in anticipating external events as well as responding to competitive trends in the external environment. Assertiveness is important because being assertive puts the organization on the front-end of the learning curve; partly by anticipating trends and partly by reacting quickly to trends. A non-assertive organization usually does not anticipate trends or fails to respond to trends adequately. The result is lost opportunities.

Goal-driven organizations use SMART type goals because SMART goals include the important elements of being measurable and time limited. Measurement enables the organization to assess performance compared to expectations (i.e. achieving the goal). Time limits create a sense of urgency among the workforce, emphasizing a "here and now" approach instead of some ambiguous future date. SMART goals have the built-in quality of providing focus, and the state of focus guides all workforce operational activities.

Too often organizations are viewed as machines, operating like a machine. Many senior leaders of some organizations operate with the premise that the organization is machine-like. However, the most successful senior leaders stress the importance of being **people focused**. These leaders realize that the success of an organization is attainable with a motivated workforce. Ensuring the well-being of the workforce results in a motivated workforce, which is tantamount to building a successful organization.

Because of the emphasis on job specialization, the formalization of the workforce's job descriptions results in a narrow focus of responsibilities and tasks to perform. Therefore, the individual efforts of employees fulfill the requirements of the job at the expense of the collective efforts of the workforce. Successful organizations take great pride in emphasizing a **team** approach to task performance. Organizations that stress the importance of a team approach develop a cooperative workforce eager to coordinate their efforts. The result is a successful organization.

The final example of a dimension of an organization's culture is the emphasis on being **detail oriented**. A detail orientation does not mean focusing on minutiae. A detail orientation refers to an organization that is thorough doing preparation work, delivering on its work efforts and satisfying customer needs. Thoroughness reduces uncertainty associated with the organization's actions by increasing the probability that actions will meet everyone's expectations.

Gillette: Part 2

Within six months of the private meeting among several senior members of the board, most analysts downgraded Gillette to a sell. This came just prior to the latest quarterly earnings announcement. In their reports on Gillette, the analysts alluded to questionable business practices, customer complaints and a bonus system that rewarded sales but not monetary sales but sales by quantity of the product. When Gillette announced their quarterly earnings, the stock price dropped precipitously. Performance was dismal. Company executives were not supported by analysts and large investors. Over the next few weeks, the negative news continued. Dividends were cut for the first time in company history. Profit margins were at historical lows, and analysts were recommending the stock as a turnaround, but this was not foreseeable in the next few years. Then, the news about the bonus system became public. The reaction was overwhelmingly negative. The company was playing with sales to influence the bonus system. Bonuses were not based on the stock's value. The Board immediately met and within days, announced that the CEO was stepping down. The Board announced the hiring of an outsider as the new CEO. The new CEO was known for being a successful turnaround specialist at other companies.

Questions

1. Why did the Board let the CEO go?
2. What was the Board trying to communicate to the outside world?
3. Why did the Board hire someone from the outside of the company? Explain.
4. What values did the Board want the new CEO to possess?
5. Identify the top three agenda items the new CEO identified to focus on? Explain.

LEARNING OBJECTIVE #4: IDENTIFY AND DESCRIBE THE DIFFERENT LEVELS OF AN ORGANIZATION'S CULTURE

Another way to approach understanding how organization's culture influences an individual's behavior involves learning about an organization's **cultural hierarchy**. A cultural hierarchy refers to different levels of influences on the behavior of individuals and an organization. Organizational culture represents an organization's values. Cultural hierarchy infers that there are distinct levels of culture, within an organization and outside of an organization; each level composed of influential values that impact behavior. An organization's attempt to change individual behavior is challenging because of the multiplicity of factors that contribute to the development of behavior shaping values.

One level of culture is represented by **national values**, embodied in the laws and regulations of national governments. A national government can be viewed as one large organization that governs the people. To create order within a nation, government sponsors laws and public policies to influence behavior. Laws and public policies reflect the national values that govern how to live, by following the behavioral standards set through the laws and public policies. Laws and public policies provide the parameters for setting behavioral standards, prescribing such issues of right from wrong, good from bad, acceptable and not acceptable behavior.

Societal values represent another form of cultural norms or ways to act. Societal values are universal customs that dictate how to behave. Societal values are non-legalistic but function much like laws and public policies but without the power of the national government to support societal customs. Societal values regulate behavior principally by influencing behavior among individuals (i.e. society). Within a society that encompasses a national boundary, there are regional and sub-regional societies that promote local values that influence an individual's behavior. For example, there is the Gullah Geechee nation of African Americans who live within a region encompassing the states of Georgia and South Carolina. These people have their own language and values as a sub-society within a larger regional society.

An industry is composed of multiple players that include suppliers, customers, economic conditions, substitute firms, international players and technology firms along with different types and sizes of competitors. These players reflect a collection of values that reflect a dynamic that influences the actions each player directly or indirectly. Successful organizations are those who can best fit within this **industry culture**.

At the next level is the **organization's culture**. As stated previously, an organization's culture encompasses the values of the organization. Organizations promote organizational values through a formal code of conduct, creating official organizational policies associated with the operations of the organization and the methods the organization uses to implement organizational policies. As an organization expands, the organization creates functional units and functional sub-units. These units have **unit cultures** because these units become homogeneous, less influenced by the organizational culture because of the segregation from other units. There is an overlap of values at the unit level, with behavior influenced by the organizational culture and by a unit's culture. The further a unit is isolated from the larger organization, the more the unit begins to develop a more unique culture of unit values.

Finally, individuals join organizations already possessing of **personal values**. The strength of these values influences the degree to which an organization can inculcate the organization's values within the individual. Over time, the organization's units' values become more influential because of the pressure to conform.

LEARNING OBJECTIVE #5: IDENTIFY AND EXAMINE THE DIFFERENT APPROACHES TO CREATE AND MAINTAIN AN ORGANIZATION'S CULTURE

Most management methods used to create and maintain an organization's culture are purposeful. But there is one situation where culture evolves from incidental actions of the organization. Dealing with external problems or **critical incidents** or **crises** forces the organization to operate outside of the organization's comfort zone. Initially, the organization responds to critical incidents originating outside of the organization using management methods learned from dealing with prior critical incidents. However, organizations soon learn that what worked in prior situations no longer lead to similar successes. Consequently, the actions of the organizations need to change to successfully manage the critical incidents. An organization's actions always reflect values because values influence all individual behavior within an organization. Actions manifest the organization's efforts at altering the organization's behavior to satisfactorily deal with critical incidents.

There are a several ways an organization can purposefully create and perpetuate the organization's culture. The original culture evolves to reflect the mark of the **founder(s)** values. Founder's actions reflect the founder's personal values that soon became the organization's values. The successors to founders and senior leaders typically role model the important values associated with the goal of maintaining the long-term success of the organization. Leadership serves as role models, demonstrating through their actions the values important to the organization's success.

The management systems represent important management methods organizations leverage to demonstrate and support the values important to the organization. The **performance management system** applies a variety of specific management methods to develop and support the values important to the organization. Individual and unit performance reviews represent formal processes that reflect values that emphasize unit/employee success by recognizing success as does failure, which leads to directives for changing behavior. The **reward system** (i.e. a sub-set of the motivation management system) is used to strengthen behavior the organization considers acceptable and important in the organization's efforts to be successful; the organization withholds rewards for non-acceptable behavior. The reward system in association with the performance management system can lead to dismissed individuals and groups of individuals if performance reflects the inability to achieve the organization's performance expectations (i.e. SMART goals and SMART operational objectives). The organization uses the **communication management system** to recognize success stories associated with individuals, units and the organization. The intent in publicizing success stories is to highlight the values symptomatic of these stories.

Organizational policies and the associated **work processes** linked to each policy reflect the values important to the organization. As the adage goes, "action always speaks louder than words." Policies serve to guide; work processes outline exactly how the organization expects individuals/units to perform a specific task.

Human Resources (HR) is an important management function in developing and overseeing the evolution of an organization's culture. HR creates the hiring policies and the hiring processes that include step(s) for learning if an individual is an acceptable fit to the organization. HR is responsible for creating the onboarding process, a process that can last up to a full year; a process that represents one of the organization's principle **socialization methods**. Socialization is an important means used by the organization to acculturate and integrate new employees to the organization. Creating job descriptions, formalizing individual performance review processes, providing guidelines for creating and managing teams and aiding in the development of an organization's code of conduct reflect HR's important role in creating and supporting the values integral to an organization's culture.

Gillette: Part 3

The new CEO met with senior leadership and announced that he was not hired to force everyone out; but that major changes in the company's business practices were necessary to reverse the negative performance trends and to re-ignite investor confidence in the company. He recorded a video for the benefit of all the employees. In the video, he discussed the dilemma the company confronted but projected a strong, positive and confident manner; emphasizing that by working together, the company can turn into a success story. There were four specifics on the "how to" at that time. Over the course of the next several weeks, the CEO made several announcements regarding important strategic initiatives to pursue. First, the Code of Conduct was modified to reflect new, important ethical values. Second, an emphasis on product innovation was THE new guiding principle. Product innovation would encourage customers to upgrade their products (e.g. new razors and new razor blades) and new products are high margin products. Cost control programs were being developed. First, cost containment was important. No increase in costs. Once successful, the focus would shift to cost reduction. Greater efficiencies lead to better margins. Management performance requirements were to change. The bonus system changed. Manager's bonuses were now based on how the organization performs, i.e. stock price increases. The performance management system will change to be numbers driven. The organization will switch to using SMART goals and SMART operational objectives. Everyone was expected to actively support the new initiatives.

Questions

1. What was the video intended to convey to the workforce?
2. What values were added to the Code? Explain.
3. What values are associated with product innovation? Explain.
4. Is cost control a value? Explain.
5. Is being numbers driven a value? Explain.

LEARNING OBJECTIVE #6: DISCUSS HOW AN ORGANIZATION'S CULTURE IMPACTS AN ORGANIZATION'S PERFORMANCE

One viewpoint among researchers regarding the association between an organization's culture and senior leaders of organizations is that an organization's culture has a tremendous impact on decisions made by senior leadership and an organization's actions. The focus of this section is to learn about and to better understand how an organization's culture impacts an organization's performance.

An organization's culture is composed of value-propositions. Values serve the organization in a similar way as values serve individuals. Values influence an individual's way of thinking which influences an individual's perceptions. Perceptions influence an individual's interpretation of observations which in turn influences how individuals act. Like the individual, an organization's values influence the organization's views as interpreted by senior leaders. An organization's view influences the organization's management processes created to respond to opportunities and threats from the organization's external environment and dysfunctional actions in the organization's internal environment. Interpreting this information is based on perceptions shaped by the values that influence the organization's viewpoint (which influences an organization's perceptions). The interpretation of the information leads to a behavioral response by the organization. Responding represents either a strategic or tactical move that positions the organization more favorably. The choice of strategy and/or tactics represents actions that synchronize with the organization's values.

Organizations have management systems and the labels used, such as information management system, organizational structure and performance management system, may be the same, but the design of these systems can vary. Variation is attributable to the values embedded within the organization's culture. What is important to know is that values influence perceptions, and perceptions (and the interpretation of what is observed) influence actions. Values influence the approaches taken in designing each type of management system. Value-based actions and value-influencing actions show in the policies associated with every management system and the work processes associated with implementing the policy.

Management systems, policies and organized work processes promote consistent types of behavior with the intent of reducing uncertainty associated with making decisions. Reduced uncertainty is associated with reducing risk by increasing the probability that the organization makes a good decision. Good decisions mean the organization is more likely to achieve the strategic goals and operational objectives. The values that support this application of management systems, policies and work processes included consistency, risk reduction and rationality. The organization seeks to follow a rational-legal model in managing the workforce. This is a guiding cultural value.

If an organization's culture is viewed as a collection of values, then the values represent the means used to improve an organization's chances of surviving into the future. Self-preservation is a value and goal because organizations live in a Darwinian world where there is no guarantee of surviving indefinitely.

An integrated workforce is viewed as an important factor associated with successful organizations. Social integration is the key link to workforce integration. A successful organization is an organization that can master the **workforce socialization process**. Understanding how the workforce socialization process operates is important because the organization learns how to apply this knowledge to improve the workforce socialization process. HR is often designated as the function that promotes social relations among the workforce. As stated earlier, designing a hiring process that includes screening candidates who can fit the social fabric is one method used to find the candidates that will best embrace the social milieu. Writing job descriptions that includes value propositions is another management method used to support the organization's culture. Selecting senior leaders who have a value proposition set that is compatible with the organization's values is another management method used to support an organization's culture. If changing values is the goal, HR looks for senior leaders with the sought-after values from outside the organization. These senior leaders serve as role models, promoting the values for subordinates to follow. The reward management system is an important management method for influencing the type of actions the organization seeks from the workforce. New values require new work processes and workers successfully implementing new work processes need to be rewarded for their efforts. Out with the old values and in with new values. Organizations cannot accept values that conflict (e.g. the value of honesty conflicts with the value of cheating customers).

An organization's culture is that hidden hand meant to influence workforce behavior, usually by appealing to an employee's intrinsic motivation, but also using performance assessments linked to the reward system.

LEARNING OBJECTIVE #7: DESCRIBE AND EXPLAIN THE LEVERS USED TO CHANGE AN ORGANIZATION'S CULTURE

If an organization's culture is instrumental in influencing an organization's performance, then making changes, when necessary, to an organization's culture needs to be a top priority of senior leadership. If an organization's culture is largely the product of a collection of values, then changing an organization's culture is a matter of changing values. Changing values can mean changing the intensity of an already held value or replacing and/or adding values.

Adding a new value, changing the intensity of a value or dropping a value is not about saying "let's be more customer-focused." Changing a value involves changing the socialization process of working together because the organization needs the workforce to commit to the proposed change. Changing the workforce's focus involves encouraging the workforce to invest the time and effort to make the change a success. The solution in gaining the workforce's commitment to change is to focus on activities associated with the new value(s). Successful performance contributes to the change in the sought-after value. In the example, the change is about being more customer focused. Changing relevant policies means changing the work processes linked to the policies.

There are levers decision-makers can use to influence the workforces' efforts; the best use of these levers will result in achieving the goal. One lever is the **performance management system**. Changing the operational objectives and the strategic goals associated with the performance management system initiates reaction in the workforce to successfully achieve these new ends. Changes in existing policies serve as new guides for the workforce to follow. With changes to policies come changes to existing work processes and/or adding new work processes. The result is the routinization of new work activities associated to achieve the strategic goals and operational objectives.

Changing work routines is insufficient to bring about the sought-after changes because the promoters of change need to overcome resistance to change. Resistance is due to the push to get the workforce to breakout of its comfort zone or routine way to perform a work process. The use of the **motivation or reward system** is necessary to influence the perception that change is necessary and that successful change gets rewarded in some form. Often, organizations use incentive programs as a motivation method. Typical incentive programs are short-term, have a measurable performance objective (e.g. 10% increase in customer sales) with a time-limit and offer a tangible reward. The combination of motivation system linked to the performance management system increases the workforce's commitment to change.

Another system for bringing about change to an organization's culture is to focus on **quality management**. Quality implies making something better or performing a service in a particular manner. To make quality improvements more substantive, quality is frequently defined using measurable standards. One of the values associated with quality management is the focus on identifying measurable standards to use as goals. For example, the performance of cashiers at a supermarket can mean saving one minute off the average time per customer served and with an increase in customer satisfaction over the time taken to process the customer's order.

Requiring workers to work together in **teams** represents another method for facilitating integration of the workforce to bring about changes to the organizational culture and sub-cultures (see the prior discussion about levels of culture). A workforce unfamiliar with working in teams, but now required to work in teams, will result in drastic change to all the relevant work processes. Even if workers already work in teams, the organization might seek to make teams a more common method for accomplishing work. Gaining a greater commitment from the workforce to the team concept is straightforward. Teams must accomplish operational objectives that force team members to work together, and the successful teams receive benefits for their success; typically, one benefit is associated with an incentive program. One aspect of management's role in moving toward a team-based model is to guide the workforce transition through the transition process.

The **knowledge management system's** purpose is to facilitate organizational learning. Seeking new knowledge is an example of a value. The knowledge management system's link to the external environment is meant to keep the organization current on activities occurring in the external environment that affect the organization's performance. Opportunities need to be pursued and threats countered. Dealing with different situations typically requires learning new approaches to successfully address the situation. New approaches result in changes to the organization's culture because of the need to adapt. The intent of organizational learning is to identify action-type ideas generated from the **innovation management system** to develop a successful response (i.e. work process(es)).

LEARNING OBJECTIVE #8: DISCUSS THE RELATIONSHIP BETWEEN LEADERSHIP AND ORGANIZATIONAL CULTURE

Suggested earlier, an organization's senior leadership is critical in maintaining an organization's culture as well as making changes to an organization's culture. At an organization's founding, the founders impress their values on the organization. Through the actions of the founders, important values dominate, and less important values are of secondary importance or diminish being relevant to the performance of the organization. Eventually, founders leave the scene. But because founders view the organization as their "child," founders make every effort to recruit successors that model the values of the founders. Founders do this by helping to prepare job descriptions for leadership positions and to involve themselves during the recruitment and hiring processes. As senior leaders retire, like their predecessors, senior leaders seek out individual successors that match these values, believing that their values are critical to the ongoing success of the organization.

Senior leaders serve as role models for subordinates, demonstrating their priorities through their actions. Because every action performed in a work process connects to one or more values, subordinates recognize that a successful, long-term role in the organization requires accepting the values by performing the work processes.

Leaders select the strategic goals for the organization to achieve. Goals often exemplify raising the performance bar, which sets in motion the necessary operational changes needed to achieve the strategic goals. For example, efficiency goals such as increasing profit margins from 30% to 35% require an examination on how to better utilize organizational resources. Cost control and profit margins become two important values now emphasized by senior leaders.

As the organization's important change agents, senior leaders are responsible for ensuring that the management systems function effectively and with purpose. Maintaining an organization's culture is one of the principle responsibilities of managers overseeing the functioning of the management systems because the systems affect the organization's performance and reinforce the culture. Two important management systems used by senior leaders to maintain an organization's culture are the motivation management system and the performance management system. Motivation management entails the use of rewards to recognize that subordinates performed the modified work processes successfully. Behavior associated with performing pre-determined work processes is associated with organizational policies that define the work processes and more often, a work process's operational objectives. Success in achieving a work process operational objective (s) is rewarded. Failure to perform leads to no rewards or even punitive actions, such as termination. Leaders leverage the performance management system to identify performance indicators that become operational objectives to assess successful performance or substandard performance.

Gillette: Part 4

Many senior managers and middle managers, near retirement, decided to leave. Internal candidates, supportive of the new initiatives and new company vision, were appointed to fill the vacant positions. Succeeding quarterly earnings reports indicated steady progress in reducing costs, increasing profits and improving market share. Analysts started showing interest in the company. Some analysts even began to recommend giving thought to purchasing shares. Part of the enthusiasm was due to positive comments coming from large retail customers and from consumer surveys. Customers liked the new business practices and consumers were extremely positive about all the new products. Analysts liked the emphasis on measuring performance by focusing on numbers and not qualitative information. Analysts also liked that Gillette practiced a new reporting system that kept analysts updated on all company news and trends. The turnaround was succeeding, and the stock price showed that investors were becoming positive about the company again.

Questions

1. What are the important values the new managers need to demonstrate? Explain why?
2. Why did analysts value a numbers focus? Explain.
3. What values does the new reporting process reveal? Explain.
4. What management methods did the new CEO use to initiate change?
5. If you were the CEO, what else would you do to build more support among customers and investors? Why investors?

LEARNING OBJECTIVE #9: DISCUSS THE APPLICATION OF THE LEWIN MODEL IN CREATING CHANGING AN ORGANIZATION'S CULTURE

The Lewin Model is a change management model intended to provide a process to following in bringing about successful organizational change. The purpose of this model is to offer a structured, systematic approach in understanding how to successfully bring about change. In this section, the focus is on describing how to apply the Lewin Model to initiate changes to an organization's culture. There are three major stages to the Lewin Model. Stage one is the **unfreeze stage**. During the unfreeze stage the emphasis is on providing **empirical evidence** to demonstrate the need for change. Empirical evidence or hard data need to demonstrate unequivocally and to provide support for changes to an organization's culture. Support from senior leaders championing the change helps to justify the need for change and initiate the process of overcoming the resistance to change. Since an organization's culture is viewed as the glue that binds an organization together, senior leaders must convince the workforce that the "glue" is less effective and likely will become less effective in the future.

Loss of market share, extended product development cycles compared to competitors, declining profit margins, a decline in same store sales, etc., represent examples of empirical, factual evidence to support change. Resistance can still occur so part of the **empirical picture** drawn must include how competitors are moving forward at the expense of the organization.

The second stage of the model is the **change stage**. During the change stage, senior leaders **pilot** specific types of programs, policies and work processes, focusing on units or sub-units most willing to advance the recommended initiatives. Piloting the new programs, policies and work processes is meant to test the changes to ensure that the new initiatives work as prescribed and that all participants understand and support the new initiatives. It is during this stage where trial and error questions arise and modifications to the new initiatives occur to ensure that the changes are successful.

Once successful changes occur during the pilot stage, stage three is the **re-freeze stage**. During the re-freeze stage successful changes, led by senior leaders, are applied extensively throughout the organization. Leaders leverage a variety of management methods to routinize the changes and to gain the full commitment of the workforce. Routinization is necessary to ensure there is no regression back to the original programs, policies and work processes. Below is a list of important management methods that senior leaders have used to champion new ideas and to ensure acceptance of the new ideas and the successful integration of the new ideas into the operations.

- **Training programs:** Training helps to educate the workforce impacted by the changes to ensure that the workforce understands the reasons for the changes; the role of the affected workforce in the change process; and how the workforce can implement the changes to the work processes successfully.
- **Motivation system:** The use of rewards associated with successful implementation of the changes is meant to strengthen the commitment of the workforce.
- **Performance management system:** Identifying operational objectives in the form of performance indicators helps keep the workforce focused and committed.
- **Co-joining professional goals and organizational goals**: Linking the goals of the workforce with the goals of the organization is meant to strengthen the workforce's commitment to the success of the organization and the organization's commitment to the workforce.
- **Communication management system**: Change is always a challenging endeavor, in part because of the workforce's resistance to change; change involves moving from the known to the unknown. The message associated with the changes helps to clarify the what's, why's and how's. Successful changes are important to publicize throughout the organization to inform resisters that successful change is doable.

The change process is meant to modify the workforce's mindset such that change becomes viewed as a positive effort to embrace and not something meant to fear.

LEARNING OBJECTIVE #10: IDENTIFY AND DESCRIBE THE MANAGEMENT METHODS USED FOR MAINTAINING AN ORGANIZATIONAL CULTURE

There are a variety of management methods available for organizations to use to maintain an organization's culture. Maintaining an organization's culture implies supporting the values reflected in the culture. The management methods that follow represent some of the most common management methods often used. Furthermore, successful organizations frequently use a variety of management methods rather than rely on only one method.

- **Employee Selection Criteria**: With guidance from HR, an organization usually includes as part of each job description personal values sought by the organization.
- **Reward System**: Organizations design the reward system to recognize the contributions of individuals and units that perform according to the organization's expectations.
- **Code of Conduct**: Developed to reflect the important ethical standards and values held in high regard by the organization. Employers often require employees to review the Code annually.
- **Training Programs**: Whether technical or non-technical training, organizations always emphasize what are the important organizational values during training.

- **Onboarding**: Onboarding represents a systematic approach to acculturate new employees over a certain period, typically no longer than one year.
- **Orientation:** Orientation is a short-term method used to familiarize new employees with the basics necessary to begin the process of assimilating within the organization. Often, orientation is the first stage of the onboarding process.
- **Goals:** The process for identifying goals forces leadership at all levels to work together because achieving goals frequently requires the collective efforts of leadership. Agreement on goals represents the mutual agreement of the values associated with the goals along with the values in following a goal-identification process.
- **Strategy and The Strategy Development Process:** Strategy represents the organization's plan for achieving the strategic goals. The strategy development process represents a systematic approach senior leaders follow to arrive at a single strategy agreeable to senior management.
- **Teams:** Teams are frequently used to force the workforce to work together to fulfill the team's purpose. Group Think is the result. A positive view associated with Group Think is that group decisions reflect the collective views of team members.
- **Loyalty Programs:** This is an example of programs, such as acknowledging an employee's length of service by publicly recognizing the individual and providing an award of some form to recognize the employee's commitment to the organization (e.g. certificate of accomplishment).
- **Policies:** Policies represent an organization's official position on a work-related issue and how organizational members need to implement the policy. Policy connotes right from wrong, good from bad and excellent from poor. Policy sets standards of acceptable versus unacceptable behavior.
- **Career Ladders:** A career ladder is meant to provide a means for encouraging employees to commit to the organization over a long period of time. A career ladder enables the organization to recognize and reward employee's dedication to the organization.
- **Career Development Programs:** Spearheaded by HR, the focus of career development programs is to provide career enhancing opportunities in return for the employee's commitment to the well-being of the organization.
- **Operational Objectives:** Like goals, operational objectives force workers to work together to ensure a successfully functioning work process because every work process creates measurable results.
- **Hierarchy:** Having a formal chain of command reinforces the commitment to an orderly, formalized approach in making decisions and communicating decisions throughout the organization.

Chapter Summary

Often referred to as the "glue" that holds an organization together, organizational culture is an elusive concept to grasp. This chapter attempts to help readers understand the concept, organizational culture, by examining the idea from a variety of perspectives. First, the chapter suggests that organizational culture is based on a collection of core values. Values are part of an organization's official Code of Conduct, which emphasizes ethical values but also there are organizational values deeply embedded with all the organization's work activities.

Values are important to organizations as much as values are important to individuals because values influence behavior. For an organization, values influence all organizational actions. Actions refer to work processes that are shaped by organizational policies; policies are organized by the type of management system associated with the policy.

Much of this chapter examines how organizational culture impacts an organization's performance. The chapter provides the reader with a dimensional view of an organization's culture to reduce the concept's complexity. An organization's dimensions can contribute to the development of an organization's culture associated with a successful organization.

Added to this issue of complexity is the notion that there are levels to an organization's culture, and that as organizations evolve and grow over time, part of the evolution includes the development of organizational sub-cultures.

Creating an organization's culture, supporting the existing organizational culture and changing an organization's culture represent important capabilities required to ensure that an organization remains adaptable to external environmental issues that offer an organization opportunities for being more successful but also can threaten the organization's competitive position. The chapter identifies and describes several management methods that enable an organization to build and maintain an organizational culture that supports the organization's ability to survive and remain competitive.

Chapter Questions

1. Explain why an organization's culture is important to an organization.
2. What are the sources of values that are reflected by an organization's culture?
3. What are the dimensions of an organization's culture and why is dimensions an important subject?
4. Identify and briefly describe the different levels of an organization's culture.
5. How can an organization create an organizational culture?
6. Discuss the association between an organization's culture and an organization's performance.
7. What are the levers to use in changing an organization's culture?
8. How do leaders impact an organization's culture?
9. Identify and briefly describe any five management methods to use in maintaining an organization's culture.
10. Why is it difficult to identify and describe an organization's culture?

Bibliography

GothamCulture (2019). What is organizational culture? https://gothamculture.com/what-is-organizational-culture-definition/.

Katzenbach, J., Oelschlegel, C. & Thomas, J. (2016). 10 principles of organizational culture. *Strategy & Business*. Spring 2016 (82). 1–47.

Kilts, J.M. (2007). *Doing What Matters*. Three Rivers Press.

Maseko, T.S.B. (2017). Strong vs. weak organizational culture: assessing the impact on employee motivation. *Arabian Journal of Business Management Review*. 7:287.

Morrison, M. (2014). Kurt Lewin change theory three step model-unfreeze, change, freeze.

July 7. Rapidbi. https://rapidbi.com/kurt-lewin-three-step-change-theory/.

Nikpour, A. (2017). The impact of organizational culture on organizational performance: the mediating role of employee's commitment. *International Journal of Organizational Leadership.* 6. 65–72.

Schein, E.H. 91990). Organizational culture. *American Psychologist.* 45(2). 109–119.

Schneider, B., Ehrhart, M.G. & Maley, W.H. (2013). Organizational climate and culture. *Annual Review of Psychology.* 64. 361–388.

Society for Human Resource Management (2018). Understanding and developing organizational culture. August 13. https://www.shrm.org/resources and tools/tools-and-samples/toolkits/ pages/understanding and developing organizational culture/.

Treven, S., Mulej, M. & Lynn, M. (2008). The impact of culture on organizational behavior. *Management.* 13(2). 27–39.

Westrum, R. (2004). A typology of organizational cultures. *Quality & Safety in Health Care.* 13(Suppl-II). Ii22–ii27.

Change Management in Organizations

OVERVIEW

"The only constant is change." Yet, organizations operate as if change is a bad thing that should never occur. Instead of embracing change, organizations too often lament disruptions to routines without realizing that change is part of an organization's lifeblood. This explains the use of the popular metaphor of organizations as machines without realizing that a machine's performance gets disrupted for a variety of reasons. The real issue is that people don't like disruptions unless the disruption is part of an overall plan.

This chapter provides the reader with an understanding of the subject, change management, and that two causes of change drive changes in the organization. The **external environment** of an organization is one source. The external environment is a dynamic and unpredictable source for disruptors that frequently compel an organization to operate outside of standard practices. This external environment is uncontrollable. The organization can only control how it responds. Second, there is the organization's **internal environment**. The organization's internal environment is a dynamic source of all types of changes as the organization becomes more ambitious by expanding its operations. This chapter describes the concept of change management because change management represents a rational-logical, systematic approach for successfully managing the change process. The goal of change management is to minimize disruptions to the organization's management systems and work processes, while leading to a better performing organization. Change management models offer theory-supported approaches an organization's senior leadership can consider in initiating organizational change. The chapter introduces the reader to the more popular change management models used by organizations to guide the change process.

Resistance to change and organizational barriers to change represent types of impediments organizations need to master to facilitate successful change. This chapter identifies and describes the causes of resistance to change by individuals and the different types of organizational barriers that change leaders need to overcome. Strategies for confronting and overcoming resistance and organizational barriers aid the reader in understanding that resistance and barriers do not need to be long-lasting impediments to change.

Accepting that change is inevitable often leads organizations to be pro-active in creating the capabilities to apply the change management models. On the other hand, many organizations, in denial that change is inevitable, act as if the situation is novel and erroneously assume that acting once the problem is solved, the situation requiring change will never re-occur. This chapter examines how organizations develop pro-active change management practices and identifies and describes the choices to follow in resolving the situation.

Finally, this chapter explores the issue of the effectiveness of organizational change practices. Most researchers claim that only 33–66% of all change management projects are successful. The critical comments of researchers about the performance results of change management projects imply that the record should be 100%. The chapter examines reasons why change management projects do not always succeed as well as offering an alternative view that 33–66% success rate might be a positive trend. Explanations to justify a positive view of the performance numbers help the reader understand an alternative viewpoint in assessing the performance of change agents.

CHAPTER 8   LEARNING OBJECTIVES

Readers will achieve the following learning objectives after reading this chapter.

1. Define, explain and discuss the issues of change and change management.
2. Identify and describe the external environmental factors that trigger the need for organizational change.
3. Identify and discuss internal organizational factors that initiate the need for organizational change.
4. Identify, describe and discuss the types of changes that require the application of a change management model.
5. Discuss why change management involves following a process approach to apply change management.
6. Identify and review the major change management models and the themes of the models.
7. Identify the different forms of resistance and explain the reasons why individuals resist change.
8. Identify and describe the organizational barriers to change and provide examples of management methods used to overcome organizational barriers.
9. Identify and describe traditional management methods used to overcome an individual's resistance to change.
10. Discuss the issues' pro-active change management and reactive change management.
11. Identify and examine the reasons for less than expected results from change management practices in organizations.

LEARNING OBJECTIVE #1: DEFINE, EXPLAIN AND DISCUSS THE ISSUES OF CHANGE AND CHANGE MANAGEMENT

Frequently heard is the phrase "the only constant is change." Too often, **change** is viewed negatively instead of as a normal function of life for individuals and organizations. What makes change unwelcome is because either the change was unplanned or intended, but the changes did not meet expectations. Change is disruptive to routines. For the organization, this means that change disrupts work processes, contributing to inefficiencies and the failure to achieve organizational goals and operational objectives.

Change can be categorized as either **planned** or **unplanned**. Causal factors for planned types of changes for individuals include change in **personal goals** and the development of a plan to achieve the personal goals. To succeed in achieving personal goals requires initiating such changes as new routines and/or modifying existing routines. A **crisis** is another cause for initiating changes in an individual's life. The extent of the changes is dictated by the scope of the crisis. The **unexpected non-crisis** is another source of change. The individual's initial reaction is to solve the situation using temporary solutions, expecting to eventually return to the status quo.

Like individuals, organizations deal with both planned and unplanned causes of change. The causes of planned changes often originate from an organization's ambitions which stem from the organization creating a new **vision, strategic goals** and **strategy** that initiate organizational change. These strategic management issues generate change because these are future-oriented. The organization needs to make **operational changes** to successfully implement the overall corporate strategy to achieve the strategic goals to accomplish the vision. Organizations often confront the unexpected as well as crises. Each of these situations occurs outside of an organization's control. The scope of each of these causes of change can vary, but an organization's size often influences the number of crises and unplanned events that can occur. Why? The larger and more ambitious the organization, the greater the likelihood of confronting a crisis and dealing with the unexpected because of the scope of the organization's activities. Doing more means more can happen.

Change management represents a proactive approach to successfully manage the change process by using a systematic, theory-based approach that focuses the organization's efforts in achieving the goals or endpoints of the **change management process**. Change management involves following a process that outlines the steps, if performed efficiently, required to achieve success in achieving the strategic goals.

What makes applying a systematic, theory-based change management methodology important is the fact that organizations are not usually successful in projects that do not fully follow change management methods. Researchers show that anywhere between 33 and 66% of projects using change management method are successful. The implications are clear. Organizations are not managing the change process as well as expected.

However, there are no research studies showing if there are certain types of change management projects that are the most successful change management projects and which types of change management projects that are the least successful. We can surmise that simple, short-term, work process types of change management projects are most likely to have a higher success rate than transformational types of change projects where the focus is nothing less than the revision of the organization's prevailing business model.

Change management is such an important activity that several organizational researchers developed **change management theories**. The purpose of these theory-based approaches to change management is to offer the practitioner of change management a better understanding of the concept of change management; the importance of following a systematic approach to change management and to provide guidelines that demonstrate an approach to successfully bring about systematic, successful changes.

The change management models emphasize several important points.

- Changing the mindsets of individuals affected by the change is critical.
- Overcoming the inhibitors of change is one of the important themes of each model.
- Managing the change process with minimal disruptions is optimal.
- A commitment to successful change management by senior leadership is essential to the potential success of a change project.

LEARNING OBJECTIVE #2: IDENTIFY AND DESCRIBE THE EXTERNAL ENVIRONMENTAL FACTORS THAT TRIGGER THE NEED FOR ORGANIZATIONAL CHANGE

The interactions with **external environmental factors** that fall outside of an organization's control initiate changes within the organization, even if the organization is unwilling to change. Organizations can be fully reactionary and wait, hoping that the external conditions change back; if not, to vary but minimally respond or the organization can anticipate potential external changes and begin the change process sooner. The former offers the advantage of knowing the actual circumstances and responding to the actual conditions. The advantage of the latter is that the organization initiates the change process to avoid the scale of the consequences that can come from waiting. What is evident is that waiting on the conditions to emerge or initiating change before the conditions become evident offer advantages and risks for decision-makers to consider when determining which approach works best.

One external factor is a **hostile takeover** attempt by another organization. Whether successful or not, a hostile takeover forces an organization to change in response. Either the organization acquiesces to the takeover and begins the process of being absorbed or the organization creates the capabilities to try and fight the takeover attempt. Change is inevitable in either situation.

A category of factors contributing to organizational change is the **industry** an organization operates within. In an industry, there are a variety of different organizations that create a **dynamic** within this network of organizations. Each organization acts independently and with only self-interest its driving force. One group of organizations includes existing **competitors** that jostle for a better competitive position as does every organization, regardless of size. Some organizations initiate change and act, and others are reactors and act accordingly. The roles of each type of competitor can change, initiators can become reactors and reactors can become initiators. Organizations of all sizes can change their competitive practices, ushering in a domino effect that involves all competitors, directly or indirectly, who respond in some way.

Suppliers to organizations in the industry represent another category of organizations. Suppliers can change their competitive approaches, initiating a chain reaction among the buyers along with other suppliers. Powerful suppliers that make major changes likely will have an impact on other suppliers as well as among organizations supplied.

The action of **powerful customers** can result in changes directly with organizations that meet their needs and indirectly to suppliers to the competitors who sell to customers. Customers that are organizations wield more power than individuals because these organizations purchase bulk quantities of items. Market segments or groupings of different types of customers can be powerful too if a market segment is large, and there are many competitors to purchase from. For example, if an organization uses a cooking ingredient that is considered potentially unhealthy for senior citizens. Senior citizens can switch to a similar competitor using a healthy ingredient during food preparation.

The prospect of **new competitors** entering an industry is always a threat unless the barriers to entry are enough to discourage entry. Organizations often change in ways to forestall the threat of new entrants, whether real or speculative. Finally, there is the threat from **substitutes** which is potentially serious. Substitutes are a real concern to an organization that might need to respond quickly if the threat is credible, real, immediate and customer interest high.

Environmental factors represent another external factor composed of elements that can hasten an organization's efforts to change. Environmental factors impact all organizations either positively or negatively. In either scenario, change must occur in response. One important element is a country's **economy**. A growing economy means that the organization needs to change to take advantage of prevailing opportunities. A declining economy requires an organization to change to withstand the duration and scope of bad economic conditions to be able to survive.

Socio-cultural factors represent another element that can cause changes to occur within an organization. Socio-cultural factors refer to demographic trends, such as an aging baby boomer group, values and beliefs of the population or values and beliefs of a significant market segment within the general population. For example, an aging baby boomer population means greater need for pharmaceuticals, medical devices, increased hospital care, increased demand for nursing home hours and additional home healthcare services. Organizations need to respond to the opportunities these trends present while other organizations might consider these trends as threats to respond to but for different reasons.

Political-legal factors force changes within organizations. The recent tariff conflict between the United States and China has an impact on all organizations directly and indirectly, caught in the struggle over trade regulations and the tariff restrictions. Here is another example. Years ago, at the height of the Vietnam War, the drinking age switched from 21 to 18 because many soldiers were under the age of 21. All types of organizations needed to respond to the lowered age limit. Several years later, the drinking age reverted to 21 because of all the vehicular accidents. All types of organizations needed to respond to the new drinking age.

International events can have a profound impact on organizations directly and indirectly. If a war or political upheaval occurred, organizations that operate in that country need to respond in some way to deal with these circumstances. If the crisis is in an oil-producing country that provides a large percentage of the world's oil, the issue in that country can impact organizations worldwide until the situation is resolved.

Finally, changes in **technology** represent either an opportunity or threat. There are three types of technology. **Process technology** aimed at creating operational efficiencies. There is **input technology** that can improve a product materially and lower a product's cost, such as using new types of materials to make cell phone glass screens. Finally, there is **product technology**. Product technology refers to adding new features to a product to enhance the products appeal to potential customers. Technological factors create tremendous opportunities for organizations that must change to take advantage of the opportunity. But technology can represent a threat to an organization that fails to take advantage of the technology or that competitors respond faster.

LEARNING OBJECTIVE #3: IDENTIFY AND DISCUSS INTERNAL ORGANIZATIONAL FACTORS THAT INITIATE THE NEED FOR ORGANIZATIONAL CHANGE

There are several internal organizational conditions that represent major causes of change that originate from within the organization. Each of these conditions represent typical and atypical types of causes of change. Successfully managing these conditions is necessary to achieve strategic goal and/or operational objectives.

New **senior leadership** is always a signal that changes in the organization are imminent. New leadership will always want to place their mark on the organization by impacting the organization's performance. The association with successful performance symbolizes that the selection of senior leaders was the correct choice. Sometimes, senior leadership is recruited from outside of the organization to improve the organization's performance. The obvious is obvious to everyone, change is coming and only the scope and magnitude of the change is open to conjecture.

Poor performance by the organization, a unit, a sub-unit or a team is always a harbinger that change is coming. Organizations are not in the business to accept poor performance over an extended period. Underperformance by even a team can begin to impact an entire organization because the neglect to correct performance begins to have a negative effect on other teams; this behavior becomes a part of the organization's culture.

The pressure to generate greater and greater **operational efficiencies** is omnipresent. One reason is to create more profits to re-invest in the business. Another reason is to offset competitive pressures that can force price reductions and therefore the need to maintain profit margin goals. Finally, an organization's culture can prioritize the value of continuous and ongoing improvement which is applicable to furthering efforts at making certain the organization has a more efficient operation.

The following represent additional internal reasons that contribute to changes in an organization.

- **Merger**: Two organizations might decide to join under one corporate umbrella. As a single entity, there is the need to integrate the two organizations' operations seamlessly.
- **Downsize**: An organization decides that earnings, profits and costs do not justify the size of the organization. Consequently, the organization institutes consolidation efforts among the workforce to streamline operations.
- **Acquisition**: An organization can decide to acquire another organization. As a result of this decision, the acquiring organization needs to craft a plan to integrate the acquisition into the operations.
- **Bankruptcy**: Filing for bankruptcy initiates various types of operational changes ranging from closing the organization to consolidating operations on a smaller scale.
- **Outsourcing**: An organization might decide that manufacturing through another organization makes for a more profitable business. As a result, the organization's manufacturing unit(s) are downsized or eliminated. Furthermore, the organization needs to create the capability to work with the manufacturing partner on a routine basis.
- **Legal**: Laws and government policies can change, resulting in the need for organizations to respond to comply with the new laws and policies.
- **Organizational Size**: Ambitious organizations grow leading to increases in the workforce. Adding more members to the workforce and adding individual's with specialized job skills result in some form of organizational re-structuring.
- **Evolution of an Organization's Culture**: Organizational cultures are not static but are dynamic, constantly evolving due to changes in the composition of the workforce, competitive conditions and in response to environmental climate organizations live within.
- **Changes to Functions**: Organizations can determine that there is a need for a new function such as inventory management and/or the need for a new sub-function such as job analysis. As a result, the organization needs to integrate these functions into the organization's existing structure.
- **Change to Management Systems**: Senior leadership and middle management constantly review the performance of the various management systems with the goal of improving operational performance.

LEARNING OBJECTIVE #4: IDENTIFY, DESCRIBE AND DISCUSS THE TYPES OF CHANGES THAT REQUIRE THE APPLICATION OF A CHANGE MANAGEMENT MODEL

The application of change management models is intended to facilitate successful change. Success is often probabilistic, with the probability of success strengthened using a team of **change agents** who possess the knowledge, skills and personal attributes as well as successful change management experiences to ensure that the recommended changes are feasible. Unfortunately, the demand for such a group of change management agents far exceeds any organization's ability to provide this capability fully. In short, the need for change typically exceeds the organization's ability to facilitate the changes using organizational experts. This does not mean that successful change cannot be accomplished. Organizations need to group change management projects into categories with major types of changes a higher priority warranting the need for a team of expert change agents. Other teams of change agents utilize less-experienced individuals assigned to the task of facilitating change. These types of change projects might involve the use of simplified, easy-to-follow change management models.

There are several types of change management projects warranting the full use of a team of change management agents using a comprehensive change management model. One type of change is **transformational change**. Transformational change involves a change in an organization's mission, vision and/or strategy. Changes triggered by these issues mean that the focus of the change is comprehensive, affecting the entire organization.

Management systems changes is another category of changes warranting the involvement of a team of experienced change management agents because even if one management system is the focus, the impact on the organization is broad. Often, a change in one management system initiates the need to make changes to one or more additional management systems. A management systems comprehensiveness in an organization means that a failed result has broad consequences as does a constructive change show strong positive result. In short, management systems link together to a larger network of management systems.

Change projects that require the active and ongoing **involvement of senior leadership** warrant the need to use a team of change management agents. Senior leadership is often over extended, always requiring the need to prioritize the use of their time. Senior leadership's ongoing involvement in a change management project implies that senior leaders recognize the value of the project and the importance of demonstrating a commitment to a successful change intervention.

Structural changes warrant the need to involve an experienced change management team because any type of structural changes likely impacts the entire workforce. As a result, significant levels of resistance will occur because structural changes involve re-configuring established social relationships, some of which might have existed for several years. Only using a team of experienced change management agents along with involving senior leadership, would the chance for successful structural changes result.

Changes in the organization that impact on a **function** warrant the need for intervention by a team of experienced change management agents. Organizations cannot afford to negatively impact customers because of organizational actions. Customers can be driven to competitors, lost forever. If not lost, customer sentiment toward the organization can turn negative, potentially impacting future customer retention.

There are change projects that are **technically complex** to manage successfully. These types of change management projects require a team of experts who possess the type of knowledge, skills, personal abilities and record of accomplishments that demonstrate the potential for successfully overseeing a technically oriented change management project.

Finally, changes to an **organization's culture** warrant the use of a team of change management agents because these types of projects are comprehensive, affect large numbers of people, involve changing the mindset of individuals and require a high level of sophistication to master changing a complicated subject such as changing an organization's culture.

Deutsche Bank: Part 1

In a meeting that included the CFO, COO and co-chairs of the Board of Directors, the CEO reviewed the final plan outlining the move to re-organize the bank. Negative publicity regarding the bank's business practices in the United States only reinforced the urgency to implement the re-organization plan, transforming the bank's focus by concentrating on core businesses that serve European companies and companies serving Europe. Profitability was always a random thing at the bank. Some years, profits were high, and in other years, profits were disappointing. Everyone agreed that more consistent performance was necessary. Everyone accepted that the bad publicity and variable profitability were due primarily to the actions of the Investment Banking Services (IBS) in the United States. The plan is to reduce the size of IBS in the United States. The bank will reduce the overall workforce by 18,000 employees by 2022. So, 9000 employees in the United States will be cut. The goal is to reduce costs and gain consistent profits. Everyone agreed that this is a risky but necessary transformational plan.

Questions

1. What makes the plan a transformational plan?
2. Why eliminate 18,000 jobs? Explain.
3. Why re-focus on Europe? Explain.
4. What did the IBS branch do in the United States that contributed to downsizing?
5. What were the reasons IBS could act as it did? Explain.

LEARNING OBJECTIVE #5: DISCUSS WHY CHANGE MANAGEMENT INVOLVES FOLLOWING A PROCESS APPROACH TO APPLY CHANGE MANAGEMENT

All actions by individuals involve some type of routine. A routine in an organization represents a **formal work process**. Formal work processes embody a standardized, logical and systematic arrangement of a series of steps or stages that have a start point, an endpoint and stages between each of these points. Processes evolve over time but by initiating the design of work processes, the organization wants to ensure that the work process adheres to a **planned, systematic methodology**. The roots of this systems perspective are the **rational-logical science-based model** in which logic and pragmatism are applicable in every type of process application. **Scientific management** provides the management roots for this model.

Researchers examining successful change management projects identified that the following factors believed to contribute to the success of these projects.

- **Well-Planned**: Change management agents followed a comprehensive approach in managing a change management project. Change management agents followed a change management model to ensure that the approach taken was comprehensive to ensure coverage of all the important issues.

- **Goal-Oriented**: Change management projects were focused by using SMART goals. SMART goals enable the change management agents to assess project progress on an ongoing basis to ensure that their efforts were meeting success or to make changes if performance was less than expected.
- **Timeliness**: By selecting a project, the assumption is that the project received the okay from all the relevant leaders and those of the workforce most affected. Everyone is eager to make the changes, and the change management agents are eager to get the project underway.
- **Integrated**: Successful change management projects show that change management agents followed a comprehensive, theory-based approach in facilitating change. Comprehensiveness involved making certain that all parts of the change management plan fit together, like pieces to a puzzle and remained linked throughout the duration of the change management project.

A formalized, standardized change management project provides the following benefits to change management agents and others with limited knowledge, skills and experience in applying change management models.

- A process orientation involves identifying all the important stages and that the stages follow a prescribed sequence. This approach aims to promote a **thorough**, routine approach to managing a change management project.
- A formalized change management project represents a **standardized model** replicable for future change management projects. This approach enables all practitioners of change management practices, experts and non-experts to hasten learning the specific project process to follow.
- **Training** individuals to learn the various change management models and change management practices is strengthened by having specific subjects to focus training on. This strengthens the training program experience. This improves the prospects of implementing successful change management projects.
- Following a process method means that there is a measurable outcome that offers a **focused** approach to process management; goal endpoint facilitates performance management practices associated with measuring a change management projects' level of success. A process method enables change management agents to report **project progress** to leadership overseeing the change management project. Leadership preference is to hear about a project's level of progress. A process approach to change management enables change management agents to apply a **checklist method** for assessing progress in completing each stage of a project.

Deutsche Bank: Part 2

Heinrich, the COO, was asked to discuss the actions associated with the planned operational changes. Heinrich began by reviewing the troubles caused by IBS in the United States. The troubles highlighted a fatal operational flaw. There was no direct link between Risk Management and Compliance and the Financial groups. The result was that IBS often pursued high risk, questionable investment activities that sometimes were illegal, sometimes un-ethical and often beyond the stated risk tolerance of the bank. The plan is to combine these groups into one unit with greater authority to oversee each of the business groups. A new leadership team will take change of all the major business groups. A clean slate was necessary to begin the process of changing the bank's image and business practices. Each new group leader was promoted from within the bank, holding a position within the group they will head. Each group leader has a stellar reputation. In addition, Heinrich men-tioned the importance of strengthening the relationship between the business groups and the cross-divisional functions. The plan includes becoming more innovative in the execution of work processes, partly by the greater use of process technology to replace the lost workers. The intent is to reduce fixed and variable costs, contributing to better margins. Everyone agreed with the parameters of the plan. The CEO added that the control system will receive substantial focus during the transformation process to ensure responsible business practices.

Questions

1. Why combine the groups into one unit?
2. Why promote from within? Explain.
3. What values are associated with a "stellar reputation?"
4. Why is it important to be innovative? What is the goal? Explain.
5. Why focus on the control system? Explain.

LEARNING OBJECTIVE #6: IDENTIFY AND REVIEW THE MAJOR CHANGE MANAGEMENT MODELS AND THE THEMES OF THE MODELS

Change management symbolizes a pro-active approach to support efforts to suc-cessfully overcome circumstances that require some form of organizational change. Random approaches to change management often result in less than optimal re-sults. Organizations seek to be successful; because change is emblematic of the prev-alence of the need to make changes, successfully managing change is critical. A **rational-logical foundation** helps change agents pursue change management that follows a systematic approach. A rational-logical focus refers to a formalized, rule-based methodology based on pragmatism. Change management models mostly are theory-based and adhere to a rational-logical foundation.

There are a variety of change management models that a change agent can select from. Most of the change management model(s) are **theory-derived**. A theory-derived change management model represents a comprehensive set of guiding prin-ciples that provide the rationale for applying that model. Some change management models are concept-based. A **concept-based** model does not possess a comprehen-sive set of empirically supported guiding principles; instead, there is a limited ide-ational support for the model.

Change management models offer change agents a structured approach to aide change agents in achieving a new **vision** by moving the focus from the here-and-now to a future condition. The models typically focus on one of the three types of change. Some models focus on changing a **work process**. Other models emphasize a **transformational approach**, where the focus is the entire organization. A select few models (e.g. Kotter's 8-Step Change Model) are meant to **apply to any situation** (i.e. work process or transformational). Each of the models provides the change agent with a systematic, routinized process to follow. The underlying assumption of each model is that by following a **process**, the change agent's efforts should be successful.

What follows is a list of all the major change management models.

- **Armenakis & Harris**: The emphasis is on preparing an organization for change.
- **Bridges Transitional Model**: The focus is on working with a team of change agents to guide the change agents through the stages of change.
- **Burke-Litwin Model**: The focus is on changing management systems.
- **Cummings & Worley Model of Change**: The focus is on identifying and achieving the vision of the change effort.
- **Kotter's 8-Step Change Model**: The focus is on working with leadership by following a process for making organization-wide changes.
- **Kubler-Ross Change Curve**: The focus is on recovering from results of change.
- **Lewin 3-step Change Model**: The focus is on facilitating all types of changes.
- **Lippett's Phases of Change Model**: The focus is on the use of external, non-organizational change agents.
- **McKinsey 7 s Model**: The focus is on leveraging seven organizational dimensions to create successful changes.
- **Prosci's ADKAR Model**: The focus is on developing the change management skills of managers.

Each of the change management models share the following themes.

- When confronted with a situation, change agents need to examine the circumstances using a big-picture microscope to gain a strategic view that sheds light on the overall requirements necessary to create a successful change.
- Each model emphasizes situations where the change agents need to create a sense of urgency; a sense of urgency gives the project a higher priority among everyone involved, especially leadership.
- The emphasis is on identifying the problem(s) to solve and avoid focusing on solving symptoms of a problem.
- A checklist methodology in checking off each stage achieved helps the change agents follow the sequence of stages and that each stage is successfully accomplished or remains ongoing before moving on to the next stage.
- Each model recommends developing a plan that represents an organized framework to follow in facilitating the change process. Each model recommends gaining the support of the plan from leadership and those most impacted by the plan.

- Engaging leadership throughout the entire change process is one of the central themes of each model. Leadership involvement symbolizes the active and continued support given to the change agents and the change plan.
- Each model supports engaging all affected individuals by involving everyone in preparing the change plan and during the entire process of implementing the plan.
- The models emphasize the importance of routinizing the changes to ensure that the changes become the new standardized work process to perform the task(s).
- Each model recommends that the change agents develop a broad vision statement to underscore what is going to be different once the change is successful. A vision provides an image of the result after completing the last stage of the change process.
- Active, ongoing communication with leadership, and with those impacted by the change process and among the change agents, is essential to avoid confusion and misunderstandings.
- Every model stresses the importance of incremental types of changes because limited changes are easier to understand, negotiate and ensure a great chance of success.

Deutsche Bank: Part 3

Ernst, the more senior co-chair, asked Heinrich to identify the first steps in the transformation plan. Ernst stated that it was important to execute the plan quickly, minimize the pain associated with the plan's execution and present a positive view of the result, after completing the major changes. Divisional leaders were going to meet with the heads of the functions to designate a team of experts tasked with the goal of identifying how to promote greater support from the functions. Divisional leaders will meet separately from the functional heads to create divisional task forces assigned to achieve the goal of identifying more effective controls over divisional activities. The head of the new risk management group will meet with department heads to create a task group with the mandate of developing a plan to improve risk management oversight and to conform with legal guidelines and the new Code of Conduct. Finally, divisional heads will meet to create two task groups. One task group will include the heads of each division's financial leader. This task group will identify additional ways to reduce costs, especially fixed costs. The second task group composed of each group CTO is assigned the task of identifying how to apply technology to improve the bank's efficiency.

Questions

1. Why create all the different teams? Explain.
2. What is the purpose of having a new Code of Conduct?
3. What type of technology will the second task group focus on? Explain.
4. Risk management needs to focus on what issues? Explain.
5. Is this a short-term project? Explain.

LEARNING OBJECTIVE #7: IDENTIFY THE DIFFERENT FORMS OF RESISTANCE AND EXPLAIN THE REASONS WHY INDIVIDUALS RESIST CHANGE

The most frequently mentioned reason for the failure of change management projects is **individual resistance** to change. Change management models provide important insights on following a process approach that is meant to either avoid resistance or to successfully overcome resistance by individuals. This section of this chapter offers readers insights into the various forms of individual resistance to overcome during a change management project.

Individuals confronted with a change management project that is **overly ambitious** will resist the changes because the individual experiences cognitive dysfunction because of cognitive limitations and/or feeling overwhelmed by a complex change plan. When in doubt, individuals will often resist changes because of the uncertainty associated with the changes.

Resistance often occurs when individuals perceive that leadership appears **less committed** to the proposed change management plan based on how individuals interpret leadership behavior; leaders are less involved in implementing the changes; leadership offers little in the way of advocacy for the changes; or some public pushback by leadership to some of the changes planned will result in individual resistance. Leadership behaviors suggest being cautious over the planned changes because of the interpretation of leadership behavior. Sometimes leaders demonstrate limited interest in the change plan. Individuals can misinterpret the behavior as not supportive of the plan when the actual reason for leadership behavior is the concern that too many change management plans that fail will negatively impact on leadership's future credibility when proposing other change management plans.

Trust in the change agents is an important issue for change agents seeking to promote a change management plan. Change agents trusted by individuals have credibility in promoting a change management plan. Trust gains the support of individuals most impacted by the proposed plan.

Trust can be of one of three types. Trust where the change agent is viewed as **honest**. There is another type of trust where the change agents demonstrate a **sincere commitment** to the change management plan. Finally, there is a form of trust where individuals consider the change agent as **credible** because of the change agent's prior history.

Job insecurity, uncertainty of role in the change process or failure to have an identifiable role in the change process represent reasons for individuals to resist change. Real or perceived threats will always be countered unless the change agents can validate the benefits of the change to individuals most affected by the plan. **Emotional factors** along with **personalities** of individuals can play an active part in resisting change because of the perceived threat that the change will have a negative impact on the individual.

Power dynamics is another factor that can lead to resistance to change. There are three different sources of power. Individuals with **formal power** conferred on their position can resist or support change by exercising the power if the change is viewed as harmful or beneficial to the individual. Individuals with **informal power** derived from their personality or status in the organization can support or resist change if the change is viewed as beneficial or harmful. Finally, there is power based on **technical expertise**. Individuals with technical expertise derive power from this knowledge. These individuals can either support or resist change using this power depending on if the individual benefits or feels harmed by the proposed change management plan.

Resistance can occur when there is insufficient **training** regarding the proposed change management plan. Also, particularly problematic is when training is limited, and the **proposed changes overlap** with the existing work process. The overlapping confuses individuals because they are asked to continue with the original work process and begin to implement the new work process, all with insufficient training. **Inadequate supervision** and the failure to adequately appeal to the **intrinsic motivation** of individuals are additional contributors to resistance to change.

LEARNING OBJECTIVE #8: IDENTIFY AND DESCRIBE THE ORGANIZATIONAL BARRIERS TO CHANGE AND PROVIDE EXAMPLES OF MANAGEMENT METHODS USED TO OVERCOME ORGANIZATIONAL BARRIERS

Change projects sometimes fail for reasons other than an individual's resistance to change. This section examines **organizational barriers** to instituting change management projects in an organization. The barriers are broad in scope, reflecting organizational attitudes toward openness to dealing with change routinely, systematically and involving the use of theory-based change management models.

Organizations can lack the **in-house expertise** necessary to improve the chances that change management projects can succeed. Purposefully excluding hiring individuals to be in-house change management experts reflects the attitude of senior leadership toward the application of change management models. However, limited oversight by leadership can be overcome by recruiting change management experts as consultants; hire change management experts with the goal of creating an in-house team of change management experts; or initiate training programs for managers with the focus on such subjects as project management, change management models and quality management. Quality management is relevant because the field of quality management emphasizes as an overall theme, continuous and ongoing improvement. Change is an essential dimension of a quality management agenda.

The organization might **lack the awareness** that change management is a specialized management field. This state of ignorance is unacceptable once an organization learns about this specialty. Once an organization becomes alerted to the ability to manage change using theory-based change management models as a guide, the organization can recruit change management specialists who can design and implement training programs for managers and non-managers to acquire the knowledge of change management models and the skills to use the change management models.

Some organizations are **habitual** with their routines (A.K.A. work processes) and that contemplating changing routines is abhorrent except under the most extreme circumstances. Being close-minded is detrimental to the long-term survival of the organization. Changing this "habit-driven" mentality begins by changing the organization's culture. A popular, credible leader needs to champion the idea that improving work processes benefits the organization.

People are motived through **extrinsic and intrinsic types of rewards**. Organizations can meet both needs of individuals. Some employees are more driven by extrinsic rewards while others by intrinsic types of rewards. By combining rewards that appeal to both types of needs, organizations recognize the behavior being rewarded is important to the organization. By not rewarding behavior associated with change management projects, organizations make a statement that change management is not an important priority. By altering the motivation management system to recognize the application of change management practices, the organization makes a statement that change management is important to the organization.

Low employee **self-esteem** is a problematic barrier to an organization seeking to institute change management practices because low self-esteem individuals find change threatening. Change disrupts the status quo and low self-esteem individuals fear that changes will result in poor work performance. Poor work performance can often lead to dismissal. Building self-esteem involves getting individuals to have successful new work experiences. An organization can select a small group of individuals with low self-esteem but with the potential to evolve over time by training these individuals in change management practices and then designating a team leader to work on small-scale change projects with a high probability of successful change. Successful experiences build self-esteem. Others will observe how their peers became successful change agents and want to participate in training to learn how to become successful change management agents too.

Some organizations are all about continuous change, whether minor or major types of change projects. The change process can be exhausting to the workforce because change projects are disruptive to work routines. **Change fatigue** is the result. To minimize change fatigue, the organization can create a metric-based system to create a process to identify only relevant, high priority change projects to undertake. This project selection methodology aims to minimize unnecessary disruptions by identifying high priority work routines to focus on.

An **organization's culture** often is a barrier to applying the use of change management practices because the prevailing values are contrary to the values associated with fostering the development and application of change management practices. One method for attempting to transform an organization's culture to support change management practices is to recruit a senior leader who is a well-recognized, successful practitioner of change management practices.

Lack of **senior leader change management role models** is a serious deterrent to implementing formal change management practices in an organization. Senior leaders with successful change management experiences can demonstrate how to successfully manage change, provide the savvy needed to promote change management practices and demonstrate the knowledge and skills that make for a credible role model. As a result, change management can become a successful management practice for an organization. Recruiting a senior leader with successful change management experiences derived from having the knowledge of change management models and the skills in applying these change management models is one of the primary methods an organization can use to introduce change management practices to the workforce.

LEARNING OBJECTIVE #9: IDENTIFY AND DESCRIBE TRADITIONAL MANAGEMENT METHODS USED TO OVERCOME AN INDIVIDUAL'S RESISTANCE TO CHANGE

Overcoming employee resistance is essential if change management projects are to have the opportunities to succeed. The most important element in dealing with employee resistance is building **trust** with the affected employees. Trust assumes that the change management project is acceptable and worth supporting. Several management methods help build trust, leading to less employee resistance to the change management project.

Designating a **credible leader** who has the knowledge, skills, personal abilities and successful change management experiences as the champion of a change management project builds the confidence that the organization is fully supportive of the change management project. Furthermore, the continued involvement of the leader with the project reinforces the view that the change management project is a high priority and that leadership wants a successful project finish.

Another management method for building trust and commitment to the change management project is to **involve employees directly** impacted by the changes during the planning stage along with having an active role in implementing the change management plan. Active involvement offers the workforce the opportunity to understand leadership intentions; providing input to the change management plan on an ongoing basis which provides confidence that their role is important and confers partial ownership rights to the plan, cementing their loyalty and commitment to the change management project.

Involving employees in the change management project requires involving employees in **creating the change management plan and during the change management plan's implementation**. Conferring upon the employee's meaningful roles in the change process by assigning meaningful tasks appeals to the intrinsic motivation of the workforce involved in the change management project. As such, employee's self-confidence increases along with a feeling of personal competency because leadership assigns them important responsibilities to fulfill.

Communication is essential element in the change process when developing and implementing a change management project because until finalized, the entire change management process remains fluid. Changes in the plan and changes during the implementation of the plan are constant as the change agents work to achieve a successful change management project. Frequent communication about goals, operational objectives, the plan and the implementation process are necessary to avoid confusion and doubt.

Routinizing both the change management planning process and implementation of the change management project provide a standardizing methodology that builds employee familiarity with the entire project. Familiarity reduces uncertainty because increased uncertainty leads to the perception of increased risk that the project will fail.

Most change management models support providing a **vision** that offers everyone a picture of what will be different and beneficial if the change management project succeeds. A vision is like a goal, providing focus, but not the specifics associated with goals. A vision offers everyone with an image of what will result from day-to-day efforts at implementing the change management project.

Short-term change management projects have a greater chance of succeeding because short-term projects reduce the chance for change management fatigue to set in. Long-term change management projects challenge everyone involved to maintain the commitment and enthusiasm because everyone has their routine work responsibilities along with the continuing responsibilities associated with the change management project.

Forming a **change management team** is crucial to increase the chances of having a successful change management project. A team represents a collection of change agents with the knowledge, skills, abilities and experiences associated with change management projects. An effective team creates a camaraderie of individuals, committed to ensuring the success of the team and the well-being of team members.

LEARNING OBJECTIVE #10: DISCUSS THE ISSUES PRO-ACTIVE CHANGE MANAGEMENT AND REACTIVE CHANGE MANAGEMENT

A **pro-active** outlook to change management is most probably influenced by the management field of quality management. There are several quality management models that could be applicable to quality management projects; the common theme among all the models is the value, continuous and ongoing improvement. The underlying belief is that every work process is improvable without the immediate requirement that only when there is a prevailing problem is intervention necessary.

Practicing a pro-active method to change management operates on the assumption that a problem is inevitable and that anticipating a problem warrants **preventative** measures to avoid a problem from occurring. Furthermore, early intervention keeps change management projects **easy-to-do** because the projects forestall the need to respond to either major or minor problems.

Pro-active change management projects present leadership with certain issues to address if a pro-active methodology is to dominate change management actions. First, a **system** needs to be developed to prioritize projects to focus on. There are far too many work processes to oversee and modify on a routine basis. Leadership needs to create a system that ranks work processes as designated **work processes** to always monitor and upgrade routinely.

A pro-active change management methodology requires that the organization develops the **in-house** capability to initiate and support change management practices throughout the organization. This capability requires routine training to provide change agents with the appropriate knowledge and skills required as change agents. Training involves identifying individuals with the motivation and potential to become change agents. As a change agent, intrinsic motivation is important because organizations cannot routinely offer tangible rewards for each successful change management project.

Finally, the **culture** of the organization needs to demonstrate the necessary values associated with creating a pro-active method associated with change management. By promoting quality management practices in the organization, the organization is promoting a set of values linked with the values underlying the theme of continuous and ongoing improvement.

A **reactive** methodology to change management is much easier to implement within an organization because there are always work process problems along with periodic strategic types of problems. In a reactive situation, the issue is prioritizing which problems to focus on. Following a **criteria-based** methodology is a common practice because criteria help rank the work-related problems to focus on. The field of **decision-making** offers examples of quantitative models for developing metric-based criteria for screening work processes. For example, urgency is one criterion, and the weight of importance is .5 out of 1.0, and the rating for the project could range from 1 to 5, with a 5 rating as critical.

Reacting to a problem automatically results in a **sense of urgency** which all the change management models support as a necessary condition to motivate leadership to act. However, if there are always problems, then leadership can be overwhelmed trying to cope with all the problems; such action often results in the failure to solve any problem fully. Consequently, leadership needs to create a system that helps to prioritize projects that warrant a change management approach.

Transformational changes typically are associated with change to an organization's strategy. A new strategy impacts the entire organization. Because of the potential scale of change, a reactive approach to transformational change is often the preferred response. Leadership needs to react to external environmental trends and then deduce how best to position the organization to respond to the trends. The ramifications for bad decisions are obvious. By waiting to get a better perspective about the circumstances, the organization increases the likelihood of making decisions beneficial to the long-term survival of the organization. Waiting too long, however, can put an organization at a competitive disadvantage.

The reactive approach is **demand-driven**, otherwise referred to as responding to issues. This is a more pragmatic approach. The pro-active approach is **supply-push** or anticipating problems before they occur. This is a riskier approach by committing resources, but if successful, highly beneficial to the organization.

Deutsche Bank: Part 4

The CEO announced that the next agenda item was Commercial Corporate Banking and the Investment Business Group with the emphasis on the Private Client Business unit within IBG. The bank saw these businesses as the best way to generate better profits among all the groups. These groups would lead the charge in boosting revenues and profits while reducing costs. The CEO discussed the reasons the focus was on these business groups. Industry and market trend analysis showed that these businesses were expected to be high growth areas for the next ten years. The bank wanted to be ranked among the top three organizations within each of these businesses by 2022. Furthermore, the bank wanted to identify potential high growth businesses with the goal of being the top player in each of these business segments. The CEO proceeded to open the floor for discussion.

Questions

1. What were the reasons for selecting the private client business unit?
2. Why focus on commercial corporate banking? Explain.
3. Why is the goal of ranking in the top three important? Is this a SMART goal? Explain.
4. Why look for new business opportunities?
5. How did people react to the CEO's announcement? Explain.

LEARNING OBJECTIVE #11: IDENTIFY AND EXAMINE THE REASONS FOR LESS THAN EXPECTED RESULTS FROM CHANGE MANAGEMENT PRACTICES IN ORGANIZATIONS

Researchers conclude that between 33 and 66% of change management projects are recognized as successful. However, there is no prevailing evidence from researchers to show the types of successful change management projects and which types of change management projects fail to achieve leadership expectations. There is anecdotal evidence as well as theory-based insights that suggest reasons why few change management projects meet leadership expectations.

Plausible reasons change management projects do not meet leadership expectations include the following.

- **Organizational Barriers**: Leadership failed to eliminate or substantially reduce the barriers that organizations often create; impeding successful implementation of change management projects.
- **Organizational Culture**: An organization's culture is critical in creating the conditions for an organization to be successful. The failure to sufficiently incorporate the values supportive of change management projects is a concern.
- **Leadership Support**: Leaders either fail to fully support change practices or offer only limited support for the application of change management models.
- **Leadership Talent**: Leadership knowledge, skills, personal abilities and prior experiences are inadequate for leading change management projects.
- **Poor Planning**: Change management projects do not adhere to any one basic change management model which provides an organized, systematic methodology that can guide the implementation of change management plans.
- **Overly Ambitious**: Large-scale, proposed change management projects are often too complex for change agents to successfully implement. Scale includes the duration of a project, the number of people involved and the many issues to deal with.
- **Expectations**: Leadership expectations of a change management project, but stated in the form of SMART goals, are ambiguous instead.
- **Incentives/Disincentives**: Disincentives to support implementing a successful change management project are greater than the incentives to support successful implementation of change management projects.
- **Vision**: The failure to provide a clear vision that illustrates the endpoint of a change management project makes focusing on the implementation process difficult because there is no sense that the changes are moving the project in the right direction.

- **Communication**: Leadership and the team of change agents fail to adequately keep everyone informed about the change management project's progress including providing a vision and goals of the project, instead providing an inadequate vision and non-SMART goals as well as few progress updates.
- **Team Membership**: The team of change agents responsible for overseeing the implementation of the change management project does not have enough change management expertise.
- **Sense of Urgency**: Leadership fails to adequately make the case that change is immediately necessary.
- **Impacted Employees**: Contrary to change management models, those individuals most affected by change management projects are not meaningfully involved in the planning and implementation of the change management projects.

Chapter Summary

The study of change management is an important management subject to learn about because managers and non-managers must frequently deal with situations that force change on everyone.

The challenges managers confronted when managing a change management project is dealing with resistance to change by subordinates along with organizational barriers that make successfully facilitating change management a challenge. This chapter provides the reader with the insight that change is inevitable and that if change agents use a theory-based change management model, the change agents can increase the chances of achieving a successful change management project. The reader learns about the major change management models and the common themes shared among the models.

Because of resistance to change and barriers to change, management methods have become omnipresent for helping leadership overcome resistance and the barriers. The chapter provides an overview of a broad sample of the management methods. Determining when to use one or more of these methods varies according to the type of changes requiring the application of a change management model. The chapter identifies and describes different types of changes warranting the need for the reader to grasp the necessity of using a diagnostic method to identify the type of change and how to apply a change management model.

To increase the likelihood of a successful change management project, the focus needs to follow a process methodology during the change management project. This is relatable to the process method advocated by project management practitioners. A process approach involves following a sequence of stages that guide the change agents through creating a successful change. The intent is to follow a systematic method that promotes thoroughness during the implementation of a change management project without guaranteeing a project's success but increasing the chances for a successful change management project.

Questions

1. Discuss the issues associated with change and change management.
2. What are the external environmental issues that trigger the need for organizational change?
3. What are the internal organizational issues that trigger the need for organizational change?
4. Identify, describe and discuss the types of changes that require the application of a change management model.
5. Discuss the reasons why change management requires a process approach.
6. What are the major themes underlying the change management models?

7. Identify and discuss the major reasons why individuals resist change.
8. What are the management methods used to overcome resistance to change?
9. What are the organizational barriers to change? What are the management methods used to overcome these barriers?
10. What are the benefits associated with taking a pro-active approach to change and what are the benefits associated with a reactive approach to change?
11. What are the five reasons identified that explain why many change management projects fail to meet expectations?

Bibliography

Aguirre, D. & Alpern, M. (2014). 10 principles of leading change management. *Organizations & People.* June 6. Summer 2014 (75). https://www.strategy-business.com/article/00255?gko=6C601/.

Austin, J. (2015). Leading effective change: a primer for the HR professional. *SHRM Foundation's Effective Practice Guidelines.* Series 1–24.

Brisson-Banks, C.V. (2010). Managing change and transitions: a comparison of different models and their commonalities. *Library Management.* 31 (4/5). 241–252.

Higgins, D. & Bourne, P.A. (2018). Implementing change in an organization: a general overview. *Scholarly Journal of Psychology and Behavioral Sciences.* August 29.

Kavanagh, M.H. & Ashkanasy, N.M. (2006). The impact of leadership and change management strategy on organizational culture an individual acceptance of change during a merger. *British Journal of Management.* 17. S81–S103.

Perkins, B. (2018). What is change management? A guide to organizational transformation. April 12. https://www.cio.com/article/2439314/change-management-change-management-definition/.

Pieterse, J.H., Caniels, M.C.J. & Homan, T. (2012). Professional discourses and resistance to change. *Journal of Organizational Change Management.* 25(6). 798–818.

Pryor, M. G., Taneja, S., Humphreys, J., Anderson, D. & Singleton, L. (2008). Challenges facing change management theories and research. *Delhi Business Review.* 9(1). 1–20.

Ryerson University. (2011). Change management resource guide. *Human Resources.* 1–30.

Saetren, G.B. & Laumann, K. (2017). Organizational change management theories and safety – a critical review. *Safety Science Monitor.* 1(2). 1–10.

Scandura, T.A. & Sharif, M. (2011). Leadership and organizational change. *Management Faculty Articles and Papers.* https://scholarlyrepository.miami.edu/management_articles/12/.

Sirkin, N.L., Keenan, P. & Jackson, A. (2005). The hard side of change management. *Harvard Business Review.* October.

Society for Human Resource Management. (2019). Managing organizational change. https://www.shrm.org/resourcesandtools/tools-and-sampes/toolkits/pages/managingorganiationalchange/.

Webster, V. & Webster, M. (2019). Successful change management-Kotter's 8-step change model. https://www.leadershipthoughts.com/kotters-8-step-change-model/.

Weiner, B.J. (2009). A theory of organizational readiness for change. *Implementation Science.* 4(67). 1–9.

Leadership and Leadership Development

OVERVIEW

The search for the Holy Grail in the study of leadership represents the long-term effort to identify a universal leadership theory. The search process, unfortunately, is like an attempt to reach for the sun, an elusive goal. However, the search continues nevertheless, identifying new ideas and assessing existing leadership theories to include additional concepts; but all these efforts serve the purpose of enriching our thinking about an important subject, leadership. Leadership is a popular subject for researchers over the centuries. The focus of researchers is to answer the following questions: "what is a leader? what makes someone a leader? how to make someone a leader?" Two historical figures, Plato, and his treaties on developing a philosopher-king to become a leader and Machiavelli's *The Prince*, standout as examples of early and important contributors to the field. Fast-forward to the 21st century, leadership is more vital today in this dynamic and rapidly changing world where organizations need to adapt to survive or disappear in that sinkhole where all failed organizations go. Organizations need effective leaders who can successfully navigate an organization through the turbulent, competitive, challenging world of the 21st century.

In addition to the myriad of leadership theories, researchers studied leadership styles which reflect an individual's personality. The purpose in studying leadership styles is to guide search committees seeking to identify and hire new leaders by matching the needs of the organization with the organization's personality as reflected by an organization's culture.

This chapter distinguishes between the term's leader and leadership, an important distinction, because each implies two different but related ideas. Simply, the term leader focuses on the characteristics of the individual. The term leadership focuses on the behaviors that effective leaders exhibit. Effective leaders are often defined as leaders who achieve the intended results.

Within the field of leadership development, identifying potential leaders represents an important process. Organizations need to identify individuals with the potential to become leaders to replace leaders who left or are promoted. Once identified, it is essential that these individuals undergo a formal and structured introductory leadership development training program, the first of many leadership development training programs. A structured type of leadership development process (LDP) is more often the exception and not what is commonly practiced because of the challenge to design this type of training program. The chapter covers the theory of andragogy, so readers understand the importance of designing a leadership development training program that represents a systematic, structured process, underscored by adult learning theory, which is the focus of andragogy.

Learning objectives guide the discussion about all the important topics associated with the study of leadership, assisting the reader in learning about the important issues associated with the subject and how to train individuals to become leaders. Even if an individual declines to be a leader in an organization, understanding the subject helps the reader learn to become a self-leader, the ability to lead themselves. The subject of self-leadership is important because self-leadership is identified as the intermediate stage in the LDP model, the evolution of an individual seeking to become a leader within an organization.

CHAPTER 9   LEARNING OBJECTIVES

Readers will achieve the following learning objectives after reading this chapter.

1. Define and describe the meaning of the term "leadership."
2. Discuss the importance of leadership in organizations.
3. Identify and describe the major leadership theories.
4. Identify and describe the primary leadership styles.
5. Discuss the process to follow and subjects to consider in identifying individuals who represent leaders.
6. Identify and describe the process for identifying individuals who are potential leaders.
7. Discuss the leader-follower relationship.
8. Discuss the role of a leader as a change agent.
9. Identify and describe andragogy, an important adult learning theory helpful in designing a leadership development training program.
10. Identify and explain the three-stage LDP model for developing leaders.
11. Identify and describe the stages in the process for designing a leadership development training program.
12. Identify and describe instructional methods associated with leadership development training programs.

LEARNING OBJECTIVE #1: DEFINE AND DESCRIBE THE MEANING OF THE TERM "LEADERSHIP"

In a 1982 study about leadership, Warren Bennis reported identifying **350 definitions** of leadership. Clearly, there was no consensus then on a definition just as there is no universal definition of leadership among today's academic and business communities. However, the lack of a universal definition is not a deterrent in stating a definition. Offering a simplified definition serves as a catalyst to initiate thought about how to begin to understand leadership and what leadership means to the reader. The initial step in making sense of the term, leadership, is to define leadership in the following way. **Leadership** refers to the actions an individual follows that involve other individuals willing to work on the individual's behalf to achieve organizational goals.

The broad range of definitions of leadership offers various topics to begin the process of learning about leadership as a concept and providing a descriptive meaning to the term. There are several categories of topics academic researchers refer to when providing a definition of leadership.

One category of definitions defines leadership as a **process**. Leadership entails conducting a series of transactions between a leader and subordinates. There are theories that broaden this definition to offer a wider range of perspectives to understand the subject of leadership. These theories are referred to as **transactional theories**. A transactional theory describes a process with an initial starting point, an endpoint and stages between the starting and ending points. Every completed process culminates in a measurable outcome. Examples of processes include the strategic planning process, budget development and review process and a meeting agenda development process.

Another category of definitions defines leadership as a series of different **group or team** interactions. Leaders achieve through the actions of organized groups of individuals often referred to as teams. Members of organizations work in teams; each team has a common focus. Leaders must work with teams to achieve the organization's strategic goals and operational objectives. Several examples include working with the organization's Board of Directors, developing an organizational strategy with the senior management team, developing an organizational vision, working with the senior management team and other teams and preparing a marketing plan or marketing plans with the different product groups responsible for putting together a marketing plan.

There are definitions about leadership that focus on the **skills** leaders possess. A skills-focus means that the leader performs something that demonstrates some level of proficiency that defines the individual as a leader. Often, the definitions delineate skills by identifying essential **core skills** that a leader needs to possess and show an expertise in performing. Within the category of essential skills, examples include technical skills, communication skills, social skills and fiscal skills.

A focus on **behaviors** exhibited by leaders represents another category of theories that define and describe leadership. Leaders demonstrate types of behaviors or actions long associated with leaders. As a further way to delineate this broad category, many definitions focus on behaviors exhibited by leaders described as **effective or successful leaders**. Examples of behaviors include **task-oriented behavior** such as short-term planning, monitoring performance and conducting meetings.

There are **relationship-oriented behaviors**, such as conducting one-on-one meetings, calling someone who is struggling with a project and volunteering to meet with a team that is struggling to achieve their goal. The emphasis on a relationship approach is to build trust, cooperation and commitment. Another example of behaviors is **change-oriented behaviors** such as initiating innovations. For example, changes to the organization's strategy, changes to strategic goals and changes to management systems, policies and work processes.

Leader **traits** represent another category of definitions to define leadership. Traits represent the personal attributes that leaders possess which differentiate leaders from non-leaders. Traits are often associated with personality characteristics. Some examples of traits frequently associated with leaders include high self-esteem, takes initiative, extroverted and assertive.

Because of perceived limitations in other definitions of leadership, some academic researchers focused on defining leadership as **situationally derived**. The situation defines who is a leader and the type of leader required. A major crisis requires one type of leader; minor crises require another type of leader; external threats to the organization require a certain type of leader to rally subordinates; a successful organization requires a leader to continue the organization's successful performance. Matching the wrong type of leader based on the situation is a recipe for problems to occur.

Leader **competencies** represent another category for defining leadership, especially **effective leadership**. Competencies refer to the abilities of leaders to be effective as a leader through achieving performance expectations. Several examples of competencies include self-development skills, social relationship development, a facilitator among others, a visionary and performance focused.

These categories of definitions of leadership represent the major approaches that define the term, leadership.

LEARNING OBJECTIVES #2: DISCUSS THE IMPORTANCE OF LEADERSHIP IN ORGANIZATIONS

Alexander the Great! Julius Caesar! Peter the Great! Winston Churchill! Franklin Roosevelt! Dwight Eisenhower! John Wooden! Steve Jobs! Jack Ma! Mary Barra! Satya Nadella! Este Lauder! Genghis Khan! What do these individuals share? Fame! What makes these individuals famous? Each is viewed as an effective leader who was a successful leader of one or more organizations. Why? The organization achieved results that benefited the country, organization(s), organizational members and those linked to the organization in some way. Do we remember the names of unsuccessful leaders? The answer is no unless that leader was Napoleon, Adolf Hitler or Joseph Stalin.

Leadership is important because leadership is viewed as a **catalyst for change**. Change is associated with making an organization effective as well as efficient in the implementation of the organization's strategy(ies). Strategy represents the organization's plan for achieving the organization's strategic goals. Achieving the strategic goals enables an organization to achieve the organization's vision. Leadership provides the impetus for developing an organization's **vision** to move the organization forward. Leadership is associated with identifying the

strategic goals to achieve the vision and the **strategic plan** to achieve the strategic goals. Leadership provides the initiative and direction during the **strategy implementation process**.

Strategy implementation is operations-oriented. Therefore, because implementation has an operations focus, leadership adheres to a **systems perspective**. An organization's operations represent a giant system, incorporating a network of various management systems functions described earlier. Management systems offer a structured approach that is commonly associated with an organization's operations. Each type of management system, for example, the information system, encompasses policies relevant to that system. Each policy identifies, describes and creates individual types of relevant work processes. A work process performs a specific work task. Every work process generates a measurable outcome. This overview is important to understand because leadership is associated with change, and leadership needs to target changes in the management systems, management subsystems, policies and work processes to move the organization forward to accomplish the strategic goals.

Leadership can imply a **group of individuals** that are leader types, but that there is a hierarchy of leaders with one individual designated as the primary leader. Leaders serve as role models for **non-leaders**. Leadership involves non-leaders in the change process because leadership is too few in numbers; leadership provides direction, guidance and feedback to keep non-leaders focused and successful in performing their work responsibilities.

Leadership is important because of the focus on **performance** through the identification of goals and objectives, along with the assessment of performance in achieving the goals and objectives. Leadership's important performance-related responsibility is to ensure that each member of the workforce knows their work responsibilities, performs their work responsibilities and performs their work responsibilities to meet the organization's expectations.

An **organization's culture** is vital in helping to create a successful organization. This is because culture represents a collection of values intended to influence the attitudes and behavior of the workforce. Leadership focuses on changing the culture by reinforcing core values, strengthening core values that emphasize performance and incorporating new values that support more effective individual, unit and organizational performance.

McDonald's: Part 1

John, Sandra, Jean and Sam and I decided that a meeting among the senior members of the Board of Directors to discuss the current situation was urgent. As chair of the Board, my concern is that McDonald's is no longer in the forefront of progressive, high-growth fast food restaurants. Sandra and Jean, as overseers of the firm's financial performance, discussed the numbers and the performance trends over the past three years. Sam, as the Board's leadership overseer, you and I conducted informal discussions about the performance of

Mike along with Mike's three predecessors. Before opening the meeting for discussion, let me briefly summarize the trends that are concerning to us.

- Revenues continue to increase at a declining rate. Next year, the trend is expected to show a net decline.
- Overall costs, especially labor and G.M. & A. costs continue to increase at an increasing rate.
- Customer surveys report negative reviews about new products and services.
- Turnover among site managers and corporate management now exceeds the average over the prior five-year period.

I am concerned. What are everyone's thoughts? Respond as if you are attending the meeting.

LEARNING OBJECTIVE #3: IDENTIFY AND DESCRIBE THE MAJOR LEADERSHIP THEORIES

An opinion indicates an individual has a theory about a subject. People understand the world around them along with the actions of others using theories. Having a theory on leadership is no different. But what is a theory exactly? A **formal theory** incorporates a set of concepts that describe the object studied; theory helps us to understand the object being studied; and theory enables people to explain or interpret some phenomenon. Theories usually are supported by empirical findings. In the case of the individual, life experiences serve to provide empirical validation on their theory about leadership. For the academic researcher, the support of a theoretical view on leadership theory originates from formal types of research studies.

This section of the chapter examines various types of leader theories. One researcher identified 16 different categories of leader theories encompassing 64 different leader theories. There are so many different theories because the subject is popular and important to researchers and organizations. Researchers look for the Holy Grail among the various leader theories that one universal leader theory that provides a comprehensive and complete understanding of the concept of leader and leadership.

Presently, there is no universal leader theory. Each existing leader theory includes conceptual weaknesses that do not fully describe or explain leadership. Furthermore, there are no empirical studies that strongly support any one of the existing theories on leadership as the universal leadership theory.

Mainstream leader theories are introduced to enable readers to learn about the wide range of theoretical interpretations of constitutes leadership. This introduction to leader theories is a catalyst to encourage the reader to develop their own personal leader theory. A corollary to the discussion on leader theories is an overview of the nature-nurture controversy associated with the subject of leadership. The controversy originates from the belief by some that leaders are born to lead. Others believe that leaders emerge through various learning experiences. Empirical evidence indicates some aspects of leadership are genetically determined but that most leader characteristics evolve from life experiences.

First, there are the various **great man leader theories**. Great man theories emerged from the school of thought that people are born leaders. There are two subsets of these theories. One group of theories is based on the individual's ancestral background. People born in the "right" family have the pedigree to be leaders. The other category is that an individual is born to be a leader with no heritage required. The evidence is clear that a person can be born into the right family and not become a leader or a successful leader. The genetic basis for determining that someone is born a leader is offset by all the examples of individuals who failed as a leader. Furthermore, great man theories do not offer a comprehensive understanding of a leader's specific personal attributes.

Trait theories represent another category of leader theory. Trait theories emphasize that a leader has unique personal attributes that differentiates leaders from non-leaders. Furthermore, trait theories focus on dichotomizing traits through identifying the unique traits possessed by successful leaders in comparison with traits exhibited by unsuccessful leaders. The usefulness of trait theory in understanding leadership is the ability to identify potential leaders for leadership development training programs.

Leader theory evolved after substantial criticism from researchers on the theoretical limitations of trait theories. Researchers focused on the actions of leaders; the actions of those leaders identified as successful leaders. This category of leader theories is referred to as **behavioral theories** because the focus is on types of behaviors of successful leaders. Behavior theories emphasize two dimensions of behavior. **Task-focused** and **relationship-focused** behaviors. Behavioral tasks emphasize the behavior associated with creating operational structures to keep the workforce focused. Relational-focused behavior emphasizes the behavior associated showing concern and consideration of the workforce who respond to these actions by maximizing their work effort.

Because empirical research did not strongly support behavioral theories, researchers pursued another line of inquiry to understand what constitutes leadership, especially the leadership of successful leaders. Out of this shift in focus came the **contingency or situational leadership theories**. These leader theories emphasize that circumstances serve as the catalyst for leaders to emerge. Non-leaders operate in an incubator, waiting for the right conditions to emerge for the non-leader to become a leader, guiding subordinates toward success. The leader adapts to the circumstances, whether internally from within the organization or externally generated from the organization's external environment, to guide the organization toward a successful performance. While receiving some empirical support, contingency leader theories did not benefit from sufficiently strong empirical support to become the pre-eminent leadership theories.

Transactional leader theories emerged as researchers pursued another approach in trying to understand successful leadership and develop a relevant theory that explains leadership from a transactional perspective. Transactions have a process focus, where the leader seeks changes in the workforce's behavior through the manipulation of rewards and punishments. Think of exchanges between a leader and non-leader. If the non-leader performs well, the leader confirms a reward to the subordinate. If the performance does not meet performance expectations, the leader can punish the subordinate. Transactional theories are criticized for their narrow focus on the use of rewards and punishments.

Transformational leader theories became popular with the focus on how leaders serve as change agents that work with subordinates to initiate organizational change. Transformationalist leaders provide a vision as the focal point of change. The vision serves to inspire subordinates to work with the leader to re-structure the organization to achieve the organization's strategic goals which leads to achieving the vision. Leaders inspire subordinates through the leader's actions. Working together leads to enhanced leader-follower behavior. Superior work performance is the result. Many researchers view the transformational theories as insufficient in explaining the complexity of the subject, leadership.

Path-Goal Leader Theory describes leaders as adaptive individual's intent on making subordinates more productive members of the organization. Leaders modify subordinate's behavior in such a way that subordinates become happier with their job, self-motived and feeling like they have greater control over their work. Leaders' adaptive abilities make for a better work environment for everyone. The end-result is a more productive and efficient organization.

A more recent leader theory is **Leader-Member Leadership Theory**. This theory emphasizes the personal relationship between a leader and subordinates. The focus is on the leader creating a bond between the leader and subordinates. The bond is more than a boss-subordinate bond. The focus is on leaders creating a personal relationship, building a trusting relationship. With higher levels of trust, subordinates become happier, more motivated, more cooperative and aspire to become more productive members of the organization. This theory emphasizes the need for the leader to proactively work to create the type of relationship with subordinates that makes for a more successful organization.

LEARNING OBJECTIVE #4: IDENTIFY AND DESCRIBE THE PRIMARY LEADERSHIP STYLES

Leadership style reflects a leader's personality and how the individual acts to lead. The study of leadership style is important to understand because of the need for a good fit between a leader(s) and subordinate's preferred leadership style along with the organization's culture. The study of leadership styles differs from leader theory because leader theory seeks to describe and explain leadership as a concept. Leadership style describes how a leader can lead.

Every leader has their own unique style in leading others. Leadership style focuses on such issues as how leaders interact with subordinates; methods used to motivate subordinates, the level of involvement a leader allows subordinates in participating in the decision-making process; and the focus on being task-driven, relationship-driven or change-driven. These factors are important to ensure an exemplary leader-organization fit.

There are several useful criteria to use within the process of selecting a leader for an organization or a unit within an organization.

1. **The level of interaction and communication needed.** Some individuals prefer working alone, and others believe in involving subordinates in daily work. Some leaders communicate as infrequent as possible and, when communicating, prefer the written form. Others are great believers in communicating, verbally

and in written form to enlighten subordinates and to be enlightened by subordinates. The leader does not want surprises.

2. **Know the leader's personality**. Learn about the leader's preferences for interacting with others because the individual's attitude on this subject reflects personal self-worth issues.

3. **Goal congruency** is important as leaders, subordinates and the organization need to collaborate to identify important goals and work together to achieve these goals.

4. **Decision-making approach** is important because there is a large time commitment associated with the extent to which a leader involves subordinates in the decision-making process. Knowing the individual's decision-making model is important in learning if there is congruence with the organization's values.

Researchers identified several types of leadership styles. The most common types of leadership styles include the following.

1. **Authoritarian/Autocratic Style**: This style involves using a directive approach in leading subordinates. Leaders using this style provide the goals and the plans for subordinates to follow to achieve the goals.

2. **Democratic Style**: A leader using this style actively involves subordinates in selecting goals and designing the plans to achieve the goals. This type of leader is open to input from subordinates.

3. **Laissez-Faire Style**: This leadership style serves a leader who is not a hands-on leader, but a leader that is non-directive. The laissez-faire leader is likely to identify the vision but let subordinates select the goals, strategy for achieving the goals and methods for implementing the strategy.

4. **Coaching Style**: A coaching style of leadership represents a leader who actively guides subordinates in performing their work responsibilities. The coaching leader works with subordinates in crafting the vision, goals and strategy and strategy implementation plan and works with subordinates to become more effective in organizing and implementing this process.

5. **Visionary or Strategic Style**: The visionary leader style provides an image of where the organization wants to be within a set time frame. This leader always keeps subordinates focused on the vision and works with subordinates to perform their work functions with the vision always the focal point.

6. **Servant Style**: The leader exhibiting this leadership style serves their subordinates. The well-being of subordinates is of primary importance to the leader. By emphasizing the subordinate, the intent of the leader is to improve employee commitment to the organization by increasing the employee's sense of personal self-worth and their value to the organization.

7. **Transformational Style**: The focus of the transformational leader is to serve as a change agent intent on guiding subordinates in making the changes themselves with the intent of changing the structure of the organization to be a better performing organization. The transformer leader breaks down barriers, upsets routines and disrupts social norms to move everyone forward because individual self-improvement only benefits the organization.

8. **Transactional Style**: Everything is about performance for a leader with a transactional leadership style. A transactional leader works to support subordinates with the intention of aiding subordinates in performing their work

responsibilities more effectively. The transactional leader emphasizes the use of rewards and punishments to influence subordinate actions.

No leader demonstrates one type of leadership style. However, every leader does show a dominant type of leadership style in combination with one or more other types of leadership styles. For example, a leader might tend to be more authoritarian but show aspects of a democratic style, willing to let subordinates have some input. However, leadership styles need to be complementary. For example, the authoritarian and laissez-faire styles would not likely go together. Organizations need to select leaders who possess a style that complements the organization's preferred leadership style as reflected by the organizational culture.

LEARNING OBJECTIVE #5: DISCUSS THE PROCESS TO FOLLOW AND SUBJECTS TO CONSIDER IN IDENTIFYING INDIVIDUALS WHO REPRESENT LEADERS

Using a **systematic methodology**, a process model to identify leaders underscores the importance of following a process because making the wrong choices can have serious, long-lasting consequences for an organization. Though there is no assurance of a correct candidate, decision-makers need a methodology to ensure a good choice is a likely outcome from the selection process. Identifying leaders is important for an organization because there are too few leader-types. Organizations want to identify leader candidates from within and outside of the organization to take advantage of the abilities and experiences these individuals offer the organization; the individuals serve as role models for subordinates; and to integrate these individuals into leadership development programs to enhance their capabilities.

An essential step in identifying a leader is to clarify the **leadership style** that fits best within the organization's culture. Decision-makers need to understand the culture and the important people values embedded in the culture to select the preferred type of leadership style. For example, an organization's values that reflect a democratic leadership style would result in problems if the organization selected and promoted leaders with an authoritarian leadership style. An organization is never able to put a round peg into a square hole successfully.

After identifying a preferred leadership style, the organization's next task is to identify a methodology for differentiating leaders from non-leaders and effective leaders from in-effective leaders. The primary differentiator separating leaders from non-leaders is feelings of **self-worth**. Leaders have strong positive feelings of self-worth which encompasses self-esteem (feelings), self-concept (thoughts) and self-confidence (belief in the self). After identifying leaders, the next step is to differentiate between effective and ineffective leaders. **Trustworthiness** is one important criterion for drawing a distinction between the two categories of leaders. Trustworthy leaders motivate subordinates to act to fulfill the leader's agenda. The other criterion for identifying an effective leader is the ability to **achieve results**. Effective leaders, by definition, achieve. Ineffective leaders talk the talk about being successful but do not achieve success by achieving SMART type goals.

Though an effective leader achieves results and is trustworthy to subordinates, there are additional personal qualities that an effective leader contributes to their effectiveness. These qualities are organized into three categories of attributes:

task-oriented, relationship-oriented and change-oriented attributes. Effective leaders demonstrate abilities that fall within each category. These groupings represent a standardized approach to organize leader abilities, all of which are captured within the three categories.

A **task-orientation** encompasses attributes that focus on performance; behavior focuses on getting results by using a structured, systematic approach. Task-orientation involves processes for identifying **goals**; **creating work processes** to achieve the goals; and **monitoring performance** routinely to learn if movement toward achieving the goals is on track. A task-orientation involves the need to **conceptualize** to understand the management systems that need to work together; **analyze and interpret** the functioning of the work processes and the outcomes associated with each work process; and **organize and implement** the various work processes. Being a **technical specialist** in a subject along with **fiscal skills** further enhance the leader's credibility among subordinates.

A **relationship-oriented** leader is a people person. This is an important point because leaders depend on subordinates to perform a variety of tasks. Significant personal characteristics of a relationship-oriented leader include actively working with and through **teams**; **support and cooperate** with subordinates; demonstrates being an **effective communicator**; and the leader relies on **personal power** more than positional power to inspire subordinates to act.

The **change-oriented** leader category of behavioral attributes focuses on a leader's efforts at moving the organization from point A to point B. To facilitate this movement requires several abilities that support being a change agent. First, a leader needs to be a **visionary** by providing a vision of what point B represents. A change agent needs to be **proactive**, initiating change and knows how to manipulate the various **management systems and work processes** to bring about organizational change. Additional personal abilities of the change-agent leader include a **pragmatic approach** to change and not theory-bound; **adaptable** to respond to different situations, especially externally initiated; **innovative** in knowing that reaching point B is achievable in more than one way. Finally, the leader change-agent is **performance-driven** by achieving SMART goals.

LEARNING OBJECTIVE #6: IDENTIFY AND DESCRIBE THE PROCESS FOR IDENTIFYING INDIVIDUALS WHO ARE POTENTIAL LEADERS

Creating a systematic search process to facilitate finding potential leaders is important because the cost associated with identifying potential leaders, training potential leaders and working with these individuals during the early stages of their development is too high to make mistakes. The search part of the process uses valuable people time; training involves the use of valuable people time. While promising leaders learn to develop their leadership skills, mistakes in selecting the wrong individuals occur; people supervising, coaching or mentoring these individuals involve valuable people time. The total costs to find a successful leader are worth the costs of the search effort, a failed leader hurts the organization.

One important aspect to creating a systematic search process is to minimize personal bias. Including several individuals in the search process increases the likelihood the recommendation is reasonable because of the greater level of objectivity. General Electric's leadership search process represents a good example of a way to introduce objectivity to the process. Managers' job descriptions include identifying potential leaders. A manager's performance review includes the identification of potential leaders. Managers can earn incentives by identifying potential leaders. When several different managers independently make the same recommendation, the probability the person identified is a high value candidate for leadership training is high.

However, as part of the search process, the organization can provide guidance to managers in recommending candidates. Human Resources (HR) can put together a list of criteria to use as a checklist to aid in recognizing potential leadership candidates. A point system helps by awarding candidates points per criterion and an overall score. Achieving a minimum score screens candidates further. Having a pool of candidates to select forces the use of a ranking system if the number of candidates exceeds the requirements.

Observing a potential candidate during the performance of their work is important because the organization wants to know how a candidate performs on the job. This can mean requesting feedback from customers, suppliers, a direct supervisor, manager's peripheral to the candidate, etc. Below is a list of the candidate abilities that a checklist might include.

1. **Extroverted**: Being outgoing is a manifestation of a person's feelings of self-worth which is an important leader quality.
2. **Innovative**: The individual can craft creative solutions to seemingly intractable problems.
3. **Problem-Identifier**: The ability to identify problems is an important skill because too often people refer to symptoms as problems, creating solutions that fail to resolve the problem.
4. **Technical Skills**: Requiring a unique skillset demonstrates that the individual developed an expertise that confers knowledge-power on the person; the authority associated with being an expert gives the individual credibility among peers and superiors.
5. **Communicator**: The individual frequently leverages their communication skills in working with others; the person is comfortable talking with others, writing and speaking in front of groups.
6. **Social Skills**: The individual actively works with others in a cooperative manner and demonstrates initiative in working with others.
7. **Pragmatic**: Flexible thinking is important because this demonstrates an understanding that there is not "one best way."
8. **Organized**: Leaders deal with many issues that require keeping focused and attentive to successfully resolve these issues. Leaders become busier moving up the organization's hierarchy.
9. **Informal Power**: If an individual gets others to work on their behalf, this is an example of using informal, non-position power. All leaders use informal power more than position power; this demonstrates the power of the individual's personal qualities.
10. **Trusted and Strong Personal Values**: Trustworthiness is an important non-ability quality possessed by successful leaders. Individuals trusted and valued

by colleagues, supervisors, customers and suppliers demonstrate qualities that are intangible; qualities that many seek; qualities that cannot be taught.

McDonald's: Part 2

Sandra, Jean, John and Sam, it has been two years since we replaced Mike with Andrea as CEO. Andrea requested a change in her bonus plan to reflect the company's performance under her guidance. I thought her request represented an opportunity for us to review Andrea's performance and the future direction of the company. For the next year, revenue was forecasted to decline; we were accurate in the forecast; actual performance was worse than expected. That was the year we let Mike go and followed up, after a careful screening process, by hiring Andrea. I propose we discuss Andrea's request by focusing on two issues. First, let us review the factors that contributed to Andrea's success as CEO. Second, I want to identify specific actions we think Andrea needs to consider in building on her success as the organization moves forward. I will start the review process with highlights of Andrea's major accomplishments.

- Revenues have increased at an increasing rate over the past two years.
- Costs have declined at an increasing rate these past two years.
- We have averaged ten new products per year and one new product category this past year.
- Sales of each new product increased in double digits.

What are everyone's thoughts? Respond as if you are in attendance.

LEARNING OBJECTIVE #7: DISCUSS THE LEADER-FOLLOWER RELATIONSHIP

The leader-follower relationship is often characterized as a **reciprocal relationship** based on the satisfaction of mutual needs. Leaders rely on subordinates to introduce organizational changes required because of new strategies to implement. Followers need leaders to ensure that the organization is successful which offers subordinates long-term job security and future work opportunities that provides subordinates with the opportunities to achieve personal goals.

Leaders and followers have **professional goals** to achieve. Though these professional goals may differ, there is a mutual interest in supporting each other to achieve these professional goals. Both leaders and followers are outcome-oriented and seek to aid each other in achieving the professional goals if the goals do not conflict. The professional goals of leaders and subordinates are linked with personal goals. Personal goals can and do vary, but the link between professional goals and personal goals is strong. For example, a subordinate's personal goal might be to buy a house. A successful organization can lead to a bonus that contributes to the individual's house savings. For a leader, a personal goal might be to buy a bigger house or to achieve a higher-level leadership position in another organization, as a sign of personal self-worth, if the current organization is successful.

Organizations represent social situations, and a leader-follower relationship represents a **social relationship**. Leaders and subordinates represent a **social dynamic**. A social dynamic characterizes a network of relationships among leaders and subordinates. The **social relations model** applies to all organizations. The social relations model describes the process within an organization where all types of relationships among leaders and subordinates are formed (i.e. social dynamic). Some relationships are temporary, and others are permanent. Some relationships are more important than other relationships. Some relationships, using the systems model, indirectly impact other leader-follower relationships. Because of the importance of social relations to the success of leaders, leaders are frequently selected based in part on their social skills. Leadership development programs frequently emphasize the development of social skills.

Leaders can and do benefit from **position power** to influence subordinates. Position power represents the formal authority to make certain types of decisions that is conferred on a position as part of the job description and not the specific individual holding the position. However, there is also **informal power** that is an important influencer for the person wielding informal power. Informal power refers to power a leader and/or follower holds because of the individual's personality and/or specialized knowledge, skills and personal abilities the individual possesses. Leaders enjoy positional power and informal power, but the application of informal power is the greater source of a leader's influence because it is personal, which is important in a social relationship. The more a leader is liked and valued, the greater the ability to leverage the use informal power. A subordinate with informal power can influence leaders because of the respect the leader holds for the subordinate's personality, knowledge, skills and personal abilities possessed.

Leadership style needs to complement the style best represented by the workforce's preferred style. A workforce influences and is influenced by the culture of an organization. For example, a command-driven culture would most likely have a workforce that seeks active direction; this leads to an authoritarian leadership style. A professional staffed organization most likely would prefer a democratic leadership style where subordinates actively participate in the decision-making process. No leader demonstrates only one type of leadership style, but every leader demonstrates a dominant leadership style. Because of the number of followers to leaders, it is better to find leaders with an adaptable leadership style to be an effective leader.

In social relations, trust is an important factor that influences how well people work together. Where people need to work together, trust is an essential quality to support a strong working relationship. Where people depend on each other, trust is critical to make for a successful working relationship. Trust enhances the informal power of leaders. Where distrust exists, leaders need to rely on positional power, a less advantageous situation for a leader because informal power is more influential. What makes informal power more influential is because of the association with **trustworthiness**. Research indicates that effective leaders are viewed as trustworthy. Subordinates follow trustworthy leaders because trustworthy leaders have credibility.

Leaders who demonstrate a transformational leadership style and viewed as trustworthy by subordinates are effective because followers trust that the leader has their best interest in mind. A transformational leader knows that subordinates need to change to be more successful in performing their work responsibilities. Change is necessary because more ambitious strategic goals and strategies to achieve these goals represent organizational change methods. Successfully implementing the strategies achieves the goals. The organization requires operational changes to succeed in meeting new competitive conditions through implementation of the strategies. Subordinates need to change because subordinates are responsible for implementing the operational changes that will contribute to the organization's efforts at successfully meeting new competitive challenges by achieving the strategic goals.

McDonald's: Part 3

Speaking before the entire Board, Andrea, as CEO these past three years, reports that staff worked admirably to implement the new strategic plan.

> However, I am not totally satisfied with the firm's overall performance or the performance of specific areas of the firm. I think we can do better, but I and senior leadership are handicapped by having too few leader types in middle management and among lower level managers including site managers. I have asked Paul, as Board chair and Sam as the Board's leadership overseer, to begin a discussion on how best we can identify potential leaders. I want to share my thoughts initially before we begin to brainstorm on the subject.

- We could make identifying potential leaders a part of each manager's performance review process.
- We could offer bonuses to managers that identify individuals who pass our introductory leadership development training program.
- We could send out self-interest survey questionnaires to learn who has an interest in entering the introductory leadership development training program.
- We could send out survey questionnaires to employees asking them if they can identify anyone with the potential to become leaders.
- We could review employee performance reviews to identify potential leaders.

"The issue before us is how to create a process to follow that helps to identify potential leaders. The process needs to include criteria to use to help identify potential leaders."

What are your thoughts? How would you respond if you were attending the meeting?

LEARNING OBJECTIVE #8: DISCUSS THE ROLE OF A LEADER AS A CHANGE AGENT

Leaders of organizations operate within a **dynamic world** with little to no control over elements external to the organization. The only control is over how leadership and the organization respond to **external influencers**. Dynamic circumstances exist because of the confluence of different environmental elements co-mingling and changing all the time. Whether economic conditions change, competitive circumstances change or market conditions change, change is the common denominator and the interconnectedness among these factors make for a dynamic world.

By default, leaders need to be **change agents** to enable the organization to successfully respond to external conditions. External conditions can represent **opportunities** that an organization can pursue to enhance the organization's competitive position or represent external **threats** that can hasten an organization's decline. External conditions require responses that range between **evolutionary**, where change evolves over time, in measured ways. At the other end of the **continuum of change** are **revolutionary** types of changes. The pursuit of revolutionary types of changes involves dramatic, major disruptions to the organization's management systems, policies and work processes because external conditions warrant major strategic and operational changes to successfully confront the threats.

The application of the **transformationalist leadership style** represents a useful model to illustrate how a leader can serve as a change agent because the transformational leadership style emphasizes changing subordinates, the organization and leadership management practices to adapt to the new competitive conditions. Furthermore, the effective transformational leader model demonstrates the application of important personal abilities that reveal why this type of leadership style is transformationalist and effective for a change agent.

The following examples of personal abilities reflect a transformationalist style of leader.

- **Visionary**: The leader provides a vision of a future that the leader wants the organization to achieve. The vision provides subordinates with an endpoint to focus on.
- **People Person**: The leader knows that successful changes can only occur through the active support and cooperation of subordinates. The leader looks for a collaborative relationship with subordinates, sharing power with subordinates to allow subordinates to act and rewarding subordinates when successful.
- **Performance-Oriented**: As a change agent, the leader is result-oriented, emphasizing achieving SMART type goals that enable the leader to assess performance objectively.
- **Initiator**: The leader-change agent does not react but is proactive in preparing the organization for the need to make changes. Once subordinates are alert to the need to change and accept the need for change, the leader initiates creating a change process involving subordinates who identify the types of changes necessary and implement the planned changes.
- **Organized:** To ensure long-lasting changes, the leader looks to modify the various management systems, organizational policies and work processes to create new routines for the workforce to follow.
- **Communicator:** The leader needs to be an effective communicator because the leader needs to convince subordinates that change is necessary; the leader needs to work with subordinates in developing a change plan; the leader must provide constant feedback during the process of implementing the change

plan; and the leader needs to discuss changes to the change plan as implementation problems emerge and circumstances dictate required changes to the plan.

- **Decision-Making Skills**: The leader needs to be decisive and avoid inaction as a result of fearing to make mistakes. Developing and implementing a decision-making process assist the leader in pursuing a pragmatic, logical approach in making decisions.
- **Problem-Solver**: An effective leader can differentiate between symptoms of a problem and a problem. After identifying the problem, the leader can offer creative solutions to the problem.
- **Conceptualizer**: An effective leader can see the "big picture," understanding all the important issues confronting the organization and the direct and indirect linkage among the issues. In short, the conceptualizer can connect the dots.

LEARNING OBJECTIVE #9: IDENTIFY AND DESCRIBE ANDRAGOGY, AN IMPORTANT ADULT LEARNING THEORY HELPFUL IN DESIGNING A LEADERSHIP DEVELOPMENT TRAINING PROGRAM

Andragogy is a theory developed to describe and explain adult learning. Applying andragogy is useful in guiding how organizations can design leadership development training programs that can benefit the trainees and the organization. By understanding the adult learning process, decision-makers can design relevant training programs.

There are four basic principles associated with adult learning.

1. Adult learners learn best when actively engaged in both the design of the learning process and with the assessment of learning outcomes.
2. Prior work experiences represent important building blocks that support future learning activities because the learner learns best when there is some degree of familiarity with the learning situation.
3. The adult learner's motivation to learn is strengthened if the adult learner perceives that the learning activities are relevant and beneficial to the adult learner's career.
4. The preferred types of learning activities are those associated with actual problem-solving situations. The adult learner prefers practical, relevant and meaningful learning activities.

Several assumptions underly the basic principles of adult learning. Knowing the assumptions aids decision-makers when creating training programs.

1. Adults want greater control over the learning process because the learning process is associated with building the adult's self-confidence.
2. Adults are more comfortable during the learning process when learning builds on the prior work experiences of the learner; familiarity is important to the adult learner.
3. Adult learners are motivated to learn when learning contributes to strengthening the learner's role in a group.

4. The adult learner's level of motivation to learn increases when the urgency to learn increases; urgency is linked to achieving work-related goals.
5. The adult learner is driven to learn more from intrinsic and less from extrinsic sources of motivation.

The adult learner shows a commitment to learning. This commitment gains greater importance as the adult learner begins to establish their career and seeks to enhance their career opportunities through learning. Consequently, the adult learner can motivate themselves to participate in any learning process that helps the adult learner achieve career goals. To keep the adult learner motivated, the subject of learning needs to be associated with achieving the adult learner's career goals.

Because the adult learner recognizes the importance of learning to achieve career goals, the adult learner seeks to influence the learning process to ensure that the learning process is personally relevant. To ensure that the learning process is relevant, the adult learner seeks to influence the design of the learning process so that the process makes use of the adult's prior work experiences. The adult learner links the acquisition of new knowledge and skills using prior work experiences. Prior work experiences provide the building blocks for further learning; the subject needs to be somewhat familiar to the adult learner consequently.

Instructional methods need to emphasize experiential learning because the adult learner prefers this type of instructional method. Experiential learning methods reduce stress associated with learning and offer the adult learner the opportunity to use their prior experiences as learning aids along with learning from other adult learners.

LEARNING OBJECTIVE #10: IDENTIFY AND EXPLAIN THE THREE-STAGE LEADERSHIP DEVELOPMENT PROCESS MODEL FOR DEVELOPING LEADERS

Leaders became leaders by evolving, following a process. If leaders are not born, then a leader emerges from the impact of the individual's environment and how the individual responds to the environment. If an individual does not suddenly move from being a non-leader to a leader, then the leader must become a leader after moving through a developmental process. Figure 9.1 identifies a three-stage process referred to as the **Leadership Developmental Process** (LDP) model.

Stage one of the LDP model is when the individual becomes a **manager**, moving from a non-management pre-stage. The selection to become a manager symbolizes that superiors recognize that the individual possesses qualities that managers and leaders seek from those holding management positions. In some instances, these individuals might be identified as potential leaders, but who need to experience the organization's leadership development training process for the organization to learn if the individual possesses leadership qualities. To become a manager, the individual needs to demonstrate performance-related qualities. Performance is assessed in two

FIGURE 9.1 Leadership Developmental Process Model

Non-Manager ⟶ Manager ⟶ Self-Leader ⟶ Leader

primary ways. First, the organization looks for individuals who achieve; **results-oriented behavior** exhibited represents the second performance measure. Behaviors such as voluntarily assisting colleagues, arriving to work early, the ability to resolve conflicts among colleagues and with customers and problem-solving skills are examples of performance types of behavior. Other qualities include possessing a set of values the organization esteems; the individual processes the knowledge that indicates the ability to demonstrate superior performance, and the individual has the skills, such as communication skills, technical skills and conceptual skills, that serve as important building blocks necessary to develop as a leader.

The next state in the LDP model is **self-leadership**. To reach this stage, the individual begins to recognize positive feelings of self-worth. Self-worth becomes an important pre-leadership insight because the individual recognizes that their career successes were a result of their personal efforts. In short, the individual begins the process of learning to succeed as opposed to the process of learning how to fail, benefiting from feedback. This insight, learning how to succeed, represents a major shift in the individual's thinking and behavior because the individual links their success with feelings of self-worth.

During the self-leadership stage which encompasses the self-LDP, the individual begins learning how to master their actions, developing stronger feelings of self-efficacy. Along with increased feelings of self-control comes self-respect. The individual associate's successful performance with positive values; the individual learns that the values they hold results in stronger feelings of self-worth along with increased feelings of self-respect. During the self-LDP, the individual begins to look ahead, with the belief that their personal road is shaped by the outcomes already achieved and future actions to pursue. Armed with these insights, the individual learns how to become a visionary by developing a personal vision for themselves that includes focusing on personal career plans.

The self-LDP never has an endpoint, and it is a continuous process; but at some point, the individual needs to decide about moving to the **leader stage**. The organization might pre-empt the individual by reaching out and assigning the individual to fill a leadership position. What makes an organization make an offer someone a leadership position? This organization's decision-makers consider the individual capable of being a change agent. Leaders are change agents because a change agent believes in themselves; the individual possesses the vision, knowledge, skills and personal abilities to succeed at improving the performance of their subordinates. Furthermore, strong feelings of self-worth reflect a positive attitude, a consequence of successful experiences. Individuals with positive attitudes influence others because people like to follow those who have a positive attitude. Positive individuals are action-oriented people; people who often succeed; followers view that supporting this type of person is in their best long-term interest. The answer to the question is obvious.

LEARNING OBJECTIVE #11: IDENTIFY AND DESCRIBE THE STAGES IN THE PROCESS FOR DESIGNING A LEADERSHIP DEVELOPMENT TRAINING PROGRAM

Knowing a leadership development training program is necessary, and it is not sufficient to design the program. The training program designers require more detailed information to learn the subjects to cover, topics to focus on within each subject and additional information to help design the training program. A **needs assessment** is the process for collecting the required information. A needs assessment represents an information gathering process that can range from being **formal** to **informal**. The difference is when the designer knows little about the subject and requires detailed information. On the other hand, an informal needs assessment involves gathering updated information on recent developments within the organization.

The next stage in the design process is to identify **training goals**. Training goals are identified through the need assessment. Designers learn from leadership their expectations of the training. From learning what leadership wants trainees to learn and/or accomplish, the designers identify specific training program goals to guide the design process.

During the need assessment information gathering process, designers also learn about the **time** leadership allocates for the training program. Time is a constraint. Designers need to know the time limits as a guide when designing the program. Learning time limits helps to ensure that the program's content meets everyone's expectations as well as achieving the training goals.

Learning objectives represent the next stage in the design process. Learning objectives focus on the specific knowledge and/or skills the leadership expects the trainees to accomplish after completing the training program. Knowledge can include learning about an individual's personal leadership style, learning leadership theories and learning about different types of leadership styles. Skills include problem-solving skills, communication skills, conceptual skills and analytical skills. Learning objectives focus training on very specific needs to achieve by the end of the training program. Information from the need's assessment provides the insights to draft the learning objectives.

After identifying the learning objectives, the designers need to identify **subjects** to cover and relevant **topics** for each subject. Designers need to be careful in selecting subjects and topics as trainees can suffer from information overload. Subjects originate from the learning objectives. The first and last stages of the training program are always the **Introduction** and **Conclusion** stages. Topics are identified for these stages too. For example, during the Introduction, the trainers can introduce themselves, cover the agenda of the program and review any administrative issues. If a learning objective focuses on learning about major leadership theories, the subject of a stage is **leadership theories**. Next, the designer needs to identify relevant topics to cover in this stage. Examples of topics for leadership theories can include purpose, behaviors, important skills and methods of applying a theory. The designers need to limit the range of topics to avoid information overload but be able to provide important insights to the trainees.

Next, the designers select **instructional methods**. Instructional methods represent the approaches used by the trainers to teach the knowledge and skills the trainees need to learn. With 150 instructional methods to select from, the choice of instructional methods is a potential challenge. However, knowledge of andragogy helps in guiding the process for selecting the optimal instructional methods for the adult learner. Lecture is always going to be one method to use for the obvious reason the trainer needs to introduce each stage and communicate other issues on a per need basis. The selection of other instructional methods is guided by understanding how best to teach the subjects. Practical, applied approaches, such as cases studies, group or team exercises, handouts and problem-solving exercises represent some of the best types of instructional methods preferred by the adult learner.

Assessment is an important element in any training program. The designers and trainers need to learn if the trainees are achieving the learning objectives and the training goals. Assessment provides useful feedback about the program. There are **informal assessment methods** (e.g. Q&A and spontaneous one-to-one sessions) and **formal assessment methods** (e.g. multiple choice exams, applied exercises and checklists). The choice of assessment methods rests with the designers. However, trainers typically need to provide an end-of-program report. Assessment helps provide information for a report to leadership, designers, trainers and any other individuals seeking information about the training program. Feedback is helpful in making modifications to the training program.

Finally, designers need to consider the time to allocate for each stage of the training program. At the start, designers know the total time allocated. Designers want to keep the time for the Introduction and Conclusion stages limited. Designers want to allocate the maximum time possible for covering the subjects. There is no standard formula for allocating time. The amount of time allocated to each stage depends on the importance of the stage and the instructional methods assigned to a stage. Consulting with the trainers is useful in aiding the designer's efforts to allocate times per stage. For example, if role playing is assigned to a stage as an instructional method, allocating more time is important because role playing is a time-consuming exercise that involves giving instructions to the trainees, conducting the role-playing exercise and allowing participants to share their insights on what was learned.

LEARNING OBJECTIVE #12: IDENTIFY AND DESCRIBE INSTRUCTIONAL METHODS ASSOCIATED WITH LEADERSHIP DEVELOPMENT TRAINING PROGRAMS

Leadership development instructional methods aid the trainers in guiding trainees to become self-leaders and self-leaders to become leaders and to enable leaders to become more effective types of leaders. Leadership training is ongoing, and instructional methods represent the means used facilitate learning during the training process.

The selection process for identifying instructional methods to use is guided by andragogy because andragogy offers insights on how adult learners learn best. The goal in selecting instructional methods is to be able to increase the trainee's feelings of self-worth. Self-worth development is an essential component of leadership development because as an individual's feelings of self-worth increase, the individual becomes more motivated, and a more motivated person becomes more ambitious. Success is associated with the need to achieve. Individuals become more success-oriented as feelings of self-worth increase. Some individuals with increasing feelings of self-worth seek to become leaders of others. The goal of training is to help trainees become more successful through achieving. The self-worth development process ends only when the individual decides to terminate the process.

Self-leadership together with leadership development emphasizes the importance of developing "core skills" associated with all levels of leadership. These skills are fundamental if an individual is going to be successful in their career. The skills include the following.

1. **Visionary**: Developing the ability to define a future in strategic terms.
2. **Decision-Making Skills**: The ability to think pragmatically and logically and then be decisive.
3. **Communication Skills**: Oral and written forms of communication are essential in guiding/working with others.
4. **Social Skills**: Getting along with others is important as leaders succeed through the efforts of others.
5. **Problem Identification/Problem-Solving Skills**: Identifying problems from symptoms is important because symptoms are not problems; finding solutions is critical in resolving problems.
6. **Conceptual Skills**: The ability to develop ideas to solve problems and identify new approaches for work processes to operate are important to succeed as a leader.
7. **Analysis and Interpretation Skills**: Understanding the relationship among facts and arriving at conclusions from the perceived relationships are important leadership abilities.
8. **Result-Driven Skills**: Leaders need to learn how to identify SMART goals and focus on achieving the goals.
9. **Team Management Skills**: Leaders work in and with teams and knowing how to work with and in a team is important for leaders to be effective.
10. **Informal Power Skills**: Exercising power derived from personal abilities is more effective than position power in motivating subordinates.
11. **Organizing Skills**: Leaders need to develop the ability to design and modify management systems and work processes.

Below are examples of instructional methods that are commonly associated with the development of an individual's leadership skills.

- **Case Studies**: Using relevant cases that draw on prior work experiences to apply.
- **Journals**: Writing about personal work experiences to include alternative ways to deal with the issues.
- **Self-Reflection Exercises**: Leaders learn about themselves through self-studies.
- **Problem-Solving Exercises**: Understanding how the individual solves problems and to identify and evaluate optional solutions to improve problem-solving skills.
- **Coaching**: Use of a trainer type of person who provides guidance.
- **Mentor**: Use of a trainer type of person who helps to facilitate self-learning from reflecting about different work experiences.

The following instructional methods represent examples of methods used in a group setting in facilitating the process of leadership development skills.

- **Case Studies**: Case studies used in a group context expose individuals to different perspectives in studying organizational problems/issues and providing solutions to the problems/issues.
- **Cooperative Learning**: Individuals work together to prepare a presentation for others.

- **Role Playing**: Participants act out different roles, using prior experiences as a starting point and then reflecting on their own actions as well as sharing their insights from observing others.
- **Problem-Solving**: A group of individuals work together to identify a problem(s) and develop solutions to the problem(s).
- **Discussion Group:** Groups are presented with topics to discuss among themselves to gain insights from learning the perceptions and insights of other group members.
- **Team Tasks:** A group is assigned a task to accomplish or select a task to accomplish; individuals rotate team leadership.
- **Presentations:** Individual and group presentations help develop oral communication skills, written skills for handouts and collaboration skills for group presentations.

McDonald's: Part 4

Paula Donovan, McDonald's Senior Executive Vice President for Human Resources, was reviewing the agenda for the upcoming meeting with her senior management team. In addition, Barbara Feldman, the head of Training and Development, was invited to the meeting. The purpose of the meeting was to discuss creating a new introductory course in leadership development for individuals recently identified as potential leaders. The group is to be capped at 20 individuals. The program was last updated ten years prior. As a first step, Paula wanted to pilot the new program first to identify issues to correct. Agenda items include the following.

- Site location for training. Under consideration was to have three different sites: classrooms at corporate headquarters; online; and classes at local sites where specific assignments were performed.
- Time to allocate is important. Should training encompass months, week, days, a day of training and the time per training session.
- Subjects to cover are important. Identifying core subjects to learn is important but keeping the number of subjects limited is necessary to avoid overwhelming trainees.
- Discussion is necessary to review potential instructional methods to use as there are "best type" of instructional methods for the adult learner who is learning to become a leader.

Folks, the floor is open! How would you respond?

Chapter Summary

With 350 definitions on leadership identified in 1982, the number of definitions has only proliferated. This chapter provides examples of definitions of leadership and themes associated with the definitions. One category of definitions of leadership is that leaders lead through work processes. Other categories of definitions of leadership explain leadership as a set of behaviors associated with being a leader. Another sample of definitions about leadership describes types of leadership traits associated with leaders. Leaders are defined by the personal traits they exhibit. Personal traits are a century-long viewpoint. Another category of definitions emphasizes that a leader is about performing tasks, an operations type of focus. There is a category of definitions that are relationship-oriented; these definitions emphasize the importance of working with others. The final category of definitions is situational types of definitions. Leaders emerge from different situations and not from any other factors.

The study of leadership in organizations continues to be an important management subject because organizations depend on leaders to ensure an organization's success. There is no alternative model to the traditional model of an organization's dependence on leaders to guide an organization in becoming an effective organization or to remain functioning as an effective organization.

Leadership theories help us better understand the subject, leader. Though there is no single, universal leadership theory, the different leadership theories offer different perspectives on the subject. Theory is meant to offer a comprehensive view on the subject, providing concepts that explain and increase our understanding of leadership. This chapter provides the reader with an overview of the major leadership theories to introduce the reader to the wide range of viewpoints on leadership as an important subject and as a process.

Personality of a leader or leadership style can determine the leader's success or failure. Leadership style introduces the reader to the understanding of the importance of a leader's personality and the culture of the organization. The purpose in discussing leadership style is to examine the importance of ensuring a good leader-organization fit. Though no leader demonstrates one pure type of leadership style, typically, there is a dominant style. Leader-organization fit is an important issue to consider during the leader selection process because no one benefits from a poor fit.

Successful leaders are not common, easy to identify individuals. Organizations often hire several different leaders until the organization finds an effective leader. The chapter identifies and describes a process that increases an organization's chances of finding the preferred leader. Identifying potential non-CEO leaders is an important issue as well for the organization because of the paucity of leader types. Identifying potential leaders enables the organization to recognize these individuals early and then place these individuals in leadership development training programs. The earlier an organization can uncover potential leaders, the earlier the individuals begin training and the sooner the organization can benefit from the development of these individuals as leaders.

The chapter examines the relationship between leaders and followers to better understand the dynamic process that exists between leaders and followers because reciprocity is critical in creating a successful relationship among leaders and followers, which can only benefit the organization.

Leaders are leaders because organizations consider a leader as a change agent. Successful leaders create effective organizations. An effective organization is an organization that can adapt to competitive conditions. Adaptation represents a change process. Successful leaders mastered the adaptation process through their role as a change agent.

This chapter examines the subject of leadership development because organizations pursue leadership development using both useful and ineffectual approaches. Designers of more effective types of leadership development training programs recognize the importance of creating relevant leadership development training programs. The chapter examines designing a leadership development training program based on the theory of andragogy, the theory that describes adult learning, because adults prefer to learn in particular ways.

The chapter concludes by describing a model on the evolution of a leader from non-leader to manager, to self-leader and then to the leader stage. Describing the model's process focus enables the reader to understand that leaders evolve following an LDP. It is important for the reader to recognize that there is an LDP along with learning about important themes associated with each stage of this developmental process.

Questions

1. What does the term "leadership" refer to?
2. What makes leadership an important subject for organizations?
3. Identify and briefly describe any five leadership theories.
4. Identify and describe any four leadership styles.
5. Describe the process for identifying leaders in an organization.
6. Describe the process for identifying potential leaders in an organization.
7. Discuss the role of the leader as a change agent.
8. Why is understanding andragogy an important subject in the field of leadership development?
9. Identify and describe the three-stage process for developing leaders.
10. Identify and describe the stages in the process for designing a leadership development training program.
11. Identify and briefly describe any five instructional methods associated with leadership development training.

Bibliography

Amanchukwu, R.N., Stanley, G.J. & Oldlube, N.P. (2015). A review of leadership theories, principles and styles and their relevance to educational management. *Management.* 5(1). 6–14.

Bass, B.M. (1999). Two decades of research and development in transformational leadership. *European Journal of Work and Organizational Psychology.* 8(1). 9–32.

Bennes, W. (1982). The artform of leadership. *Training and Development Journal.* 36(4). 44–46.

Caprino, K. (2018). The changing face of leadership: 10 new research finding all leaders need to understand. https://www.forbes.com/sites/kathycaprino/2018?02/08/the-changing......./#7e7/February 28/.

Carbery, R. & Garavan, T.N. (2016). Leadership and management development in Thomas, Garavan, Alma McCarthy, and Ronan Carbery. (Eds.). *Handbook of International Human Resource Development: Context, Processes and People.* Edward Elgar Publisher. 387–406.

Cherry, K. (2019). Leadership styles. https://psychology.about.com/OD/leadership/

Cote, R. (2017). A comparison of leadership theories in an organizational environment. *International Journal of Business Administration.* 8(5). 28–35.

Day, D.V. (2001). Leadership development: a review context. *Leadership Quarterly.* 11(4).581–613.

Day, D.V. (2012). Leadership in *Oxford Handbook of Organizational Psychology, Volume 2 – Oxford Handbooks.* Oxford University Press. Chapter 22.

Day, D.V., Fleenor, J.W., Atwater, L.E., Sturm, R.E. & McKee, R.A. (2014). Advances in leader and leadership development: a review of 25 years of research and theory. *The Leadership Quarterly.* 25. 63–82.

Dinh, J., Lord, R., Garnder, W., Meuser, J., Liden, R.C. & Hu. J. (2014). Leadership theory and research in the new millennium: current theoretical trends and changing perspectives. *Leadership Quarterly.* 25(1). 36–62.

Kundor. (2019). Leadership skills. Kundoc.com/pdf-leadershp-skills-8BB4443FFODE4F6BC56A4BE2265BA4FB55779.html./

Leadership-Central.com. (2019). Leadership theories. https://www.leadership-central.com/leadership-theories.html/. 1–7.

Oracle. (2012). Seven steps for effective leadership development. *An Oracle White Paper.* June. 1–20.

Pryor, M.G., Taneja, S., Humphreys, J., Anderson, D. & Singleton, L. (2008). Challenges facing change management theories and research. *Delhi Business Review.* 9(1). 1–20.

Ross, S. (2015). *The Road to Self-Leadership Development: Busting Out of Your Comfort Zone.* Emerald Publish.

Ross, S. (2018). *Training and Development in Organizations: An Essential Guide for Trainers.* Routledge Publishing.

Society for Human Resource Management. (2016). Leadership development: the path to greater effectiveness. EFMD. *Network of Corporate Academics.* Network of Corporate Academics. November. 1–81.

Yukl, G. (1989). Managerial leadership: a review of theory and research. *Journal of Management.* 15(2). 251–289.

Yukl, G. (1999). An evaluation of conceptual weaknesses in transformational and charismatic leadership theories. *The Leadership Quarterly.* 10(2). 285–305.

Yukl, G. (2012). Effective leadership behavior: what we know and what questions need more attention. *Academy of Management Executive.* November. 66–85.

Yukl, G., Gordon, A. & Taber, T. (2002). A hierarchical taxonomy of leadership behavior: integrating a half century of behavior research. *Journal of Leadership and Organizational Studies.* 9(1). 15–32.

Organizational Development and Training

OVERVIEW

This chapter examines two subjects associated with improving an organization's performance. First, Organizational Development (OD) represents a management theory about facilitating organizational change as well as providing a methodology to follow to create a process to bring about organizational change. OD's long-term purpose is to be a guide to implementing organizational change with the goal of improving the organization's ability to successfully compete more effectively.

Training represents a second management approach to bring about change. Training's emphasis is to serve as one of the primary methods to facilitate employee learning with the goal of improving workforce performance. Formal by intent, training programs focus on educating the workforce or segments of the workforce by increasing employee knowledge, adding to or developing employee skills and improving an employee's personal abilities. The overall goal in improving the workforce is to better the organization's performance.

The chapter offers the reader an in-depth overview of OD which includes a description of the different OD models. Often organizations draw on the expertise of OD consultants to help manage the change process. This chapter identifies and describes the knowledge, skills and personal abilities OD consultants need to be successful change agents.

The remaining focus of this chapter's coverage of OD is to identify and describe core values linked to OD; explain the application of systems theory integral to OD initiatives; and identify and describe the expected impact OD is meant to have on individuals, groups and the organization.

The second part of this chapter covers training. In particular, the chapter identifies the important benefits associated with training. Furthermore, this chapter introduces and describes the Ross Instructional Systems Design Process (RISDP) model to help understand all the important issues associated with creating a training program. The chapter also describes the Ross Systems Training Program Design (RSTPD) model. This model describes the process training program designers can use to design an actual training program. The chapter ends by identifying and describing important themes (e.g. instructional methods) associated with the design and implementation of training programs.

CHAPTER 10   LEARNING OBJECTIVES

Readers will achieve the following learning objectives after reading this chapter.

1. Identify and describe OD, the definition and role of OD.
2. Identify, describe and explain the OD models.
3. Identify and describe the knowledge, skills and personal abilities needed by an OD consultant.
4. Identify and explain the objectives of OD.
5. Identify, describe and explain the core values associated with OD.
6. Describe and explain the systems perspective associated with OD.
7. Describe and explain how OD is meant to impact individuals, groups or teams, and the organization.
8. Identify, describe and explain the benefits of training.
9. Identify, describe and explain the RISDP.
10. Identify, describe and explain the RSTPD.
11. Identify, describe and explain the Kirkpatrick four-level model for evaluating the effectiveness of training.
12. Identify, describe and explain the importance of instructional methods.
13. Identify and describe the benefits of training for individuals and the organization.
14. Identify, describe and explain the best types of subjects to cover in training.

LEARNING OBJECTIVE #1: IDENTIFY AND DESCRIBE ORGANIZATIONAL DEVELOPMENT: THE DEFINITION AND ROLE OF ORGANIZATIONAL DEVELOPMENT

Organizational Development (OD) is unique in that OD is both a theory and a prescriptive model that describes how to facilitate organizational change. OD theory emphasizes two major themes. First, OD identifies and describes the antecedent external environmental conditions that are a catalyst for the organization to initiate organizational changes. Second, as stated already, OD provides a broad conceptual overview to describe and explain the change process to follow when an organization initiates change. OD theory provides a change management model that offers a step-by-step guide to follow in implementing systematic, routinized changes within an organization. Though there are different permutations of OD theory, each model variation offers the OD change agent a model to follow in designing and implementing changes within an organization.

   OD represents a sub-category within management theory; OD originated out of the humanistic school of thought where the emphasis was on individual self-improvement. Though initially, the focus was on effecting change among individual members of an organization's workforce, the scope of the focus evolved to include making improvements to the organization. OD theory includes a paradigmatic representation of a process for implementing organizational change along with individual change. Consequently, the focus on organization-wide change continues the evolution of the self-improvement process which is the fundamental focus of OD theory.

OD is grounded on a humanistic set of values that emphasize positive individual change and change to the organization that will benefit both the members of the workforce and the organization. OD theory's foundation represents a composite of concepts originating from a variety of disciplines such as sociology, psychology and anthropology to demonstrate that OD's multi-dimensional roots, demonstrating an eclectic and inclusive approach to better describe, understand and guide the change process.

One of the disciplines associated with OD is biology. Biology offers a system's perspective (derived from General Systems Theory) to understand why OD emphasizes a comprehensive approach to change in response to the impact that external environmental forces have on the organization and various units within the organization. Systems theory, open systems theory, posits that the external environment has an impact on the organization, organizational units and individuals directly and indirectly. Furthermore, because of the open systems perspective, OD postulates that any action to make improvements in one or more areas of the organization will indirectly impact related areas of the organization. Action research, an important component of OD, focuses on the important role collecting empirical information plays to identify organizational problem areas. The action research model serves to guide the collection of empirical data to assess the impact of OD intervention initiatives.

Another important element of OD is OD's process orientation during the implementation of an OD intervention strategy. All OD models adhere to a process focus when implementing intervention strategies with the goal of improving organizational performance. A process orientation means that OD initiatives adhere to a stage-by-stage or step-by-step approach; intervention follows a sequence of actions that build on preceding actions (i.e. stage-by-stage).

The role of OD as a model for facilitating change is explicit. OD is meant to create a cultural shift by linking changes with a series of values derived from the humanistic school. The fundamental belief is that by making the life of individuals better, the performance of the organization improves as a result. Second, the process for implementing an OD intervention strategy is meant to be an ongoing process and not a one and done application. A long-term goal of OD is to build and/or strengthen the organization's abilities at self-management and self-improvement (both values) by incorporating OD humanistic perspectives into the organization's operations. Third, OD emphasizes developing leadership's capabilities to develop leaders as change agents who oversee and guide the ongoing change management process indefinitely. Finally, OD is a result-oriented change management theory. OD emphasizes the importance of creating a performance management system that conducts empirically based performance assessments, identifies problems and assesses the impact of OD intervention strategies. Empirically derived data provide objective-based evidence to support leadership's views on identifying problems and on the effectiveness of the changes to the organization.

LEARNING OBJECTIVE #2: IDENTIFY, DESCRIBE AND EXPLAIN THE ORGANIZATIONAL DEVELOPMENT MODELS

Four OD models help to exemplify implementation strategies to facilitate organizational change. Each model offers a different approach in guiding the organizational change process. Each of the models follows a stage-by-stage approach to change management, with specific types of task activities to perform at each stage. Other than Lewin's three-force change model, the other three models emphasize a process with more discrete stages; the focus of each stage is to generate specific types of outcomes for each stage.

There are three basic parts to each of the models. The first part represents the **diagnostic phase**. Diagnosis assumes that the organization is not functioning as expected. **Action research** represents a data collection methodology used during the diagnostic phase. Action research quantifiably assesses an organization's performance. The information is used to compare the findings with leadership's expectations. The difference between the actual findings compared to the expected findings signals what leadership needs to focus on. OD consultants work with leadership to assist leaders in identifying solutions that lead to improved performance, meeting leadership's expectations. Goals represent leadership's expectations.

The next part is the **action phase**. During this phase, the organization's leadership works with the support of an OD consultant or OD consulting team to begin to identify solutions to close the gap between actual performance and expected performance. Solutions move through a process of trial and error to learn what solution works best to improve performance. Solutions or actions pursued focus on changing individual behavior, group behavior and organizational behavior (through changes to organizational work processes).

The third part of the OD change process is **program management**. Program management involves routinizing the changes made to organizational work processes identified during the action phase, requiring changes to close the performance gap. This means that the organization's goal during this phase of the change process is to standardize the modified work processes. The new work processes represent building blocks that the organization leverages for further development because OD is meant to institutionalize the change process so that change is continuous. One of the important foci of OD is to transform an organization's culture to support ongoing changes efforts by emphasizing the values associated with performance management. Such values as performance assessment, goal-oriented, self-motivation, self-development and accountability represent some of the most important values associated with the change process.

Lewin's **force field OD model** is a three-stage change model. Lewin recognized the importance of making a strong case for the need to change because of the countervailing forces that seek to maintain the status quo. The first stage in Lewin's model is the **unfreeze stage**. This stage emphasizes making a strong case for the need to change. The use of action research during this stage is meant to gather performance data as well as data on the performance of competitors to overcome advocates who want to maintain the status quo. During the **change stage** new work processes are designed and implemented to initiate specific changes. Feedback on the impact of the work processes informs leadership and

OD consultants on the effectiveness of the changes to the work processes. Modification to the work processes refines the work processes by eliminating the dysfunctional elements of the modified work process. During the third stage, **re-freeze**, leadership formalizes the new work processes, using organizational policies, training and a change in values to ensure the continuity of the changes to the work processes.

The **action research OD model** focuses on solving organizational problems by learning how to identify problems and then develop solutions that solve the problems. Collecting data is meant to identify symptoms of problems at the initial step in the search for causal factors (i.e. problems). After identifying the problems, leadership along with OD consultants develops solutions. The solutions represent new work routines that lead to improve performance.

The **appreciative inquiry OD model** focuses on examining an organization's capabilities and not problems. The goal is on self-improvement through identifying strengths and developing solutions that build on strengths. The model examines individuals, groups and the organization's strengths or capabilities with the goal of creating more effective strengths. Routinizing the changes is meant to forestall any chances of backsliding. Changing the organization's culture involves strengthening the values that support the changes which reduces the chance of relapses from occurring.

The **general OD model of planned change** emphasizes identifying problems as well as identifying an organization's strengths. This model has two goals. First, identifying solutions to the problems is essential to improve an organization's performance. Second, identifying strengths is meant to find solutions that create a core competency from a strength. This OD model is meant to offer the OD consultant a comprehensive range of subjects to cover in working with an organization's leadership.

LEARNING OBJECTIVE #3: IDENTIFY AND DESCRIBE THE KNOWLEDGE, SKILLS AND PERSONAL ABILITIES NEEDED BY AN ORGANIZATIONAL DEVELOPMENT CONSULTANT

There are several subjects an OD consultant must be knowledgeable about.

- **OD Theories:** Theory provides the consultant with different perspectives about organizational change and change management strategies.
- **Process Management:** OD theories mostly adhere to a process orientation in working with clients and recommending solutions; this means following a client-consultant process and offering solutions that create or re-design organizational work process to routinize change.
- **Organizational Culture:** Organizational activities are influenced by the organization's culture; an organization's culture is composed of a collection of important values.
- **Motivation Theories:** Understanding the variety of motivation theories helps the OD consultant understand the relationship between the individual and existing organizational reward system as well as being able to offer ideas on re-designing the organization's reward system.

- **Strategies to Overcome Resistance:** Resistance is a natural reaction to change initiatives; the OD consultant needs to know the various strategies used to overcome resistance.
- **Behavioral Analysis:** OD consulting involves changing behavior, especially the behavior of individuals; knowing how people act and the influences on behavior is important to the consultant's work.
- **Team Management Theory:** The OD consultant needs to understand how to form and manage teams and common types of team-related management issues to advise clients.
- **Change Theories:** Understanding change and the different perspectives about change enable the OD consultant to offer their perspective about the antecedents of change.
- **Organizational Theories:** The OD consultant needs to understand the structuring of organizations, organizational behavior and common structural problems experienced by organizations.
- **Research Methods:** All OD intervention strategies require the collection of data, data analysis and data interpretation to validate the need for change and to evaluate the results of organizational changes.
- **Systems Theory:** The OD consultant needs to think strategically to guide clients in understanding the impact of change in other parts of the organization.
- **Business and Business Functions:** Working with business organizations requires that the OD consultant understands how a business operates.

The OD consultant must develop skills that enable the consultant to successfully work with clients.

- **Problem-Solving Skills:** Distinguishing between a symptom of a problem and a problem is an important skill when trying to identify solutions to a problem.
- **Social Skills:** Developing social skills is important because OD consultants must work with people to be successful.
- **Communication Skills:** Effective writing and oral presentations along with client planning sessions require good communication skills.
- **Working with Teams:** Often, OD consultants work with teams of decision-makers; the consultants need to be skilled in the application of group management strategies.
- **Diagnostic Skills:** Problem-solving is only one aspect of diagnosis; the OD consultant needs to know how to understand patterns of interactions among individuals along with the impact of change solutions on the organization.
- **Applied Research Methods:** Know how to conduct research is important for the OD consultant but knowing how to use research methods is critical to the success of the OD consulting process.
- **Intervention Strategies:** The ability to apply intervention strategies when confronting resistance is an important aspect of the OD consultant's role.
- **External Analysis:** The OD consultant needs to be able to assist the organization's leadership in understanding how the organization's external environment impacts the organization.

The personal abilities necessary to succeed as an OD consultant include the following.

- **Education:** The OD consultant needs to gain the necessary knowledge and skills necessary to work as an OD consultant and be credible.
- **Training and Experience:** Specialized training in specific OD topics and the development of an OD consultant's expertise; working with a practicing OD consultant offers an OD consultant the opportunity to learn from experience and tutelage.
- **Interpersonal Skills:** Effective interpersonal skills provide the foundation for further development of social skills.
- **Self-Knowledge:** Knowing oneself helps in understanding human dynamics when working with people.
- **Strategic:** The ability to think "big picture" provides a solid foundation to build on for the OD consultant who needs to think strategically.
- **Self-Leader:** Working with others to bring about individual change and organizational change requires an OD consultant who has a strong set of positive values, a positive attitude and strong feelings of self-worth.
- **Communication Skills:** Natural oral skills are particularly important because of the frequent use of conversation in working as an OD consultant.
- **Organized:** OD consulting is a complex process, potentially working with scores of different individuals and groups of individuals. The OD consultant needs to be well-organized to keep abreast of all ongoing work projects.

LEARNING OBJECTIVE #4: IDENTIFY AND EXPLAIN THE OBJECTIVES OF ORGANIZATIONAL DEVELOPMENT

The goals of the organization's practitioners of OD and OD consultants are to improve the organization's long-term performance and the performance of individual members of the organization's workforce. To achieve these goals, OD practitioners and OD consultants focus on accomplishing the following objectives.

- **Guide Organizations Seeking Change** by creating an awareness that change is necessary by preparing a roadmap to follow by identifying initiatives that serve as a catalyst for organizational change.
- **Routinize Changes to Work Processes** because organizations operate using work processes. To ensure the long-term benefits of the changes, organizations need to incorporate the changes within a work process because work processes standardize the work performance of individuals.
- **Leadership Development** represents one of the important objectives in implementing OD methods because change must start among leadership and changes initiated must come from leadership. Leadership needs to learn how to succeed as OD change agents.
- **Build an Organization's Capabilities to Initiate Organizational Change** because change is an ongoing work process that never stops, so the organization needs to create in-house OD change agents to spearhead change and the change management process.
- **Prepare the Workforce that Change** is coming because people will either resist change or fail to embrace the benefits of change. Change is ongoing but

people are creatures of habit, following routines in performing their work. Individual's need to understand the need for change and the benefits of change to embrace change, which is disruptive to routines.

- **Create a Learning Organization** because a learning organization constantly seeks to acquire new knowledge and skills to aid the organization in successfully managing the organization's change processes.
- **Increase an Organization's Effectiveness** because change management's focus is on improving performance to enable the organization and individuals to achieve goals and to become more success oriented by setting ambitious goals.
- **Increase an Organization's Efficiency** in performing work routines to enable the organization to perform faster, with fewer mistakes and at a lower cost; lowering costs increases the organization's profitability which enables the organization to invest more money into building the capabilities of the organization to meet future competitive challenges.
- **Create an Organizational Culture that Embraces Change** through the development of a value-based culture where the values associated with the support of change, initiating change and managing change become part of the fabric that represents the organization's culture.

Eldridge Corporation – Part 1

Paul Ryan, Executive Vice President of Human Resources, was meeting with his senior staff to discuss problematic behavior trends among the workforce. Included in the meeting was Janet Simpson, a senior OD specialist with Monroe Organizational Development Consultants. Paul asked Margaret, the firm's conflict resolution manager, to review the issues that occurred during the past year that contributed to serious organizational performance problems. Margaret's list was extensive. The attrition rate exceeded the baseline by a considerable amount. Complaining was rampant among managers and non-managers. Lateness to work and to meetings was a problem as was extended lunch breaks and personal conflicts among workers and between workers and managers. Unit performance trends were abysmal. Units and groups were rarely meeting their performance goals. When Margaret finished, Paul turned to Janet for her thoughts.

Question

Describe how Janet responded.

LEARNING OBJECTIVE #5: IDENTIFY, DESCRIBE AND EXPLAIN THE CORE VALUES ASSOCIATED WITH ORGANIZATIONAL DEVELOPMENT

Though the list of values that follow is not exhaustive, the sample of values showcases the more important values OD consultants seek to promote within a client organization. OD consultants advocate the acquisition of values, or if a value is present, to strengthen the commitment to that value within the organization.

The list of values includes the following.

- **Change is Good:** OD attempts to put change in a broader context; change is constant, and the organization needs to embrace change as a common activity.
- **Improve Performance:** OD is all about improving the performance of the workforce and the organization. Improving performance is one of the "golden rules" for an organization.
- **Increase an Individual's Feelings of Self-Worth:** Individuals that value themselves and have a positive attitude are self-motivated, striving to do more and aim to succeed at what they want to accomplish. This is another organizational "golden rule."
- **Systems-Oriented:** Systems represent organized management methods that support and promote organizational performance by being well-organized and emphasizing the broader impact of a management system.
- **Working Together:** Cooperation among the workforce contributes to greater performance successes than working solo.
- **Process-Oriented:** All work follows a structured process. Accepting this fact focuses all change efforts on instituting changes to the organization's work processes.
- **Structure:** The design of an organization attempts to create a network of linked work groups hierarchically and vertically to strengthen coordination, cooperation and locus of functional authority.
- **Employee-Focused:** Improving employee performance contributes to improved performance of the organization.
- **Learning:** Creating a learning organization leads to an organization capable of successfully responding to external environmental conditions the organization needs to respond to.
- **Models:** Acquiring a model mentality aids the organization in developing a framework that guides performance of any activity. A "how to do something" focus.
- **Theory-Oriented:** Theory helps to bring understanding to observed phenomena.
- **Communication:** Emphasizing clear and concise writing and oral presentations reduces confusion and aids in achieving goals.
- **Goal-Oriented:** Emphasizing goals provides focus and enables performance management system to function at a high level because effectiveness is about achieving goals.
- **Efficiency:** Improving performance to reduce costs is important in improving profitability.
- **Leadership:** Leadership at all organizational levels is a must to promote change initiatives meant to improve an organization's effectiveness and efficiency.
- **Self-Improvement:** By encouraging individuals to focus on themselves, the organization aims to directly benefit from members of the workforce's efforts at strengthening their ability to perform their jobs.
- **Decision-Making:** Involving the workforce in making decisions provides workers with the opportunity to share their perspective, strengthening their commitment to an organization devoted to employee involvement.

- **Performance Assessment:** OD is a result-oriented method for facilitating organizational change and change needs to lead to measurable results.
- **Continuous Improvement:** Change management is not a one-time event. Change is ongoing, and the organization needs to create the capabilities to manage change continuously.
- **Ethical:** A commitment to moral principles strengthens an organization's dedication to the workforce; the organization serves as a role model for individuals to follow.
- **Teamwork:** A devotion to working with others increases an organization's efforts at coordinating work through the cooperative effort of the workforce.
- **Adaptability:** Rigid thinking is bad for an organization that needs to change in response to external environmental conditions that require the organization to change to remain successful.
- **Empirically Based Research:** Knowing how to collect data, analyze data and interpret the analyses is essential in developing empirically supported recommendations for changing a work process as well as identify the need for change.
- **Client-Centered:** The OD consultant needs to ensure that the client and assisting the client remains the most important goal driving the OD consultant's efforts.

LEARNING OBJECTIVE #6: DESCRIBE AND EXPLAIN THE SYSTEMS PERSPECTIVE ASSOCIATED WITH ORGANIZATIONAL DEVELOPMENT

OD focuses on pursuing a comprehensive, organization-wide impact in making changes. Systems theory is part of OD because systems theory requires a strategic, big picture focus. Strategic because changes are meant to have a broad impact. An organization is composed of units or collections of people organized into units. Small organizations have fewer units, while larger organizations have more units. OD actions targeting one or several units will naturally impact additional units because all units are either directly or indirectly linked through various work processes.

The systems approach in facilitating organizational change forces the OD consultant to be cognizant of the potential impact when applying intervention strategies. Awareness of the possible implications of change, OD consultants need to consider planned changes carefully to anticipate the impact of the planned changes as well the consequential unplanned effects. That is why OD theory emphasizes the use of a planned, stage-by-stage approach to change management, including assessing if the changes trend in the predicted direction. Moving too fast without assessing the impact of the changes is a recipe for additional problems. Worse because now, workers and leaders might have a negative impression of OD theory and the OD methodology for change.

Systems theory involves the use of SMART goals that make performance measurement easier to accomplish. Systems thinking, where all units of the organization are directly and indirectly linked, means that all the connected units are in some way impacted by the change process. OD's focus is on changing existing work processes and routinizing the changes within the affected work process. Work processes include processes linking other units within a larger process. The focus on changing a work process can include within unit processes and/or the processes that link units. Regardless of the focus, the impact of changes is broad. Minor changes like throwing a pebble in the water, small ripples occur and the ripples stop quickly. The larger the stone, the larger the ripples and the further the ripples spread.

An organization's systems perspective is intuitive. Therefore, organizations create different types of management systems identified and described in prior chapters. Organizations recognize the importance of organizing the workforce into groups and units, organizing groups and units into larger units and onward until all units fall under one large system of interconnected units referred to as the organization. Management systems are organized around themes, such as the information system, performance management system and reward system. A systems perspective guides the organizing process that is intuitive, but this does not minimize the need for more structure and focus in the organizing process. The organization's management systems serve to link all the units together in one overall organizational structure.

LEARNING OBJECTIVE #7: DESCRIBE AND EXPLAIN HOW ORGANIZATIONAL DEVELOPMENT IS MEANT TO IMPACT INDIVIDUALS, GROUPS OR TEAMS, AND THE ORGANIZATION

OD's focus on individuals emphasizes promoting an individual's sense of self-worth. The OD approach is to teach individuals how to become successful change agents in performing their work responsibilities. Success leads to an individual who changes their self-view to one in which the individual's perception of self-worth increases. An individual with a strong understanding of their self-worth develops a positive attitude about themselves, their work and their workplace. A positive attitude leads to a self-motivated individual who values achieving, leading to the individual's pursuit of new work opportunities that result in more successful accomplishments. Success contributes to the development of a set of values that reinforce the individual's attitude, self-motivation and ambitions. The result is the individual's feelings of self-importance to the organization increases. The individual commits to doing more for the organization's benefit. A successful individual along with a successful organization strengthen the bond with each other.

Groups or teams benefit from OD initiatives because the perception of people successfully working together confirms the perception of the value of the group or team to the organization. Group/team dynamics changes from ongoing OD initiatives to ensure that the group/team continues to succeed in meeting their responsibilities; groups/teams use the knowledge of OD principles to overcome roadblocks that can lead to failed efforts. Groups/teams create a set of values that strengthen the group/team members commitment and loyalty to the group/team and among each group/team members, along with reinforcing the idea of the importance of working as a group/team.

The organization benefits from OD interventions in four important ways. First, OD focuses on changing an organization's culture through the promotion of values that emphasize the importance of the individual, the group/team and the ability to successfully initiate and manage change on an ongoing basis. Second, OD demonstrates the importance of routinizing organizational changes to ensure the longevity of the changes by incorporating the changes within organizational work processes. Third, OD provides the knowledge necessary for an organization to create the capabilities of confronting external threats and opportunities, successfully responding to each. Finally, OD works with leadership to help leadership understand their importance to the organization as role models to the workforce. As role models, leadership demonstrates the characteristics of change agents who can successfully lead the organization in confronting problems, pursue opportunities and confront external threats in becoming visionaries and provide a picture of what the organization can become through change.

Eldridge Corporation – Part 2

Bob Aldridge, CFO, Katherine Parker, COO and Paul Ryan, Executive Vice President of Human Resources were meeting with Janet Simpson, the senior OD specialist with Monroe Organizational Development Consultants. Janet is an expert in assisting organizations in developing a team model for organizing work. Bob, Kathleen and Paul were explaining to Janet that they realized the need to organize the workforce into teams. They believed that a team approach would generate more synergies from the workforce. However, they were uncertain how to begin. Furthermore, they were concerned that instead of valuing a team approach in performing their jobs, the workforce would reject the idea. Resistance from managers was a real issue as informal discussions with managers about the proposal were met with push-back. Bob asked Janet her thoughts. Janet responded by proposing to follow the Lewin model for change.

Questions

1. How did Janet present the Lewin model?
2. Why did Janet recommend following the Lewin model? Explain.

LEARNING OBJECTIVE #8: IDENTIFY, DESCRIBE AND EXPLAIN THE BENEFITS OF TRAINING

An example of a proactive effort by organizations to improve the performance individuals is the creation and implementation of formal training programs. Qualitative improvements to the workforce directly benefit the organization. One important advantage associated with training's impact on the organization is to improve the organization's ability to achieve strategic goals. Achieving strategic goals comes from the application of increased knowledge that contributes to the workforce's ability to perform their jobs.

Skill development or skill enhancement represents another payoff from training. Workforce skills are associated with performing a job. There are several different types of skills, such as problem-solving skills, communication skills, cognitive skills along with specific technical skills associated with the ability of an individual to perform a job.

Another advantage of training is to improve the workforce's level of knowledge and skills by using performance types of learning objectives. Performance types of learning objectives represent learning objectives that set a standard that trainees need to achieve. For example, trainees need to know a subject sufficiently to pass a test with a score of 80 or higher. Another example, call center operators need to manage each call in under three minutes. A final example, the keyboardist must type 300 words in nine minutes or less with no more than one error. Achieving higher performance standards leads to superior work performance.

Superior work performance is another advantage of training. The purpose of many organizational training programs is to enable the trainee to apply learning on the job with the result being superior work performance. The challenge for the trainer and the trainee is to ensure that the training experience is relevant and applicable, resulting in the trainee applying what was learned to the job.

A further advantage of training is that training can enable the trainee to gain mastery in a subject or skill. Mastering a subject will lead to increased feelings of self-efficacy which results in improved perception of self-worth. Self-worth contributes to the development of a positive attitude which advances an individual's self-motivation; the self-motivated worker pursues more work responsibilities as a direct benefit of increased feelings of self-worth.

Training individuals to become leaders is crucial to developing leaders which justifies the organization's creation of leadership development training programs. Organizations that believe leaders are developed and not born emphasize the use of leadership development training. Organizations gain by having more leaders and better leaders; more effective leaders contribute to a happier and more focused workforce which benefits the organization.

Finally, most organizations today promote the use of teams in performing complex work tasks. Forming and managing teams is not a natural ability. Training team leaders in **team development** and **team management** enables team leaders to be more successful. Successful team leaders lead successful teams which benefits the organization.

LEARNING OBJECTIVE #9: IDENTIFY, DESCRIBE AND EXPLAIN THE ROSS INSTRUCTIONAL SYSTEMS DESIGN PROCESS MODEL (RISDP)

A successful training program begins with the understanding that having a comprehensive overview about the training purpose is essential; the methods to use in designing a training program are crucial; and the importance of implementing a training program correctly is critical. A model of the training program design process ensures that the training program designers consider all the important issues during the design process. The **RISDP** (see Figure 10.1) provides the designers with a framework of a process to follow, the stages in the process and the sequence the stages.

The RISDP model follows a **systems theory** perspective in creating the training program design process. Each stage of the process links directly and indirectly with every other stage in the process, creating network of stages sequenced in an ordered, systematic way. Failure at any one stage negatively impacts other stages. Failure results in a less than optimal training program that does not reflect the intentions of decision-makers.

In addition to systems theory, there are three other types of theories for training program designers to consider. **Motivation theories** provide designers with

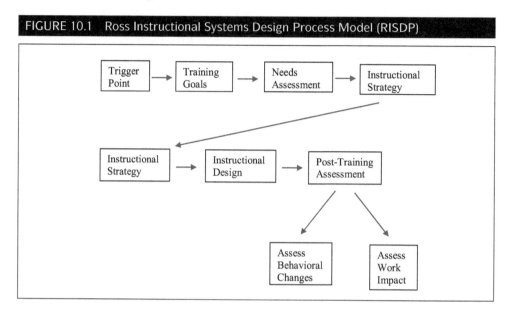

FIGURE 10.1 Ross Instructional Systems Design Process Model (RISDP)

insights on how best to design a training program to keep trainees motivated to learn and willing to apply the subjects learned post-training. To learn about the receptiveness of the trainees to the upcoming training program along with the importance of the training program to the organization, decision-makers and the trainee, a **needs assessment** enables the designers to learn about the issues associated with the training subject. A needs assessment provides training program designers with vital information to assist in creating a well-designed, relevant training program.

Learning theories represent another category of theories designers need to consider during the design process. There are three sub-categories of applicable learning theories to apply. **Behavior-based learning theories** focus on how to influence the types of behaviors trainees need to exhibit post-training. **Cognitive theories** help the designers create a training program that influences the type of analytical abilities to develop. **Constructivism theories** enable the designers to consider the practical needs of the trainee. **Andragogy** is an example of a constructivism theory because the emphasis is on designing a training program that considers the learning styles adult trainees use to learn best. Problem-solving, group learning, use of prior experiences, etc. represent examples of the contextual issues that the learning experience needs to emphasize to maximize learning.

The stages of the RISDP model follow.

1. **Trigger Point:** The issue or issues that trigger the idea among decision-makers that a type of training program is necessary.
2. **Training Goals:** Decision-makers identify the goals the training program needs to achieve.
3. **Needs Assessment:** Training program designers collect information from decision-makers about their expectations, the subject matter to cover, the type of trainee and the comprehensiveness required of the training program.

4. **Instructional Strategy:** This strategy reflects the specific plan the designers will follow in designing the complete training program.
5. **Instructional Design:** Identify and show the linkage among all the training program components.
6. **Post-Training Assessment:** Assessment refers to the methods used to determine if trainee behavior changed as a result of training; learning if the trainees applied what was learned in their job.

LEARNING OBJECTIVE #10: IDENTIFY, DESCRIBE AND EXPLAIN THE ROSS STRUCTURED TRAINING PROGRAM DESIGN MODEL (RSTPD)

The **Ross Structured Training Program Design model (RSTPD)** provides training program designers with a systematic approach to follow when designing a training program. The approach to designing a training program for adults needs to rely primarily on the learning theory, **andragogy**, because andragogy provides a useful framework that considers the needs of the adult learner.

Table 10.1 provides a visual overview of the RSTPD model. The RSTPD training program design model follows a process composed of **stages**. Each stage is numbered for referencing a stage, showing the sequence of stages along with the number of stages in the training program. Designers next focus on identifying the **learning objectives** of the program. Learning objectives state the specific **knowledge** trainees need to know or the **skills** trainees need to perform or **performance-based** learning objectives that define how well a trainee needs to know a subject or how well a trainee needs to perform a skill. For example, a knowledge-based learning objective is phrased as follows: Trainees can identify and describe five different types of motivation theories. A skill-based learning objective is stated as follows: Trainees can demonstrate how to start and operate a self-propelled lawn mower. A performance-based learning example follows: Trainees can demonstrate an understanding of expectancy theory by scoring an 80 or higher on a test that assesses the knowledge about expectancy theory.

After designers identify the learning objectives for each stage following stage one and prior to the final stage, designers identify a subject to cover during each stage. Typically, a subject originates from the learning objective. For example, "three motivation theories" could be a subject for a stage. Stage one will always be the

TABLE 10.1 Ross Structured Training Program Design Model (Rstpd)						
Stage	*Time*	*Learning objectives*	*Subjects*	*Topics*	*Instructional methods*	*Assessment methods*
1			Introduction			
2						
3						
4						
5						
6						
7			Conclusion			

Introduction stage. The last stage in the training program is always the **Conclusion** stage. After identifying subjects, designers identify the **topics** to cover during each stage. A topic refers to a specific element of a subject. Topics can vary, but the designer needs to strike a balance between too few and too many topics to include. For example, three topics associated with motivation theories can focus on the important concepts, applications and limitations of each theory. The designers select topics based on what trainees need to know according to the feedback from decision-makers through the need's assessment.

    Instructional methods represent the next item designers must consider. Designers rely on their knowledge of andragogy for guidance in selecting instructional methods. In addition, the purpose of the training program influences the type of instructional methods to consider; the designer selects those methods with the goal of optimizing learning. There are approximately 150 different types of instructional methods to select from.

    Designers next need to consider assessment of learning. **Assessment methods** can vary from formal, such as a multiple-choice exam to the informal (e.g. a spontaneous Q&A session). There is a **formative assessment** type; trainers need to learn if trainees are learning during training. Post-training assessment methods (i.e. **summative methods**) are used to learn if trainee behavior changes because of training and/or if trainees applied what was learned during training while performing their work responsibilities.

LEARNING OBJECTIVE #11: IDENTIFY, DESCRIBE AND EXPLAIN THE KIRKPATRICK FOUR-LEVEL MODEL FOR EVALUATING THE EFFECTIVENESS OF TRAINING

Kirkpatrick's s four-level model is meant to offer a roadmap for assessing learning as a result of trainees participating in a training program. Assessment of learning is part of the process for establishing accountability within a training program. Organizations expend resources to conduct training that leads to results. Training program designers, trainers and trainees are accountable for fulfilling their responsibilities for the organization's benefit.

    The Kirkpatrick model recommends the use of different approaches to assess learning and the trainees learning experience. The first evaluation level in the Kirkpatrick four-level model is to learn the trainee's **reaction** to the training program. A survey questionnaire and focus groups represent two common methods used to gauge trainee opinions. Valuable insights can come from using these methods. However, the potential for trainee bias is strong. Trainees can either say that they learned a lot and benefited from the training or that they learned little and training was a waste of time. These are opinions that might be accurate, but they don't really show to what extent learning did or did not occur.

    Training programs typically have measurable learning objectives. **Assessment of learning** is the second level. Assessment of learning can occur during training or immediately after training ends. The intent of assessment at this level is to learn what trainees learned, the depth of learning and whether trainees met the expectations of decision-makers as to how much what was learned. Examples of assessment to learning at the second level include multiple-choice exams, essay tests and checklist when assessing skills. Decision-makers need to justify the use of resources devoted to training. Training program costs are easy to quantify, but training program benefits are a challenge to quantify. Also, trainees may demonstrate that learning occurred, but the impact of training is unclear.

Because of the limitation associated with the second level, level three involves assessing whether training impacted the **work behavior** of the trainees' post-training. Decision-makers expect some degree of impact, and a change in work behavior represents an example of how to assess the impact of a training program. Changes in work behavior can be assessed by surveying trainees, surveying supervisors of trainees or through direct observation by a trainer trained in observation techniques.

Changes in work behavior show that training had an impact, but changes in work behavior offer no assurance that changes in performance outcomes. Effort might change but did training lead to improved **work performance**? Did training lead to increased productivity or greater efficiencies? These are the questions to address in a **level four assessment**. If baseline data was collected prior to training, then post-training data is collectable. For example, if trainees were call center operators and the goal of training was to reduce by ten seconds the average amount of time spent on each call, this is measurable. In fact, most call centers automate the various work processes to assess the performance of individual operators and all aspects of the call center's operations. Assessing work performance results represents an optimal assessment approach when feasible. Resource constraints limit how often an organization can perform level-four assessments.

Cambridge Connections – Part 1

Rapid growth led to a workforce of 100 full-time employees. By the end of the next year, the goal was to employ 200 employees and within five years employ at least 1000 employees. Sandeep Singh, CEO, was pleased with the overall performance of the company. However, in a meeting with Sandra Ferris, Vice-President of Human Resources, Sandeep expressed his concerns over the high-attrition rate among new hires. Early hires remained with the firm. But, after passing the 35-employee mark, circumstances changed. Sandeep noted that the organization was in transition, moving from mostly informal operations to more formal operations. Sandra stated that this was a natural process as organizations grow. One area that remained mostly informal was the hiring process. A casual approach to selecting new employees resulted in hiring either unqualified candidates or overqualified candidates or candidates with a bad work ethic. A hiring freeze was put into effect to provide Sandra time to develop a new hiring process. Several weeks later, in a meeting with Sandeep and a select group of managers, Sandra presented a model hiring process to implement. Her presentation covered the various activities organized in sequential stages. Sandra proposed learning objectives to achieve in training individuals directly involved in the hiring process.

Questions

1. Identify each possible stage of the hiring process proposed by Sandra.
2. Identify learning objectives that Sandra proposed to focus on achieving during the training program.

LEARNING OBJECTIVE #12: IDENTIFY, DESCRIBE AND EXPLAIN THE IMPORTANCE OF INSTRUCTIONAL METHODS

The goal in the selection of **instructional methods** to use in a training program is simple, select instructional methods that lead to trainee learning. But there are approximately 150 different types of instructional methods to choose from. Training program designers require a selection rubric to follow to guide the process for selecting instructional methods.

There are several criteria that are commonly used to guide the selection process. **Andragogy**, the learning theory on adult learning, is a useful guide to the selection process. Andragogy helps the designer understand the needs of adult learners when trained; adult learning styles and the various methods to motivate the adult learner. Adult learners follow the **WIFM learning model** (What is in it for me?). The adult learner learns best when the purpose of training is perceived as self-beneficial. The motivation of the adult learner is heightened by perceived personal benefits of the training.

Adult trainees' motivation to learn increases if the selection of instructional methods links to the learning styles of the trainee. **Relational learning** is the primary learning style of the adult trainee because the adult trainee prefers linking a new situation with prior experiences so that there is some familiarity with the issues.

Multiple use of instructional methods simultaneously keeps the adult learner motivated and focused. Keeping focused during the learning process is always a challenge for any type of learner because of **cognitive fatigue**. To address concerns about cognitive fatigue, the training program designer ensures that multiple instructional methods are used concurrently. For example, the trainer can lecture, use PowerPoint and provide a handout during a stage of the training process.

Another criterion to include in the selection process is the **level of learning** expected. Bloom's Taxonomy of learning is a useful paradigm for understanding that each level of learning benefits from different types of instructional methods. For example, analytical thinking is well-matched with the use of the case method approach for learning.

Constraints represent another criterion to consider when selecting instructional methods. **Time constraints** for training, **motivation** of the trainees, **resource limitations, facility limitations,** the **knowledge and/or skill level** of the trainee along with a trainee's **personal abilities** represent examples of constraints that influence the selection of instructional methods.

Actively involving the trainee in the process of selecting instructional methods is based on the **theory of experiential learning**. This theory promotes the idea that learning is best achieved by involving the learner in selecting instructional methods along with conducting their own self-assessment of learning.

Learning objectives represent another criterion to use in selecting instructional methods. Designers select learning objectives to accomplish during the training. Designers identify the optimal instructional methods that help the trainees achieve the learning objectives.

Finally, the preferred criterion is the **impact** trainees are expected to demonstrate because of the training. The greater the potential impact sought along with the long-lasting benefits of training, the more the designer needs to consider the choice of instructional methods. Following Kirkpatrick's four-level model, there is short-term learning, learning that shows post-training, learning that leads to changes in behavior and learning that shows if the trainees perform their work differently as a result of training. Training program designers need to consider the importance of training impact to determine the choice of instructional methods to use.

Cambridge Connections – Part 2

Sandeep and Sandra were more than satisfied with the new hiring process. Since implementing the new hiring process, attrition among new hires was nearly negligible. However, Sandeep and Sandra started meeting to discuss the problems with the new supervisor managers. Sandeep agreed with Sandra that the need for creating middle-manager positions to oversee operations was necessary, freeing top management to focus on strategic issues. Problems quickly became apparent. Supervisory managers were quitting; people were complaining that the supervisors would not make decisions, allowed team meetings to turn into unproductive social events and team members complained that teams were not performing well. Sandra and senior management met to discuss Sandra's solution to the problem. The problem was self-evident, the policy of promoting from within meant that supervisory managers had insufficient management experience or training as a manager. Sandra presented a leadership development training program for new supervisory managers. During Sandra's presentation, Sandra emphasized the importance of certain types of instructional methods to use.

Questions

1. Why did Sandra consider instructional methods to be a critical part of the training program? Explain.
2. What types of instructional methods did Sandra consider using in the training program? Explain.

LEARNING OBJECTIVE #13: IDENTIFY AND DESCRIBE THE BENEFITS OF TRAINING FOR THE INDIVIDUAL AND THE ORGANIZATION

Individuals benefit from training through the acquisition of new knowledge, new or improved skills and better performing personal abilities (e.g. communication skills and problem-solving skills) which should lead to improved work performance. Better work performance can result in **rewards** such as promotions, financial rewards and greater job security.

Another benefit of training for individuals is the development and strengthening of **self-management** skills. The ability to self-regulate originates from the individual's judgment of self-worth. Training provides the knowledge, skills and improved personal abilities that can lead to success on the job. Success leads to an improved assessment of self-worth which contributes to developing a positive attitude, which leads to a self-motivated person who derives greater pride in their work accomplishments. A happy person is the result of this process, and happy people seek greater control over their lives.

Organizations always seek to become more **effective** through achieving goals. Training is one of the important levers intended to contribute to making an organization more effective. Improving the quality of the workforce only serves to benefit the organization.

Another benefit for the organization is that **work processes** improve through various process management projects. Training the workforce by focusing on work process management practices provides the knowledge and skills that can contribute to greater operational efficiencies. Improved operational efficiencies lead to better profit margins. More profits provide additional resources to invest in building a stronger organization.

Training benefits the organization through the development of the workforce as a **competitive advantage**. A high-performance workforce contributes to the long-term growth of an organization; training can sustain growth almost indefinitely.

LEARNING OBJECTIVE #14: IDENTIFY, DESCRIBE AND EXPLAIN THE BEST TYPES OF SUBJECTS TO COVER IN TRAINING

Selecting subjects to offer in training programs is determined primarily by assessing the potential impact a subject can have on an organization's performance. Subjects are derived from the training program's learning objectives. Training costs are easy to assess quantitatively, but the impact of training on an organization is difficult to quantify in a cost-benefit analysis. Instead, the organization needs to consider subjects with a **strategic scope**.

1. **Increase Organizational Revenue**: Subjects intended to increase the organization's revenues are optimal.
2. **Reduce Organization Costs**: Subjects that focus on learning how to reduce/ eliminate costs are important because cost reduction results in wider profit margins.
3. **Create a Competitive Advantage**: Subjects that enable the workforce to develop an expertise in specialized knowledge and/or specialized skills enhance the organization's capabilities to compete.
4. **Conform to Legal Guidelines**: Subjects that enable the workforce to implement policies that helps an organization adhere to legal guidelines.
5. **Reduce Conflict**: Subjects, such as conflict resolution strategies, lead to more harmonious social relations that result in fewer work disruptions.
6. **Coordination and Cooperation**: Subjects that are essential elements in building successful work relations are important; training offers trainees an opportunity to develop useful social relations based on trust. Trust contributes to a workforce that is effective in performing job responsibilities and avoids competing with work colleagues.

7. **Improved Sense of Self-Worth**: Training subjects that build the self-worth of the workforce strengthen the capacity of the organization to improve because of a positive, self-motivated workforce.
8. **Enhanced Personal Abilities**: Strengthening the personal abilities of individual members of the workforce leads to happier workers who are more productive employees.

Chapter Summary

Organizations must change to survive, and planned change is preferable to random, ad hoc and poorly thought out changes. The focus of this chapter is change management because change management is essential for an organization to respond to environmental opportunities and threats. OD and training represent two important management methods organizations use to expedite organizational change.

This chapter provides an in-depth understanding of the importance of the theory of OD associated with organizational change, along with OD's connection with systems theory. Both theories enable the reader to understand the strategic worldview of the importance of OD in managing the change process. A strategic worldview emphasizes the need for management to consider pursuing change as an organization-wide effort when applying OD to bring about long-lasting organizational change. OD is an approach that can spearhead successful organizational change. Though there are different OD models, each model applies a process approach to planned change. Each model emphasizes the importance of making changes to work processes to ensure that the changes become routinized.

Training represents another management method to bringing about change by focusing on individual members of the workforce. One goal of training is to provide useful knowledge and skills that the individual acquires with the expectation that the organization benefits too. Another goal of training is to develop personal abilities of individuals with the expectation that improved personal abilities leads to greater feelings of self-worth; improved self-worth contributes to better employee performance.

The chapter's focus on training includes identifying and describing both the RISDP and the RSTPD. The RISDP model examines training in a broad context, starting with the catalyst for the need for training and showing the overall steps an organization needs to follow in designing and implementing a training program. The RSTPD model provides an overview of the actual process training program designers need to follow in designing a training program.

Questions

1. Explain the meaning of the term OD.
2. What are the major OD models? Identify and briefly describe each model.
3. What is the knowledge, skills and personal abilities an OD consultant needs to possess?
4. What are the important objectives of OD?
5. Identify and describe any ten of the important values associated with OD.
6. What is the systems perspective underlying OD? Explain.
7. Who and how is OD meant to impact? Explain.
8. What are the important benefits associated with training?
9. What is the Ross Instructional Systems Design model? Explain.
10. What is the Ross Structured Training Program Design model? Explain.

11. Identify and describe the Kirkpatrick four-level model.
12. What are instructional methods? Why are instructional methods important?
13. How do individuals and organizations benefit from training?
14. What are the preferred subjects to cover in a training program? Identify and describe any five.

Bibliography

Agunis, H. & Kraiger, K. (2009). Benefits of training and development for individuals and teams, organizations and society. *Annual Review of Psychology.* 60. 459–474.

Arthur, Jr. W., Bennett, Jr., W., Edens, P.S. & Bell, S.T. (2003). Effectiveness of training in organizations: a meta-analysis of design and evaluation features. *Journal of Applied Psychology.* 88(2). 234–245.

Asumeng, M.A. & Osae-Larbi, J.A. (2015). Organizational development models: a critical review and implications for creating learning organizations. *European Journal of Training and Development Studies.* 2(3). 29–43.

Austin, J.R. & Bartunek, J.M. (2003). Theories and practices of organizational development in William C. Borman, Daniel R. Ilgen and Richard J. Klimoski (Eds.). Volume 12. *Handbook of Psychology: Industrial and Organizational Psychology.* John Wiley & Sons.

Baldwin, T.T. & Ford, J.K. (1988). Transfer of training: a review and directives for future research. *Personnel Psychology.* 41(1). 63–105.

Banutu-Gomez, M.B. & Banutu-Gomez, S.M. (2016). Organizational change and development. *European Scientific Journal.* 12(-22). 56–67.

Borman, W.C., Ilgen, D.R. & Klimoski, R.J. (Eds.). (2003). *Handbook of Psychology: Industrial and Organizational Psychology.* Volume 12. 309–332.

Burnes, B. & Cooke, B. (2012). The past, present and future of organizational development: taking the big view. *Human Relations.* 65(11). 1395–1429.

Choi, M. & Ruona, W.E.A. (2011). Industrial readiness for organizational change and its implications for human resource and organizational development. *Human Resource Development Review.* 10(1). 46–73.

Edmondson, W. & Myungweon, C. (1996). Introduction: Organizational learning as a source of competitive advantage in Choi Myungweon and Wendy Edmondson (Eds.). *Organizational Learning and Competitive Advantage.* Sage Publications. 7–37.

Francis, A. (2019). Four major theories of training and development. *Human Resource Management.* https://www.mbaknol.com/human-resource-management/four-major-theories-of-training-and-development/.

Kulkarni, P.P. (2017). A literature review of training and development and quality of work life. *Researchers World-Journal of Arts, Science and Commerce.* 4(2). 136–143.

MBA Knowledge Base. (2019). Four major theories of training and development. *Human Resource Management.* https://www.mbaknow.com/human-resource-management/four-major-theories-of-training-and-development/. 1–4.

Ross, S. (2019). *Training and Development in Organizations: An Essential Guide for Trainers.* Routledge.

Salas, E., Tannenbaum, S.I., Kraiger, K. & Smith-Jentsch, K.A. (2012). The science of training and development in organizations: what matters in practice. *Psychological Science on the Public Interest.* 13(2). 74–101.

Society for Human Resource Management Online Staff. (2012). Seven trends expected to influence training in 2013. *SHRM Online Organizational and Employee Development.* 1–4.

Weick, K.G. & Quinn, R.E. (1999). Organizational change and development. *Annual Review of Psychology.* 50. 361–386.

Worley, C.G. & Mohrman, S.A. (2015). A new view of organizational development and change competencies: the engage and learn model. *Center for Effective Organizations.* June. 1–15.

Worley, C.G. & Feyerherm, A.E. (2003). Reflections on the future of organizational development. *The Journal of Applied Behavioral Science.* 39(1). 97–115.

PART IV

PEOPLE DYNAMICS

Team Development and Team Management

OVERVIEW

Over the past 25 years organizations have increased the use of teams as a management method for achieving goals and operational objectives. The proof that organizations value teams for improving an organization's performance stems from the wide use of teams and the emphasis on team training to teach individuals how to improve the effectiveness of teams. This chapter describes the differences between groups and teams because many assume these are one in the same subjects. The chapter examines why the subject of teams represents an important management topic, and the chapter examines how organizations use teams to improve an organization's performance.

This chapter identifies and describes the common skills needed to create teams as well as the management skills needed to successfully manage a team. Included in the chapter's discussion about teams is the identification and description of typical problems that occur during the team development process and during the on-going management of a team. Associated with the identification of team-related problems is the review and description of the strategies for solving these problems. This chapter also identifies and describes strategies useful in improving a team's performance.

Team meetings represent an important method that teams use to conduct team business. Time constraints will impede a team's effectiveness if team leadership does not know how to manage team meetings effectively. There are skills linked to learning how to effectively manage team meetings. This chapter covers these skills along with describing the issues associated with team leadership during team meetings and team leadership outside of team meetings.

Experience is an effective teacher in developing and managing teams along with conducting team meetings. However, challenges occur during the process of gaining this type of experience. This chapter describes a process for teaching individuals how to successfully develop and manage teams; learn how to conduct team meeting; team leadership; and strategies for dealing with team-related problems including conflict management strategies. This chapter introduces the reader to a model for teaching these subjects that, if successful, achieves the goal of improving team performance.

Determining when a team is necessary along with the type of team needed are important issues to consider. Leadership is loathed to the idea of creating a team with no purpose. This wastes time and resources. This chapter identifies and describes criteria that leadership can consider when contemplating in creating a team, whether a long-lasting team or a temporary team.

Team climate is an important subject associated with understanding the way teams perform and the influences that affect team performance. By understanding the issues that explain team climate, the reader acquires a better grasp of the complexities associated with creating teams and managing teams.

Finally, teamwork theory, using Tuckman's stages of team development as an example, enables the reader to understand the application of theory by examining the team development process teams commonly follow from inception to dissolution. Tuckman's theory is universally accepted as an overall characterization of the team developmental process and the four primary stages this process follows.

CHAPTER 11   LEARNING OBJECTIVES

Readers will achieve the following learning objectives after reading this chapter.

1. Define and explain the differences between groups and teams.
2. Identify and describe the skills associated with team development.
3. Identify and describe team management requirements.
4. Identify, describe and explain the problems in creating and managing teams.
5. Identify and describe strategies for resolving team development and team management problems.
6. Identify and describe management methods for improving team performance.
7. Identify and describe the important issues in successfully managing a team meeting.
8. Explain the role and importance of team leadership.
9. Identify and describe the process for teaching teamwork skills.
10. Identify and describe the circumstances that can determine the need to create a team.
11. Describe the different types of cultures and how culture can impact team performance.
12. Identify and describe Tuckman's teamwork theory about the stages of team development.

LEARNING OBJECTIVE #1: DEFINE AND EXPLAIN THE DIFFERENCES BETWEEN GROUPS AND TEAMS

Often, the terms **group** and **team** are used synonymously. However, there is a distinction between the two terms that is important to clarify. Within an organization, a group of individuals is a **work group**. Work group members provide information to each other, without necessarily any formal effort to coordinate the information sharing among all the group members. The information enables group members to perform their respective work responsibilities. There is no attempt to coordinate the passing of information among individuals because there is no shared or common purpose such as a group goal. Group members are not mutually interdependent on each other.

A **team** represents a collection of individuals, and everyone on the team has a unique set of knowledge and/or skills that require the individuals to coordinate their efforts because team members are bound by common team goals. Team members are mutually accountable for performing their individual team responsibilities and shared team responsibilities to enable the team to achieve the team's goals. Team success in achieving the goals leads to the organization rewarding team members. Failure to achieve the team goals can result in negative consequences for team members. Team size typically ranges between 8 and 12 members, but some teams can be smaller and other teams larger, depending on the organization's team requirements.

Functional teams are teams that serve a specific purpose for the organization. One purpose can involve the team members working together to **prepare a recommendation**. For example, teams might evaluate proposals from different suppliers with the mandate to recommend the best supplier to contract with. Second, a team can have the mandate to **make or do something**. For example, a company might want a new model retail store, and the team develops a prototype of the relevant store according to the decision criteria presented to the team. The other option is for a team to develop the criteria to use in recommending a new type of retail store. Finally, a team might be organized to **operate something** such as a machine or a section of an assembly line or use of heavy earth moving equipment that requires several individuals to coordinate all their related actions to achieve a performance goal.

Another defining characteristic of a team is that a team acts following a structure created specifically for the team. The purpose of the structure is to keep team members focused, working together, facilitate communication among team members and arrange routine meetings to ensure that the team is moving forward to achieve the team's goals. A structural issue that guides teams is team policies, both formal and informal policies, to keep team members focused. Groups do not necessarily operate with the same type of structure associated with teams because groups function with a different purpose.

Teams are task-focused because the successful performance of tasks moves the team forward in achieving the team's goals. The team breaks down the goals into definable tasks that need to be completed to achieve the goals. A team's success in achieving the goals is linked to the organization's support of the team's efforts. There is a **hierarchy of goals** that can link the action of teams throughout the organization to achieve unit goals and organization goals. Groups don't necessarily have the same focus. For groups, an individual's success might not contribute directly to the success of the unit the group falls within or to the organization.

LEARNING OBJECTIVE #2: IDENTIFY AND DESCRIBE THE SKILLS ASSOCIATED WITH TEAM DEVELOPMENT

The pre-stage initiates the process of forming a team. The pre-stage involves identifying the team's goals. Team goals can vary; because of this variation, decision-makers need to consider the type of knowledge and skills team members need. Additionally, decision-makers must consider the personal abilities individual team members need if team members are to integrate well and work together to achieve the team goals and team objectives.

There are different types of goals a team can achieve. There are **routine goals** that require the performance of **routine tasks**. Organizing an annual event, providing a standard report and hiring several new employees using the hiring process are examples of goals that require routine work process to accomplish. There are **innovation types** of goals. These goals require individuals that can think and operate outside-of-the-box by demonstrating creative abilities. There are work tasks that involve the need for individuals possessing personal skills that enable the individual to demonstrate their creative talents and apply these creative thinking talents in developing and performing different work processes in performing team tasks. Examples of innovation goals include creating a new product, developing a new store design, creating new meals and designing new work processes. **Problem-solving goals** represent a third category of goals. A solutions-oriented focus requires individuals with personal attributes that emphasize the need to have answers. Work tasks involve the need to eliminate a problem. Examples include changes in the economy that impact demand, entry of new competitors, a merger of major competitors, etc. the team needs to identify problems and respond to these problems with solutions.

After identifying team goals, decision-makers initiate the process, first stage of the team development process, forming the team. This stage involves assessing the **size** of the team required by identifying the **knowledge, skills and types of experiences** needed to achieve the team goals. The ideal team size is to keep the team within eight to ten members. This makes working together easier; but the size is dictated by the requirements needed to achieve the team's goals. **Values** represent an important consideration in selecting team members. Values drive individual thinking and behavior. As much as possible, decision-makers need to consider an individual's values to ensure compatibility which can lead to success in achieving the team's goals. Once formed, a team begins the process of creating a team culture that reflects team values. Decision-makers need to avoid creating a toxic team culture that can contribute to the failure of the team to achieve the team's goals and team objectives.

Included in the process of identifying potential team members is an assessment of the **strengths** an individual contributes to the team's efforts. Strengths enhance the team's ability to be successful and operate with less conflict. The **motivation** of an individual is another factor decision-makers need to consider when selecting team members. Team goals may inspire or discourage candidates. Knowing the effect goals can have on the potential performance of individual's is important as successful goal achievement is the overarching intent of decision-makers.

After selecting individual team members, the next stage of the team development process is to arrange for the **team to meet** for the first time. The meeting initiates the discussion of establishing a team structure to follow. Structure evolves over time but creating a team structure early on enables the team to begin working sooner. Structure includes formulating the **basic rules** for the team to follow. Rules can focus on such issues as creating decision-making processes, designing a reporting process, determining meeting frequency and meeting format issues, leadership of the team and initial tasks to perform. **Role identification** and/or role clarification begins during this stage but remains an ongoing issue as roles can evolve once the work of the team begins. Roles eventually become clarified though there is often an informal component to role identification because of the ad hoc nature of performing some aspects of the team's work. Team members need to be open-minded about roles because the circumstances often require flexible roles.

After identifying the team goals, the team begins to identify **objectives** to achieve. Objectives represent milestones to accomplish during the process the team follows to achieve the team's goals. Objectives are quantifiable measures that provide focus to the work. Time is an important element in identifying team goals and team objectives because imposing time limits creates a sense of urgency on team members to continue to remain focused, maximize work effort and be achievement-oriented. Achieving involves creating either a formal or informal **performance assessment process** to promote team accountability. The use of time and measurable objectives represents basic building blocks of a performance assessment management system.

Part of the process of creating a team structure includes providing an agenda for each **team meeting.** Team meetings represent an important method in the process of achieving the team goals and team objective because important business occurs during team meetings. Report updates, coordination efforts, planning, delegating responsibilities, conflict management and assessing performance represent examples of the issues addressed during a team meeting. Because face-to-face team meetings do not occur often, meetings require a structure to ensure the highest level of productivity when the team meets.

Finally, once the team achieves team goals, decision-makers need to determine the **next stage in the life of the team**. Because some teams are ongoing, decision-makers assign new goals for the team. A review of the team's prior performance is often conducted (either formally or informally) to eliminate problems that might handicap the team during the next assignment. If a team is to dissolve, team members use the time to **reflect** on the experience. Reflection offers individuals the opportunity to learn about the benefits of the experience and how the lessons learned help in serving on another team.

LEARNING OBJECTIVE #3: IDENTIFY AND DESCRIBE TEAM MANAGEMENT REQUIREMENTS

Creating a team is an important first step in providing the elements needed to become a high-performance team. These elements are the knowledge, skills, personal abilities and motivation of individual team members. Developing the team is fundamental in ensuring that the team takes advantage of the talents of the individual team members.

One of the important early steps in developing a team is the identification of team **leadership**. Effective team leadership keeps team members focused, motivated, facilitates role identification, initiates efforts to create team structure and applies conflict resolution strategies to help build trust by resolving differences among team members.

A team's focus is the achievement of team goals and team objectives. Team goals often emphasize a broad, long-term focus. Teams use **objectives** linked to the team goals because objectives are short term and measurable. Objectives function as milestones that provide teams with the necessary focus while performing team tasks.

An important step in the team development process is the creation of the team's **structure**. Structure is the organizing component that teams need to achieve team goals and team objectives. There are several elements to the structuring of a team. One element is the creation of work processes associated with performing team tasks to achieve team objectives. Every objective requires one or more successfully performed work processes to achieve the objective. As stated earlier, a process represents a series of stages that follow a planned sequence. Success in moving through the process contributes to achieving the objective. Part of a team's efforts in creating structure is the development of **team management processes**. Team management processes represent formal management functions associated with creating team structure. Important team management processes include **decision-making processes, performance monitoring, communication, coordination, cooperation and trust building processes**.

One of the essential management methods teams use to aid a team as the team moves forward to achieve a team's goals and team objectives is **face-to-face meetings**. Mostly, teamwork is performed by individual team members or sub-groups of team members. Team members can easily report their efforts using email and/or memorandums. However, the benefits gained from face-to-face meetings are not replicable with alternatives. Face-to-face meetings provide the team with an important opportunity to gain real-time contact with each other to discuss various issues and needs that are best addressed through face-to-face meetings. However, because of the challenges that limit face-to-face meetings (e.g. distance, work schedules and other work obligations) face-to-face meetings need to be well-organized to ensure that the meetings benefit the team's efforts at achieving the goals and objectives.

The **Input-Process-Outcome model (IPO)** illustrates the importance of the composition of a team and the management of the team because the two elements link together lead to positive outcomes. Briefly, the IPO model describes the organization's commitment of resources to the team, the management of the resources to achieve the team's goals and team objectives and whether the team's performance met the organization's expectations. Team performance is measured by the ability of successfully applying the IPO model, such that the team achieves the team's goals and team objectives.

LEARNING OBJECTIVE #4: IDENTIFY, DESCRIBE AND EXPLAIN THE PROBLEMS IN CREATING AND MANAGING TEAMS

In forming a team there is an ideal approach where decision-makers can select individuals with the preferred attributes. However, in most circumstances, the **pressure of time** does not allow decision-makers to be selective. Often, teams need to form in haste, which results in the selection of individuals limited in the preferred personal characteristics. Timing is not a critical issue for standing teams, but team members might not possess the characteristics decision-makers prefer. Adding new members to provide the needed **knowledge, skills, personal abilities, motivation and experience** is disruptive to the established team culture. Adding new team members is disruptive because new members need to be absorbed into the team's culture. Too often, decision-makers do not consider the impact on a team's culture when adding new team members. New members bring new values that the team must assimilate.

Besides needing to consider the knowledge, skills, personal abilities, motivation and experiences of potential team members, decision-makers need to consider if potential candidates are **self-managers**. Self-managers are important because this type of person can function independently, which enables other team members to have the confidence that this type of person will follow through with their responsibilities.

Team size is an important consideration for decision-makers as teams that exceed the optimal size of 8–10 members can expect to struggle integrating all members together, attempting to create a uniform team culture. More members can function as an inhibitor; with some team members reluctant to share their thoughts and ideas because the necessary level of trust among team members is missing or insufficient. Trust building takes longer the larger the team because gaining familiarity among team members is more challenging with larger numbers of people. Less contact makes trust building more difficult to accomplish without the use of trust building exercises.

Another potential problem associated with the creation of a team is when decision-makers fail to create a **process** to follow in creating a team. A selection process, by definition, forces decision-makers to consider essential issues to consider when selecting team members. One of the issues decision-makers might overlook is the issue of **team diversity**. Too often, diversity is synonymous with a negative outlook. However, diversity can offer a team a broader set of viewpoints as the team considers ideas for performing actions that lead to the achievement of team objectives and team goals.

There are several problems that can impede an established team from achieving team goals and team objectives. One type of problem is a culture that incorporates values antithetical to the values that support team members working closely together. A related issue is that **cultural dysfunction** can contribute to an insufficient level of **trust** among team members. Incompatible values can contribute to the polarization among team members. Sub-groups form around these values, and the result is distrust. Trust is essential in minimizing team conflict; trust helps in overcoming conflict; and trust is the glue that supports the efforts of team members to work together.

Limited **interpersonal skills** among team members represent another potential problem that can inhibit a team from achieving team goals. Team members need to work together, and team members with limited or dysfunctional interpersonal skills challenge the team's ability to successfully resolve the differences when differences emerge.

Competing goals is another potential problem teams need to confront. Team members' **personal goals and the team's goals** may conflict. If the team is unable to resolve this issue, the team is unlikely to succeed in achieving the team's goals.

Vague **roles and responsibilities** of team members represent another type of potential problem that can interfere with a team's ability to perform the tasks necessary to succeed as a team. Vagueness inhibits action because team members remain conflicted over each team members' areas of responsibility. Along with the failure to clarify roles and responsibilities of team members is the possible conflict over performing important **tasks and making decisions**. Unclear roles complicate the issue, but even where roles and responsibilities are clear, team members can disagree over how **best to perform a task** because of the inability to overcome **problematic interpersonal relations.**

Weak **team leadership** is another potential problematic team issue because leadership provides focus to the team, helps manage conflict, spearheads change initiatives and provides the self-management abilities required of leadership when making decisions.

Kellogg Pharmaceuticals – Part 1

Kellogg Pharmaceuticals recently acquired Phillips Pharma, a 200-person company that specializes in the development of early stage prostate cancer treatment drugs. The company has one drug performing well in the market with several promising drugs in the drug development pipeline. Kellogg acquired Phillips to extend its product portfolio of specialty cancer drugs. Bob Mack, CEO of Kellogg and Sandra Dickerman, CEO of Phillips are meeting with their Vice Presidents of Human Resources and the Vice Presidents of R&D to determine how best to integrate the two companies. Everyone realizes that their goal is to identify key individuals to participate in a temporary undertaking to identify an integration plan. Bob and Sandra need an integration plan within 45 days. One integration model to follow was the plan Kellogg used in its last acquisition. Everyone agreed that this makes good sense.

Questions

1. What was the knowledge and skills required of members of the integration team?
2. Who from Kellogg would participate as a member? Explain.
3. Who should Sandra recommend being a member of the integration team? Explain.

LEARNING OBJECTIVE #5: IDENTIFY AND DESCRIBE STRATEGIES FOR RESOLVING TEAM DEVELOPMENT AND TEAM MANAGEMENT PROBLEMS

There are several possible strategies to consider when attempting to create a team. First, leadership can approach forming a team by treating the process like a **hiring process**. Leadership develops a list of the important knowledge, skills, personal abilities and experience candidates need to possess. Then, using a **checklist** approach, following these attributes, leadership can begin the process of searching for qualified candidates. A related strategy is to consult with supervisory managers to learn who possesses the qualifications along with relevant experiences and motivation. Another strategy is to send out a **"team member job description"** with all the relevant qualification requirements and let potential candidates apply for the team positions.

After forming the team there are a variety of strategies to consider using in dealing with potential or actual team problems. **Training** is a strategy that offers team members the opportunity to learn strategies for dealing with potential or actual team problems. Training can focus on teaching the following subjects.

- Creating team structure to include established rules to follow and developing process management skills.
- Strategies for improving interpersonal skills.
- Strategies for improving communication skills.
- Strategies for managing face-to-face meetings successfully.
- Develop problem-solving skills.
- Develop team leadership skills.

There are several **intervention strategies** to use in managing team issues that limit team performance. These intervention strategies include the following.

- Clarify team member **roles and responsibilities**.
- Clarify the **role and responsibilities** of team leadership.
- Promote team-strengthening **values** by focusing on tasks linked to specific values. For example, require small groups of team members to work on a group project that forces individuals to cooperate and coordinate their efforts.
- Create **performance management assessment processes** to evaluate team and individual performance and make these results a component of an individual's annual performance review process (this is a structural issue).
- Involve all **team members in working together** to resolve differences.
- Identify a non-team member who could serve as a **coach** for the team.
- Serious team management issues might warrant the need for intervention by an outside **decision-maker**.
- Use of **SMART goals and SMART objectives** to clarify expectations of the team.
- Increase the use of **face-to-face meetings** to work on building trust among team members.
- Ensure that **personal goals are linked** in some way to team goals.

LEARNING OBJECTIVE #6: IDENTIFY AND DESCRIBE MANAGEMENT METHODS FOR IMPROVING TEAM PERFORMANCE

Methods for managing a team's performance can determine the success or failure of a team's ability to succeed. Problems can occur, some outside of the team's control. However, to put a team in the position of succeeding involves the use of standard methods associated with improving team performance.

- **Goals**: a team needs goals to provide focus to the team's efforts. The preferred types of goals are SMART goals because a SMART goal is measurable and time-limited. Measurement provides a quantitative means for assessing progress. Time-limited creates a sense of urgency that keeps team members focused.

- **Objectives**: Objectives represent operational milestones linked to achieving the team's goals. Objectives need to be SMART type to assess progress and create a sense of urgency.
- **Structure**: Structure represents the methods a team uses to systematically organize the team. Included in the creation of **structure** are team **policies**, team **rules**, formal **work processes** for performing team tasks (i.e. tasks to achieve objectives and tasks for managing the team), a **reward system** for team and individual performance, **communication methods** and **communication processes** and **problem-solving processes.**
- **Context Issues:** Teams never operate independently. A team functions within a broader context. Teams can only respond to context issues; never able to control the context a team operates within. One context issue is the **unit** a team operates within. Unit needs to take precedence over a team's needs. A team operates within an **organization**. Organizational need satisfaction will always supersede meeting a team's needs. Finally, there is the organization's **environment**. Environmental issues, such as a changing economy, will always impact the organization, affecting teams as well. Teams need to learn and apply adaptation strategies to succeed in achieving team goals and team objectives.

LEARNING OBJECTIVE #7: IDENTIFY AND DESCRIBE THE IMPORTANT ISSUES IN SUCCESSFULLY MANAGING A TEAM MEETING

Face-to-face meetings represent one of the more important functions of a team, but also one of the most challenging to make effective. Face-to-face meetings provide the team with the opportunity to join in real-time discussions about team issues. However, too often, team meetings lead to few if any positive results, dissatisfaction among team members, discouraged team members and a general feeling that the team won't achieve team goals or team objectives based on the experiences in face-to-face team meetings.

Maximizing the benefits of face-to-face team meetings requires that team leadership be cognizant of the important methods to use in conducting successful team meetings. The important issues associated with successfully managing face-to-face team meetings include the following.

- **Team Leadership**: Team leadership needs to know how to conduct a team meeting, the knowledge of the issues associated with conducting successful team meetings and that leadership can conduct successful team meetings. Keeping team members focused, resolve conflict and being decisive are the essential qualities required of team leadership.
- **Objectives**: Face-to-face meetings require meeting objectives, stated at the start of the meeting. Stating meeting objectives and gaining team agreement on the objectives create a sense of urgency to limit unproductive discussions to accomplish the meeting objectives.
- **Agenda**: Having an agenda puts team members on notice about the topics to cover during a meeting. An agenda provides the team with focus and enables

leadership to re-focus the discussion if the team digresses. Sending the agenda to team members in advance of the meeting educates the team about the issues the meeting will cover.

- **Format of the Meeting**: Providing a structure to team meetings creates an orderly process to follow and avoids the necessity of developing a structure at each meeting. Formal and informal rules help to create a systematic process to follow. Use of rules helps the team save valuable time that is better spent on covering the agenda of the meeting.
- **Communication**: Reporting is always an essential component of a team meeting. Leadership can update team members on recent issues; sub-groups can report on the status of projects each group is working on. Face-to-face meetings offer the team the opportunity to discuss issues together and to gain the benefit of real-time discussions that stimulate thinking that is found wanting using emails and memos.
- **Task Assignments**: Team meetings often uncover issues the team needs to address. As a result, leadership can either request volunteers or assign to specific team member(s) the responsibility to perform an assigned task and report back on progress in completing the assignment.
- **Actions to Take**: Even the most successful team meetings might not cover all the agenda items and decisions might lead to other items to cover in future meetings. Leadership can provide a brief preview of the agenda topics to cover in the next team meeting.

LEARNING OBJECTIVE #8: EXPLAIN THE ROLE AND IMPORTANCE OF TEAM LEADERSHIP

High-performance teams are typically associated with high-performance leaders. What makes an individual a high-performance leader is essential to learn as decision-makers go about selecting team leaders. The importance of selecting individuals for team leadership positions cannot be understated. This section examines the important characteristics associated with high-performance leaders often lead their teams in achieving team goals and team objectives.

Self-manage is often referred to as an important personal ability of team leaders. If an individual is unable to lead themselves, it is questionable that this person can lead others. What makes someone a self-manager is a positive attitude that is an outcome of strong feelings of self-worth. Equipped with a positive attitude, a self-manager is primed to be motivated, channeling this drive to be an ambitious, action-driven individual. Some self-managers seek official leadership positions and others prefer serving as an informal leader who can contribute to a team's success in their own way. What makes a self-manager team leader important to a team is their ability to provide teammates with the **affective support** many team members require because a self-manager is a giver because of their own perceptions of their self-worth.

Additional factors that make a high-performance team leader a successful team leader include the following.

- **Team Boundaries**: Team leaders keep a team focused on team goals, team objectives and the team's agenda allowing few distractions.

- **Structure**: Leaders provide the guidance in developing a structure for the team to operate within. Important elements of structure include team policies, team rules and teamwork processes associated with performing important team tasks.
- **Important Team Processes**: Team leadership processes that are important in influencing the team's ability to succeed include: making decisions, creating communication processes, creating processes for identifying team objectives and task performance work processes.

Meeting the needs of team members is an important factor contributing to the high level of participation by team members, which ensures the success of the team. High-performance team leaders meet the needs of team members in the following ways.

- **Shared Goals**: Team leaders attempt to link personal goals of team members with the goals of the team.
- **Team-Building Actions**: Building trust is an essential element of a successful team because team members bond together when there is trust and bonding leads to less conflict and more cooperation. Creating boundaries and structure contributes a culture that promotes trust among team members.
- **Conflict Resolver**: Conflict is inevitable even among the most integrated teams. Team leadership provides the insights, strategies and affective support to resolve conflict in a way that retains, if not strengthens, the trust among team members.
- **Decision-Maker**: Sometimes, a team needs a leader to step forward to make decisions that break's an impasse among team members.
- **Result-Oriented**: A team leader that is result-oriented assures the team that the team will successfully cross the finish line as a direct benefit of the collective efforts of team leadership and team members.

Kellogg Pharmaceuticals – Part 2

Bob Mack and Sandra Dickerman, CEO's, respectively, of Kellogg and Phillips Pharma, agreed with the integration team's plan for integrating Phillips within Kellogg. However, left open for further discussion was the issue of integrating the two companies R&D units along with the existing product development projects of Phillips. Bob and Sandra decided that the best approach was to meet with the heads of R&D of the two companies. Paula Vossburg of Kellogg and Jim Spitzer from Phillips had met already, anticipating that a team of experts was necessary to recommend the best approach for integrating the two units along with the existing project groups of Phillips. Paula and Jim presented their recommendations for a R&D integration team to Bob and Sandra for discussion.

Questions

1. Discuss the model for creating a team to develop an integration plan for integrating the two R&D units.
2. The prior model used by Kellogg with other acquisitions was found non-applicable with the Phillips acquisition. Discuss what to do.

LEARNING OBJECTIVE #9: IDENTIFY AND DESCRIBE THE PROCESS FOR TEACHING TEAMWORK SKILLS

For first time, **team members training** is essential to educate them on the important subjects associated with ensuring team success. Also, individuals need to become knowledgeable about the pitfalls that can impede a team's success along with learning the strategies for overcoming these pitfalls. Furthermore, new team leaders benefit from developing a better understanding of the roles and responsibilities of team leaders and the attributes that make for an effective team leader.

A one-time training program lasting several hours or a day is insufficient for individuals to absorb and comprehend all the necessary information. A training program divided into stages, with time between each stage for the trainees to better absorb the learned information is ideal. Decision-makers need to determine the time allocated per stage along with the time designated between stages.

There are four identifiable stages labeled **pre-team** for stage one; the **demonstration stage** for stage two; and the **application stage** for stage three. Stages two and three can occur prior to the initial meeting of the team or subsequent to and early in the team's history. There is a separate stage that covers the knowledge and skills for **team leaders** to learn.

Stage one is like a typical classroom event. Suggested instructional methods include lecture, PowerPoint, handouts, guest presentations and discussion. **Stage two** can include such instructional methods as lecture, PowerPoint, video, demonstrations and evaluation methods to assess learning. **Stage three** is an application stage. Training involves in-class training as well as homework assignments. Lecture, role play, group discussions and individual and team presentations represent the instructional methods suggested to use in this stage. **Team leadership** training involves the recommended use of instructional methods such as lecture, PowerPoint, group discussion, role play and cognitive mental model imagery.

Covered in more detail in prior sections, important training subjects to cover include:

- Building effective communication skills
- Developing group decision-making skills
- Developing project management skills
- Team tasks include planning, coordinating, time management and creating structure
- Goal-oriented using SMART type goals
- Building trust among teammates
- Learning conflict management strategies

Subjects to cover in written handouts, in addition to the above subjects, include a discussion about the importance of clarifying roles and responsibilities, the stages of a team's development based on Tuckman's teamwork theory and the concept of mental models or using cognitive imagery to conceptualize issues.

Team leadership training subjects should cover the following issues.

- Creating team structure
- Creating team task work processes

- Keeping team members motivated
- Using team goals and team objectives to keep the team focused
- Providing the team and individuals on the team with performance feedback
- Effective communication strategies for team leaders
- Effective conflict management strategies for team leaders
- Methods for managing face-to-face meetings

Kellogg Pharmaceuticals – Part 3

Bob Mack and Sandra Dickerman were meeting with John Roche and Carl Segal, co-managers of the team formed to identify who was to receive notice of discharge at Phillips Pharma once the integration plan was approved. John and Carl sit at opposite ends of the table. The tension in the room was palpable. When invited to speak, both John and Carl responded, each with accusations about the other and the views of each team. Abruptly stopping the discussion, Bob reminded both John and Carl of the need to reduce labor costs but not to harm the product development process.

Questions

1. Identify the issues that prevent the team from making recommendations.
2. What strategies do you recommend moving the team forward in developing a plan for recommending specific job cuts?

LEARNING OBJECTIVE #10: IDENTIFY AND DESCRIBE THE CIRCUMSTANCES THAT CAN DETERMINE THE NEED TO CREATE A TEAM

Teams form when decision-makers determine the need for a team. The creation of a team and the purpose of the team is often decided in response to circumstances that warrants an approach that existing operational units are not able to perform based on the thinking of decision-makers. However, decision-makers need to determine if the team's existence is for a short period of time or that the longevity of the team needs to be open-ended. Frequently, decision-makers initially designate the team's status as "short term" and let the circumstances dictate the term of the team's existence.

There are three primary types of teams decision-makers can recommend. One type is a team formed to **recommend** some action. Another type of team is when decision-makers need a team to **make something or perform some action**. For example, the team is a project team formed to develop a prototype or concept for a new store model; assign the team with the goal to develop a strategic or marketing plan; or form a team to draft a proposal when responding to a government Request for a proposal or a proposal request from an organization soliciting suppliers. The third type of team is a team formed to **perform a work process** on a temporary or long-term basis. For example, a team replaces when the unit becomes dysfunctional or create a group of teams to manage a newly acquired business or the organization merged with another business, and the team's goal is to facilitate the process of integrating the two organizations. In these latter two examples, teams have specific agendas to follow so the organization creates a governing team that oversees the performance of the other teams.

There are four identifiable types of circumstances that can initiate the need for decision-makers to form a team.

- Changes in **competitive conditions** warrant a quick response by the organization, and the response requires the input from several units of the organization.
- Organizations often **consolidate their operations** as a result of a change in strategy or change in economic conditions. The use of a team approach to oversee the consolidation process requires going outside traditional procedures to ensure greater objectivity in making decisions that objectify the re-organization process.
- Projects often require the need for **expertise** that is only found among multiple organizational units or within a large organizational unit. A team approach pulls together a group of experts who share the knowledge, skills, experiences and motivation to successfully work together.
- Organizations operate within an environment that is not controllable. The organization can only **adapt** to changing economic conditions, new laws or government policies, changing demographics or changing values. Finally, different technologies can provide an organization with opportunities but also represent existential threats. Organizations that determine the need for a **quick response** is best served by a team that follows a novel approach in response to the situation.

LEARNING OBJECTIVE #11: DESCRIBE THE DIFFERENT TYPES OF CULTURES AND HOW CULTURE CAN IMPACT TEAM PERFORMANCE

An organization's culture influences team behavior, impacting a team's performance results. Because of the role of culture and culture's impact on team behavior, understanding the subject is essential for the reader to learn about. Briefly, culture is defined as a constellation of values that shape the actions of the collective whole which encompasses the organization, organizational units, teams and individuals within the organization. However, there is an external culture to the organization that is referred to as societal culture.

Figure 11.1 presents the value chain which illustrates the initial beginning point of an organization's culture and that of teams. Societal values influence an individual's values. Individuals create organizations, and part of the process of creating an organization is the creation of an organization's culture. The organization's culture originates as a reflection of the values of the founders of the organization. The organizational values influence the values of individuals in two ways. First, during the hiring process, the organization looks for employees who possess values compatible with the organization's values. Second, the organization's culture

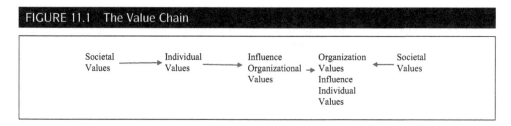

FIGURE 11.1 The Value Chain

operates to ensure that individuals conform to the values of the organization. People either adjust to the organization's culture or leave the organization. Societal values can continue to impact the organization's culture but to a lesser extent because one aspect of the role of an organization's culture is self-maintenance through the support of the core values of the organization.

There are levels of culture within an organization that reflect the team's collective internal climate. There is the organization-wide culture with a set of core values that encompass the entire organization. Within an organization, the design of most organizations incorporates some type of network of interconnected units that can vary size. Units have their own culture that can differ to some degree from the organization's culture. For example, a unit that thrives on creative development emphasizes values that include innovativeness. Whereas the organizational culture might discourage creativity by promoting values linked to conformity and standardization. The more isolated the unit the more the unit's culture can differ from the organization's culture. For example, a unit located in another part of the United States or outside of the United States will develop a culture at greater variance from the organization's culture. Within units, there are teams. Temporary or permanent, a team establishes a culture that reflects the cultural values of team members. Short-lived teams are less likely to develop their own culture that varies from the unit's values because of its temporary status. The culture of a permanent team evolves into a sub-culture with team values separate but overlapping with the unit's values.

Figure 11.2 displays the complexity of the dynamic interplay between the external societal culture and the organization's culture. Dynamic best characterizes the ongoing interchange between societal values, organizational values, unit values, team values and the values of individuals, and how this network of cultural values influences the development of an organization's management systems, organizational policies, work processes and the arrangement of an organization's structure to include the creation of teams and team oversight. After creating the structural configuration, structure begins to influence an organization's, unit's and team's cultures along with the values of individual members of the organization because structure's focus is to create some degree of uniformity or conformity of actions through the standardization of business practices.

Organizations evolve continuously because of the dynamic linkage among the different cultures. Change, under these circumstances, is inevitable. Teams and team actions are a part of this dynamic process, influencing and being influenced.

FIGURE 11.2   Culture and Culture's Impact on Teams

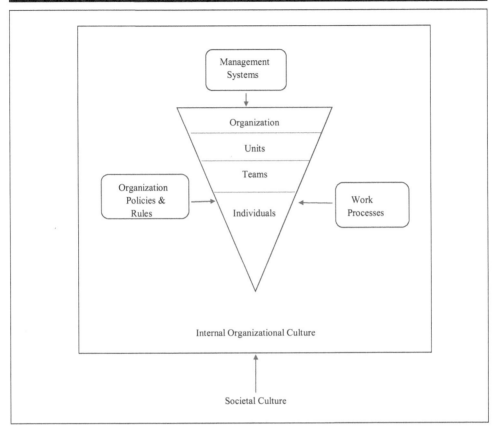

Kellogg Pharmaceuticals – Part 4

The vice presidents of Human Resources for Kellogg Pharmaceuticals and Phillips Pharma were asked to head a small team with the mandate of determining which senior executives from both companies would receive a Golden Parachute upon their termination. Bob Mack, CEO of Kellogg, has the impression that several senior executives of Phillips were worth keeping. He also knew that none of the senior executives of either company would accept a demotion. The team needed to identify criteria for determining who would stay. Bob Mack would make the decision using the criteria. There are 12 senior executive positions not including the CEO position. Sandra Dickerman, CEO of Phillips, was planning to leave. One of the challenges is that there was no need for two Vice Presidents of Human Resources. There are 23 senior executives between both companies excluding Bob Mack.

Questions

1. What criteria should the team use to determine who stays?
2. Should the two vice presidents of HR make the decision about themselves? Explain.
3. What potential issues might arise that makes deciding who leaves difficult?

LEARNING OBJECTIVE #12: IDENTIFY AND DESCRIBE TUCKMAN'S TEAMWORK THEORY ABOUT THE STAGES OF TEAM DEVELOPMENT

Team development researchers that teams evolve by following a process from the creation of the team to some endpoint unless a team retains the status as a permanent team. Development is frequently described in the context of stages of team development. **Tuckman** popularized the concept of **stages of team development** by identifying four principle stages that characterized the development of all teams. There is no uniform time frame that characterizes the length of a stage or that the process of development will always move forward. Dysfunctional teams are common, and the reasons have to do with unresolved issues that handicap the evolution of a team's development, arresting the ability of a team's efforts to achieve team goals.

Tuckman's first stage in a team's development is the **forming stage**. Forming involves the initial efforts of team leadership to begin the process of identifying, selecting and organizing team members. Learning about the purpose of the team, team member roles, structural issues and other related start-up issues dominate the focus of this stage of the team development process.

The forming stage lasts a brief time before moving to stage two, the **storming stage**. Storming implies conflict because differences among team members emerge. Conflict occurs because during this stage, roles and relationships begin to be clarified and formed; team goals and the team objectives linked to the goals are determined beyond the goals set my decision-makers; work processes to perform the team tasks are identified and formalized along with defining other team organizing issues. There are **two categories of work processes**. There are work processes that focus on the tasks associated with **achieving** the team's goals. **Achieving processes** characterize these processes. The other category of work processes is **maintaining processes** that focus on supporting the team's efforts at performing the achieving work processes. Examples of maintaining processes include conflict resolution processes, problem-solving processes, role clarification processes and organizing team meeting processes.

After team roles and relationships become established and structural issues defined and become an integral part of the team's operations, the team moves into the **norming stage**. With the settling on routines, work relationships and the team culture established, the team transitions to increase the team's efforts at performing the primary work of the team. Norming stresses increase the cooperation and coordination among team members because increased cooperation and coordination are essential elements in achieving the team's goals. Along with the team's structure, the team's culture, in the form of team values, is instrumental in contributing to greater coordination and cooperation among team members because of the emphasis on building trust, which is the primer for increased cooperation and coordination.

The final stage in the team development process is the **performing stage**. During this stage, the team's efforts at working to achieve the team's goals and team objectives move forward. The team does not allow differences among team members to thwart the team's efforts. Established conflict resolution strategies and conflict resolution processes, along with problem-solving processes, help to resolve differences among team members. An established team structure incorporates the formal and informal policies that dictate what can and cannot be done. Again, the primary focus of this stage is achieving the team's overall goals and team objectives.

The reader can now better understand why teams too often fail to achieve team goals. Weak team leadership, an unsupportive team culture, the unwillingness of decision-makers to intervene when teams lose focus and extreme personal feelings of individual team members can hinder a team's ability to accomplish team goals. Finally, external environmental conditions can make a team's mandate irrelevant. The result is that the team loses the drive to continue striving to achieve the team's goals and team objectives.

Chapter Summary

Studying team development and team management are important management subjects because teams represent a common management method used to help organizations achieve organizational goals. Unfortunately, the performance record of team's achieving team goals is not good. It is estimated that less than 50% of teams achieve their goals. Given the complex issues associated with forming and managing teams successfully, such a performance record should not be unexpected.

This chapter provides the reader with an in-depth understanding of the role and functioning of teams. Included in the discussion is a description of the important role of teams in organizations. Identified and described are the issues associated with forming a team. Once established, a team requires organizing. The chapter identifies and describes the organizational issues decision-makers and team leadership need to consider in managing a team toward being successful.

Teams confront problems. The chapter identifies and describes common problems that can impede a team's performance. The chapter identifies and describes strategies associated with solving team problems.

Finally, the chapter identifies and describes Tuckman's theory of team development because Tuckman popularized the concept of a team development process with the idea that team development occurs through a series of stages. Each stage serves a particular purpose in organizing and managing the team to perform successfully.

Questions

1. What is the difference between a group and a team?
2. Identify and describe the skills needed to develop a team.
3. What are the requirements for managing a team successfully?
4. Identify and briefly describe the problems associated with creating and managing a team.
5. Identify and briefly describe the strategies to use in resolving team development and team management problems.

6. What are the methods used for guiding team performance?

7. Identify and discuss the important issues associated with successfully managing team meetings?

8. Identify and describe the process for teaching teamwork skills.

9. Why is the role of team leadership important? Explain.

10. Identify and describe the circumstances for determining the need for creating a team.

11. What is meant by the term "collective climate of a team"?

12. Identify and briefly describe Tuckman's four stages of team development.

Bibliography

Bishop, J.W., Scott, D., Maynard-Patrick, S. & Wang, L. (2014). Teams, team process, and team building. *Clinical Laboratory Management*, 2nd Edition. Loyola eCommons School of Business: Faculty Publications and Other Works. 373–391.

Bushe, G.R. & Coetzer, G.H. (2007). Group development and team effectiveness. *The Journal of Applied Behavioral Science*. 43(2). 184–212.

Chartered Management Institute. (2015). Steps in successful team building. *Checklist088*. http://www.managers.org.uk/.

Guzzo, R.A. & Dickson, N.W. (1996). Teams in organizations: recent research on performance and effectiveness. *Annual Review of Psychology*. 47. 307–338.

Harris, P.R. & Harris, K.G. (1996). Managing effectively through teams. *Team Performance Management: An International Journal*. 2(3). 23–36.

Harvey, S., Millet, B. & Smith, D. (1998). Developing successful teams in organizations. *Australian Journal of Management & Organizational Behavior*. 1(1). 1–8.

Hwang, M.I. (2018). Relationship between teamwork and team performance: experiences from an ERP sim competition. *Journal of Information Systems Education*. 29(3). 157–168.

Kozlowski, S.W.J. & Ilgen, D.R. (2006). Enhancing the effectiveness of work groups and teams. *Psychological Science in the Public Interest*. 7(3). 77–124.

Lacerenza, C.N., Marlow, S.L., Tannenbaum, S. I. & Salas, Eduardo. (2018). Team development interventions: evidence-based approaches for improving teamwork. *American Psychologist*. 73(4). 517–531.

Levasseur, R.E. (2011). People skills: optimizing team development and performance. *Interfaces*. 41(2). 204–208.

Pentland, A. (2012). The new science of building teams. *Harvard Business Review*. April. 1–21.

Rico, R., de la Hera, C.M.A. & Tabernero, C. (2011). Work team effectiveness, a review of research from the last decade (1999–2009). *Psychology in Spain*. 15(1). 57–79.

Salas, E., Shuffler, M.L., Thayer, A.L., Bedwell, W.L. & Lazzara, E.H. (2014). Understanding and improving teamwork in organizations: a scientifically based practical guide. *Human Resource Management*. 1–23.

Society of Human Resource Management. (2019). Developing and sustaining high-performance work teams. https://www.shrm.org/resourcesandtools-and-samples/toolkits/pages/developingandsustaininghigh-performanceworkteams/.

Wilson, C. (2010). Bruce Tuckman's forming, storming, norming & performing team development model. *Culture at Work*. www.coaching cultureatwork.com.

Yeager, K.L. & Nafukho, F.M. (2012). Developing diverse teams to improve performance in the organizational setting. *European Journal of Training and Development*. 36(4). 388–408.

Zaccaro, S.J., Rittman, A.L. & Marks, M.A. (2001). Team leadership. *The Leadership Quarterly*. 12. 451–483.

Group and Individual Decision-Making

OVERVIEW

Making decisions is one of the most common activities in any organization. Therefore, studying the subject decisions and the decision-making process is an essential management subject to learn about. This chapter offers the reader in-depth coverage of the subject, decisions including decision-making and the decision-making process because organizations attempt to rationalize the decision-making process to reduce the risk of making a bad decision. Understanding the issues associated with decision-making is important because of how decisions impact an organization's performance. Through a detailed discussion of the issues, the chapter attempts to elucidate for the reader the complexity, importance and challenges associated with decision-making. The study of decision-making in organizations provides the reader with insights to understand why organizations devote considerable resources and time attempting to improve decision-making. The logic of studying decision-making is clear, and good decision-making leads to effective decisions.

Identifying and describing a routine decision-making process, examining the role of decision models and reviewing the management methods used in decision-making represent important chapter subjects in understanding the influences of decision-making.

Additional subjects covered in the chapter focus on introducing different types of decisions, centralization and de-centralization of decision-making authority, the association between the elements of time and decision-making, managing the decision-making process and the linkage between problem-identification, problem-solving and decision-making. Because many decisions reflect the need to solve problems, the chapter offers a detailed overview of the network of linked decisions associated with the problem identification process and the problem-solving process.

CHAPTER 12   LEARNING OBJECTIVES

Readers will achieve the following learning objectives after reading this chapter.

1. Define and explain the terms decisions, decision-making and the decision-making process.
2. Identify, describe and explain the different types of decisions.
3. Identify and describe the different types of decision-making models.
4. Identify, describe and explain the different types of decision-making techniques.
5. Identify and describe the stages of a structured decision-making process.
6. Describe and explain the evolutionary process in the formalization of a decision-making process.
7. Describe and explain the relationship between centralization, de-centralization and decision-making.
8. Identify and explain the reasons making decisions do not ensure a successful outcome.
9. Identify and describe the levels of decision-makers in an organization.
10. Describe the relationship between time and decision-making.
11. Identify and discuss the issues associated with managing the decision-making process.
12. Identify, describe and explain the relevance of the steps, problem identification and problem-solving, with decision-making.

LEARNING OBJECTIVE #1: DEFINE AND EXPLAIN THE TERMS DECISIONS, DECISION-MAKING AND THE DECISION-MAKING PROCESS

What is a decision? Why is understanding decision-making important? Why is the creation of a decision-making process important? How are decisions and decision-making significant to an organization? These are important questions that need answers because organizations function according to the outcomes of decisions made by decision-makers. Organizations succeed or fail based on decisions made by organizational decision-makers.

A **decision** represents a cognitive choice between two or more alternatives that either create change or reinforce a programmed decision. A **programmed decision** represents the organization's official position, commonly referred to as a **policy**, on how to respond to a situation by designating a select choice response (decision) approved by the organization when a predictable situation or situations occur. For example, a business customer fails to provide payment within the prescribed contractually set time frame, the organization's policy dictates a specific response that represents the organization's official decision on the issue.

A decision represents the established position of the person or persons making the decision. A temporary status is not relevant nor is the gravity of the decision, a decision is a decision regardless of the circumstances, though a decision can have a time context and a degree of importance or level of impact significance. In short, a decision is a mental response to a situation, often framed as a problem needing a solution.

There are several definitions for decision-making. A useful definition is that **decision-making** represents a "cognitive process that results in in the selection of a course of action among several alternative scenarios" (Donelan, 2013). What is important to understand is that decision-making is first an intellectual exercise that leads to a decision-maker stating their preference between two or more options. If there is a policy, then the decision-maker must decide based on the organization's officially required decision that is the focus of the policy. A policy can provide the decision-maker some decision-making flexibility by prescribing a range of decisions linked to different situations. For example, if a customer does not respond with a payment within 30 days, this can lead to a decision such as sending a reminder notice. If the customer does not respond within 45 days of the second notice, a warning notice is sent. If a partial payment is sent, this trigger sending a notice that full payment is required on receiving the most recent notice.

Decisions are determined after following a process referred as a decision-making process. A **decision-making process** represents a series of linked, sequenced stages or steps, with a start point and finishing at an end stage. The end stage represents the outcome of the process and the outcome is a decision. The start point of the decision-making process is a situation that triggers the need for a decision.

By using a process approach, the intent of the decision-maker(s) is to influence cognitive functioning with the goal of identifying a specific outcome(s) to act on. Following a **process** imposes a degree of rationality to decision-making. **Rationality** aims to minimize bias to decision-making and to select a decision that moves the organization forward. Because the decision-making process represents sequenced, linked stages, each stage is a foundation for the following stage. A systematic decision-making process is an attempt at making decision-making easier and to increase the certainty that the decision represents the optimal choice among the choices available to a decision-maker.

LEARNING OBJECTIVE #2: IDENTIFY, DESCRIBE AND EXPLAIN THE DIFFERENT TYPES OF DECISIONS

There are different **types** of decisions decision-makers can make. The types of decisions vary based on the level of impact and focus of the decisions. Understanding how decisions stand apart is an important distinction because the differences are important to learn and understand; decisions are not homogeneous but are heterogeneous because the expected impact of a decision ranges in importance for the organization units and for individuals. A decision can range from having an organization-wide focus with the intent of impacting the organization to decisions made by individuals which can indicate that the decision has a narrow focus of limited importance to the organization.

One type of major decision is a **strategic decision**. Strategic decisions impact the entire organization or a substantial segment of an organization. A strategic decision is meant to have a substantive effect on an organization's performance. This means that strategic decisions focus on how best the organization can achieve the organization's **strategic goals**. A strategic decision can include selecting a new strategy, modify the organization's strategic goals and/or change how the organization implements the strategy.

Tactical decisions represent another type of decision. The dominant focus of tactical decisions is to improve the efficiency of an organization's operations. Mid-level managers are tactical managers who identify unit and sub-unit objectives intended to improve the organization's performance during the organization's efforts toward achieving the strategic goals. Achieving the strategic goals, but doing so inefficiently, negatively affects the organization's profitability. Efficiency focuses on the improvement of work processes (A.K.A. operations management) because work process improvements leads to fewer errors, less time spent performing a task and greater levels of productivity.

The next type of decisions is **operational decisions**. Operational decisions represent matter of fact day-to-day work activities that affect the organization's performance at the micro organizational level. Self-improvement is not the focus nor is the focus expected to impact the organization in any substantive way. Operational types of decisions represent decisions made by individuals and teams in the normal course of performing work tasks.

Mentioned earlier are **programmed decisions**. A programmed decision represents a decision or a group of decisions incorporated in an organization's policy. A policy represents the organization's official position on how to perform a task or deal with a situation and the acceptable decision(s) a policy implementor needs to follow. Organizations create policies to deal with re-occurring situations that warrant a response. The organization dictates that form of response within the context of a policy. The intent for having policies is to avoid the unnecessary wasting of time. For example, if an organization has a layoff policy, when a decision is made to reduce the workforce by "X" number of employees, the organization implements relevant work processes and related decisions to fulfill the requirements needed to implement the policy correctly. Time limitations, forms to complete by a specific date, notification times and specific methods to follow, etc. represent several examples of decisions and work processes associated with a layoff policy.

Another type of decision is a **non-programmed decision**. A non-programmed decision is a decision without a policy for guidance because the situation is novel, with no existing policy or no policy sufficiently relevant to apply. A variation of a non-programmed decision is a **semi-programmed decision**. A semi-programmed decision reflects the fact that a decision-maker(s) confronts a new situation that is not unlike prior situations when a policy was created to deal with the situation, but the circumstances are new enough that the policy is not fully applicable. Decision-maker(s) need to determine if a relevant policy is applicable as the basis for making an ad hoc decision based on a broad interpretation of the policy. If decision-makers think that the new situation will re-occur with some degree of regularity, the decision-maker(s) begin the process of updating the relevant policy.

LEARNING OBJECTIVE #3: IDENTIFY AND DESCRIBE DIFFERENT TYPES OF DECISION-MAKING MODELS

A model represents a guide with a specific purpose. A decision-making model is a guide to understand the decision-making process. Decision-making is described as following a process. A process, discussed in a prior chapter, represents a systematic approach with a starting point (first stage) and an outcome stage (in this application, the product of the decision-making process). The use of decision-making models represents an attempt to characterize a decision-making process and to influence an existing organization's decision-making process in specific way(s). The goal in using a decision-making model is to assist decision-makers in dealing with circumstances that challenge decision-makers to produce better decisions.

There are several types of decision-making models developed to serve as a guide for decision-makers to select from.

- **Rational Model**: Each decision option is identified and evaluated using quantitative decision criteria and scoring system; the selected option is chosen after considering all factors.
- **Bounded Rationality Model**: Because decision-makers lack the information and time to consider all possible decision options, the decision-maker arrives at a choice that **satisfies** the basic decision quantitative and non-quantitative criteria of the decision-maker.
- **Incremental Model**: Limited information and time constraints make even the preferred choice an uncertain selection. Decision-makers make decisions which provide feedback on whether the decision moves the organization/unit/ individual forward. The feedback influences the choice of the next decision in the decision-making process.
- **Organizational Procedures Model**: Decisions result from following a decision-making process identified in relevant organizational policies.
- **Political Model**: The selection of a decision among a range of choices is a product of a negotiating process, characterized as a decision-making process.
- **Garbage Can Model**: Problems require solutions; the problems fill the garbage can which disappears after a decision is reached. The faster a decision is made, the quicker the garbage can disappear.
- **Individual Differences Model**: Decision-making is about selecting a decision option that solves a problem(s). Problem-solving behavior is influenced by the decision-making style of the individual, the individual's background and the individual's personality.
- **Naturalist Decision-Making Model**: The decision reached follows a decision-making process that begins with the recognition of a similar situation from the decision-makers' past; the prior decision is evaluated, and the type of decision being considered evolves through constant assessment until the decision-maker is prepared to select an option.
- **Multiple Perspectives Model**: This model applies systems theory to the decision-making process. The decision-maker needs to solve a network of linked problems using technical, organizational and individualistic approaches guided by ethical considerations.
- **Ambiguity Model**: Because the probabilities of events being inaccurately characterized, decision-makers follow the **multiple-perspective evaluation process** to make a choice.
- **Psychological Decision Model**: The decision-maker processes information associated with alternative decision options and makes interpretations of the information, choosing that alternative that is most sanguine.

LEARNING OBJECTIVE #4: IDENTIFY, DESCRIBE AND EXPLAIN THE DIFFERENT TYPES OF DECISION-MAKING TECHNIQUES

Decision-making techniques represent the tools that decision-makers can use to facilitate decision-making. Decision-makers use tools to increase the certainty that the chosen decision represents the best choice given the circumstances. Decision-making techniques help to introduce a systematic, structured approach to the decision-making process. Decision-making techniques run the gamut from qualitative approaches to quantitative approaches. Decision-making techniques can be used by individuals and groups. Often, only one type of technique is used in any given decision situation. However, when decision-makers confront a complex situation, decision-makers will use multiple decision-making techniques to increase the likelihood of making a good decision.

Several types of technically oriented decision-making techniques include the following.

- **Multicriteria Decision-Making**: Use of criteria along with applying weights to the criteria to show the importance of each criteria and the use of values to rate each criteria of a decision alternative by the decision-maker.
- **Mathematical Programming**: Use of mathematical methods to use in selecting from a range of decision alternatives.
- **Artificial Intelligence**: This method involves the use of technology to eliminate or minimize the human element in the decision-making process.
- **Analytical Hierarchy Process (AHE)**: Combining the use of mathematics and psychology, the aim is to analyze criteria using the experiences of the decision-maker to value each of the criteria used to assess each decision alternative.
- **Analytical Network Process (ANP)**: A variation the AHP approach, the ANP method links all the important decision criteria, goal and each decision option to find the best choice among the alternative options.
- **Data Envelopment Analysis**: This method is used in identifying more efficient decision alternatives from less efficient alternatives. There are times when this method is used along with the **multicriteria decision-making method** when the decision-maker wants to rank order the decision choices.

There is another category of decision-making techniques when a group decision is preferred, and the problem is not a technical problem. One or more of these techniques are useful for the group to apply. For example, choosing between several suppliers using multiple criteria, weights for the criteria and values used to demonstrate a decision-maker's opinion regarding each of the criteria applied to each decision alternative. Each group member's scores are averaged together, and the alternative with the higher score is selected.

Examples of decision-making techniques for a group decision include the following.

- **Brainstorming**: The group lists all possible decision alternatives and then proceeds to evaluate each choice. The process continues until there is only one alternative option remaining.

- **Nominal Group Technique**: The group identifies decision alternatives, evaluates the alternatives and then votes; the next stage follows using a similar approach until there is only one decision alternative remaining.
- **Delphi Technique**: Decision alternatives are requested from many individuals but not discussed face-to-face; everyone's comments are circulated among all the participants. Votes occur and the decision alternative receiving the most votes is selected. Consensus sometimes is required for very important decisions.
- **Devil's Advocacy**: Decision alternatives receive critical reviews from all participants in the decision-making process. The intention is to avoid groupthink when selecting a decision alternative.
- **Dialectical Inquiry**: Each group within a large group reviews and critiques the decision alternatives generated by other groups; the process continues as more decision alternatives are identified and evaluated. The large group identifies decision rules to use in guiding the process and in selecting a decision option for the group.
- **Paired Comparison Analysis**: Decision-makers use pair-wise analysis to eliminate all alternatives except one. Starting with the alternative options, one option is eliminated, and a new option is used for comparison.
- **Decision-Trees**: A structured approach that identifies the problem lists the decision alternatives, identifies the likely consequences for each alternative and assigns a probability rating for each possible consequence. The probability rating is multiplied by a value for each alternative. The decision alternative with the highest value is chosen.
- **Pros and Cons**: The decision-makers make a list of the advantages and disadvantages for each decision option. This process is based on the subjective assessments of the decision options; the option that offers decision-makers the best advantages is selected.
- **Game Theory**: Decision-makers seek to assess the possible actions of competitors for each decision alternatives. Decision-makers select the alternative that least benefits competitors and benefits the organization the most.
- **Multi-Voting**: All the decision-makers vote on the alternatives, with the alternative receiving the highest number of votes selected.
- **Heuristics**: The decision alternatives are evaluated based on hypothetical trial and error in assessing the choices drawing on the prior experiences of the decision-makers. The process continues until there is only one decision alternative remaining.

LEARNING OBJECTIVE #5: IDENTIFY AND DESCRIBE THE STAGES OF THE STRUCTURED DECISION-MAKING PROCESS

Throughout the organization, decision-makers try to impose order to the decision-making process. Order implies developing a systematic approach in making decisions. Even if a decision is ad hoc in nature, decision-makers develop and follow a cognitive application to the decision-making process. This ad hoc approach represents a spontaneous application of the decision-making process, but still, the decision-maker follows a cognitive process. By creating a formal, standardized decision-making process for major types of decisions, decision-makers seek to rationalize the decision-making process with the goal of increasing the certainty that the decision represents the best choice at that time.

There are seven major stages to the decision-making process.

1. **Identify the Problem**: Too often, decision-makers identify symptoms as problems without realizing that the solutions are unlikely to be effective. Symptoms represent signals that there are one or more problems causing the symptoms. Much like a doctor, the decision-maker needs to develop effective diagnostic skills to differentiate between symptoms and causes of the symptoms (problems).

2. **Identify and Assign Weights to the Criteria**: Not all decision alternatives are relevant. Sorting among the alternatives helps by identifying the criteria to indicate what decision choices to include, but also weight each criterion because not all criteria are equal in importance. For example, in looking to buy a used car, miles per gallon might be more important to the decision-maker than miles on the odometer.

3. **Identify the Alternatives**: The criteria aid in identifying the decision alternatives to select from. Using the purchase of a used car as an example, if the preferred color is white and miles per gallon is important, then only white cars and cars exceeding a minimum number of miles per gallon are considered.

4. **Evaluate the Alternatives**: Here, the decision-maker can assign values to each of the criterion for each decision alternative. Since a value of a "5" might be less important for one criterion than a value of a "4" for another, the decision-maker calculates the value by the weight given. For example, miles per gallon might have a weight of .30 and color a weight assigned of .05 but each choice earns a value score of "4." Miles per gallon criterion receives the higher score.

5. **Select an Alternative**: Whether the decision-maker uses an objective or qualitative approach to evaluate each decision alternative, the next stage is to select that decision option considered to be the optimal alternative. An objective approach is to choose that option with the highest score. For a qualitative approach, the decision criteria are influenced by prior experiences and the application of heuristics.

6. **Implement the Choice**: Once the decision-maker selects a decision alternative, the decision-maker follows by putting the decision into effect. Implementation can range from an informal, spontaneous approach to a formal, structured process in putting the decision into effect.

7. **Assess the Effectiveness of the Decision**: Feedback is necessary for the decision-maker to learn if the decision worked as expected. Feedback is important for several reasons. If the decision was not the best choice, a new decision can be identified. Feedback helps the decision-maker develop a more effective decision-making process or validate the existing process as well as the decision-maker's judgment. Feedback helps the decision-maker apply the decision-making process in future situations with confidence that the decision-making process represents an effective approach to use.

Whitney's Contemporary Clothing – Part One

Carolyn Jones, CEO of Whitney's Contemporary Clothing, Paula Renault, VP of Marketing, Jane Briggs, VP of Sales, and Kendra Walker, VP of Human Resources, were meeting to discuss a vexing problem. Sales staff were reporting a dramatic increase in the number of angry customers. The causes were easily identifiable. The advertising of clothes not available, advertised sales prices that were not available in stores and limited sizes of advertised clothing were the primary reasons. Carolyn was working on learning the reasons for these problems, but the process was taking longer than expected. Meanwhile, sales staff needed to deal with angry customers. The four decided that if a customer came in and requested an advertised item, a sales price for an advertised item or a size that was not available, the sales staff can offer an alternative equivalent item at the sales price. If the custom remains dissatisfied, the sales staff must immediately direct the customer to store management. Store management is empowered to supplement the initial offer made by the sales staff with a $50 dollar gift certificate.

Questions

1. What were the programmed decisions?
2. Will the decisions mollify customers? Explain.
3. What additional assistance could benefit the sales staff in making on-the-spot decisions?

LEARNING OBJECTIVE #6: DESCRIBE AND EXPLAIN THE EVOLUTIONARY PROCESS IN THE FORMALIZATION OF A DECISION-MAKING PROCESS

Why create a decision-making process? Situations always require a decision because making decisions is one of the most common actions undertaken at work or outside of work. Having a decision-making process provides an individual with a model to follow, regardless of the circumstances. When the decision-maker confronts a re-occurring situation, a decision-making model becomes more essential because the decision-maker's goals are to perform on a consistent basis, use time efficiently, ensure making an effective decision (i.e. achieve the decision-maker's goal(s)) and conform to the ethical guidelines of the individual decision-maker and the organization's code of conduct.

An established, structured decision-making process (using policies) represents an attempt by individuals and the organization at applying a rational approach to the decision-making process. The application of rationality to decision-making aims to create an organized, ordered, reasoned and systematic process. In addition to providing better, more effective decisions, a systematic decision-making process offsets the **cognitive limitations** and **cognitive biases** of the individual. All individuals have cognitive limitations and cognitive biases, though these phenomena vary in severity among individuals. The more challenging the situation, the more likely the cognitive limitations and cognitive biases make decision-making more difficult. Cognitive biases represent the prejudices held by individual decision-makers. Created over time, cognitive biases prejudice the decision-maker toward making subjective types of decisions. A structured, systematic and inclusive decision-making process helps to offset the effects of cognitive limitations and cognitive biases.

Learning objective #5 provides a model decision-making process, identifying a sequence of stages that guide the decision-maker from problem identification through to the outcome stage. In applying the decision-making model, the approach taken can vary according to the circumstances. For example, when there is need for a simple decision, the decision-maker moves rapidly through the process, relying on pre-established **decision rules** derived from "best practices" and the use of policy. When there is the need for a complicated decision, the decision-maker is inclined to move patiently through the decision-making process, relying on policy and input from others in to arrive at a decision. If the circumstances dictate a complex type of decision with multiple parts, the decision-maker can modify the structure of the decision-making process to generate more input from others so that more decision alternatives are available to the decision-maker. The decision-maker moves slowly through the decision-making process because of the importance of the decision. While established policy remains important, typically, a complex decision requires the need to move beyond policy because the situation is new, without a clear precedent and the situation might not repeat itself.

LEARNING OBJECTIVE #7: DESCRIBE AND EXPLAIN THE RELATIONSHIP BETWEEN CENTRALIZATION, DE-CENTRALIZATION AND DECISION-MAKING

Centralization of decision-making often referred to as the top-down approach refers to decisions made among senior management of an organization. Subordinates primarily execute decisions made by senior leadership. Frequently viewed as an autocratic model of decision-making, the type of decisions made by top leadership often impacts the entire organization. Leadership accesses information provided by lower management, seeking to acquire the knowledge to boost leadership's confidence in making good decisions. The use of prior decision-making experiences along with heuristics contributes to leadership's self-confidence in making decisions. Leaders rely on prior experience which provides feedback on the success rate of earlier decisions. Prior experiences help leadership in developing and using heuristics as an aid in decision-making. Heuristics involves the use of simple decision-making approaches, such as consulting with a select group of subordinates, to make decisions that rely on intuition and commonsense. The goal is to reduce the risk of making bad decisions by exercising control over the decision-making process.

Centralization of decision-making is a self-limiting decision-making approach in a complex organization with an external environment that is often changing and an internal environment where understanding and overseeing the complexity of the organization's operations is challenging. Because of leadership's reliance on experience and heuristics, decision-makers tend toward a narrow, less innovative approach in deciding. New ideas for improving organizational performance are slow to evolve. Decision-makers maintain tight control over the organization, which can limit the organization's efforts at changing in response to external circumstances. Finally, a proclivity toward tight control can lead to a dictatorial form of leadership with the corresponding ethics that come with a dictatorship.

De-centralization of decision-making is a form of decision-making that is often characterized as bottom-up decision-making. In a de-centralized organization, lower management levels are empowered to make many types of decisions. Though the type of decisions are not strategic decisions (A.K.A. subordinate decisions), the decisions can impact individuals, groups and units. These subordinate types of decisions provide feedback that moves up through the organization's hierarchy, eventually reaching senior leadership in some form. Decision-making at a subordinate level is meant to begin the process of positioning the organization to respond to external conditions. Decisions often are innovative at this level, varying from programmed types of decisions because the circumstances require an "outside-of-the-box" type of decision. At the subordinate level, decisions frequently reflect the collective wisdom of a group. Group decisions can offer better choices to the organization if **groupthink** is avoided. Groupthink occurs when there is no disagreement or careful evaluation of the decision under consideration. De-centralized decision-making can increase morale because participants affect their own destiny, contributing as important participants in helping to make the organization more competitive.

However, there are limitations to a de-centralized or bottom-up decision-making approach. Too often, decision-making is constrained by the reliance on programmed decisions and programmed decision-making because of concern about deviating from an organization's policies. Second, decisions are often slow to evolve because identifying a decision made by a group takes time to develop as the group needs to involve all group members in the decision-making process and the group's decision-making rules commonly require consensual group decision. Furthermore, there is always the concern that the group's decision might reflect the negative side of group think. Finally, instead of viewing making decisions as an opportunity, subordinates lacking in self-confidence likely do not view the situation as a privilege and opportunity. Finally, subordinates can feel burdened because the performance and reward systems do not recognize the positive decisions made by subordinates.

LEARNING OBJECTIVE #8: IDENTIFY AND EXPLAIN THE REASONS MAKING DECISIONS DO NOT ENSURE A SUCCESSFUL OUTCOME

Decisions do not always result in the expected outcomes. Too often, the expectation is that a decision made will always be a successful decision. Unfortunately, the expectations are frequently unrealistic. A better approach in making decisions is to think like a baseball hitter. Aim for a better batting average.

Improving decision-making outcomes requires making better decisions and good luck. By understanding the reason decisions do not always achieve the anticipated outcomes, and the decision-maker can learn to improve decision-making to achieve the planned outcomes.

The **Ethics** of a decision-maker and the **values** embedded within the corporate culture can limit the effectiveness of decisions. The moral development of top decision-makers influences decision-making by filtering the decision-making process through a value-based filter that recognizes, evaluates, creates intentions and leads to actions influenced by the values of a decision-maker(s). Top leadership's values quickly become incorporated into an organization's culture. Changes to an organization's culture influence decision-making throughout the organization. The result is biased, value-influenced decisions that are not likely to lead to an outcome compared to that derived from an objective-based decision-making process.

Cognitive limits and **cognitive biases** challenge the decision-maker in making decisions that lead to the planned outcome. All decision-makers have cognitive limitations that challenge their ability to assess information objectively and to make sense of the information. Intellectual limitations can occur because of cognitive bias. A bias is a pre-conceived position regarding a subject. One author identified four types of biases: belief bias, hindsight bias, omission bias and confirmation bias. Each type of bias functions as a filter that influences the decision-maker's perspective and interprets information according to the decision-maker's biases.

Many times, decision-makers involve a group of individuals to make a group decision, offsetting the individual's cognitive limitations and cognitive biases in making a more objective decision. However, **groupthink** is a potential inhibiter in making unbiased decisions when the group feels the need to conform, acting irrationally during the decision-making process, thereby resulting in a bad decision. Pressure from leadership, lack of confidence among the group and uncertainty about the type of outcome expected are the more common reasons for groupthink.

Organizational politics is a common cause for bad decisions. Power does not signal superior decision-making abilities. Power is used to influence others. Where power is exerted in direct and indirect ways, the decision-making process can become corrupted. The result is fewer effective decisions.

Additional reasons that contribute to decisions that do not achieve the expected outcomes include the following.

- **Prior Experience**: Decision-makers rely on prior decisions that achieved the intended results but fail to consider new information that makes a prior decision less relevant.
- **Unstructured Decision-Making Process**: Decision-makers do not create an orderly decision-making process to follow, whether for themselves or for others. This allows for a less than thorough, subjective decision-making process.
- **Autocratic Leadership**: Autocratic leaders impose their decisions and the methods used to make decisions. A biased decision often is the result.
- **Misdiagnosis of the Problem**: Too often, decision-makers develop solutions to deal with symptoms of a problem and not the problem(s) associated with the symptom. Miss-diagnosis is the issue.
- **Time**: Either a hasty decision is reached because of the pressure to decide immediately or a delayed decision results in the inability to take advantage of an opportunity or to deal with a threat successfully.
- **Non-Diverse Workforce**: Hiring is often a biased process; the intention is to select certain types of individuals. A homogeneous workforce limits the perspectives of decision-makers during the decision-making process.

LEARNING OBJECTIVE #9: IDENTIFY AND DESCRIBE THE LEVELS OF DECISION-MAKERS IN AN ORGANIZATION

Organizations create formal organizational designs to influence and improve the structure of the decision-making process throughout the organization. Structure represents the intent to provide order by standardizing an organization-wide decision-making process to exercise great control over the making of decisions throughout the organization. There are four primary levels to an organization's structure: senior or top management, middle management, supervisory management and non-management. Each level's type of decisions has a specific focus. The structure is sometimes referred to as a hierarchy of authority. Though some researchers view existing design models ineffective in facilitating decision-making to deal with prevailing market conditions, the hierarchical design models continue to be dominant (see Figure 12.1).

Senior management's decisions, referred to as strategic decisions, are meant to impact the entire organization. Strategic decisions focus on improving the organization's performance with the goal of survival in a Darwinian World of dynamic changes because of globalization and reduced trade barriers. Strategic decisions are broad, general statements meant to encompass the entire organization.

Middle management is the level below top management. Middle management's primary role in the organization-wide decision-making process is to implement top management's strategic decisions by converting the strategic decisions into more narrowly focused operational decisions which concentrate on specific operational or functional areas of the organization (e.g. marketing, R&D and accounting). For example, top management might decide that building a partner-network of organizations is an effective approach to diversify revenue sources as well as increase revenue. Middle management decides on which operational units need to be involved in finding partners, formalizing relations with partners and oversee the partner-organization relationship. Middle management determines the decision-making rules to follow by the levels below middle management. Decision rules are incorporated in policies, guide decision-makers when dealing with re-occurring and non-reoccurring situations. Middle managers develop decision rules that influence how

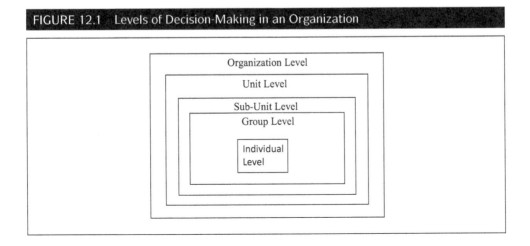

FIGURE 12.1 Levels of Decision-Making in an Organization

middle management ensures compliance to decisions by lower levels and identifies decision rules that guide middle management's interactions with top management when in consultation with top management.

Supervisory management is the lowest management level in the organization. Supervisory management makes decisions regarding how subordinates need to perform their work responsibilities per their respective job descriptions and assigned tasks. Decisions focus on ensuring consistent work efforts, greater operational efficiencies and improved operational effectiveness. When crises occur, the supervisory manager assesses the situation using the decision rules as a guide, involving middle management as needed.

At the individual level, individuals adhere to the decision rules associated with policies regarding work performance. Decision-making at this level involves focusing on performing the various job-related work processes to meet performance expectations. Decision-making at this level concentrates on dealing with immediate operational issues that are frequently one-time events. Situations considered to be re-occurring get passed up through the hierarchy. Typically, middle management decides how to proceed. The decision often involves either creating new decision-rules or improving existing decision rules. Developing or modifying existing policies can be part of the process associated with the decision rule development process. If the change is major, organization-wide change, middle management recommends a decision for top management to consider and finalize on.

Whitney's Contemporary Clothing – Part Two

Jane Briggs, VP of Sales, Phil Montague, VP of Store Management, and Pam Cousins, Sales Staff Manager were meeting to discuss how to increase sales per customer. The consensus was to promote the concept of upselling with the emphasis on getting the customer to purchase additional, complementary items. During the discussion, they agreed to an upselling work process for sales staff to follow. Designing a training program was the next item on the agenda for discussion. The agreed-upon upselling process for sales staff follows:

Step 1: Work with the customer to finalize a selection of an item(s).

Step 2: Ask if the customer was considering a complementary item(s).

Step 3A: If the answer is no, suggest considering an item to enhance the look.

Step 3B: If the answer is yes, find out the type of item and move to the store location for the item.

Step 4: After selecting the item, promote the idea of buying the top two items.

Step 5A: Encourage the customer to consider an additional complementary item to enhance the overall look.

Step 5B: Do not wait for the customer to say yes or no to the question, immediately guide the customer to the location of the recommended item (e.g., jewelry and shoes).

Step 6: Encourage the customer to try on items.

Step 7: Compliment the customer's look with their preferred choice.

Step 8: Close the sale by directing the customer to the cashier station, accompanying the customer to the station, complimenting the customer's purchases.

Questions

1. Why should the company create an upselling work process?
2. What is the benefit of having an upselling work process?
3. Are there ethical issues to consider? Explain.

LEARNING OBJECTIVE #10: DESCRIBE THE RELATIONSHIP BETWEEN TIME AND THE DECISION-MAKING

Time and speed of decision-making are closely linked because the circumstances frequently lead to greater or lesser uncertainty in how and when to respond. The irony is that too often, there is pressure to decide hastily. There is one type of decision that can make the decision-making process extend out in time. The answer is a complex decision because a complex decision requires a careful response to a complex situation. The types of decisions can be conceptualized using the concept of a continuum. Simple decisions on one end and complex decisions at the other end of the continuum. Superseded over this continuum is the certainty-uncertainty continuum. Certainty is at one end (parallel to simple decisions) and uncertainty at the other end (parallel to complex decisions). Certainty and simple decisions work in parallel, likely dealing with a re-occurring situation. At the other end of the continuum, uncertainty and complex decisions mate because the decision involves dealing with a complex, non-re-occurring situation (see Figure 12.2).

FIGURE 12.2 Relationship Between Risk, Information Needed, Cost of Information and Time Available

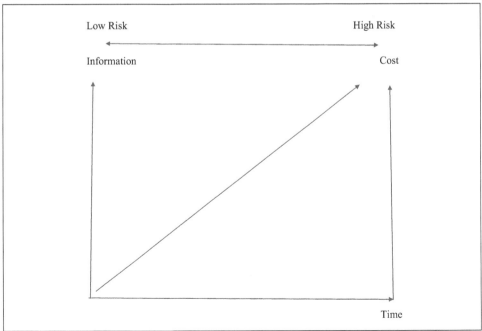

A familiar, repetitive situation means that more than likely the organization created a policy for the decision-makers to use in making a quick decision. Typically, the decision-maker develops follows decision rules that are incorporated in the policy. With the rules/policy in-place and a simple decision required, the decision-maker can respond quickly.

Faced with atypical situations uncertainty escalates and increases further if the circumstances become more unusual. This is a result of the fact that the decision-maker confronts an atypical situation that has no prior precedent or is at variance from previous situations. This means that there is no policy to follow nor decision rules to guide the decision-maker. Because of the uncertainty associated with the circumstances, the decision-maker relies on the decision-making process to impose a structured process for the decision-maker to follow. The intent of extending the time involved with the decision-making process is to reduce if not eliminate the uncertainty associated with making the wrong decision. The goal is to make a decision that leads to the preferred outcome.

One of the principle ways a decision-maker can reduce uncertainty involves benefitting from the insights of experts. Soliciting input from experts is time-consuming; the amount of time depends on the degree of involvement required. The more complicated the situation, the greater the likelihood the decision-maker will involve more and not fewer experts to provide their input as part of the expanded decision-making process (see Figure 12.3).

A complex situation warrants a complex response which takes time to identify. But a complex situation often requires a quick response as the situation usually is of an urgent nature. As a result, one form of response by the decision-maker is to pass on making one decision as the outcome of the decision-making process. The decision-maker makes a series of incremental decisions linked sequentially as the

FIGURE 12.3   The Relationship Between a Decision's Importance, the Need for a Formal Decision-Making Process and the Need to Involve Others

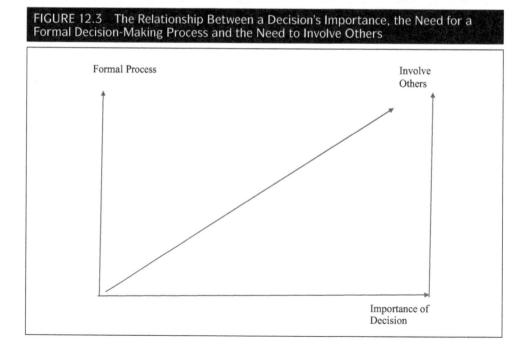

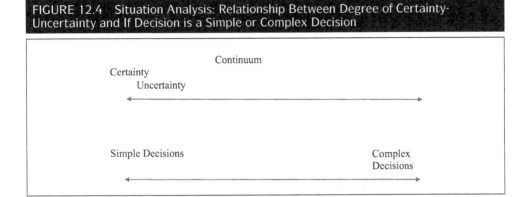

FIGURE 12.4 Situation Analysis: Relationship Between Degree of Certainty-Uncertainty and If Decision is a Simple or Complex Decision

decision-maker(s) benefits from feedback on the results of prior decisions. This incremental decision-making approach extends the entire decision-making process time frame. The intent of extending the time by making a series of decisions is to reduce the uncertainty associated with seeking a specific outcome. Feedback offers the decision-maker performance results that help the decision-maker(s) move forward with impactful and effective decisions (see Figure 12.4).

LEARNING OBJECTIVE #11: IDENTIFY AND DISCUSS THE ISSUES ASSOCIATED WITH MANAGING THE DECISION-MAKING PROCESS

There are a several management issues a decision-maker or a group of decision-makers need to think about during the management of the decision-making process. The more important the decision, the more substantive the management issues; the more people needing to be involved in the decision-making process, the more comprehensive and complicated are the management issues. Presented below are the major management issues decision-makers need to consider. The complexity of each issue is tied to the importance of the decision.

- **Decision-Making Process**: Regardless of the importance of the decision, the decision-maker needs to adhere to and follow some types of formal or informal decision-making process.
- **Task Management**: The decision-maker needs to identify relevant tasks to perform the sequence of tasks and perform the tasks while proceeding through the decision-making process.
- **Discretion**: The type of decision dictates the extent to which the decision-maker needs to involve others in the decision-making process.
- **Ethical Code**: The decision-maker needs to adhere to and follow their personal code of conduct concurrent with the organization's code of conduct.
- **Input from Others**: Gather information from individuals that need to be involved in the decision-making process as either active participants or in a passive role.
- **Problem Identification**: The decision-maker needs to develop and manage a problem-solving process to identify a problem(s) separate from symptoms of a problem.

- **Transparency**: The decision-maker needs to determine and oversee the approach to pursue in making the decision-making process open to others to follow while a decision is under consideration.
- **Communication**: The greater the importance of the decision, the greater the need to keep all the important stakeholders updated during the decision-making process.
- **Clear Decision Rules**: Clarifying the guidelines to follow is necessary, even if the decision is a simple decision and the rules need only be informal. Often decision rules are found in policies.
- **Cognitive Bias**: Decision-maker prejudices need to be offset to ensure an objective decision-making process.
- **Decision Audit**: Identify and apply methods to generate objective assessments that provide feedback about the results of a decision.
- **Decision Techniques**: Decision-makers often use techniques designed specifically for use in facilitating decision-making during the decision-making process.
- **Time Management**: Some decisions require haste and other types of decisions warrant a patient approach to decision-making. The decision-maker must monitor the decision-making process to ensure that an outcome occurs within the expected time frame.

Whitney's Contemporary Clothing – Part Three

Carolyn Jones, CEO of Whitney's Contemporary Clothing, Paula Renault, VP of Marketing, Jane Briggs, VP of Sales and Vanessa Forsberg, VP of Finance were meeting to discuss one issue, the average sales revenue per customer was declining. This trend began three years prior, with each succeeding year showing further declines. The meeting originally intended to develop a plan to increase sales per customer. However, Vanessa asked the questions "Why are sales trending this way? What are the reasons?" All were stunned because no one had a direct answer. Everyone agreed that what they thought was a problem was really a symptom. Everyone agreed to take the following steps to learn what are the cause(s) of declining average sales revenue per customer. The steps included:

Step 1: Poll store managers for their thoughts.
Step 2: Conduct a customer survey with the goal of learning why their purchases were declining.
Step 3: Meet with industry analysts to learn about new market trends and their perceptions of Whitney's Contemporary Clothing.

Questions

1. Why aren't declining sales per customer a problem? Explain.
2. Why take a multiple approach to identify the problem(s)?
3. Is there a missing step(s) to the problem identification process they planned to follow?

- **Information Management**: Decision-makers need to identify, locate, collect, analyze and report information either formally or informally to arrive at a decision outcome.

LEARNING OBJECTIVE #12: IDENTIFY, DESCRIBE AND EXPLAIN THE RELEVANCE OF THE STEPS, PROBLEM IDENTIFICATION AND PROBLEM-SOLVING, WITH DECISION-MAKING

The preponderance of decisions made by an organization involves following a process for identifying problems and a process for identifying solutions to problems along with a process for implementing the solutions to the problems. The standard decision-making process model's first stage is to identify a problem or problems (see above). All the decision-making models incorporate a process to identify a problem.

The link between problems and decisions is clear. Identifying a problem incorporates the use of a structured problem identification process. Whether a simple or complex situation, decision-makers need to make different types of decisions during the process of identifying a problem. This includes deciding on questions to ask, analytical methods to use, people to consult and other types of decisions associated with identifying a problem. The problem identification process also includes the ranking of problems if this is a relevant and necessary issue. Problems generate symptoms. A symptom is something seen or experienced. The problem(s) is the cause of a symptom. Rising costs and declining revenues are symptoms that the decision-maker needs to learn the cause(s) of these negative trends.

Developing solutions to problems comprises a series of decisions linked together by the stages of the problem solution process. Again, the decision-maker needs to determine how best to proceed, who to involve, questions to ask, analytical methods to consider views along with any other useful aids that can help in developing a plan to solve a problem(s). If these are optional plans, the decision-maker needs to decide on a process to follow for evaluating each option and a methodology to use to assist in selecting the best plan.

Finally, the decision-maker needs to implement the selected problem-solving plan. The implementation plan can range from a simple process, with few stages to an implementation process encompassing many stages and sub-stages. Regardless of the complexity of the plan, each stage in the plan involves some type of decision.

For an organization, there are two primary categories of problems. **Strategic problems** can occur for several reasons. First, the organization's external environment can change. For example, a declining economy results in different consequences the organization needs to respond to. Second, market issues can result in problems that the organization needs to resolve. Even if market trends are positive, the trends can lead to problems, such as an insufficient supply of products, insufficient inputs to produce products, changes in brand loyalty and rising costs. Third, new initiatives by competitors can lead to problems that the organization needs to confront. Finally, problems with suppliers are disruptive to the organization, requiring decisions to deal with these problems.

Operational problems represent another category of problems. Operational problems can include problems with individual management systems and the links that connect the management systems together; potential problems that might be anticipated because of certain actions taken at the operational level; or there is no policy to guide decision-makers in responding to an operational problem; and work processes that need changes to contribute more consistent performance, create operational efficiencies and improved operational performance (increased productivity, fewer defects, etc.).

In sum, the link between the problem identification process, the problem-solving process and decision-making is clear. Making decisions is a fundamental aspect of the problem identification process and the problem-solving process.

Whitney's Contemporary Clothing – Part Four

Carolyn Jones, CEO of Whitney's Contemporary Clothing, met with Paula Renault, VP of Marketing, and Jane Briggs, VP of Sales, to discuss the results of the problem identification process intended to learn why sales revenue per customer was declining. The findings follow.

1. The targeted demographic group was declining in numbers.
2. Existing products were not among the top preferred styles.
3. Customer style interests were changing more rapidly than in prior years.
4. The frequency of customer surveys declined from six per year to three times per year.
5. The advertising and promotions budgets were cut each of the past three years.
6. The market wanted clothes with new types of material that provided a different feel and look.
7. Customers were increasing their online purchases.

Questions

1. How should senior leadership respond to the findings? Explain.
2. Are there short-term and long-term responses? Explain.
3. What is the preferred decision-making model to apply? Explain.

Chapter Summary

Studying the subject, decisions, is an essential subject for the reader to learn about because making decisions is the most common activity in any organization. The goal in decision-making is to bring about a positive outcome. This means that for any decision-maker, making a good decision is very important. Learning about what improves decision-making and the factors that contribute to making effective decision-making a challenge are important subjects for any decision-maker to learn about.

This chapter discusses the importance of having a decision-making process to follow, regardless if the decision is a major or minor decision. Any decision represents an outcome from a decision-making process. This chapter makes the case for developing a rational, systematic decision-making process to provide the decision-maker with a structured method to follow. The chapter identifies and describes a traditional decision-making process model.

Decisions are not monolithic but are polylithic. The chapter identifies and describes different types of decisions to cause the range of decision types, so the reader understands the challenges associated with making effective decisions. To educate the reader further, the chapter presents different types of decision-making models for the reader to understand; there are a broad range of models regarding the decision-making process. The chapter includes the identification and description of decision-making techniques that decision-makers can use as tools to aid the decision-maker in making decisions.

The hierarchy of authority or organizational structure represents levels of decision-making within any organization. Each level of the organization is responsible for fulfilling a specific role along with the types of decisions made at each level. The chapter identified and described the different levels, the types of decisions made at each level and the linkage among the decision levels.

Managing the decision-making process is important chapter topic because of the importance of decision-making to the

organization. Describing how to manage decision-making provides insights on how best to manage the decision-making process.

Most decisions deal with problems, and one of the contributing factors for failed decisions is that decisions are frequently made to deal with symptoms of problems and not the actual problems that generate symptoms.

The chapter examined the issue of problem-generated symptoms; provided a model problem identification process and described the relationship between the problem identification process and the decision-making process.

Studying decisions is an important subject because of the role decision-making plays in all organizations. The goal of this chapter was to provide the reader with a better understanding of decision-making with the intention of strengthening the reader's understanding of the subject.

Chapter Questions

1. Define and explain the terms decisions, decision-making and the decision-making process. Why should decision-makers use decision-making techniques?
2. What are the different types of decisions? Explain.
3. Identify and briefly describe any five of the different types of decision-making models.
4. Identify and briefly describe any five of the different types of decision-making techniques.
5. What are the stages of a structured decision-making process?
6. Describe the process typical in creating a decision-making process.
7. Describe and explain the relationship between centralization, de-centralization and decision-making.
8. What are the reasons making a decision does not guarantee a successful decision?
9. Identify and describe the different levels of decision-making in an organization.
10. How is time and the decision-making process linked? Explain.
11. What are the issues associated with managing the decision-making process?
12. What is the connection between problem identification, the problem-solving process and decision-making?

Bibliography

Blenko, M.W., Mankins, M. & Rogers, P. (2010). The decision-driven organization. *Harvard Business Review*. June.

CAPTIO. (2015). The eight stages of the decision-making process within a

company. August 8. 1–5. Blog/the eight stages of the decision-making process within an organization.

Chai, J., Liu, J.N.K. & Ngai, E.W.T. (2013). Application of decision-making techniques in supplier selection: a systematic review of the literature. *Expert Systems with Allocations*. 40. 3872–3885.

Cox, K., Strang., L., Sondergaard, S. & Monsalve, C.G. (2017). Understanding how organizations ensure that their decision making is fair. *Rand Europe*. 1–74.

Dietrich, C. (2010). Decision-making: factors that influence decision making, heuristics used, and decision outcome. *Inquiries Journal*. 2(2). 1–11.

Donelan, R. (2013). Good decision-making practice in the regulatory arena. *Regulatory Reporter*. 10(6). 4–5.

Eby, K. (2018). Which management style is right for you: top-down or bottom-up approach? *SMARTSHEET*. June 28.

Gibson, F.P., Fichman, M. & Plaut, D.C. (1997). Learning in dynamic decision tasks: computational model and empirical evidence. *Organizational Behavior and Human Decision Processes*. 71(1). 1–35.

Janczak, S. (2005). The strategic decision-making process in organizations. *Problems and Perspectives in Management*. 3. 58–70.

Lunenburg, F.C. (2011). Decision-making in organizations. *International Journal of Management, Business, and Administration*. 15(1). 1–9.

Mykkanen, M. & Tampere, K. (2014). Organizational decision-making: the Luhmannian decision communication perspective. *Journal of Business Studies Quarterly*. 5(4). 131–146.

Negulescu, O.H. (2014). Using a decision-making process model in strategic management. *Review of General Management*. 19(1). 111–123.

Oliveira, A. (2007). A discussion of rational and psychological decision-making theories and models: the search for a cultural-ethical decision-making model. *Electronic Journal of Business Ethics and Organization Studies*. 12(2). 12–17.

Panpatte, S. & Takale, V.D. (2019). To study the decision-making process in an organization for its effectiveness. *The International Journal of Business Management and Technology*. 3(1). 73–78.

Trevino, L. (1996). Ethical decision-making in organizations: a person-situation interactionist model. *The Academy of Management Review*. 11(3). 601–617.

Turpin, M. & Marais, M. (2004). Decision-making: theory and practice. *ORION*. 20(2). 143–160.

Wu, A. (2015). Organizational decision-making and information: angel investments by venture capitalists. *Department of Business Economics & Public Policy. The Wharton School of the University of Pennsylvania*. November 10. 1–70. Unpublished.

Zeiger, S. (2020). Decision-making styles for organizations. Chron.com. htpps://smallbusiness.chron.com/decision making_styles_organizations_24385.html.

Motivation and Effective Work Performance

OVERVIEW

A performance management system includes an organization's formal approach in creating the methods for motivating the organization's workforce. A motivated workforce is a critical element in the long-term success or failure of an organization. The goal in designing a performance management system and reward system is to increase workforce productivity with the intent of improving the organization's effectiveness.

This chapter covers the subject of motivation and effective workforce performance because of the critical link between the workforce's motivation and the workforce's contribution to the success of an organization. The chapter enables the reader to fully understand the definition of the term, motivation, in its technical application. Because of the importance of the subject, it covers a wide range of motivation theories to aid the reader in understanding what drives individuals to act in particular ways that reflect a motivated or unmotivated individual. Motivation theories help to understand the different motivators of a motivated workforce. But theory is only one of three focus points of emphasis.

In understanding the concept of motivation, what is crucial for the reader to learn about is the association between motivation and work performance; work performance results, indications of motivated employees and the antecedent factors that influence employee work performance.

This chapter introduces the reader to the issues of intrinsic and extrinsic motivation. Furthermore, the chapter describes the differences between intrinsic and extrinsic motivation along with identifying and describing the issues that result because some workers are more motivated by intrinsic factors and other workers are more motivated by extrinsic factors.

Another important topic covered in this chapter is levels of motivation. A performance management system's design needs to encompass the different levels, such as motivating individuals, motivating groups and motivating units.

An organization's culture and cultural factors contribute to creating an effective, productive and motivated workforce. Learning about the role of culture and how cultural factors contribute to creating a motivated workforce enables the reader to learn and understand how an organization's internal culture contributes to enable the organization to motivate the workforce. Culture is a relevant topic to understand because cultural factors influence the design of the performance management and reward systems.

Another important factor in understanding the motivation of individuals is the association between an individual's sense of self-worth and the motivation of an individual. The subject of self-worth is important to study because the design of a performance management and reward systems will differ when the focus is to build an individual's self-worth to positively impact the individual's work performance. Self-worth is an important factor that influences an individual's choice of goals. Achieving can be an individual's goal because of the link between motivation and achievement. The more motivated the individual, the more the individual becomes achievement-oriented. The chapter examines the factors individuals need to become more motivated; this enables the individual to select and pursue ambitious goals that require outside-the-box behavior.

Finally, this chapter examines the link between the performance management system and the reward system by learning how a reward system is integral to the functioning of a performance management system and contributes to a motivated workforce.

CHAPTER 13   LEARNING OBJECTIVES

Readers will achieve the following learning objectives after reading this chapter.

1. Describe and explain the term motivation and its importance to organizations.
2. Identify and describe examples of the most common motivation theories.
3. Describe and explain the relationship between motivation and work performance.
4. Identify and describe the antecedent conditions that influence motivated employee work performance.
5. Describe, explain and compare intrinsic motivation with extrinsic motivation.
6. Identify and describe the levels of motivation in an organization.
7. Describe and explain the relationship between organizational culture and motivation.
8. Discuss the relationship between self-worth and motivation.
9. Describe motivation as a goal and the process factors associated with achieving the goal.
10. Discuss the link between the performance management system, the reward system and motivation.

LEARNING OBJECTIVE #1: DESCRIBE AND EXPLAIN THE TERM MOTIVATION AND ITS IMPORTANCE TO AN ORGANIZATION

There are many definitions for the term **motivation,** but the most salient and concise definition is to define motivation as the active engagement of an individual's cognitive and affective domains with the intent to behave or act in particular ways to achieve a specific goal or outcome.

There are a several reasons for an organization to want to understand the importance of motivation and the relationship between motivation and an effective organization. The positive association between a motivated workforce and an effective organization is supported by numerous empirically based research studies. In learning about the link between a motivated workforce and organizational performance, the organization can pursue an agenda that contributes to creating and maintaining a motivated workforce.

First, there is the need to create an environment conducive to inspiring the workforce to be motivated. The organization's **culture** is an essential internal environmental issue because the culture of an organization reflects the important values an organization seeks to promote. Identifying and promoting the values that inspire the workforce to work harder and smarter include the following examples of such values.

- Demonstrating through actions that employees are **important** to the organization.
- Employees can **trust** that the organization has their best interest in mind.
- The organization demonstrates through actions a **commitment** to the well-being of the workforce.
- The organization demonstrates through its actions the importance of treating employees **fairly.**
- **Job security** for employees is an essential aspect of an organization's policies and practices.
- Employees perceive that **wages and wage scales** aim to support the well-being of the workforce.

Employee engagement is a term often associated with the motivation of an organization's workforce. The engagement of the workforce to achieve an organization's goals is critical to an organization's ability to achieve the long-term goal of survival within a competitive external environment. Examples in how an organization can contribute toward creating an engaged workforce include the following.

- Designing a **performance management system** that results in a highly motivated workforce represents the vision associated with creating and improving the performance management system.
- The careful selection of new employees by designing a **selection process** that includes identifying a set of criteria that encompass being able to discover motivated individuals. A critical mass of motivated employees can counter a group of unmotivated employees helping to influence the values of an organization's culture.
- **Training** the workforce on an ongoing basis shows an organization's commitment to enable employees to succeed in performing their work responsibilities.

- Providing a formal method to offer employees **feedback** during the performance evaluation review process enables the workforce to understand the organization's expectations and assessment of current work performance.
- Knowing the **personality of the workforce** is critical in signaling interest and concern for the workforce; the interest and concern is demonstrated by designing the management systems along with managing the management systems with an employee focus.
- As an organization grows, the workforce **diversifies** both in terms of ethnicity and sex, but also in terms of education, knowledge, skills, personality and intelligence. The organization's management systems need to evolve to reflect the diversity of the workforce and meet the needs of a diverse workforce along with taking advantage of a diverse workforce.

LEARNING OBJECTIVE #2: IDENTIFY AND DESCRIBE EXAMPLES OF THE MOST COMMON MOTIVATION THEORIES

Theory offers a set of principles intended to explain some phenomena. Theories of motivation provide principles for understanding human behavior characterized as motivated behavior. Motivated behavior is purposeful with the goal of generating an outcome. Behavior can fall within a continuum ranging between **action and inaction**. Inaction is purposeful as the individual makes a choice to not behave in a way other than to do nothing, acting by choosing to do nothing. Action refers to behavior intended to accomplish a goal that requires some form of action, which leads to an outcome. Where an individual falls on the continuum is a measure of the degree to which the individual is motivated in general or for achieving a specific purpose.

Motivation theories vary because there are different perspectives developed to help understand the factors that drive individuals to act. These perspectives help in understanding the complexity of individuals because organizations need to learn how to encourage an individual and the workforce to be motivation. A motivated workforce is engaged in performing work responsibilities. An engaged workforce is achievement-oriented; an achievement-oriented workforce contributes to the making of a productive organization.

When an individual is characterized as "lazy," this is a mischaracterization of the individual and a negative label. The individual is far from being lazy, and the individual is not motivated to act but motivated to not act.

The variety of motivation theories that follow are organized into three categories. **Content theories** describe individual's motivation as an attempt at fulfilling a need. **Process theories** focus on the individual's manifested behavior triggered by the attempt at satisfying personal needs. **Contemporary theories** are derived from empirical studies whereas content and process theories largely originate from basic assumptions about human behavior and the link to causality.

Content theories follow.

- **Maslow's Hierarchy of Needs**: Individuals have needs to satisfy. Needs are ranked within a basic hierarchical framework from the need to satisfy basic needs first before attempting to satisfy higher-order needs.
- **Herzberg's Two-Factor Theory**: A job's characteristics can lead to an individual being satisfied or not satisfied with the job. To achieve a motivated employee,

the organization needs to appeal to the individual's intrinsic motivation to motivate the employee to greater levels of performance.

- **Alderfer's Existence, Relatedness and Growth Theory (ERG)**: An individual's needs are grouped into three categories. Existence needs motivate the individual to act to survive. Relatedness needs refer to the actions of the individual to fulfill social needs. Growth needs represent the individual's efforts toward self-improvement.
- **Theory X and Theory Y**: Theory X characterizes workers as lacking ambition, dislike work and prefer to be free of work obligations. This type of worker does the minimum. Theory Y characterizes workers as enthusiastic about work and derives tremendous satisfaction from work responsibilities, seeking greater control over work responsibilities to generate higher levels of self-satisfaction.
- **McClelland's Needs or Achievement Theory**: The individual acquires certain needs based on life experiences. All individual's fall within one of three categories of needs, the need to achieve, the need to seek power or influence or the need to have strong personal relationships with others. Each category represents the purpose of being motivated. Process theories follow.
- **Porter-Lawler Motivation Theory**: Individuals pursue goals based on the likelihood that successful performance leads to rewards commensurate with the effort expended. The types of rewards can be intrinsic-driven and extrinsic-driven, but the rewards need to meet the individual's expectations to motivate the individual.
- **Vroom's Expectancy Theory**: The individual will act to achieve an outcome or goal if the individual perceives that the effort will likely lead to success.
- **Equity Theory**: An individual assesses if the rewards offered are commensurate to the rewards offered to others for comparable behavior. If equal or better, the individual will act to earn the reward.
- **Job Design Theory**: Worker motivation increases based on a job's characteristics. Important job characteristics include the variety of skills required, the importance of the job and the degree of autonomy offered in performing the job responsibilities and performance expectations.

Contemporary theories follow.

- **Agency Theory**: An individual or agent acts in the best interest of the organization when the organization confers incentives valued by the agent.
- **Goal Theory**: Individuals prefer working to achieve goals. The best goals are goals that require the individual to act using outside-the-box methods to be successful.
- **Reinforcement Theory**: An individual's behavior is influenced by the rewards received because of acting in particular ways. The reward needs to be sufficiently important for the individual to act.
- **Life-Span Development Motivation Theory**: Individuals select goals to achieve according to the developmental stages an individual is in at any point in time. Motivation occurs as the individual adjusts to the circumstances of a developmental stage to achieve the goals associated with a specific stage.
- **Socioemotional Selective Theory of Motivation**: Individuals move through developmental stages, selecting goals that lead to "ego-transcending goals"

but the choice of goals become less risky as the individual ages and social/emotional gains become less important than social/emotional stability.

- **Theory of Self-Worth**: External environmental factors impact the individual such that feelings of self-worth increase from successfully responding to these factors. As a result, individuals choose to act to generate new experiences to increase feelings of self-worth.
- **Social Cognitive Theory**: The individual is driven to pursue new knowledge and skill development because of external environmental factors requiring such action. The individual learns to become self-efficacious, gaining greater control over their ability to be successful learners, apply what was learned and therefore succeed at achieving outcomes.

LEARNING OBJECTIVE #3: DESCRIBE THE RELATIONSHIP BETWEEN MOTIVATION AND WORK PERFORMANCE

The assumption that a motivated workforce leads to better work performance is supported by empirical evidence. What contributes to a motivated workforce is an important issue to learn about because organizations can be proactive in championing a motivated workforce. Another way to think about the subject is to consider the idea that motived workers are **engaged employees**.

An engaged employee is **cognitively** committed to their employer and job because the engaged employee is mentally involved in performing work responsibilities in the best way possible. An engaged employee is **emotionally** committed to their job, work associates and the organization. An emotional commitment is reflected by the individual's loyalty to work associates and the organization. Finally, an engaged employee demonstrates through **behavior** a commitment to their job, work associates and the organization.

Behavior is the physical manifestation of an engaged employee. Through behavior, an organization learns whether an employee is motivated and the extent to which an employee is motivated. One example of an engaged employee is retention rates. **Committed**, happy employees remain at the same organization even though moving to another organization can lead to a better position with more appealing benefits and greater career opportunities. An engaged employee is actively involved with their job. **Involvement** is often associated with such behaviors as volunteering for an assignment, speaking out without prompting, assuming a leadership position and voluntarily assisting others. These examples highlight an individual's active involvement with their job. **Satisfaction** is another trait common to an engaged employee. Behavior associated with a satisfied employee is length of service, choosing to remain in the same position, social engagement with peers on the job and outside of work, and someone who is active in training programs to improve their knowledge, skills and personal abilities in performing work responsibilities. Another example of an engage employee is an **enthusiastic** employee. Enthusiasm suggests an emotional commitment which is exemplified by a low absentee rate, arriving at work on time or early, leaving work on time or later, taking few breaks and short lunches or initiating working lunches with colleagues. Finally, a productive worker reflects an engaged employee and a productive worker is an **achiever**. Achievement is measured by accomplishing goals. The preferred goals are "stretch goals" that are SMART type goals. Stretch goals are goals that require a self-motivated individual to move outside of their comfort zone by adapting new approaches to succeed in achieving the goal.

One of the important ways to create an engaged employee is through work empowerment. **Work empowerment** involves modifying an individual's work responsibilities. Changing job responsibilities can include expanding job responsibilities, conferring greater decision-making authority, allowing an employee to take initiative or self-direction, granting greater autonomy, believing that the employee knows best how to perform work responsibilities better. The approach is typically associated with the application of Theory Y. By creating an engaged employee, the organization creates a self-motivated employee, and self-motivated employees are productive employees. The benefit of having self-motivated employees is a productive organization.

Design Clothing for the Young – Part One

Kate Hudson, Vice President of Marketing, Kate's assistant Paul Cruise, Kim Novak, Associate Vice President of Incentive Programming, and Bill Foster, Vice President of Human Resources were meeting because Kate thinks that an incentive program is necessary for the new line of leggings, Desirables Plus. The line came out in the early spring with great expectations. Unfortunately, sales were well below expectations. Customer feedback was positive. The other major concern was that the advertising campaign was not having the intended impact. Everyone decided that a two-prong approach to boost sales was the answer. Stores with the highest sales would receive gift certificates for each customer service representative. Top customer service representatives would receive gift certificates too. What everyone needed to decide was whether to create a program where all stores and all top performing customer service representatives were eligible for more prizes by surpassing a minimum amount of sales within a specified time frame or make the program stricter when only certain top performing stores and customer service representatives were eligible to receive the gift certificates.

Questions

1. What are the advantages and disadvantages of enabling full eligibility or limited eligibility?
2. What is the best way to determine an approach to follow?
3. How long should the program last? Explain.

LEARNING OBJECTIVE #4: IDENTIFY AND DESCRIBE THE ANTECEDENT CONDITIONS THAT INFLUENCE MOTIVATED EMPLOYEE WORK PERFORMANCE

Antecedents represent the factors that influence the extent to which an individual is an engaged employee. Extent implies that there are degrees of engagement which is accurate. An engaged or motivated employees' degree of commitment can range between non-engaged to the opposite end of the continuum, fully engaged. Learning about and understanding the factors that influence employee engagement is important because an organization can attempt to exercise control over these factors. The antecedents are organized into three main categories: the individual's contribution, job characteristics and the internal environment of the organization.

The **individual** contributes several types of antecedent factors, as an example, that can determine the degree of self-motivation demonstrated by behavior exhibited in performing a job. The individual's factors include:

- **Cognitive Abilities**: The individual's intellectual capabilities to deal with varying degrees of abstract thinking.
- **Affective Abilities**: The individuals' degree of happiness with themselves and with their immediate environment.
- **Personality Characteristics**: The ability of the individual to get along with others and to maintain homeostasis.
- **Skill Variety**: The individual's range of skills and skill performance that enables the individual to apply skills under varied circumstances.
- **Interpersonal Relations**: An individual that values social relationships seeks out work that involves frequent and ongoing contact with others.

Job characteristics represent another category of antecedents directly controllable by an organization seeking to support efforts toward the creation of an engaged workforce. Job characteristics include:

- **Task Importance**: How important are the tasks performed in fulfilling job requirements.
- **Autonomy**: Workers prefer being able to decide how best to perform work responsibilities.
- **Interpersonal Relations**: Workers work best when working with others or a job that minimizes social contacts for the individual who prefers this type of arrangement.
- **Access to Resources**: Performing job tasks without the necessary resources is discouraging because this is often a recipe for underperformance.
- **Job Responsibilities**: Overspecialization is often discouraging because the individual typically prefers lots of responsibilities to maintain strong interest in performing the work.

Finally, an **organization's internal environment** is an important contributing factor to influence the degree of employee engagement. An organization's internal environmental issues include:

- **Safety**: The organization creates an environment in which the individual expresses the feeling that work conditions lead to safety from work-related injuries, harm from others and threats such as work-related pollutants.
- **Support Provided**: The organization offers workers the means to successfully perform their work responsibilities as well as a sense of well-being from such company programs as maternity leave, paternity leave, counseling services and other employee-support programs.
- **Fairness**: Akin to equity theory, the workforce believes that the organization attempts to treat everyone equally the same by being respectful, trusting and transparent in all actions.

- **Leadership**: Leaders can inspire the workforce by being visionaries, describing what everyone can achieve which is uplifting.
- **Performance Review System**: The performance review system's design is perceived as functioning to benefit the workforce through honest and objective work assessments.
- **Training**: The organization creates a variety of training opportunities to enhance the workforce's capabilities to perform their work responsibilities successfully.
- **Policies**: The organization develops policies that are biased-free and intended to facilitate fair, equitable and reasonable work practices.
- **Supervisors**: Supervisors are trained to provide oversight that strengthens employee commitment to the position and to the organization.
- **Reward System**: The organization creates a reward system linked to the performance management system, one system is designed to recognize and the other system to reward employee successes.
- **Work Conditions**: Lighting, temperature levels, colors, decorations and workstations are examples of what an organization can control to support the workforce's efforts at optimizing work performance.

LEARNING OBJECTIVE #5: DESCRIBE, EXPLAIN AND COMPARE INTRINSIC MOTIVATION WITH EXTRINSIC MOTIVATION

Understanding what motivates individuals is important because an organization can create the conditions associated with motivating the organization's workforce. There are no absolute factors that motivate. Instead, there are a range of factors that can motivate the workforce. The motivating factors can be categorized as **extrinsic motivators** and **intrinsic motivators**. The continuum shown in Figure 13.1 reflects that individuals can range from being primarily extrinsically motivated or intrinsically motivated but can also include some factors from each category. For example, an extrinsically motivated individual will find incentive programs an appealing motivator but also feel good (intrinsically motivated) by winning the incentive. An intrinsically motivated individual will not only take personal satisfaction from winning an incentive contest but also value earning the reward associated with the incentive contest. Understanding the psychology of the individual is important in an organization's efforts at creating the conditions for motivating the workforce.

Extrinsic motivation represents the use of external rewards intended to influence worker behavior in particular ways. Money, non-monetary rewards (e.g. gift

FIGURE 13.1 Continuum Between Extrinsic and Intrinsic Motivation

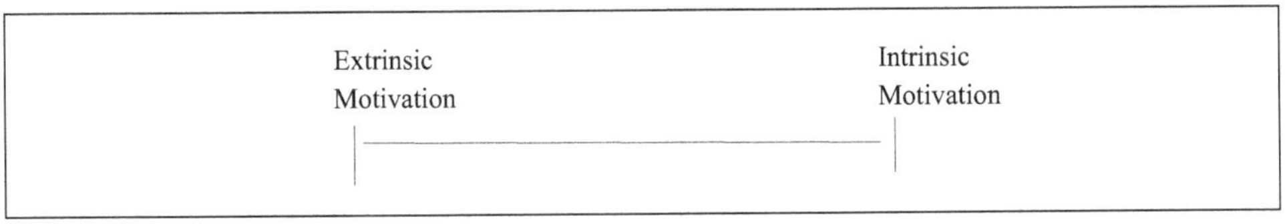

Extrinsic
Motivation

Intrinsic
Motivation

certificates and trips), promotions and positive performance reviews represent examples of external motivators. **Intrinsic motivation** involves influencing the behavior of individuals by appealing to the individual's sense of self-satisfaction through the individual demonstrating acceptable behaviors. Acceptable behavior is defined by the individual's personal standards and/or the performance standards set by the organization.

There are four major personality characteristics that determine if an individual is primarily extrinsically motivated or intrinsically motivated. **Introversion, extroversion, self-efficacy** and **self-worth** represent the primary personality characteristics. Figures 13.2 and 13.3 show the relationship between introversion/extrinsic motivation, extroversion/intrinsic motivation and self-efficacy and extroversion/intrinsic motivation introversion/extrinsic motivation and self-esteem.

An introverted individual is characterized as shy, withdrawn and anti-social, preferring to work autonomously. Feelings of self-efficacy or control over life and work are low. Feelings of self-worth are low as the individual is generally not a happy person with low affect. As a result, this type of individual is less performance-oriented which translates into behavior less than expected. For this type of individual, the organization designs a job with few responsibilities, repetitive type of tasks and tasks generally easy to learn. Incentive programs are effective as well as setting low-level performance goals that are easily accomplished.

An extroverted individual is characterized as outgoing, enjoys working with others and socializing with peers. An extrovert demonstrates behavior reflecting someone who feels more in control (e.g. self-efficacy) of their life. Feelings of self-worth are opposite those of an introvert. An extrovert demonstrates behavior indicating feeling happy with their life and life's circumstances. An extrovert is achievement-oriented because they enjoy being successful; the extrovert likes setting stretch-types of goals. An organization can cultivate a work environment that

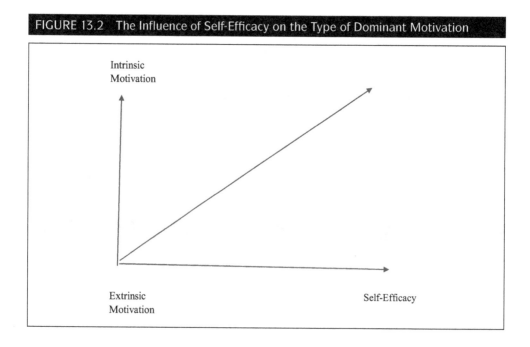

FIGURE 13.2   The Influence of Self-Efficacy on the Type of Dominant Motivation

FIGURE 13.3 The Influence of Self-Esteem on the Type of Dominant Motivation

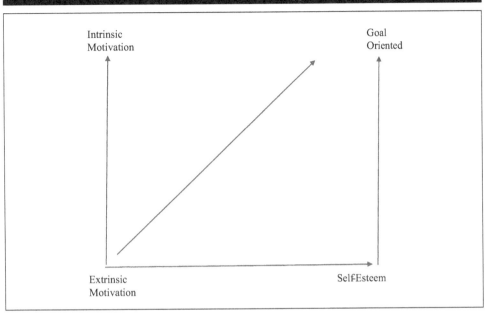

appeals to an extrovert's performance standards by using high-level performance goals, design jobs that confer greater responsibilities and decision-making authority on the position along with creating jobs that are part of a team of individuals performing interconnected jobs.

Design Clothing for the Young – Part Two

Kate Hudson, Vice President of Marketing, and Bill Foster, Vice President of Human Resources arranged to meet at Kate's request. During the past year, turnover among customer service representatives at all store was substantially higher than the base rate. A strong economy accounts for some of the additional loss because customer service representatives have alternative job options. However, the problem seems more serious, according to Kate. Kate received anecdotal feedback that customer service representatives were unhappy with their job responsibilities. That was the substance of the feedback. Kate's concern is that the negativity might impact sales and the recruitment of new customer service representatives. A strong economy is tough to compete against without the negative perceptions of customer service representatives. Kate and Bill discussed the issue for over an hour, attempting to determine a process to follow.

Questions

1. What is the process referred to?
2. What are the major tasks to perform during the process?
3. What is the best way to implement the process?

LEARNING OBJECTIVE #6: IDENTIFY AND DESCRIBE THE LEVELS OF MOTIVATION IN AN ORGANIZATION

Many empirical studies and theoretical papers focus on the individual when study-ing the motivation of the engaged employee. The emphasis on the individual was meant to understand motivation as a concept through identifying and discussing different themes of motivation as applied to individuals; the antecedent factors that motivate individuals; and the methods organizations can use to motivate individu-als. However, organizations need to approach understanding motivation of formal groups of individuals because individuals work in a broader context. Individuals work as members of a team, members of a unit and members of an organization (see Figure 13.4).

Organizations rely on several primary methods to motivate **individual** em-ployees to turn the individual into an engaged employee or to keep an engaged em-ployee engaged. Job design, covered previously, involves modifying an individual's job in several different ways to motivate the job holder. The use of goals is another method for motivating employees. Goal theory and expectancy theory underscore the use of goals. Goal theory promotes the idea of setting ambitious goals, but ex-pectancy theory moderates the goal setting process to ensure that the individual views themselves as able to achieve the goal. The performance management system linked with the reward system represents formal ways to motivate individuals. In-dividuals know that the organization is assessing their behavior and that positive feedback will result in some form of reward. For example, positive performance reviews, promotions and bonuses.

FIGURE 13.4   Levels of Motivation in an Organization

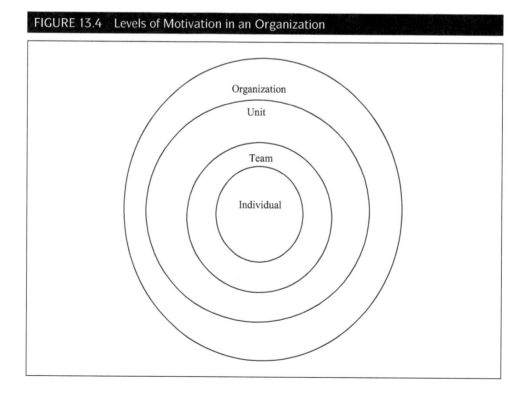

Team motivation has become more important to organizations in the 21st century because most organizations utilize teams of high value specialists in planning, solving problems and developing new products and services; and designing work processes. Ensuring that a team remains focused and engaged is important to fulfill the team's mandate, whether short term, long term or indefinite. Team leadership and team oversight are essential in keeping team members engaged and focused. Empowering a team with decision-making responsibilities increases the team's sense of self-efficacy. Using team goals creates targets for the team to focus on, but goals need to be realistic as expectancy theory suggests that a team, like an individual, needs to think that achieving the goal is realistic. Creating performance management system team performance indicators aids in monitoring team performance and keeps a team focused and persistent remain accountable and to benefit from successfully achieving goals to earn a reward.

Unit motivation continues the examination of another level of motivation to consider. Organizations are grouped into work units. As an organization expands in size, there are more units and units within larger units. Organizations need to keep units focused and persistent by motivating unit members. Leadership, in the form of transformational leadership, attempts to inspire unit members. Units are expected to achieve goals that are deemed achievable if the unit can make decisions that lead to a unit's success. The performance management system and reward system include standards of performance for a unit to achieve, and the unit creates a process to follow in ensuring successful performance and reporting results. Earning rewards for successfully achieving the performance goals is common.

Finally, organizational motivation represents the next level of motivation; organizational motivation encompasses the entire organization. Transformational leadership is an essential factor in inspiring the entire workforce to commit to achieving the vision identified by leadership. Organizational leadership model's critical values associated with motivating the workforce. Values, such as achievement, work ethic, problem-solving and goal-oriented, contribute to motivating the workforce. Setting realistic stretch goals keeps the organization focused and achievement oriented. The performance management system includes a formal process for assessing and reporting an organization's performance. Use of the **balanced scorecard** represents one type of management method to use in assessing performance. The balanced scorecard's most important focus is financial performance, operational performance and customer trends. An organization's reward for success in achieving short-term goals is achieving the organization's long-term goal of survival. Survival is every organization's long-term goal. The workforce benefits by having job security and a career in the organization.

LEARNING OBJECTIVE #7: DESCRIBE AND EXPLAIN THE RELATIONSHIP BETWEEN ORGANIZATIONAL CULTURE AND MOTIVATION

Reports on the top 100 companies to work for are common. The findings originate from employee surveys. The implications are obvious. These companies represent great companies to work for because of the way the organizations treat employees. The corollary is that working for a great employer represents an opportunity to remain employed at a liked organization. Continuing to work for such an employer means that an employee values the treatment received and reciprocates by actively contributing to the organization's success.

The way an organization treats employees makes the organization a desirable place for employees to work at. "Take care of me and I will take care of you" might be a common phrase used by employees. An organization demonstrates interest in having happy, satisfied employees through the organization's actions, showing concern in the well-being of employees. What contributes to these actions is an **organization's culture** which reflects the **values** associated with these actions. Values are essential; values are manifested by the actions of an organization because values influence all an organization's actions.

Actions, labeled as management methods, are common outcomes of values reflected in an organization's policies, work processes and management systems. These management methods reflect the important values of the organization by the type of methods formalized and the way the organization implements these management methods.

Organizations that promote relationship building, greater employee empowerment and strong feelings of well-being have the best interests of employees because important motivators include social relationships, self-efficacy and self-worth. Policies that advocate teamwork, support equal treatment for all, show blindness to prejudices of all types and forms, in formulating policies, focus on meritocracy in work evaluations and open communication are examples of supporting and promoting the importance of social relations in building a successful organization. An organization that encourages self-efficacy of the workforce demonstrates a culture that is flexible in its work practices, especially in the design of jobs. As described earlier, the intent in modifying a job's design is to enable employees to assume greater control over their job responsibilities which promotes greater feelings of empowerment. This contributes to employees owning the results of their work efforts, seeking to perform at or above expectations. Finally, an employee-centered organization seeks to assist employees' efforts in succeeding at work because a successful employee's sense of self-worth benefits. The achievement of goals becomes more meaningful and impactful to an employee because of increased feelings of self-worth associated with achieving goals.

A **people-oriented organizational culture**, more flexible and accommodating in its practices, will appeal more to the individual who thrives on intrinsic forms of motivation. This is because individuals thrive on self-reinforcement primarily. A **mechanistic, programmed organizational culture**, controlling every action in specific ways, is a **controlling culture** that uses management methods for those employees who find extrinsic motivators more appealing than intrinsic motivators. This is because those individuals are less able and less willing to self-reinforce. Evidence indicates that the benefits of extrinsic forms of motivation diminish in value over time, however. A non-mechanistic, loosely programmed organizational culture does not seek total control over all actions, but prefers using general guidelines, empowering employees to take greater responsibility for their actions.

Design Clothing for the Young – Part Three

Senior management was about to meet with Karen Bloom, CEO. Karen called for the meeting because she wanted to discuss how to increase employee productivity. Karen decided that as a first step, a brainstorming session among senior leaders might result in a plan to follow. Prior to the meeting, Karen had dinner with several of her peers from other companies where the issue of worker productivity was discussed. Karen knew that the issue of worker productivity is a constant theme in retail. At the start of the meeting, Karen reminded everyone of the purpose of the meeting and that no final decisions were expected. However, Karen did want an outcome to result from the meeting.

Questions

1. What outcome do you think would satisfy Karen? Explain.
2. What are the top three ideas for increasing productivity? Explain.
3. What are the top three ways for assessing productivity? Explain.
4. Should everyone also consider how to recognize and reward productivity during the discussion? Explain.

LEARNING OBJECTIVE #8: DISCUSS THE RELATIONSHIP BETWEEN SELF-WORTH AND MOTIVATION

The theory of self-worth is often referred to as a motivation theory. **Self-worth theory** represents a self-assessment by the individual. Self-worth involves an individual's assessment that the individual varies along a competence incompetence continuum. As depicted in Figure 13.5, as the perceived level of competence increases so does the self-assessment that the individual's self-perception of self-worth increases. **Perception** is a critical factor, but judgment is filtered by the individual's past interpretation of self-worth.

The stronger the judgment of competency, the stronger the feelings of self-worth. The greater the self-perception of self-worth and competence, the greater the degree of self-motivation. The use of goals becomes an important method of motivation when the judgment that competency is increasing because the individual perceives that success is achievable according to the individual's perceived degree of competency.

Why individuals pursue some goals and no other goals is explainable as the individual does not consider themselves able to successfully achieve the goal because the level of **competency** associated with achieving the goal is lacking. Organizations need to be more flexible in assigning goals to individual's because unrealistic goals lead to the failure in achieving the goals. This process of assigning unreasonable goals can setback the individual whose self-perception of incompetency is reinforced by failure, resulting in the downgrading of the individual's perceptions and feelings of self-worth. The result is a less-motivated individual.

Competence and self-worth reinforce each other as does incompetence and low self-worth. Organizations need to learn how to create a different paradigm that

FIGURE 13.5 Perceived Level of Competence and the Impact on Self-Worth

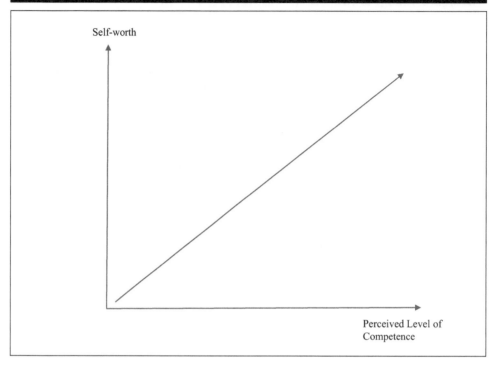

reinforces and strengthens the competence self-worth link. Organizations can focus on job re-design to improve an individual's work performance; the organization can transfer an individual to a job more reflective of the individual's abilities; or the organization can identify more relevant job-specific goals.

Design Clothing for the Young – Part Four

Karen Bloom, CEO and senior management were meeting to discuss how to create a culture whereby trust is one of the critical values of the organization. Routine employee surveys provided senior management with feedback on employee attitudes and impressions of the organization. Everyone knows that trust is an essential quality that enables people to feel more comfortable working with others without fear of negative implications. The byproduct of a trusting culture is greater openness, a willingness to work with others and strong interest in contributing to the well-being of the organization. Half-way through the meeting, there was a collective sigh. Karen became startled. Kate Hudson, Vice President of Marketing spoke on behalf of everyone when she said, "trust is critical but how do we make trust a part of our daily operations?" Karen agreed with Kate, thinking to herself that this was a major challenge to overcome.

Questions

1. Why is senior management confused by the issue? Explain.
2. Identify and describe methods for making trust part of the organization's operations.
3. Can senior management go back to their departments and talk about trust without doing anything specifically? Explain.

LEARNING OBJECTIVE #9: DESCRIBE MOTIVATION AS A GOAL AND THE PROCESS FACTORS ASSOCIATED WITH ACHIEVING THE GOAL

Developing engaged employees is a goal of all organizations because engaged employees symbolize motivated employees. Motivated employees, organized well, are productive employees. The productivity of the collective whole of the workforce results in a productive organization. Productive organizations achieve performance goals and an organization achieving performance goals continues to achieve the only long-term goal that counts to an organization, the goal is to survive. The focus of this learning objective is to understand how organizations purposefully create work processes that can influence workforce behavior typically associated with motivated employees. Creating and sustaining a motivated workforce has no concluding outcome. The motivating process is ongoing, only the individuals involved change. This section offers insights on a process for understanding how to **motivate** an organization's workforce and the levers to pull that represent catalysts to motivate employees.

Maslow's hierarchy of needs represents a useful theoretical model of motivation in that facilitates the understanding that the process of fulfilling a need signifies a motivated individual. DNA programming as well as learning (based on social learning motivation theory) helps provide the context, everyone has needs to fulfill. What differs among people is the type of need to satisfy and the methods the individual learned to use to satisfy the need. Satisfying needs is always a dominating issue for individuals, but once an individual learns how to successfully satisfy a need, the individual moves forward to initiate a motivational process for satisfying the next higher level of needs. For example, when an individual satisfies basic physiological needs, the next level of needs to learn how to satisfy are safety needs. An organization working with the individual begins learning how to satisfy the individual's safety needs, attempting to achieve the individual's goal of the individual feeling safe at work.

The process for satisfying needs results in experiences that contribute to learning by the organization and employee. The organization and individual learn what methods worked to satisfy specific needs, resulting in a motivated individual and a motivated workforce. Learning can occur as a product of negative experiences as well. Satisfying needs represents a **trial and error learning process** until the individual and the organization learn what works best to satisfy a need. In addition to learning what methods work and the methods that do not work, both the individual and organization develop a series of values that influence future actions associated with motivating individuals. For example, engaging in social relations represents a value that leads to behavior linked to motivation. Using another example, the organization can create the conditions that promote socialization at work using teams, project groups, action plan teams and other similar types of management methods.

Values influence the outcome(s) an individual and organization seek to achieve by influencing behavior in different ways. Self-actualization and self-maintenance represent useful values. Using a continuum helps explain the issues; there are two extreme forms of values that can influence the type of outcome sought. **Self-actualization** represents one end of the continuum; the focus of self-actualization is **self-improvement**; there is no final point to self-actualization. The end comes when the individual stops pursuing self-actualization activities. At the other end of the continuum is **self-maintenance**. Self-maintenance involves the motivation to maintain an **individual's homeostasis**. A self-actualizer is most often influenced by intrinsic reasons because a self-actualizer learned to self-motivate. An individual focusing on homeostasis is motivated most often by extrinsic reasons because this individual has not learned how to self-motivate, preferring external rewards from external sources. Because the focus of the continuum is the extremes, realistically, everyone is motivated by a combination of extrinsic/intrinsic or intrinsic/extrinsic antecedent types of motivators.

Additionally, the individual's development process, from birth onward, follows a sequence of developmental stages, culminating in the death stage. All stages emphasize the theme of **self-efficacy**. The most important focus of an individual is shaping their destiny. Even a self-maintainer seeks to exercise self-control required to maintain their status quo and avoid atrophy.

Experience leads to the development of values and the strengthening or elimination of existing values. Values influence the decisions individuals and organizations make when selecting goals to accomplish. Achieving goals results in positive experiences which lead to greater feelings of self-worth. Bad experiences can lead to lowered feelings of self-worth. Lessened feelings of self-worth can lead to the avoidance of being goal-oriented or the decision to select less ambitious goals. In sum, self-worth represents a motivation theory. Valuing the self can lead to greater interest in achieving higher-level goals because of an individual's expectation of achieving higher-level goals.

Reinforcement theory in tandem with self-worth theory, expectancy theory, goal theory and needs theory helps to understand why individuals follow a certain path that either leads toward self-actualization or self-maintenance. Reinforcers strengthen the behavior of the individual and the path the individual follows, either toward self-actualization or self-maintenance.

Ongoing experiences can lead to new values, strengthen existing values and reduce or eliminate less useful values. The changes are reasonably predictable. If the individual follows the path toward becoming a more self-actualizer, there are certain types of values associated with self-actualization. The self-maintenance path and the behaviors associated with this path are influenced by relevant values.

How organizations can create a more productive workforce is self-evident. Organizations need to promote the idea of moving individuals to follow the self-actualization path because this path is associated with the **self-development process** which is linked to self-actualization. Organizations can create the means for supporting self-development and the values associated with self-development in four ways. First, organizations can create **training programs** designed to maximize learning by the adult learner. The focus of training is acquisition of new knowledge, new skills, enhancing personal abilities and learning strategies to succeed in achieving work goals. Second, organizations can **modify jobs** to create a more challenging and rewarding experience for the individual. Third, organizations can increase an individual's feelings of self-worth from **positive experiences** developed from successfully achieving achievable goals. Finally, organizations can use **stretch goals** that force individuals to be challenged to succeed and utilize new strategies to follow to achieve the goals; the result is positive experiences with the concomitant values.

LEARNING OBJECTIVE #10: DISCUSS THE LINK BETWEEN THE PERFORMANCE MANAGEMENT SYSTEM, THE REWARD SYSTEM AND MOTIVATION

Organizational designers link the **performance management system** and the **reward system** to achieve the goal of increased **employee and organizational productivity**. By increasing the productivity of the collective workforce, the organization benefits through achieving organizational goals. The performance management system represents a formal process that an organization uses to monitor employee behavior linked with the need to achieve job-related goals.

There are several requirements in designing a formal performance management system. First, the performance management system needs to be conceptualized as a process to follow in assessing individuals. The process follows a sequence of steps. Responsibilities of all participants require defining and clarifying along with a description of task activities to perform during each step. For example, sending out notifications for a performance review and scheduling a meeting. Organizations define the process, the steps in the process and the task activities associated with each step.

An individual's job description, which should be behavior-focused and/or outcome focused, helps to identify the subject matter to consider. Furthermore, a set of standards, such as a rating scale, helps to assess levels of acceptable behavior and degree of outcome performance. A face-to-face step includes task activities to help to structure the meeting. A final recording of the assessment review creates a paper trail for everyone to access on a per need basis. The result of finalizing the last step in this process is the contribution to an individual's increased feeling of competency, which leads to greater sense of self-efficacy; this leads to a stronger sense of self-worth. Increased self-worth leads to a more motivated, achievement-oriented individual.

The reward system's link to the performance management system symbolizes the importance of applying reinforcement theory. If the individual performs to expectations, the individual benefits from the successful performance with some type of reward. The purpose in using rewards is to strengthen the performance of acceptable behavior and extinguish undesirable behavior. The linkage with the reward system is included in the design of the performance management system. Rewards can be tangible, such as a bonus, positive performance reviews and promotions. These forms of rewards are extrinsic motivators. An award, supervisor comments and public recognition are examples of intrinsic forms of rewards. By reinforcing intrinsic motivation, the intention is to stronger feelings of self-worth.

The design of a performance management system, linked with the reward system for individuals, functions as a model that an organization can use in other applications. Organizations develop sophisticated performance management-reward systems for team assessment, organizational unit assessment and assessing organization performance. The benefit in applying the model throughout the organization is to show the benefits of developing a formal process that achieves the purpose of motivating all levels of the organization.

Chapter Summary

Motivation is an important subject to study because a motivated workforce is often the difference between a high-performance organization and a low-performing organization. An organization can have great products, a solid strategy to follow and a well-designed operation, but it is people that make success possible.

This chapter examines the important issues associated with the subject of motivation. The chapter provides a definition of motivation and explains the role motivation plays in an organization. Theories of motivation presented in the chapter help to illustrate the complex nature of people in understanding the various dimensions identified to describe what motivates individuals. Examples of antecedents that function as motivating catalysts serve to demonstrate how to initiate motivation in individuals. Learning about antecedents enables the organization to understand how best to push the workforce's motivation button.

An important consideration in seeking to motivate the workforce is to know whether to create the conditions that emphasize an extrinsic focus or an intrinsic focus of motivation. Knowing the character of the organization's workforce helps decision-makers determine whether to emphasize a motivation system that is pre-dominantly intrinsic-oriented or extrinsic motivation-oriented.

An organization's culture represents an organization's value system and values shape how an organization performs. The chapter examined the link between cultural values and the motivation of an organization's workforce. Culture, through values, can and does influence the promotion of self-improvement. By seeking to assist employees in the process of self-improvement, the organization intends to directly impact the individual's sense of self-worth through the individual's accomplishments. Because of the importance of self-worth for the individual, many consider the issue of self-worth as the single most important factor to emphasize in creating a productive workforce.

Finally, this chapter examined how organizations formalize the various processes intended to create a motivated workforce. Examined is the role of the performance management system, the reward system and the connection between each of these systems and how these systems contribute to motivating the workforce.

Questions

1. What does the term motivation mean? How is the term relevant to an organization?
2. Identify and describe any five motivation theories.
3. How is motivation linked to the concept of work performance?
4. Identify and describe any five factors that can influence employee work performance.

5. Compare and contrast intrinsic and extrinsic motivation.
6. Identify and describe each of the levels of motivation.
7. How is an organization's culture linked to motivated employees?
8. Self-worth is often described as a motivation theory. Explain.
9. Motivation is a goal. Identify and discuss the process factors associated with achieving the goal.
10. How are the performance management and reward systems linked to motivation of the workforce? Explain.

Bibliography

Badubi, R.M. (2017). Theories of motivation and their application in organizations: a risk analysis. *International Journal of Innovation and Economic Development.* 3(3). 44–51.

Bodman, S.A., Lashinger, H.K.S., Wong, C. & Clarke, S. (2018). Effect of transformational leadership on job satisfaction and patient safety outcomes. *Nursing Outlook.* 66. 180–189.

Comaford, C. (2018). Why leaders need to embrace employee motivation. January 20. 1–7. https://www.forbes.com/sites/christinecomaford/2018/01/20/why-leaders-need-to-embrace-employee-motivation/#29d9b47a1272.

Curtis, C.R., Upchurch, R.S. & Severt, D.E. (2009). Employee motivation and organizational commitment: a comparison of tipped and non-tipped restaurant employees. *International Journal of Hospitality & Tourist Administration.* 10(3). 1–28.

Dobre, L. (2013). Employee motivation and organizational performance. *Review of Applied Socio-Economic Research.* 5(1). 53–60.

Elona, L. (2010). Chapter 4: Motive, manage and reward performance in *Better Workplaces-Employer Resource Kit.* Business.tas.gov.au. 68–86.

Isen, A.M. & Reeve, J. (2005). The influence of positive affect on intrinsic and extrinsic motivation: facilitating engagement of policy, responsible work behavior, and self-control. *Motivation and Emotion.* 29(4). 297–325.

Kanfer, R. & Chen, G. (2016). Motivation in organizational behavior: History, advances, and prospects. Organizational Behavior and Human Decision- Making. *Processes.* 136. 6–19.

Lai, E.R. (2011). Motivation: a literature review. *Research Report.* Pearson. April 11. 1–43.

Lee, M.T. & Raschke, R.L. (2016). Understanding employee motivation and organizational performance: arguments for set-theoretic approach. *Journal of Innovation and Knowledge.* 1. 162–169.

Locke, E.A. & Latham, G.P. (1990). Work motivation and satisfaction: light at the end of the tunnel. *Psychological Science.* 1(4). 240–246.

Molden, D.C. & Dweck, C.S. (2000). Meaning and motivation in C. Sansone & J. Harackiewicz (Eds.). *Intrinsic and Extrinsic Motivation.* Academic Press. 131–159.

Nuckcheddy, A. (2018). The effect of personality on motivation and organizational behavior. *Psychology and Behavioral Science.* 9(2). 1–5.

Pradhan, R.K. & Jena, L.K. (2017). Employee performance at workplace: conceptual model and empirical validation. *Business Perspectives and Research.* 5(1). 69–85.

Shuck, B. (2011). Four emerging perspectives of employee engagement: an integrative literature review. *Human Resource Development Review.* 20(10). 1–25.

Stajkovic, A.D. & Luthans, F. (2003). Social cognitive theory and self-efficacy: implications for motivation theory and practice in L.W. Porter, G.A. Bigley & R.M. Steers (Eds.). *Motivation and Work Behavior.* McGraw-Hill Irwin. 126–140.

Tokarz, A. & Malinowska, D. (2013). From psychological theoretical assumptions to new research perspectives in sustainability and sustainable development: motivation in the workplace. *Sustainability.* 11(2222). 1–16.

PART V

SPECIAL
ORGANIZATIONAL
TOPICS

■ ■ ■ ■ ■

Communication Management

OVERVIEW

Communication is the ubiquitous function that dominates all activities within an organization, among organizations and with other important stakeholders of the organization. Because of the role of communication in supporting an organization's well-being, it is important to understand the purpose and function of communication. This chapter begins by introducing the reader to a detailed explanation of communication. The chapter identifies and describes the basic elements of the two-way communication process; a model communication process that involves two people.

The chapter continues with an overview of the major types of communication channels, one of the basic elements of the communication process. Communication strategies is another important topic covered in this chapter because organizations and individuals need to carefully consider how best to facilitate communication to achieve organizational and personal goals. One of the important issues associated with understanding the communication process is to learn about the barriers that can interfere, disrupt or prevent effective communication. Paired with the discussion about communication barriers is the topic on strategies that lead to effective communication, overcoming and/or preventing barriers from emerging. Communication skills is the last major topic covered in the discussion about the communication process.

This chapter introduces and describes the formal aspects of communication within an organization. One formal issue is the topic of communication flows, the process describing how organizations structure communication within the organization, vertically, horizontally and diagonally, mirroring an organization's structure. Continuing the discussion is the examination of the topic of communication networks which originates from systems theory. Communication flows represent formalized methods of communicating within an organization; all methods are directly and indirectly connected, the networks increasing in complexity as the organization expands.

Organizations create an information system to routinize the collection, analysis and movement of information throughout the organization. Understanding the purpose of an information system is an essential aspect of understanding organizational communication.

Another important subject in this chapter is managing communication within an organization. Communication management ensures that an individuals and organization's performance meet the expectations of decision-makers.

Over the years, the role of communication oversight expanded because of the growing importance of communication. The importance of the new role of communication is reflected by organizations creating new positions and units that focus exclusively on organizing an organization's communications.

In addition, communication oversight includes the process of creating a communication strategy to support the workforce's effort in achieving the strategic goals. A communication strategy represents a functional strategy that supports the organization's efforts in the implementation of the organization's corporate strategy.

CHAPTER 14   LEARNING OBJECTIVES

Readers will achieve the following learning objectives after reading this chapter.

1. Describe and explain communication and the elements of a two-way communication process.
2. Identify and describe the major communication channels.
3. Identify and describe the process for creating communication strategies.
4. Identify, describe and explain the barriers to effective communication.
5. Identify and describe the strategies for creating effective verbal, non-verbal and written communication.
6. Identify and describe the major communication skills.
7. Identify and explain the concept of communication flows that move downward and upwards through levels of an organization; flows that move horizontally within and between units on the same level and diagonally through the organization.
8. Describe and explain the concept of communication networks within an organization and among organizations and individual stakeholders.
9. Explain the importance of an organization's information system in facilitating formal reporting of organizational activities.
10. Identify and describe the important role of communication management within an organization.
11. Identify, describe and explain the different types of communication theories.

LEARNING OBJECTIVE #1: DESCRIBE AND EXPLAIN COMMUNICATION AND THE ELEMENTS OF A TWO-WAY COMMUNICATION PROCESS

There is no universal definition for the term, communication. A simple **definition** suffices. Communication is a method for converting ideas into useful information that influences the action(s) of another person or persons. An **effective** communication process represents a process that achieves the sender's goals that the communication was intended to achieve.

In general, there are three major organizational goals associated with all forms of communication. One goal is to increase the **engagement or involvement** of others in keeping focused on achieving work processes. Second, communication aims to increase the **collaborative efforts** among all the participants of the communication process to achieve the goal of increased worker productivity. Finally, communication helps to **build trust** by breaking down psychological barriers. As these barriers decline, workers experience the development of a closer interpersonal bond. A closer bond strengthens the work relationship which can contribute to the ongoing success of the workforce.

The simple two-way communication model shown in Figure 14.1 reflects the basic model of the communication process. There is a **sender** who initiates the communication process. Starting with an idea or message, the sender **encodes** the idea or message. Encoding involves putting the idea or message into a form that the sender thinks will help the receiver fully understand the message. After encoding the message/idea, the sender selects the optimal **communication channel** to use in sending the message. Communication channels represent the media the sender can use to provide the message/idea to the receiver. The **receiver** is the recipient of the message/idea sent by the sender. Upon receiving the message/idea, the receiver **decodes** the message/idea. Decoding involves translating the message/idea to understand the meaningfulness to the message/idea. After decoding the message/idea, the receiver encodes a response, referred to as **feedback**, and selects a communication channel to use to send the feedback. Feedback represents the receiver's message/idea that either conveys an understanding of the message/idea received, seeking clarification of the message/idea or showing how the receiver plans to act in response to the message/idea.

There are **barriers** that can hinder the communication process. Barriers challenge both the sender and receiver in learning how to overcome the difficulties with barriers that can impair hearing, understanding and responding to the message/idea in accordance with the expectations of the sender and receiver. Several types of barriers can include internal barriers such as psychological issues, personal prejudices, status of one of the communicators or other factors that can exist between and among the communicators. External barriers can include other people talking, organizational and/or external cultural factors, physical types of barriers and sound types of barriers.

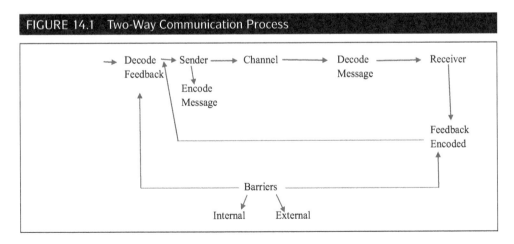

FIGURE 14.1   Two-Way Communication Process

LEARNING OBJECTIVE #2: IDENTIFY AND DESCRIBE THE MAJOR COMMUNICATION CHANNELS

A **communication channel** represents one of the elements integral to the functioning of a communication process. The communication channel's role within the communication process is to prioritize methods to use by communicators in sharing and exchanging information. The channel represents the choice of media to use in the sharing/exchanging step during the communication process.

There are three types of communication processes; each type includes the element, communication channel. **One-way communication** process represents a process that is unidirectional, moving from the sender to the receiver only. Another type of communication process is **two-way communication**. As described earlier, both the sender and the receiver share/exchange information using a communication channel(s). The choice of channel(s) between the sender and receiver can vary. The third type of communication process is a **multi-dimensional communication** process. In a multi-dimensional process, there are three or more participants involved in the communication process. Participants can include senders and receivers; participants can use several types of communication channels.

There are formal types of communication channels and informal types of communication channels. The difference between the uses of either types depends on the purpose of the communication process. Spontaneous communication tends toward the informal, using face-to-face, texting, telephone/cell or email. Use of formal types of communication channels is influenced by the planned purpose of the message/idea and the preferred method(s) for delivering the message/idea, as influenced by **cultural factors**. Organizational culture represents established norms and routines developed by organizational values associated with the exchange of different types of messages/ideas. For example, providing a plan of some type will be presented in written form but a complementary channel is an oral presentation.

The selection process for choosing a communication channel(s) is important because the type of channel(s) used can improve the receiver's comprehension of the message/idea or weaken the receiver's understanding of the message/idea. There are five identifiable criteria to use in guiding the communication channel selection process. **Reliability** of the channel is important. Reliability of a channel means that the channel functions on a consistent basis, secure to use. **Speed** of delivery is another criterion in selecting a communication channel. If the sender or receiver needs to send a message/idea quickly, the choice of channels is limited to face-to-face, text and calling as examples. **Effectiveness** of a communication channel is another criterion for the sender or receiver to consider because the communicators have goals to achieve, and the choice of communication channel can increase or decrease the likelihood of achieving the goals. **Reach** is another criterion. The number of participants during the communication process dictates the choice of communication channels to use. Examples include video conferencing, email, newsletters and written reports.

Finally, the **complexity** of a message/idea determines the choice of communication channel. The greater the complexity of the message/idea, the more likely one of the channels is in written form paired with an oral type of channel. Communicators might find the need to have several communication exchanges involving the use of multiple types of communication channels necessary when there are many participants involved in the process.

There are **indirect** and **direct** forms of communication channels. Indirect forms of communication channels represent media with no specific intended person and/or department as the recipient. These can include newsletters, videos and emails. Direct forms of communication channels represent sharing a message/idea with a specific individual(s) and/or department(s). Examples of direct communication channels include face-to-face, email, texts, telephone/cell and faxes.

A multi-dimensional communication process can include the use of the following types of communication channel media: department meetings, staff meetings, virtual meetings, reports, conference calls and video conferencing. The number of communicators increases the complexity of the communication process and potentially can have the effect of diminishing the effectiveness of the media without the use of an imposed structure to the communication process.

LEARNING OBJECTIVE #3: IDENTIFY AND DESCRIBE THE PROCESS FOR CREATING COMMUNICATION STRATEGIES

A **communication strategy** represents a plan for influencing others in particular ways using select communication channels that convey the form of a message/idea intended for the audience to receive and understand. An organization's communication strategy can represent a simple communication plan with a singular purpose. But an organization can have a multi-faceted communication strategy depending on the complexity of the business and the purpose of the message/idea. Logically, the complexity of an organization's communication strategy increases along with the increase in an organization's size.

The use of a communication strategy to influence recipients of the communications is straightforward. However, knowing if the communication strategy is effective requires the need to assess impact using some form of metrics to assess impact. Metrics can come in different forms. There are employee metrics, typically measured using employee surveys, but quantitative metrics are feasible, such as attrition rates of new hires within three months of hiring. The most common type of employee survey uses some types of scale, such as strongly agree to strongly disagree. Communication channel effectiveness metrics has a specific focus, evaluating the method(s) used in the communication process. Surveys are a common type of assessment method to use in this situation. What the organization wants to learn about is the feedback from different constituencies about the type of channel media used to fine tune the use of specific channel media and to learn if another form of media might be potentially more effective.

Often, organizations communicate to promote improved performance, either at the strategic level, which means achieving the strategic goals. There is also operational performance which refers to achieving non-strategic goals and operational objectives. If organizations use SMART goals and SMART objectives, a communication strategy's effectiveness is measurable by whether the SMART goals were achieved or if ongoing, do the trends show movement in the direction for achieving the SMART goals and SMART objectives.

To facilitate an effective communication strategy or communication strategies, the strategy formulators need to consider several issues. First, knowing the **audience or audiences** is important in the process of creating an effective communication strategy. Knowing your audience helps to answer three questions. What to say? What not to say? How to say what you need to say? Listening carefully to the audience(s) helps the strategy formulators gain answers to these questions.

Another issue to guide the strategy formulators is to always keep communications **professional** and never personal. Personal communications often push "hot buttons" of individuals whereas professional messages keep to an objective form of presentation. This does not mean agreement to the message, but a professional approach avoids involving a negative emotional reaction as much as possible. **Reflection** is often used to fine-tune a strategy. Often, the organization's grapevine is useful in testing ideas informally or gain insights about an existing strategy informally. Reflection helps the formulators improve the strategy that guides the communication process.

Avoiding a communication strategy that creates **divisiveness** is important. Differences of opinion are a common occurrence without stoking the fires of conflict needlessly. Differences of opinion often lead to superior ideas through a give and take process. But creating conflict unnecessarily only makes working together more challenging because defenses increase, trust decreases and trust is an essential quality for people to work close together.

Frequent communications stem from an organization's leadership. During the strategy formulation process, leadership is responsible for their messages/ideas conveyed to the organization's internal and external constituents. **Clear, concise and relevant messages/ideas** direct from a leader(s) enable constituents to know and understand leadership's positions on the issues communicated. Constituents can then know how best to respond.

Therapeutics Products, Inc.: Part 1

Paul Hinkle, Chief Financial Officer, was meeting with senior managers. The purpose of the meeting was to discuss how to prepare a new monthly budget report. The impetus for the project came from the CEO, Sarah Brinkley, who was responding to the Board's and senior managers' request. Everyone agreed that a change was necessary as the current report format was created five years earlier. The consensus was that there needed to be two forms of the monthly budget report. A detailed version for the Board and senior managers and a simpler version for middle management. In addition, everyone's opinion was that it would be helpful to show projections, actual numbers and the differences between the actual and projections with each of the major line items. Also, the preference was to cut back on the report's minor categories and cover major budget items only.

Questions

1. Why have a monthly budget report?
2. Why have the monthly budget report in a written format?
3. Why involve the Board as recipients of the monthly budget report?
4. Why include middle managers as recipients of a scaled-down version of the monthly budget?
5. Why simplify the monthly budget report?

LEARNING OBJECTIVE #4: IDENTIFY, DESCRIBE AND
EXPLAIN THE BARRIERS TO EFFECTIVE COMMUNICATION

Barriers represent issues that interfere with the ability to create and/or deliver effective communication. Preventing barriers from occurring and eliminating barriers is important to improve communication. Solutions to eliminate barriers require learning and understanding what constitutes a barrier and the type of barrier(s) that disrupt the communication process.

Below are categories of barriers.

- **Physical Barriers**: Anything that is tangible that disrupts or otherwise hinders the communication process. Examples include geographic distance, sounds, disrupted internet connection, closed doors and machinery represent examples of physical barriers.
- **Semantic Barriers**: Communicators can use words that have different meanings for different people; there is technical language that only experts in a specialized field understand; there is a jargon such as sayings and slang that not everyone is familiar with. For example, "a bird in the hand is worth two in the bush." This is an example of a saying.
- **Process Barriers**: At any point during the communication process between a sender and receiver, disruptions can and do occur. The sender might not know how to organize an idea; the sender might not know how to encode an idea for greater clarity and conciseness; the choice of communication channels might not be appropriate in the context; the receiver might not know how best to interpret the message (decode); the receiver might not be sound intellectually or sufficiently experienced to understand the message; and the receiver might not provide feedback or provide feedback that is not sent in a timely manner.
- **Psychosocial Barriers**: These types of barriers represent issue(s) with either the sender or receiver or both that interferes with the communication process. Communication experiences can vary, such that communication does not come easily. Because the sender/receiver can function as a filter, hearing and understanding the communication can be selective and not fully understand the intended message/idea. The sender/receiver can demonstrate psychological distancing, the practice of not listening carefully. For example, if the receiver considers the sender to be an inferior, then the message is of less value. Poor listening skill is another example of a psychosocial barrier.
- **Cultural Barriers**: Cultural barriers is a complex subject because there are different forms of cultures. For U.S. organization, there are cultures dealing with international organizations and people living in other countries. The less developed the country, the greater the cultural differences from the United States. In the United States, there is the American culture, but there are regional cultures that lead to cultural barriers. Finally, there is an organization's culture. The larger the organization, the greater the probability of distinct organizational sub-cultures. Sub-cultures represent differences in outlook. For example, an R&D unit involves individuals with certain types of personalities such that the policies and work processes can differ substantially from other units. The uniqueness can function as a barrier when communicating with non-R&D individuals and groups.

LEARNING OBJECTIVE #5: IDENTIFY AND DESCRIBE THE STRATEGIES FOR CREATING EFFECTIVE VERBAL AND WRITTEN COMMUNICATION

Being an effective communicator is essential if the sender is going to influence the receiver(s) in a specific way. The goals that guide the process for creating effective communication include increasing the engagement of the audience, getting the audience to collaborate more and increasing the audience's trust with the sender.

Organizations approach creating effective communications by **knowing the audience** and design the message/idea based on the described profile. The organization selects the communication channel preferred by the audience. Whether following a policy or other reasons, organizations use a formal approach in communicating, being systematic in the approach taken. Systematic involves keeping the message to one dominant theme, standardize the approach by using **models** to demonstrate how to present different types of messages and **routinize** the process to ensure using approaches the audience would welcome. Common communication channels used by an organization include reports, memorandums, emails, newsletters and videos.

The general guidelines or model for individuals planning to write anything is to plan it, write it and edit it! All forms of communication should benefit from careful thought. Writing a draft puts an idea on paper which is an effective way to learn if the author has a good understanding of the subject. Editing is critical. Editing involves a careful review of the draft. Editing needs to consider the following factors.

- Spelling, grammar and punctuation
- Ensure that the message will likely appeal to the audience
- Ensure that the message is clear, concise and thorough
- Checking to eliminate unnecessary jargon
- Avoiding or minimizing the use of technical language
- Avoiding long, wordy sentences
- Ensure that the message avoids the excessive use of details

Sometimes, senders use the **verbal approach** in sending a message. There are certain rules or guidelines to follow to ensure effective verbal communication.

- Be clear and concise
- Avoid using a monotone voice
- Avoid the use of jargon, especially biased jargon
- Speak up so the audience can hear
- Avoid excessive detail; provide details in a handout to accompany the verbal presentation
- Listen by providing feedback that demonstrates listening
- Be aware of non-verbal body language that is bothersome to the audience
- Ask questions

Non-verbal communication is an important component in the communication process, complementing and reinforcing verbal communication. Non-verbal communication either reinforces the verbal message or undercuts the verbal message. Methods to consider improving the non-verbal form of communicating include the following.

- Be aware of the attitude of the sender. Attitude influences everything
- Be aware of the tone of voice used because tonality is a metric of attitude, like a thermometer
- Face the person or audience
- Look at the person's eyes to connect with that person or select someone in the audience to look at their eyes
- Look for other non-verbal cues that can reflect attitude
- If sitting, lean forward to show interest

LEARNING OBJECTIVE #6: IDENTIFY AND DESCRIBE THE ORGANIZATIONAL STRATEGIES TO IMPROVE THE MAJOR COMMUNICATION SKILLS

Too many people think communication skills are natural talents. What is natural are creative communication skills. Otherwise, basic communication skills such as writing skills and oral skills can be learned. Attitude can enable individuals to develop effective communication skills or hinder developing effective communication skills.

An organization can promote learning to improve the basic communication skills, writing and oral skills, in any of four different ways. An organization can design **training programs** in-house using organizational trainers or hire experts to deliver the training programs. No training program should exceed a 2–4-hour time frame because the type of skill to learn is cognitively tiring. An organization can subsidize the cost of supporting the return to college to take a **business writing course or a business speaking course**. The principle advantage is that the course is already developed, saving the organization the time and expense of developing and delivering this type of course. A third approach is to offer training **online**. Online training provides trainees with greater flexibility for when to take the course. **One on one coaching** is the fourth approach. The organization recruits in-house candidates able and willing to coach individuals on their communication skills. This is an expensive approach, often used for selecting recipients, such as senior managers.

Strategies for developing written and verbal communication skills involve the use of a pedagogical model to structure and guide the learning process. The model's roots are the learning theory, **andragogy** and the field of **adult learning theory**. Organizations develop their own unique model for structuring the learning process but using andragogy as the pedagogical model helps in designing an effective program. There are basic features that a training program needs to include.

- Use of **learning objectives** provides focus to the training process.
- Use multiple types of **instructional methods** to engage the learner, keeping the learner interested and motivated.
- Every training session should include an **introductory stage** as the first stage to provide a good initial start to training. A **conclusion stage** as the final stage to the training program brings closure to the training program. Between these two stages are other **stages**, and each stage could focus on one of the learning objectives.

Instructional methods need to vary to keep trainees motivated. Popular instructional methods include lecture, PowerPoint, hands-on, demonstration, self-correction and guest speakers. Instructional methods for verbal skills development include the use of video and role playing.

Lectures should follow the Talk, Show, Do and Feedback method (TSDF method). A brief discussion, followed by some type of demonstration, and then practice, followed by feedback. The use of repetition of the same body of work is useful to support the learner's efforts at moving up the learning curve. The learning curve focuses on using repetition to improve performance each time the activity is repeated.

Video is a useful instructional method for developing verbal skills. Watching others and then the individual watches themselves is helpful feedback in supporting the learning process.

Therapeutic Products, Inc.: Part 2

Sarah Brinkley, CEO was meeting with Tim Considine, Senior Vice President of Human Resources and Talent Management and Patricia Owns, Vice President of Talent Management. Sarah called the meeting because of the substantial number of complaints from department managers, suppliers and commercial customers complaining about the poor quality of different types of written communications. Poor grammar, misspellings and punctuation errors were only part of the problem. Vagueness, wordiness and confusing statements were the more serious problems. Time was wasted trying to decipher communications. The meeting focused on how to design an effective training program to begin training all personnel. Everyone recognized that the solution needed to be ongoing and cover multiple training subjects. The focus was on developing four different types of training programs. Each program would have a theme. Each program would last four hours. After all personnel completed the four programs, a survey would seek feedback to learn if the goals were achieved.

Questions

1. Why is written communication important?
2. What are the themes of each of the training programs? Explain.
3. Why make each training program four hours maximum?
4. Why focus on one theme for each training program?
5. Why conduct a survey? What do they hope to learn from the survey? Explain.

LEARNING OBJECTIVE #7: IDENTIFY AND EXPLAIN THE CONCEPT OF INFORMATION FLOWS THAT MOVE DOWNWARD AND UPWARD THROUGH LEVELS OF AN ORGANIZATION; FLOWS THAT MOVE HORIZONTALLY WITHIN AND BETWEEN UNITS ON THE SAME LEVEL AND DIAGONALLY THROUGH THE ORGANIZATION

All organizations organize their workforce into some type of **structural configuration**. The structure represents the organization's efforts to **rationalize and systematize** the linkage among all members of the workforce. The structure creates **formal**

authority relationships among the workforce. Authority encompasses two issues: **reporting relationships** and **areas of decision-making responsibility**. Policies dictate the reporting relationships, who reports to who, and dictate decision-making responsibilities, who reports to who. At the micro level, this involves creating job descriptions. At the macro level, this involves creating **units** and **sub-units** within a larger unit, each with specific types of responsibilities. For example, a unit could be Human Resources. Sub-units under Human Resources could be Benefits, Training, Recruitment and Healthcare.

Throughout the organization-linking units, sub-units and individuals are the information management system, the decision-making management system and the performance control management system. The information management system represents the organization's formal approach at routinizing, systematizing and controlling the movement of information throughout the organization. The goal in formalizing the movement of information throughout the organization is to increase the organization's effectiveness and efficiency in predictable ways.

Organizations refer to the movement of information as **flows**. Information flows follow set patterns identified and described in relevant policies. There are different types of information flows introduced in different policies. The major types of information flows include the following.

- **Performance**: Information on how well a unit is performing using financial and/or operational metrics (e.g. monthly sales, attrition rate and defect rates).
- **Decision-Making**: Stating decisions made by superiors.
- **Accountability**: Ensuring that every unit, sub-unit and individual performs according to expectations.
- **Routine**: Reporting activities performed according to schedule (e.g. weekly calls and weekly meetings with clients).
- **Organizing**: Information related to changes in job descriptions and unit/sub-unit linkages and areas of responsibilities.
- **Leadership**: Information from leadership covering such issues as strategic goals, vision and strategies.

There are three types of information flows in an organization. Vertical flows, horizontal flows and diagonal flows. There are **downward vertical information flows** where information moves down through the chain of command, starting with senior management. The most common types of downward information subjects include the vision statement, strategic goals, strategies to follow, operational guidance issues, policy development and policy implementation issues and feedback on performance. **Upward vertical information flows** cover such subjects as operational problems, operational recommendations, performance reports, new ideas, complaints, and unit financial and operational information.

Horizontal information flows are the exchange of information among sub-units within a unit or an exchange of information between or among units. For example, Human Resources might share information among the sub-units, Benefits, Retirement, Payroll and Healthcare. Horizontal flows help to facilitate coordination and collaboration efforts and/or deal with problems.

Diagonal information flows represent the exchange of information between functional units or units such as divisions at different levels. For example, Human Resources Recruitment unit might share headcount information with the managers of Marketing and R&D units. Diagonal information flows are meant to facilitate co-ordination among different functional units and to deal with operational problems. For example, Human Resources sharing information on low headcount with Marketing's manager of sales can be used to initiate the recruitment and hiring process in the sales unit.

LEARNING OBJECTIVE #8: DESCRIBE AND EXPLAIN THE CONCEPT OF COMMUNICATION NETWORKS WITHIN AN ORGANIZATION AND AMONG ORGANIZATIONS AND INDIVIDUAL STAKEHOLDERS

A **communication network** represents an array of formal and informal communication processes that involve the use of various types of communication channels (see Figure 14.2). The term network is meant to characterize all the various forms of communication processes created by the organization. Network is a widely used term. Though often referred to in official communications, the term is frequently used to include the broad array of informal communication processes that evolve to meet user needs that the formal network of communication processes does not fulfill.

Network evolutionary theory helps to explain the changing nature of formal and informal communication processes. Communication networks evolve over time in response to changing organizational circumstances. The circumstances vary by type. There are **endogenous factors** that influence network configurations. Endogenous factors can include changes in leadership, new strategies and changes in work responsibilities as examples of factors that can influence the design of a network and changes to a network. **Exogenous factors** refer to external elements to the organization that contribute to the development of an organization's communication network and to modifications to the organization's existing communication network. Examples of exogenous factors include changes to the economy, changes in government regulations, changes in consumer tastes, new competitors, war and new products produced by competitors.

A communication network can link people who work together on a permanent or temporary basis. The purpose of creating a network of communication processes is to support the organization's efforts at achieving the organization's strategic goals. The informal aspect of a communication network aims to accelerate the flow of information among critical decision-makers who need the information to help plan and need to make quick decisions (see Figure 14.3). For example, a company developed a new drug for dogs to be used during the early springtime. In the past the company prepared a detailed, technically oriented brochure for sales staff to

---

FIGURE 14.2   Continuum Between Informal and Formal Communication Processes

Informal
Communication

Formal
Communication

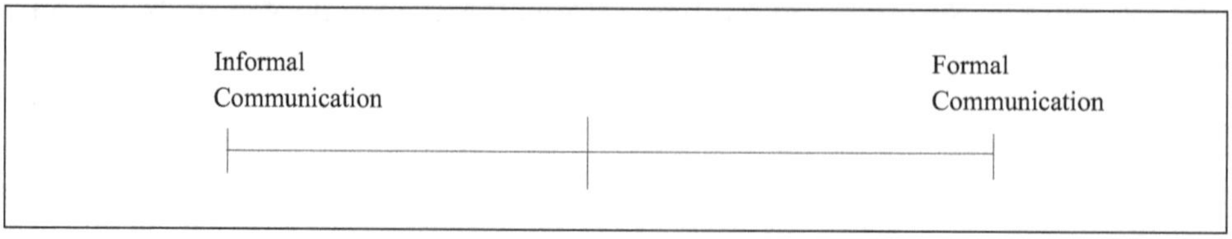

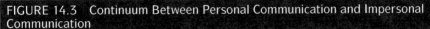

FIGURE 14.3 Continuum Between Personal Communication and Impersonal Communication

distribute to veterinarians. On this occasion the company took a cost-savings approach and relied on the sales staff to describe the new drug supplemented by a one-page brochure. Through standard reporting, the company learned that sales were well below expectations. One of the senior executives reached out to the head of U.S. operations and together they polled sales representatives to learn why sales were low. What they learned was that the veterinarians always rely on reading detailed technical brochures have a new drug before prescribing its use. The company quickly developed a "cheat sheet" and shipped this directly to each sales representative to distribute to veterinarians.

Standard reports, each report with a central theme, are a common communication channel used in organizations such as hospitals. In a hospital, like other organizations, reports help to define links among the units/people who need the report's information to support decision-making. For example, in a hospital, a category of reports is "incident reports." Incidents occur in hospitals but if incidents are repetitive types of incidents, the hospital creates a standardized report and a report network communication process. For example, assaults occur. There can be patient assaults, non-patient visitor assaults, staff assaults and other types of assaults. Since safety is an important hospital value, reporting assaults and the type of assaults is necessary in formalizing a policy to deal with the problem and then learn if the policy was effective in helping to reduce assaults. What could result is a new communication process added to the network or a temporary communication process added to the network or an additional report added to the existing communication process.

Therapeutics Products Inc.: Part 3

Paul Heard, Senior Vice President of Manufacturing, was meeting with his staff to discuss the need for better coordination among all the departments. The mandate, coming from the CEO, was that the firm needed to get products to customers faster. Customers were complaining that orders took too long to receive, resulting in lost sales. Manufacturing was identified as the bottleneck. Paul and his staff determined that the primary cause of delays was the difficulty in arranging for face-to-face inter-departmental meetings to coordinate all activities. The result of the meeting was the identification of the need to create a reporting process and a report format that eliminated the need for frequent meetings. Only periodic meetings would be necessary, but meetings are not vital to the actual manufacturing process.

Questions

1. The departments reflect a network. Explain.
2. Why create a report? What is the purpose of the report?
3. Who should initiate the report starting point? Why?
4. Does the new report change the way departments interact? Explain.
5. What problems are likely to occur because of the new report and new reporting process?

LEARNING OBJECTIVE #9: EXPLAIN THE IMPORTANCE OF AN ORGANIZATION'S INFORMATION SYSTEM IN FACILITATING FORMAL REPORTING OF ORGANIZATIONAL ACTIVITIES

An organization's **information system** serves a critical role in contributing to the survivability of an organization. An organization without information operates blindly. Information represents feedback, and this enables decision-makers throughout the organization to make decisions.

There are several specific purposes served by creating an organized information system. First, **decisions** occur because of receiving information. The more complete the information, the greater the probability of an effective decision. Second, some information involves the assessment of organizational performance. This type of information helps to assess the **impact** of decisions. Decision-makers need to know if decisions lead to the expected results. Decisions on strategies implemented along with operational decisions require validation to continue in the same way. The preferred type of performance information is **objective-based information** because this type of information is measurable. Measurability validates decisions made and makes writing reports easier because metrics are more concise.

A well-designed information system can increase the level of **trust** among the workforce if the information promotes transparency. Honest information leads to increased workforce commitment because the workforce appreciates that upper management considers the workforce as a valuable partner, with no intention to dupe anyone. When workers think the organization shows trust and respect, the workforce responds by committing to strengthen the organization's performance (see Figures 14.4–14.6).

An information system supports decision-makers in maintaining **control** over the organization and the different parts of the organization. Control is an important management function because decision-makers need to know if the organization's performance is trending in the expected direction. Assessing organizational performance is determined by achieving SMART goals and SMART objectives or by demonstrating trends that demonstrate the likelihood of achieving the goals and objectives.

Another reason that organizations develop an information system is to facilitate **organizational learning**. Organizations generate a lot of activity, the bigger the organization the more the intensity of the activities. Decision-makers need to remain alert about the organization's performance by assessing performance to learn if the planned changes were occurring along with the expected results. Also,

FIGURE 14.4   How Mutual Attraction Improves a Relationship, Resulting in More Personal Communication

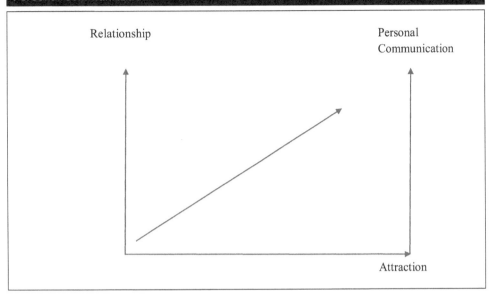

FIGURE 14.5   Where There is Greater Formal Communication, There is Less Personal Communication

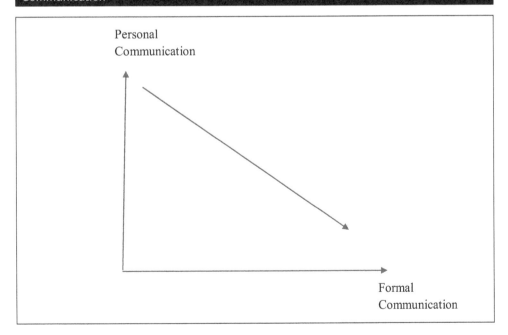

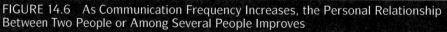

FIGURE 14.6 As Communication Frequency Increases, the Personal Relationship Between Two People or Among Several People Improves

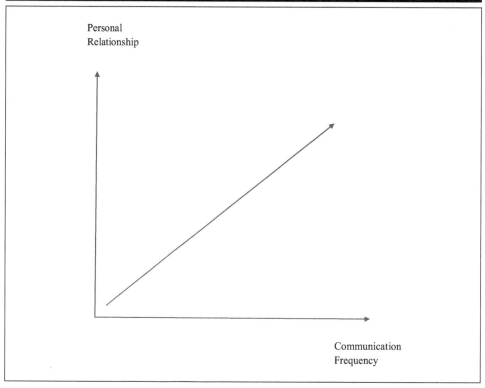

the faster an organization learns of problems the quicker the organization can respond, strengthening the organization's ability to successfully manage the change process.

Mentioned earlier, to ensure a steady flow of information, organizations create an **organized information system**. There are several characteristics that the structuring process focuses on. **Filters** help to screen the myriads of information an organization generates. Filters control for the type of information to collect. Filtering involves defining the types of information needed. For example, sales per store, sales per product and selling costs per month represent a small sample of the possible types of information to collect. **Frequency** of information is also a characteristic of an organized, information system. Standard, routine reports often have a time frame or schedule to follow, such as daily, weekly, monthly, quarterly and so on. For example, daily reports on product defect rates, daily reports on products manufactured or daily calls received at a call center. **Non-routine** reports often deal with requests by decision-makers for reports that cover a specific topic of interest. The **types** of information reported are often standardized by decision-makers; decision-makers prefer objective, measurable types of information. Finally, the organization frequently identifies the type of **communication channels** to use when reporting. Many reports are written, but sometimes, routine reports can include an oral report to complement the written report. Written reports provide a record to refer to and enable the decision-maker to reflect on report content issues and then ask follow-up questions.

LEARNING OBJECTIVE #10: IDENTIFY AND DESCRIBE THE IMPORTANT ROLE OF COMMUNICATION MANAGEMENT WITHIN THE ORGANIZATION

Communication management represents an important organizational function. The purpose of communication management is to oversee the linkage among all types of communication channels to strengthen the organization's efforts at achieving organizational goals and to implement the organization's strategies. Because of the importance of the role played by the organization in the strategy implementation process, organizing the communication processes is one of the critical responsibilities of senior management.

Often, communication management is considered a **strategic management function** because of the importance of communication. Communication management structures the **information flows** to ensure that the movement of critical information reaches the right individuals, within the optimal times and in the expected form. This means that communication management includes being responsible for the selection of the **communication channels**.

Another important responsibility included under the auspices of communication management is the structuring of **decision-making flows**. Decisions are either strategic types of decisions associated with identifying a vision, goals, strategies or operational decisions associated with the strategy implementation process. The structuring of the decision-making flows (or processes) represents a critical organizational function, operating in tandem with the communication processes.

As an organizational function, communication management operates in several ways.

- Communication management assists in the **design** of an organization's structure along with designing other management systems such as the information system to ensure effective communication.
- Communication management aids in the **integration** of each of the different types of management systems.
- Communication management assists in the **evaluation** of the performance of the other management systems and related work processes to ensure that the systems and work processes perform to expectations.

Communication management's attention primarily focuses on the work processes within each management system because work processes are designed to perform specific tasks associated within and between systems. For example, quarterly financial report preparation represents a work process within the financial reporting system, a sub-system which operates under the information system. Communication management's evaluative responsibility means that the communication management is **results-oriented**. A work process generates measurable outcomes; as such, the organization uses these outcomes as work process objectives to measure the effectiveness of a work process in comparison with the performance expectation. Work process outcomes represent information about the work process that is packaged within a communication channel, moving to the recipients who use the information to make decisions if necessary. For example, making black dry erase markers generates two outcomes, the number of markers produced within a planned time frame and the number of defects per random sample. Each type of information is important for decision-makers to learn and to determine how to respond to the findings.

Therapeutic Products, Inc.: Part 4

Sarah Brinkley, CEO, was meeting with her senior staff. The agenda was singular in focus. The proliferation in the number of company-wide reports and department reports was overwhelming the decision-making process. Specifically, it was taking too long to make decisions and reports often came at inconvenient times and provide conflicting information. Everyone realized that the need to rationalize the management of reports was critical. The issue confronting Sarah and everyone else was the question 'How to begin and what to focus on?"

Questions

1. Why is the issue of communication management important to focus on?
2. How would you recommend starting the process of re-designing the reporting process?
3. What are the topics to focus on in re-designing the reporting process?
4. Should an ad hoc committee be formed, tasked with the responsibility to make recommendations. If yes, why? If no, why not?
5. Why is information critical in an organization's performance?

LEARNING OBJECTIVE #11: IDENTIFY, DESCRIBE AND EXPLAIN THE DIFFERENT TYPES OF COMMUNICATION THEORIES

References to communication theory imply that there is one universal theory that describes the fundamentals of communication. There is no universal communication theory. There are **communication theories** that cover different aspects of communication. The variety of theories offers a comprehensive overview of communication and the variety of ways to describe and understand what constitutes communication.

What follows is a brief introduction to the different types of communication theories.

- **Network Evolutional Theory**: This theory explains the patterns of communication processes that exist within an organization; the formalization of new communication processes; and how communication processes change in response to a change in an organization's structure.
- **Organizational Information Processes Theory**: Within an organization, the organization creates formal communication processes for the purpose of disseminating information throughout the organization.

- **Structural Symbolic Interaction Theory**: This theory describes communication as a function for understanding how people interact using communication and explain how communication influences behavior.
- **Social information Processing Theory**: This theory describes the way individuals communicate using technology and how the use of technology during communication functions without the use of non-verbal cues.
- **Social Learning Theory**: This theory explains how communication is used to facilitate learning among people.
- **Organizational Information Processing Theory**: The focus of this theory is the organization's attempts at reducing uncertainty by creating information processes intended to provide the necessary information an organization needs to meet performance expectations.
- **Multi-Level Theory**: This theory describes the variety of vertical levels within an organization and how the vertical levels are linked using formal communication processes, serving to disseminate information between the levels.
- **Interpersonal Communication Theory**: This theory describes the one-to-one communication process and group communication with a description of the elements of the communication process for exchanging information.
- **Rational Communication Theory**: This theory describes the pattern of interactions between individuals or patterns among individuals within a group, with the emphasis on communication roles, dominant roles and submissiveness and how each person influences others when communicating.
- **Strategic Communication Theory**: This theory describes how individuals in an organization use communication to organize themselves for specific purposes. The process evolves as the needs of the individuals change.
- **Emergent Communication Theory**: Communication processes often start as informal processes which do not serve the purpose of providing decision-makers with timely, needed information. Decision-makers seek to create more rational communication processes to improve organizational decision-making.
- **Critical Communication Theory**: The proponents of this theory examine the role of technology and social media in re-shaping the communication processes within organizations, between organizations and between individuals. New forms of communicating overshadow traditional forms of communicating by changing the way people communicate.
- **Reciprocal Communication Theory**: This theory explains how the frequency of communication leads to more trust and openness among communicators. As such, standardizing communication processes promotes more frequent forms of communicating to build trust and openness.

Chapter Summary

Communication is the lubricant for getting organizations and the people in an organization to perform. Without communication, leadership would not be able to guide others in performing their work responsibilities to meet expectations. Organizations use all types of communication channels to manage and guide the workforce, so the workforce performs in ways necessary to achieve the organization's vision and strategic goals.

Communication is essential to ensure that the operations or strategy implementation process meets the expectations, contributing to a successful strategy which results in the organization achieving the vision and strategic goals.

This chapter focuses on all the important issues associated with communication and the communication process. The importance of communication, written and oral communication, is reflected by organizations that sponsor training programs to improve the communication skills of the workforce. These types of training programs focus more on the organization's leadership because leaders need to be effective communicators to guide the workforce in sustaining the organization's competitive position.

The importance of effective communication and the value of organized communication processes are described through the chapter's focus on how organizations create structured, systematic communication processes to ensure that recipients of the communication benefit from the information received. This means that communicators need to know the type of information to send, the form in presenting the information and the schedule for sharing information. Furthermore, organizations provide recipients with standard types of information, often in a written report, to ensure that the recipients receive the type of information needed to successfully perform their work responsibilities.

Questions

1. Identify and describe the elements of a two-way communication process.
2. Identify and describe the major communication channels.
3. Describe the process for creating a communication strategy.
4. What is a communication barrier? Identify and describe any three types of communication barriers.
5. Identify and describe the strategies for creating effective written communication.
6. What are the strategies for improving communication skills?
7. What does the term "communication flows" refer to?
8. There are communication networks within an organization and between organizations. Explain.
9. What makes an organization's information system important? Explain.
10. Describe the role and function of communication management within an organization.
11. Identify and describe five types of communication theories.

Bibliography

Abudi, G. (2013). Managing communication effectiveness and efficiency. Paper presented at *PMI Global Conference 2013-North America*. October 29. 1–12.

Bell, R. L. & Roebuck, D. (2015). An increasing usefulness for managerial communication research on the main topics of management. *Journal of Management Policy and Practice*. 16(2). 71–108.

CEB HR Leadership Council. (2015). *Effective Communication Strategies*. CEB. 1–8.

Dainton, M. & Zelley, E.D. (2010). *Introduction to Communication Theory in Applying Communication Theory for Professional Life: A Practical Introduction*. Sage Publications. Chapter 1.

Eddie, W. F. & Goret, R. (2013). Theories and models of communication: foundations and heritage in Paul Cobley and Peter J. Schultz (Eds.). *Theories and Models of Communication*. De Gruyter, 1–32.

Erven, B.L. (2016). Overcoming barriers to communication. *Department of Agricultural Environmental, and Developmental Economics*. Unpublished. 1–6.

Fulk, J. & Boyd, B.K. (1991). Emerging theories of communication in organizations. *Journal of Management*. 17(2). 407–437.

IFAC Policy Position 8. (2017). Enhancing organizational reporting: Integrated reporting K. *International Federation of Accountants*. January. 1–9.

Illia, L. Lurarti, F. & LaRocca, A. (2006). Communication flow, channels, content, and climate in downsizing. *European Academy of Management Conference*. May. Paper #1.

Keyton, J. (20017). Communication in organizations. *Annual Review Organizational Psychology and Organizational Behavior*. 4. 501–526.

Lunenberg, F.C. (2010). Formal communication channels: upward, downward, Horizontal and extern focus on colleges, universities. *Schools*. 4(10). 1–7.

Lunenberg, F.C. (2010). Communication: the process, barriers, and improving effectiveness. *Schools*. 1(1). 1–11.

Mishra, K., Mishra, A.K. & Walker, K. (2019). Using innovative internal communication to enhance employee engagement in Anthony Normore, Mitch Javida and Larry Long (Eds.). *A Strategic Communication, Leadership and Conflict Management in Modern Organizations*. Business Science References. Chapter 22.

Monge, P. & Margoin, D. (2017). Organizational communication networks. *Center for Effective Organizations*. CEO Publications G 07–15 (525). May 17. 1–14.

Munter, M. & Hamilton, L. (2014). Communication strategy in *Guide to Managerial Communication: Effective Business Writing and Speaking* (10th Edition). Pearson. Chapter 1.

Raupp, J. & Hoffjann, O. (2012). Understanding strategy in communication management. *Journal of Communication Management*. 16(2). 146–161.

Rider, E. (2002). Twelve strategies for effective communication and collaboration in medical teams. *Career Focus*. August 10. 545.

Ross, S.C. (2019). *Training and Development in Organizations: An Essential Guide for Trainers*. Routledge.

Ruler, B.V. (2018). Communication theory: an underrated pillar on which strategic communication rests. *International Journal of Strategic Communication*. 12(4). 367–381.

Sadiku, M.N.O., Shaoare, A.E. & Musa, S.M. (2016). Information overload: causes and cures. *Journal of Multidisciplinary Engineering Science and Technology*. 3(4). 1–3.

Sanina, A., Balashov, A., Rubtova, M. & Satinsky, D.M. (2017). The effectiveness of communication channels in government and business communication. *Information Polity*. 22. 251–266.

Solar, A. (2019). Best practices for your initial communication strategy. *Sprout Social*. September 23. 1–16. https://sproutsocial.com/insights/internal-communications-guide/.

StarupNation. (2019). 4 Effective communication strategies in business. April 24. https://startupnation.com/sponsored-content/effective-communication-strategies/.

Wabisabi Learning. (2020). The path to improving student communication skills. January 21. https://wabisabilearning.com/blogs/inquiry/8-methods-improving-student-communication-skills/.

Waner, K.K. & Winter, J.K. (1993). The multidimensional communication process: a communication paradigm for the 21st century. *U.S. Department of Education, Office of Educational Research, and Improvement*. ED 363 907. 2–16.

Technology and the Organization's Workforce

OVERVIEW

The interface between people and technology symbolizes a century-long relationship starting with primitive people's use of cutting tools, weapons development and cooking and eating utensils. Fast forward to the 21st century, the relationship remains essential in supporting the evolution of humankind. The bond between people and technology transcends many facets of people's lives. Technology is the term mean when describing the "man-machine." Technology is all pervasive, at work and in people's personal lives. Technology helps to make workers more productive and efficient. Technology enables people to enjoy many of the benefits life can offer. Technology represents the means to achieve goals. For organizations, technology is used to benefit people at work and in their private lives. Technology enables an organization to assess an organization's level of workforce productivity and enhance the organization's efforts at identifying greater operational efficiencies.

This chapter examines the important issues associated with technology, ranging from the management of technology, the technology development process and the impact technology can have on an organization's workforce. The chapter examines the role of the workforce in contributing to the development of new technology. To understand the role of technology for organizations, knowing that there are three major types of technology is important. There is process technology used in an organization's work processes; there is product technology, represented by new products or upgraded products; and there is input technology, which is used in the production process. Examples of input technology are different, healthier cooking oils; modal used in making clothes; and sweeteners used in beverages instead of sugar or sugar cane.

Human Resources (HR) importance to an organization has expanded over the years along with the increased use of technology by organizations. HR's role is examined to learn how HR uses technology to screen resumes, as an example; the use of technology to conduct interviews and use of technology in the individual performance assessment process along with developing job descriptions to assist the organization's pursuit of knowledge workers, sometimes referred to as high-value employees. This represents a brief overview of HR's expanded role and importance to an organization.

Other subjects covered in the chapter include the examination of the role of individuals in the innovation management system, knowledge management system and the performance management system. These systems are important for an organization where technology represents an output or technology is process technology used in the organization's work operations. Innovation management is essential in developing new approaches for an organization to become more productive and efficient, along with increasing sales. Innovation management is important to the organization developing new, technology-based products. Knowledge management focuses on creating a more productive learning organization that can benefit advanced knowledge applied to the organization's activities. Performance management focuses on how an organization can use technology to improve operational performance.

In this chapter, the reader gains important insights on the important role of technology in how organizations try to survive in a Darwinian World.

CHAPTER 15   LEARNING OBJECTIVES

Readers will achieve the following learning objectives after reading this chapter.

1. Define and explain the meaning of the term "management of technology."
2. Describe the scope of the management of technology process.
3. Identify, describe and explain the differences between supply-push and demand-pull influences on the management of technology.
4. Discuss the differences between creativity, innovation, R&D, science and the management of technology.
5. Identify and describe the purpose and function of the innovation management system and the people-technology interface.
6. Identify, describe and explain the differences between process technology, product technology and input technology.
7. Identify and describe the role of the people-technology interface in the knowledge management system.
8. Identify and describe the role of the people-technology interface and the performance management system.
9. Discuss the meaning of the term "creative destruction" and the relevance to the management of technology.
10. Describe and explain the impact of technology on the workforce.
11. Identify, describe and explain the role of HR in the management of technology.
12. Discuss and explain the impact of technology and social relations in an organization.

LEARNING OBJECTIVE #1: DEFINE AND EXPLAIN THE MEANING OF THE TERM "MANAGEMENT OF TECHNOLOGY"

Whether the organization produces technology products or integrates the use of technology in making products or delivering services, technology requires **pervasive technology management (PTM)**. PTM refers to the need to involve technology management throughout the organization because the role of technology evolved over the years, but most rapidly since the industrial revolution.

Organizations incorporate the use of technology in their operations. The purpose of integrating technology into an organization's operations is to create greater operational efficiencies through the reduction of costs; increase productivity of individual workers and gain competitive advantages over competitors. The organization that makes technology products values technology because of the revenue derived from selling useful technology products; the development of technology products typically involves the use of technology in the production process.

Because of the expanded importance of technology, the **management of technology** has become an important theme to focus on by organizational leaders. For many organizations, the importance of technology shows in the strategic planning process and in the output of that process, the strategic plan. Whereas technology was once only a functional strategy (i.e. technology strategy), now technology is often included the organization's overall strategy. As an element of the organization's strategy, technology also serves an important role in the strategy implementation process. Strategy implementation involves the changes in an organization's operations to successfully implement the strategy. By definition, a new strategy always impacts an organization's operations. In particular, the focus is on how to better structure relationships among units and between units and how to build competencies through the changes in operational work processes. Changes in work processes first require changes in policies that shape the design of a work process. Policies now promote greater use of technology in work processes because technology is an important contributor to the organization's efforts to achieve strategic goals and achieve operational objectives. By reducing costs, increasing worker productivity and increasing revenues from new technology products, organizations learn to survive.

LEARNING OBJECTIVE #2: DESCRIBE THE SCOPE OF THE MANAGEMENT OF TECHNOLOGY PROCESS

Management of technology (MOT) emphasizes the oversight and management of the **developmental process** for creating new technology. The first stage of this process is the act of scientific inquiry where the search for new ideas occurs, with the organization intent on improving a structure to the idea development stage to minimize wasted resources and increase the productivity of the idea generators. The last stage in the process focuses on demand estimation along with determining potential product profitability.

After creating the conditions for generating ideas, the next stage is the innovation stage. Innovation involves innovation management (discussed in detail later). Briefly, innovation management involves a process for converting ideas into feasible products. Prototypes or working models are created to assess if the actual technology works as expected. Following this stage is the production stage. Production entails the actual producing of the first generation of a product. Often, products are produced in limited quantities to be beta tested by external independent individuals and organizations. Beta testing represents an objective step to ensure that bias did not distort the perceived value of the technology. After successfully completing the beta testing stage, producing the product begins. This stage usually incorporates product modifications based on beta test results. Here, the organization also seeks to learn about the market's receptiveness and willingness to purchase the product. Profitability of the new technology is the final stage in the process. During this stage, the organization learns if profitability targets are achievable, and the organization begins to look ahead to the next generation of the technology if sufficiently profitable.

MOT follows a process that incorporates the use of process technology. Briefly, process technology represents technology used in support of work processes. Process technology helps to gain increased operational efficiencies and increase worker productivity. During the industrial revolution, the use of technology moved organizations away from a reliance on the use of artisans to the standardization of the production and assembly processes to reduce the labor costs of production. The end result is that society benefited from access to less-expensive products, organizations benefited from increased revenues, lower costs and increased profits; people benefited by having more and better jobs (loss of farm jobs due to increased use of technology in agriculture) and a healthier and happier life.

The initial stage of the developmental process involves identifying technology that the organization can use in the operations. Organizations create, in varying degrees, the search capabilities needed to learn about **operational technologies**. One of the important organizational capabilities is **scanning** or searching outside of the organization for how other organizations incorporate the use of technology in the organization's operations. Scanning is a multi-dimensional activity because the organization seeks to gain insights from a variety of sources. These sources can range from academic think tanks, competitors, non-competitors and the academic community. Another source for new ideas is the organization's employees who frequently think of a more useful technology to use and pass this idea on to management to consider.

Both types of processes have the same outcome focus, profitability. Each stage of the process has an outcome focus. These work process stage outcomes are framed as **operational objectives**. Easily measured, the organization creates the structure within each stage to ensure achieving the operational objective.

Because each of these processes represents stages that are separate and different but related steps with other stages in the process, coordination and collaboration are important issues. The pass-off from stage to stage needs synchronization to occur to ensure that the process continues to move forward. As an example, Xerox' Palo Alto research team developed the original idea that became Windows, but the idea languished because there was no champion to move the idea forward through Xerox development process. No one could see the future of the idea.

As the reader can gather, both processes involve the use of the information system, knowledge management system and the performance management system. Information management occurs within a stage among teams that share information using reports and presentations and between stages during the pass-off from one stage to the next stage. Knowledge management operates within each stage through facilitating organizational learning, serving as a depository of knowledge for individuals to access. Performance management is relevant because the organization needs to ensure that each stage achieves operational objectives and provides feedback to aid management's efforts at improving a stage's performance in achieving operational objectives.

LEARNING OBJECTIVE #3: IDENTIFY, DESCRIBE AND EXPLAIN THE DIFFERENCES BETWEEN SUPPLY-PUSH AND DEMAND-PULL INFLUENCES ON THE MANAGEMENT OF TECHNOLOGY

Supply-push technology represents a disruptive type of technology that lacks a specific target market. An organization that focuses on developing supply-push technology seeks to create a new product category within a product category or a totally new product category. For example, Motorola created the original cell phone in 1983. This was the start of a new product category. There was no defined target market. Instead, a supply-push technology product is a product in search of a market. This approach offers an organization greater risk of failure, but if successful, greater potential rewards. Apple created the iPhone, a smart phone which is a new product category within the cell phone product category.

Demand-pull technology is a sustainable form of technology product. There is a clear target market, and the organization develops a product for this market that was designed to meet the specific needs of the target market. This approach begins within a specific product category, such as the laptop sector, but developing a superior laptop to meet the needs of a niche target market, offering less risk of failure to Apple but usually the financial results are less than sought.

An organization with the determination to pursue more types of supply-push technology products tend to create a less-structured environment within the unit responsible for developing new ideas that serve as the start point for these types of products. Structure can often constrain the creative process; less structure allows for greater creative freedom. Demand-pull products focus on creating a structured idea generation process because the organization emphasizes evolutionary types of products. In both instances, the organization creates units composed of the type of creative individuals best able to generate the kind of ideas needed for these types of products.

Supply-push technology requires more creative, free thinkers who can generate all sorts of ideas to pass on to those involved with the innovation process. There is an innovation process for demand-pull organizations. But for individuals participating in the innovation process, the type of ideas to work with are familiar because the ideas represent product upgrades or products where there is an established product category, often already individual products.

Strategic management applies to both types of product forms, but the implementation process differs. In particular, the marketing function operates differently. For a supply-push product, marketing needs to identify potential users and demonstrate the value of purchasing this type of product. For demand-pull products, the market is familiar with the product; marketing needs to convince users of the value of upgrading or convince non-users of the benefits of purchasing the new product.

Home Science Biotechnology: Part 1

Sarah Lawrence, newly installed as CEO, was meeting with her new CFO, Paul McDonald and the chair of the Board of Directors, Paul Douglas. Included in the meeting was the strategic consultant, Harriet Beacham, who worked for Worldwide Consulting, a consulting firm that works with small biotechnology and pharmaceutical companies. Harriet's strategic specialty area is small business start-ups. The discussion was important because everyone knew that a good start is important to the success of a start-up. Start-up biotechnology firms have a notorious history of burning up. The focus of the discussion was on three drug research projects in development. Each project had a different path. There was no interest in pursuing different paths for each drug. The same path for each drug development process to follow was the consensus. Harriet opinioned "you can pursue a demand-pull or a supply-push strategy." Everyone looked at Harriet. Sarah asked Harriet to explain what she meant.

Questions

1. What is a demand-pull strategy?
2. What is a supply-push strategy?
3. Why would an organization consider a demand-pull strategy? Why would an organization consider a supply-push strategy?
4. How would you respond to Harriet?
5. What type of strategy would you recommend? Explain.

LEARNING OBJECTIVE #4: DISCUSS THE DIFFERENCES BETWEEN CREATIVITY, INNOVATION, R&D, SCIENCE AND THE MANAGEMENT OF TECHNOLOGY

To be creative is to develop new ideas. **Creativity** implies that there is a process to follow with an outcome, a new idea(s). Organizations can conduct the creativity process informally with no organized attempt to formalize the creative process, allowing the development of new ideas to evolve from all areas of the organization. However, an organization can formalize idea-generating throughout the organization. This would occur by forming teams with the mandate of developing new ideas that focus primarily on improving work processes. The goal in improving a work process is to modify the process, and this can include changing personnel, training personnel and adding new technology. An alternative to creating organization-wide teams is to formalize the creative process within a functional area, typically R&D or Product Development within Marketing. Groups within R&D or project teams formed within R&D have the goal of generating ideas with the intent to develop sustainable products or disruptive technology products or products of either type.

 Innovation is an inclusive term that encompasses the creative process but transcends the creative process by developing an idea that results in a finished product or service ready to offer to customers or potential customers or a decision to cancel the project. The intent of being innovative is to create competitive advantages through developing new products and services without any direct competitors. Innovation can also focus on enabling the organization to have more efficient work processes and to increase the productivity of the workforce. Any individual, group, team or unit can be innovative.

R&D represents a functional area of the organization. R&D is set apart by the organization to concentrate all activities associated with developing new ideas and converting new ideas into a finished product or determine that the product is not viable. R&D specialists can make the decision to stop work on a new idea, move an idea forward in the developmental process, create a prototype for market testing or provide the product for sale. At this point, R&D's role ends except for working on the product upgrade if sales warrant a product upgrade.

R&D is typically organized into different specialty groups. These groups consist of specialists who work temporarily on project team. Project teams are organized on a "one idea per team basis." A project team either develops a new product or drops the idea in consultation with the project's manager and senior R&D managers.

Science is typically a common word used in biotechnology and pharmaceutical companies. These companies employ specialized employees, often with doctorates, who conduct science-based research. These individuals lead teams of lab technicians. Teams can include senior scientists and junior scientists depending on the importance of the project. The process for developing new products is formalized, applying the scientific method to guide the research. The scientific method is a formalized research model that provides a research process to follow. The end goal is to develop a profitable product. Scientists can conduct **basic research** which starts with an idea or **applied research** which starts with a prototype product idea; applied research focuses on one idea. Researchers are organized by research groups or teams. Applied researchers follow the scientific method but with a singular focus.

Google is a good example for the reader to understand the creative process and innovation processes. In Google's early days, employees were encouraged to set aside one day a week to work on personal ideas. When a new CEO was hired, he learned that few new, useful products emerged from this approach. He introduced a new model, where each person needed to present their ideas at various stages of development and meet certain criteria. If met, the project moved forward. If not, the person could continue or drop the project. This innovation development process model led to a better use of resources and resulted in more profitable outcomes.

LEARNING OBJECTIVE #5: IDENTIFY AND DESCRIBE THE PURPOSE AND FUNCTION OF THE INNOVATION MANAGEMENT SYSTEM AND THE PEOPLE-TECHNOLOGY INTERFACE

The purpose for an organization to create an innovation management system is to develop the organization's capabilities to access new ideas from the external environment and from within the organization. By creating an innovation management system or a comparable type of system, the organization prioritizes the importance of learning ideas that can benefit the organization. A system is composed of policies and work processes. Therefore, the policies and work processes of an innovative management system essential in guiding (policies) the process on where to search, how to search, how to access the information, how to collect the information, how to analyze the information and how to report the information. The work processes represent the routines that individuals follow per the policies.

The innovation management system links with the knowledge management system because this system's purpose is to act as a depository or library for the organization, supporting the organization's efforts at supporting continuous learning. In part, the system looks for marketing opportunities that focus on demand-pull types of ideas because demand-pull products are lower risk products, responding to specific needs of the market.

The innovation management system reflects unique characteristics important for this type of system. First, the system has an entrepreneurial focus with all the necessary values to support being entrepreneurial. Entrepreneurial because being entrepreneurial is about taking initiative. The cultural values that support being entrepreneurial include risk taking, having a vision, innovativeness, achievement-oriented, ambitious and opportunistic to name several important values. Always, the focus of all work processes is to gather and process new ideas for the organization to consider for products, services and aids to improve work processes. Second, the system is well-managed because the search for new ideas can run into many false leads. A well-organized operation helps to make the system more efficient while getting results. A well-organized system imposes a discipline over the process using operational objectives as a focus point, reinforcing the need for a disciplined process to follow. Finally, the system's structure is designed to identify ideas with a high probability of leading to an outcome that can lead to cost reductions for a process idea or revenue gains for a new product or new service idea.

There are two major categories of innovation ideas. Technical innovations emphasize ideas for new products, new services or new work processes (i.e. process technologies) used to make new products (e.g. robots) or new services (e.g. voice recognition software). The second category is administrative innovations. This type of innovation focuses on new way to design all part of an organization's structure, new or different ways to modify the decision-making processes (e.g. de-centralize authority, centralize authority and change job descriptions) or change to work processes (e.g. re-configure processes).

Future Electronic Toys: Part 2

Paul Drake, Senior Vice-President of Product Development, was meeting with his senior management team. Paul started the meeting by sharing feedback from the CEO. The focus of the feedback was the failure to develop enough new products to feed the appetite of the market, and too many of the new products did not achieve the sales targets. Paul followed by stating that the new product development pipeline was smaller than in prior years. Furthermore, almost all these products represented product "upgrades." Paul stated, "We need new ideas for the new product development pipeline; new ideas need to result in the form of new products or new product categories."

Questions

1. As a member of the senior management team, how would you react to Paul's comments?
2. How would you use SMART goals? Provide an example.

3. What would you recommend doing to generate new ideas? Explain.
4. How would you change the innovation process? Explain.
5. Why was Product Development underperforming? Explain.

LEARNING OBJECTIVE #6: IDENTIFY, DESCRIBE AND EXPLAIN THE DIFFERENCES BETWEEN PROCESS TECHNOLOGY, PRODUCT TECHNOLOGY AND INNOVATION TECHNOLOGY

An organization responsible for managing technology will likely focus on three types of technology: process technology, product technology and input technology.

Process technology refers to a form of technology used in support of a work process either in making a product or providing a service. The goals for using process technology are to increase worker productivity and control costs by increasing the performance of a work process. For example, McDonald's was suffering from several problems years ago, one of which was food provided at inconsistent temperatures, labor shortages and time delays in providing a meal to a customer. McDonald's used new technology to help keep waiting food at a consistent temperature while completing the meal, re-designed the kitchen and incorporated the use of technology to speed up the food preparation process; McDonald's also introduced the use of a self-service beverage machine to reduce the demands for additional labor and reduce the time waiting on each customer. A call center relies extensively on process technology to monitor call volume and to track call center activity and call center operator's work performance, such as average time spent per call. Manufacturers rely on introducing technology into the manufacturing and assembly process to provide more uniform performance, fewer mistakes and eliminate boring, tedious work that can lead to human error and human injury.

Product technology involves the incorporation of technology in a product or if the product is an existing technology product, with new technical features added. For example, Apple upgrades the iPhone by incorporating new camera features to enhance the photographic capabilities of the iPhone. New products can range from incremental or sustaining types of products such as the upgrades to the iPhone. There are radical or disruptive types of technology that often eliminate industries but lead to the creation of new industries. The automobile created a host of new industries but contributed to either the elimination or shrinkage of industries (e.g. carriage industry and horse bridle industry).

A third type of technology is **input technology**. Input technology is technology used in making a product. This could include new types of ingredients to make healthier foods, new clothing material to change the look, feel and fit of new clothes and new armor protection for military tanks. The list of new types of input technology is almost endless. Some of the ideas for new input technology originate from suppliers, competitors and the market. For example, the market might look for new look clothing, and the manufacturer develops a new input to use to make the look.

Essentially, in the 21st century, all organizations are involved in the management of technology.

LEARNING OBJECTIVE #7: IDENTIFY AND DESCRIBE THE ROLE OF THE PEOPLE TECHNOLOGY IN THE KNOWLEDGE MANAGEMENT SYSTEM

All organizations possess some type of a **knowledge management system** but an organization that integrates technology into products and work processes usually develops a sophisticated, organized knowledge management system to maximize the benefits of learning how to use technology. The management of technology includes the development of the knowledge management system because this is a system designed specifically with the goal of maximizing learning and applying learning, both in product development and in improving the performance of work processes; both areas involving the use of technology.

Human capital development is one of the important activities associated with the knowledge management system. The purpose is to add knowledge workers to the workforce because knowledge workers contribute to an organization's learning through the knowledge, skills and personal abilities possessed by knowledge workers. Furthermore, knowledge workers demonstrate the motivation and interest in contributing to the interests of the organization. Knowledge workers are prime candidates for advanced training to add to their knowledge and skills along with developing their personal abilities.

Knowledge management is purposeful. The intent of knowledge management is to maximize gaining new knowledge that is applicable to product development and in improving the performance of work tasks. Through the application of learning the dynamic capabilities of the organizations are strengthened, contributing to the organization's efforts at creating competitive advantages.

Knowledge acquisition and knowledge application efforts impact the workforce in different ways. The profile of a knowledge worker changes to someone that possesses the knowledge, skills, personal abilities, self-confidence and self-motivation to contribute to the organization's pursuit of competitive advantages. Low-level workers are in less demand, leading to few types of low-level workers. A middle group of workers, with some of the talent of knowledge workers but less so, are marginal employees who need to advance their knowledge, skills and personal abilities or eventually become low-value employees that the organization can no longer use. Employees need to contribute to the success of the organization to benefit from the success of the organization. Knowledge development by the individual reflects the knowledge development process of the organization, advances forward or confronts the consequences of becoming marginal.

LEARNING OBJECTIVE #8: IDENTIFY AND DESCRIBE THE ROLE OF PEOPLE-TECHNOLOGY AND THE PERFORMANCE MANAGEMENT SYSTEM

Organizations create and design the **performance management system** to assess the performance of individuals, groups, teams, units and the organization through the collection, storing, analyzing and reporting of performance information. The intent is to learn about performance effectiveness during the strategy implementation process. Technology has become a useful tool in creating sophisticated performance management systems for monitoring the changes occurring within an organization. For example, virtual teams telecommuting. These activities remove individuals from the worksite and can cover different time zones. The performance management system needs to respond to assess performance of the individuals participating in these activities. Technology has become one of the tools used to assess performance where workplace activities devolve into new ways to perform work.

As organizations expand their geographic reach, expand their product lines and services and broaden target markets, the performance management system needs to evolve coincidental with this growth. Assessing productivity and efficiencies from a micro level (i.e. individuals) to a macro level (i.e. the organization) are important activities to perform routinely to ensure that the organization remains focused.

The performance management system operates under a broad mandate than only assessing operational productivity and efficiencies. Organizations create policies that attempt to direct actions of individuals, groups, teams, units and the organization. Determining a policy's effectiveness is an important requirement of a performance management system. For example, computer security and access to computers. A policy on computer security can be assessed by measuring computer security breakdowns. Another example is employee safety from physical and mental harassment. A policy developed to curtail these situations is in effect. Performance management collects information that is analyzed to determine the effectiveness of the policy. Finally, government laws mandate non-discriminatory hiring practices. Organizations create policies to conform to these laws. Organizations need to create the means to generate information, analyze the information and report the information to HR for internal evaluation. HR passes the collected information to relevant government agencies who monitor organizations to learn if the organizations are conforming to government legal mandates.

Technology's role in the people-technology relationship has only increased within the context of the performance management system. As an example, a call center's operation at a major health insurer sheds insight on the people-technology link. Every call center operator's workstation is linked to a central computer system. Each operator's average time per call and number of calls handled was recorded. The information was aggregated into different forms for different uses. The organization assessed the average time spent per call per person; the average number of calls per person per day; the average number of calls per hour, per time of the day and per day. In addition, benchmark performance data was created as performance objectives. Training programs helped to improve the collective efforts of the call center operators. When important changes occurred, such as adding a new client, training helped call center operators successfully deal with the changes to achieve the benchmarks.

Finally, the performance management system's focus includes evaluating the performance of new products compared with expectations (i.e. goals), market development (e.g. change in market share and market receptiveness levels) and work process effectiveness (e.g. product development process and sales per sales representative). The link between people and technology is expanding because of the organizational needs to assess performance activities but with the intent to reduce the human element in the process.

LEARNING OBJECTIVE #9: DISCUSS THE MEANING OF THE TERM "CREATIVE DESTRUCTION" AND THE RELEVANCE TO THE MANAGEMENT OF TECHNOLOGY

Creative Destruction is a term that originated from the economist, Joseph Schumpeter, to describe the impact new products and innovative technologies can have on the economy of a nation and among organizations within an industry. Technology resonates as the single most important disruptor to the long-term well-being of an organization, industry and nation. Examples include the automobile, the electric light, computers, aircraft and nuclear energy. This list of breakthrough technologies is almost inexhaustible.

Once the process of creative destruction commences, the process is continuous, leading to new, growing organizations and at the same time, the process contributes to the downward spiral of many organizations, unable or unwilling to adapt. Benefits for organizations that are in the forefront of innovative development associated creative destruction are positive and negative. Using Microsoft as an example, Microsoft's operating system was new and a minor player in a field dominated by the CPM operating system. CPM lost the battle and is no more. There are many other similar stories.

Society benefits from the effects of new products and technology impacted work processes by adding new jobs, expanding personal wealth but many traditional jobs are lost. What happens is the rise of new types of jobs that require better educated, more skilled and broad personal abilities of workers (i.e. problem-solving skills and positive attitude). The legion of workers lacking in what the new workers possess results in a disenfranchised group of workers.

Creative destruction represents an economic force that is not respectful of boundaries. It is the powerful bull in a China shop. Managing technology is in part about managing the impact of technology but not stopping a process that is unstoppable. Organizations promote planned change by providing an organized, structured innovation process that is less disruptive to the organization. Once the technology genie is out of the bottle, the organization needs to continue onward in the process of benefiting from the new technology or suffer the consequences. Organizations that resist using new technology face the prospects of being pushed aside by new competitors with new products and new technology infused work processes.

The major effort to sustain the organization's products and new work processes developmental process is by monitoring the organization's external environment. New ideas represent new opportunities but if not pursued, the opportunities can become threats. Organizations develop the organizational capabilities to be tuned in on new developments; learning from competitors, customers, suppliers and researchers to identify new technology trends. Then, the organization needs to decide which new trend has the potential to be a growth opportunity to access. Partnerships, mergers and acquisitions investing as a VC represent important methods an organization can use to gain access to new technologies that can lead to new products and new technologies to use in work processes.

LEARNING OBJECTIVE #10: DESCRIBE AND EXPLAIN THE IMPACT OF TECHNOLOGY ON THE WORKFORCE

Technology is the driving force propelling changes to the workplace. Whether the focus is new product technology, new process technology or new input technology, the organization is impacted. The workforce is the direct or indirect focal point of the impact. Between looking for a certain type of worker to changing the way the workforce works, the impact of technology is significant for organizations and for an organization to succeed.

Discussed earlier was the importance of **human capital development**. Organizations look for well-educated, technically trained, creative, curious, highly motivated, self-confident and independent types because this profile meets the requirements of organizations seeking innovative, idea people, especially idea people who can develop an idea through an idea development process (innovation process) that results in a planned outcome.

Innovation can include ideas about new technology to support increasing the workforce's productivity and efficiency and identifying new inputs to use to make superior products. Unfortunately, the search for a technology-oriented workforce results in less employment for low-skilled workers who show little upside potential to a technology-driven organization.

Middle management suffers from the increased focus on process technology. Technology is available to facilitate communication, monitor performance through all levels of an organization and support collaboration efforts between middle management and senior management and between senior management and subordinates. As a result, fewer middle managers are required, but the **new** middle manager type is needed: technically skilled, highly educated, flexible and able to work with large numbers of people with diverse backgrounds. A flatter organization is the consequence. Senior management can reach out to lower-level managers, and lower-level managers can initiate contact with senior managers. Authority relationships are becoming less defined and more flexible; these changes accelerate the decision-making process.

Once hired, technology-skilled workers' technical skills begin to become obsolete as technology evolves. However, the experience and personal qualities of technology-skilled workers or **high-value** workers influences the organization's efforts at retaining these employees. Organizations develop training programs or contract with outside organizations to develop knowledge-based and/or skill-based training programs to keep high-value employee's technical skills and technical abilities current with the organization's needs. Organizations do not ignore the technical development of managers. Organizations develop training programs for managers at all technical levels to keep managers current on the use of communication technology, information management technology and performance management technology.

Organizations attempt to increase the workforce's productivity and the workforce's ability to reach greater levels of efficiency. There are four ways organizations can promote the goals of increased productivity and increased efficiency. Communication technology helps workers connect with colleagues regardless of the location, time or distance. Communication technology makes everyone reachable and available. Many organizations use virtual teams with individual members from

California, Massachusetts, Brazil, India and Taiwan on the same team, collaborating on a project. Information technology empowers high-valued employees with the knowledge accessible in an organization's knowledge library. Knowledge management is a sub-system of the information management system. High-value employees know how to access the knowledge, analyze the knowledge and report on their work to team members and management. Performance management technology enables the organization to monitor the performance of individuals, groups, teams and units. Performance information moves rapidly through the organization with the use of enabling technology. Technology is available to collect and report performance information and enable managers to report performance ratings to other managers and non-managers. Access to performance information enables the organization to target problems for intervention efforts and to enable managers to target how to use technology to improve sales, profitability and cost analysis. The impact of technology on the workforce is huge.

Fairbanks Automotive Manufacturers: Part 3

Jim Haskell, CEO, was telling his managers of the manufacturing division that making mufflers for Ford was becoming a major challenge. Ford continued to reduce order sizes because in response to the market and expected better prices for finished products with no changes to product specifications. This means that Fairbanks needed to fill smaller orders for better prices. Fairbanks was a company that lived on its margins. Margins were always a strategic goal. With smaller order sizes, Fairbanks buyer orders from suppliers were smaller which contributed to higher costs per unit. Changes were necessary to drive down costs and at the same time meet quality standards. Sam Pickens mentioned that he recently learned about a new input that was a better quality but priced lower than the product sold by the current supplier. Jim asked Sam to investigate this and present a proposal to the group at the group's first meeting of the next month. Jim asked for other ideas from the group.

Questions

1. What questions will Sam ask the supplier? Why these questions?
2. What suggestions are the team likely to offer? Why these ideas?
3. What are other ways of learning new ideas? Explain.
4. The focus on margins and keeping the same margins or increasing margins means the organization needs to focus on what issues? Explain why?
5. What ideas can you offer as an outsider? Explain.

LEARNING OBJECTIVE #11: IDENTIFY, DESCRIBE AND EXPLAIN THE ROLE OF HUMAN RESOURCES IN THE MANAGEMENT OF TECHNOLOGY

In the 21st century, HR role expanded to become one of the most important management functions of all organizations, but in particular, organizations that make technology featured products along with the extensive use of process technology within most work processes. The reason for the added responsibilities is clear, and these organizations need to attract, hire and retail high-value employees. The role of HR is multi-faceted. HR's areas of expertise make HR an essential function for building and sustaining a high-value organization that relies heavily on technology.

Two important duties of HR include conducting **job analyses** and designing **job descriptions**. Working with other units, HR performs extensive job analysis of existing jobs or, if a new position, discusses the job requirements with the relevant unit along with looking outside of the organization to learn if the job exists in other organizations. After collecting the information, HR prepares a draft job description for review by all the involved decision-makers. After finalizing the job description, this becomes the organization's de facto official job description.

Another critical HR duty is **recruitment**. HR possesses the knowledge on how best to recruit the type of candidates in demand. HR knows how to post job announcements, use outside recruiters such as hiring agencies and collect resumes. Once resumes are collected, HR begins the **staffing** process. Staffing involves screening resumes for acceptable candidates, conducting initial interviews and organizing the remaining stages of the hiring process. HR can use technology to perform an initial resume screening. HR coordinates with the relevant unit to determine HR's role in the interviews and if necessary, testing candidates. HR conducts reference checks, background checks and drug tests. HR usually is responsible for sending out the hiring letter and arranges for a candidate to move through an HR unit designed **onboarding process**. Onboarding's purpose is to help to successfully integrate new hires into the organization and place of work in the organization.

Training and development programs represent additional duties of HR. HR conducts need assessments to identify training requirements, design the actual training programs and arrange to implement training. All these activities are done in collaboration with the unit(s) requesting training. Training usually focuses on new knowledge, new skills, advance knowledge and skills, and leadership training. Development focuses on building on the personal abilities of trainees. For example, problem-solving skills, self-leadership, decision-making and organizing skills along with other types of abilities.

HR works with senior management and unit management to design or modify the **performance management system**. HR's specific focus is to assist the organization and organizational units in being able to conduct individual performance reviews. HR functions like an in-house consultant, assisting the organization in keeping the performance management system relevant and useful in meeting the organization's needs as well as unit requirements.

Another HR duty is the design and modification of an organization's **motivation or reward management system**. HR works with senior management and unit management to ensure that the system meets management's needs and requirements. HR, acting like an in-house consultant, helps in designing incentive programs, developing a list of benefits to offer employees, and develops employee support programs. Career management development is an additional topic to include in a motivation management system because the goal in creating career development programs is to retain high-value employees.

HR's last important duty is to ensure that organizational policies conform to government laws and regulations and that the organization adheres to these policies and report organizational activities to government agencies showing how the organization conforms to government laws and regulations.

Fairbanks Automotive Manufacturers: Part 4

Jim Haskell, CEO, and Patrick Summers, Vice President of Manufacturing, and Katherine Givens, Vice President of HR were meeting to discuss upcoming changes at the company. Katherine knew about specific changes and the reasons for the changes. She received a copy of the proposed operations plan the previous month. Jim asked her to develop a plan for how best to implement the operations plan. Jim wanted a short-term plan and a long-term strategic plan to prepare for the future because the market has become unpredictable.

Questions

1. What issues did Katherine's short-term plan cover? Explain.
2. What issues did Katherine's long-term plan cover? Explain.
3. Why is HR important in successfully implementing the operations plan? Explain.
4. What should Jim consider as important elements in the long-term strategic plan because the markets are unpredictable? Explain.
5. What role, if any, will HR play in the implementation of a strategic plan? Explain.

LEARNING OBJECTIVE #12: DISCUSS AND EXPLAIN THE IMPACT OF TECHNOLOGY AND SOCIAL RELATIONS IN AN ORGANIZATION

An organization represents a social system because an organization represents a collection of individuals interacting with other individuals either as part of their work responsibilities or independent of work responsibilities. Technology changes the people dynamics in substantive ways. More people interact with other people in the form of virtual teams, videoconferencing and telecommuting to identify several types of technologies that contribute to social interaction. However, though social contacts increase, the closeness that existed from personal connections derived from face-to-face meetings declined.

Trust and trust-building, which is one of the fundamental requirements of a close working relationship, is more challenging to develop with the advent of the technology where people are more isolated. Building trust needs alternative methods to substitute for face-to-face contact. Relying on measurable performance represents an important trust building activity. Measuring performance represents assessing the results of an individual's actions. The more an individual performs successfully the more the individual shows credibility. Credibility builds trust this way.

Some technology leads to job loss and individual productivity gains. Where several people might need to be involved in a project, advanced software enables an individual's productivity to increase but at the cost of fewer meaningful, useful social relationships. What was learned years ago in the **Hawthorne Effect** studies was the importance of social relationships as a contributing factor in creating a happy, productive workforce. Organizations have not learned effective alternative methods to support social relationships in the age of technology.

Chapter Summary

For centuries people used technology to make their lives easier to live and safer. Cooking utensils, storage containers, weapons, hunting tools and skinning knives represent only some of the early technologies contributing to the advancement of civilization. However, the industrial revolution accelerated the advancement of civilization as technology become a more dominant force affecting civilization, organizations and people in different ways. Solar power, the electric car, self-driving cars, drones for delivering packages, space stations and new vaccines developed in scientific labs, the use of voice recognition technology; these technologies represent only a small sample of society shaping technologies. More are coming, and organizations need to be prepared or suffer the consequences.

The term, management of technology, originated to describe the attempt by organizations to assume more control over technology development so organizations can harness technology for the organization's benefit. Organizations want to avoid suffering from the effects of what Schumpeter referred to as "creative destruction," a situation that can occur from uncontrolled technological development.

Organizations can oversee any one of up to three different types of technology. One type of technology is process technology, which is technology used as an aid to the workforce as the workforce performs their work responsibilities in a productive and efficient way. Next, there is product technology or products that represent technology. Cell phones, laptops and televisions are examples of product technology. Finally, there is input technology which refers to the use of new types of inputs to use in creating a product. Examples include modal used in clothing, graphene nanocoating, colored conductive inks represent new types of inputs to use in making products.

Because technology has such an important role in society and for the future of organizations, many organizations create advanced management systems to aid in managing technology. The innovation management system, the knowledge management system and the performance management systems were developed and continue a developmental path to access the benefits of technology in the evolution of organizations and to avoid the negative consequences of technology. The chapter focuses on how an organization's workforce benefits from technology usage and how some workers suffer from being unprepared to work with advanced technology.

Questions

1. What does the term "Management of Technology" refer to?
2. Why would you prefer a demand-pull strategy? Explain.
3. What are the advantages of a supply-push strategy? What are the disadvantages? Explain.

4. What is the purpose of the innovation management system and the people-technology interface?
5. How is technology important to the knowledge management system?
6. How is technology important to the performance management system?
7. Creative destruction. How is this an economic concept? Explain.
8. How does technology impact the workforce?
9. Explain the positive benefits of technology's impact on the workforce.
10. Identify the important duties HR performs in the management of technology? Are these any different from a non-technology company? Explain.

Bibliography

Bin, A. & Salles-Filnoa, S. (2012). Science, technology, and innovation management contributions to a methodological framework. *Journal of Technology Management & Innovation.* 7(2). 73–86.

Burke, R. & Ng, E. (2006). The changing nature of work and organizations: implications for human resource management. *Human Resource Management Review.* 16. 86–94.

Carayannis, E.G. & Alexander, J. (2020). Technology management-strategy, organization, system, examples, advantages, manage, definition, school, model. https://www.referenceforbusiness.com/-technology-management.html/

Cascio, W.F. & Montealegre, R. (2016). How technology is changing work and organizations. *The Annual Review of Organizational Psychology and Organizational Behavior.* 3. 349–375.

Chanaron, J.J. & Jolly, D. (1999). Technological management: expanding the perspective of management of technology. *Management Decision.* 37(8). 613–620.

Dukes, E. (2019). 5 ways technology in the workplace has improved our lives. Iofficecorp.com. May 24. 1–9. https://www.iofficecorp.com/blog/-5-ways-technology-has-changed-the-modern-workplace/

Durnd, T. (2003). The strategic management of new technology in *Bringing Technology and Innovation into the Boardroom: Strategy, Innovation and Competencies for Business Value* by The European Institute for Technology and Innovation Management. Springer. Chapter Three.

Ernst, H. (2003). Patent information for strategic technology management. *World Patent Information.* 25. 233–242.

Espinosa-Cristia, J.F. (2019). Managing innovation based on studies in science, technology, and society: toward a constructionist and critical perspective of innovation management. *Cadernos Ebape. br.* 17(1). 68–83.

Gopalakrishnan, S. & Damanpovr, F. (19997). A review of innovation research in economics, sociology, and technology. *Omega International Journal of Management Science.* 25(1). 15–28.

Harvey, G. (2019). How does technology affect the work environment today? *Chron.com.* March 16. 1–9. https://smallbusiness.cchron.com/technology-affect-work-environment-today-27299html/

Lekchiri, S. (2016). Impact of technology of workforce development. *The Association of Technology, Management, and Applied Engineering.* April. 1–9.

Levin, A.Z. & Barnard, H. (2008). Technology management routines that matter to technology managers. *International Journal of Technology Management.* 41(1/2). 22–37.

Montealegre, R. & Cascio, W.F. (2017). Technology-driven changes in work and employment. *Communications of the ACM.* 60(12). December. 60–67.

Prasad, A. (2018). 10 ways technology has reshaped the modern workplace. October 8. 1–15. https://www.quickfm.com/blog/how-technology-has-reshaped-the-workplace/

Syryamkin, V.I. & Syryamkina, E.G. (2015). Technology management as a tool of innovation strategy of education and cognitive management. *Procedia-Social and Behavioral Sciences.* 166. 468–471.

Unsal, E. & Cetindamar, D. (2015). Technology capability: definition and its measurement. *European International Journal of Science and Technology.* 4(2). 181–196.

Ware, J. & Grantham, C. (2003). The future of work: changing patterns of workforce management and their impact on the workplace. *Journal of Facilities Management.* 2(2). 142–159.

INDEX

Note: *Italic* page numbers refer to figures.

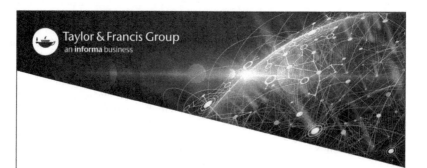

Taylor & Francis Group
an **informa** business

Taylor & Francis eBooks

www.taylorfrancis.com

A single destination for eBooks from Taylor & Francis
with increased functionality and an improved user
experience to meet the needs of our customers.

90,000+ eBooks of award-winning academic content in
Humanities, Social Science, Science, Technology, Engineering,
and Medical written by a global network of editors and authors.

TAYLOR & FRANCIS EBOOKS OFFERS:

A streamlined
experience for
our library
customers

A single point
of discovery
for all of our
eBook content

Improved
search and
discovery of
content at both
book and
chapter level

REQUEST A FREE TRIAL
support@taylorfrancis.com

 Routledge
Taylor & Francis Group

 CRC Press
Taylor & Francis Group